No Settlement, No Conquest

A History of the Coronado Entrada

Richard Flint

University of New Mexico Press ■ Albuquerque

© 2008 by the University of New Mexico Press
All rights reserved. Published 2008
Printed in the United States of America
14   13   12   11   10   09   08   1   2   3   4   5   6   7

Library of Congress Cataloging-in-Publication Data

Flint, Richard, 1946–
No settlement, no conquest :
a history of the Coronado Entrada / Richard Flint.
    p. cm.
Includes bibliographical references and index.
    ISBN 978-0-8263-4362-8 (cloth : alk. paper)
1. Coronado, Francisco Vásquez de, 1510–1554.
2. Southwest, New—Discovery and exploration—Spanish.
3. Southwest, New—History—To 1848.
4. Indians of North America—Southwest, New—History—16th century.
5. Historic sites—Southwest, New.
6. Excavations (Archaeology)—Southwest, New.
7. Southwest, New—Antiquities.
8. Southwest, New—Discovery and exploration—Spanish—Sources.
I. Title.
    E125.V3F58 2008
    979'.01—dc22
                2007047694

Cover painting: *1541–Battle of Basalt Point Pueblo*, gouache on paper, by Douglas Johnson.
Designed and typeset by Mina Yamashita.
Composed in Minion Pro, an Adobe Original typeface designed by Robert Slimbach.
Printed by Thomson-Shore, Inc. on 55# Natures Natural.

*With my utmost appreciation

and affection to

Carroll L. Riley and

Brent Locke Riley*

The only thing worth my writing

or anyone's writing is a book that says,

hey, this seems to have been

left out of the picture.

—Bernard DeVoto to Garrett Mattingly

Contents

Acknowledgments / xi

Introduction: *The Mechanics of the Event* / xiii

Chapter 1: Whys and Wherefores / 1

Chapter 2: Precious Goods of Greater India, China, and Antilia / 17

Chapter 3: Cíbola, a Name for the Goal / 27

Chapter 4: License from the King and His Council / 39

Chapter 5: Raising a Force and Paying for It / 49

Chapter 6: Avoiding Provocation, Demanding Submission / 65

Chapter 7: Almost a Highway / 75

Chapter 8: By Sea to Chichilticale / 87

Chapter 9: Inside Cíbola / 97

Chapter 10: Refusal to Submit / 107

Chapter 11: In the Wake of Disillusionment / 117

Chapter 12: Overture from Cicuique / 127

Chapter 13: The Heart of the Land of Flat-Roofed Towns / 139

Chapter 14: Vassalage Denied / 145

Chapter 15: To the Farthest Edge / 155

Chapter 16: What Was Seen and What Was Not / 171

Chapter 17: Disintegration and Withdrawal / 183

Chapter 18: Upshot / 195

Chapter 19: One of a Hundred and Thirty / 205

Chapter 20: Discontinuity at Mid-Century / 219

Chapter 21: Enduring Life of Rumor / 227

Chapter 22: Violence, Expected but Not Sought / 237

Maps / 249

Appendix 1: Major Spanish-Led Expeditions in the Western Hemisphere, 1492–1598, by Date, Leader, and Area / 261

Appendix 2: Chronological Context of the Coronado Entrada, A.D. 700–1609 / 267

Abbreviations Used in the Notes and References / 271

Notes / 273

Glossary / 321

References / 329

Index / 347

Acknowledgments

ALTHOUGH MY NAME APPEARS as sole author of this book, and indeed I am responsible for its writing, much of the research on which it is based derives from projects undertaken during the past twenty-six years in partnership with Shirley Cushing Flint. Were she not currently at work on a book-length project of her own, this book would have been a more collaborative effort than it already is. Even so, it has benefited from her editorial scrutiny, without which it would be a different and impoverished product.

I also owe sincere appreciation to the members of the Santa Fe seminar, who read and commented on several chapters in the book. Thanks are due especially to Sandra Lauderdale Graham, Richard Graham, and Carroll Riley, who read the entire manuscript and offered many helpful suggestions. My particular gratitude goes to Suzanne Flint, who also read and commented on the entire text. I have often written with her in mind as a well-educated, non-historian reader. And I am grateful to John L. Kessell and David J. Weber for their continuing support and encouragement.

The dust jacket illustration is a painting by Douglas Johnson, who lives in Coyote, New Mexico, titled *1541—The Battle of Basalt Point Pueblo*. The subject of the painting is an encounter in early 1541 between García López de Cárdenas, the second *maestre de campo* of the Coronado expedition, and three Pueblo men at the pueblo of Moho—possibly the ruin now known as Basalt Point Pueblo on Santa Ana Mesa, overlooking modern San Felipe Pueblo in New Mexico. After López has been persuaded to leave his weapons behind, he and the Indians approach one another on foot, at least two of the Indians concealing clubs behind their backs. As the lead Indian embraces López, the two others draw their clubs and beat him over the head. Immediately, several Spanish horsemen race from nearby to the *maestre de campo*'s aid, narrowly preventing his being dragged off to the pueblo and, presumably, killed. This incident is recounted in chapter 14. ■

Introduction

The Mechanics of the Event

IN THE COURSE OF LITTLE MORE THAN A CENTURY, from 1492 to about 1600, armed parties from the Old World, aided crucially by large cohorts of Native American men, forcibly took control of many peoples of the vast twin continents that have come to be known as the Americas. Propelled by desire for status, honor, and wealth, energized by unquestioned certainty about the principles governing the natural and social worlds, expeditionaries fanned out over the southern two-thirds of the Western Hemisphere. Toward the middle of the sixteenth century the tide of conquest reached what is today northwestern Mexico and the American Southwest in the form of the Coronado expedition.

Between 1539 and 1542, that Spanish-led expedition of some 2,000 people, mostly Indians from what is now central and western Mexico, made an armed reconnaissance of a place they knew by the name Tierra Nueva. They intended to seize control of the people who lived there, in places called Cíbola (seeBohla), Marata (MahRAHtah), Totonteac (TohTOHNteyahc), Tiguex (TEEwesh), Tusayán (ToosighYAHN), and Quivira (KeeVEErah). In exchange for the local Indians' surrender of control, they would offer to initiate the new vassals into the religion, economy, and way of life of sixteenth-century Spain. In return for such a priceless favor, the natives of Tierra Nueva were expected to accept and support don Francisco Vázquez de Coronado, captain general in the name of King Carlos I of Spain, as their overlord. All the nearly 400 European men who accompanied Vázquez de Coronado expected roles in running and sustaining the new Spanish *provincia*.

When the expedition reached Tierra Nueva, its resident peoples were exposed for the first time to the customs, beliefs, mores, and institutions of Europe and Africa. Interaction between Indians and Old World natives was not invariably confrontational, but on the whole, discord between the groups far outweighed the moments of congeniality. Fighting broke out often. Sullen stand-offs were the norm. People on both sides were killed and maimed, although American natives bore a disproportionate share of the casualties. Everyone suffered.

The promise of lucrative and prestigious colonial offices went unfulfilled. Most of the Europeans who survived the *entrada*, or armed reconnaissance, returned south to Nueva España disillusioned and heavily in debt. They left behind in Tierra Nueva dislocation and destruction in most places where the expedition had spent more than a few days. As a result, suspicion and wariness, even hostility, characterized each group's perception of the other. The stage was set for further friction when next the two peoples would meet.

How the Coronado *entrada* was conducted and why it unfolded as it did; what the responses of the natives of Tierra Nueva were to the expedition and why they pursued the options they did; what effects the expedition had on its own members and the Indians it sought to control; how the events and outcomes of the expedition fit with those of similar, contemporaneous undertakings—I explore all these subjects in this book.

Drawing from documentary and archaeological sources, I develop a chain of explanatory narratives that account in significant part for the actions of people of the Coronado expedition and of the American natives they met at critical junctures during the expedition's course. To do that, I highlight selected words and actions of many members of the Coronado expedition and of indigenous persons, in order to understand why members of each group made certain choices and why those choices produced the outcomes they did. Although evidence relating to individual people fills this book, my main intent is to tell the aggregate story.

The remainder of the book is arranged chronologically, to follow the sequence of events of the expedition. Each subsequent chapter includes, besides a narrative of events drawn from sixteenth-century documents and archaeological and ethnographic data, an explanatory argument in which I marshal evidence from those same sorts of sources that convincingly, I think, accounts for why events happened as they did, how they relate to other events of the period, and what their consequences were.

Some readers will be familiar with—indeed will have grown up imbued with—the general outline of events of the Coronado expedition of 1539–42. To others it will be a revelation. In either case, I offer evidence that will be new to both groups and interrogate "old" evidence for fresh purposes. I do not simply retell what has become part of the lore of the Southwest. Instead, I reconstruct that story as amended, expanded, and recolored by more than a quarter century of my own research about the expedition and that of my wife and collaborator, historian Shirley Cushing Flint, not to mention the work of scores of other historians, archaeologists, anthropologists, geographers, folklorists, and linguists.

For those familiar with earlier versions of the history of the expedition, some common misconceptions may impede the reading of this book. I talk about those misconceptions throughout the book, at scattered places where each seems most pertinent. But they are widespread and pernicious enough that going over them briefly at the beginning may be helpful. The Coronado expeditionaries have commonly been portrayed as a small army of Spanish knights in armor dispatched by the king of Spain to look for gold. Every element of that characterization is inconsistent with what is now known about the expedition and the traditions and conditions from which it sprang. The expedition was instead very large and was not an army in any modern sense. Its membership was not entirely or even predominantly Spanish, and almost no one on the expedition possessed metal armor. The idea for the expedition originated in the New World, not in Spain, and it was paid for by its members, without significant financial support from the king. The expeditionaries were not in a literal sense looking for gold.

As a historian, I do not repeat what other, earlier historians have said about the Coronado *entrada* without carefully reexamining the bases for their conclusions. Accounts of the past are not settled, fixed, and permanent. Researchers regularly discover new sources of information about the past, new manuscripts, new archaeological data. Each new item affects the understanding of past events, provokes new questions, may require new methodologies, and demands accommodation within an ever-growing and evolving comprehension. Collating new elements with the previous understanding of past events reshapes the outline of that understanding, reveals hitherto unimagined connections, exposes misinformation, and adds crucial information and links that previously were unknown, ignored, or slighted.

This book is no more the "final answer" about the Coronado expedition than its predecessors were. For one thing, Shirley and I continue to work. Unless the practice of history comes to an end, we and others after us or alongside us will continue to uncover significant information about the *entrada* and the human and physical context in which it took place. That new information will again necessitate reevaluation of our understanding of how and why the events of 1539–42 transpired.

Ultimately, the discipline of history concerns understanding the range of human behavior. Although the past may not precisely repeat itself, past and present often share parallel elements. Studying the past does not predict the future, but it does present us with the only real-life cases we have of attitudes, choices, actions, and outcomes similar to those in play today. We humans are fools if we willfully ignore and dismiss the examples of the past, if we insist that "the past is past, get over it." The past always has ramifications in the present. The Coronado *entrada* and indeed the Spanish Empire of the sixteenth century as a whole offer striking parallels to circumstances and events of our own time. I have written this book with that observation as a powerful and urgent motive.

I do not offer a minute and exhaustive recounting of the details of the expedition. For that, readers should consult *Documents of the Coronado Expedition, 1539–1542: "They Were Not Familiar with His Majesty, nor Did They Wish to Be His Subjects"* (Southern Methodist University Press, 2005) and *Great Cruelties Have Been Reported: The 1544 Investigation of the Coronado Expedition* (Southern Methodist University Press, 2002). Together those volumes make available most of the principal manuscript sources concerning the expedition. Moreover, readers who look for a detailed reconstruction of the route followed by the expedition will not find it here. Neither of these possibilities is uninteresting or unimportant, but my purpose is to explore why things happened as much as to reveal what happened. Either facet—explanation or narration—is sterile without the other, and I have sought to balance the two, providing enough narrative to make clear what took place but always asking, Why was this so?

History can be immensely enjoyable as entertainment, but it can be much more than that. At its best it offers the prospect of learning from the behavior of our forebears. Learning from them sometimes means rejecting, in whole or in part, their rationales and actions, being appalled and turning away. At other times it means embracing those actions and striving to follow or modify them, proudly building on what seems a wisely laid foundation. The history of the Coronado *entrada* that I offer here contains instances of both.

Readers who refer to the notes at the end of the book will notice the many references to Pedro de Castañeda de Nájera's *Relación*. They highlight the huge debt modern students of the expedition owe to that former expeditionary. For many episodes in the story, his lengthy narrative, written more than 20 years after the events it describes, provides the only contemporaneous evidence known to exist. It is always unwise, however, to rely heavily on a single source, because of the potential for error, bias, and even purposeful distortion. Whenever possible I have preferred and cited contemporaneous sources other than Castañeda de Nájera, in order to incorporate as many voices and points of view as possible. Nevertheless, Castañeda de Nájera's narrative is an extraordinary source without which historians' understanding of the events and people of the Coronado expedition would be little more than skeletal.

People connected to and affected by the Coronado expedition, like most other people, rarely recorded or even thought about the reasons behind their actions. Moreover, their infrequent statements about their motivations are unlikely to represent full and complete lists of what moved them. Indeed, psychologists have amply shown that many human motives do not ordinarily reach the level of consciousness. And there is always the possibility that persons or groups knowingly hide or disguise their genuine motivations.

How, then, can any historian presume to specify the factors that drove thousands of persons nearly 500 years ago? Except in extraordinary instances, I cannot hope to know the purely personal drives that originated in the intimate experiences of individual expeditionaries. I assume, though, that people of a given age cohort, ethnicity, social class, vocation, and gender broadly shared goals and ambitions, although specifics varied. When important individual variations in motivation can be discerned, I make that point. I also take it for granted that the expeditionaries' behavior, and thus their choices, like that of all people, suggests possible reasons underlying their actions.

In inferring motives from actions, caution is mandatory. The standard to which I try to adhere to is that inferences must be credible, convincing, and faithful to the preponderance of the evidence. Inferences must not be significantly contradicted by any portion of the existing body of evidence. And inferences are only as trustworthy as the gathering of evidence has been free ranging. The research that generates the evidence must be guided by the goal of thoroughness rather than the intention of building a specific forensic case. In a history of the Coronado expedition, although the only immediate casualty of such a practice might be understanding, in the long run it can contribute to disaster. Misunderstanding the past gives us a false perception of the present. ■

CHAPTER 1

WHYS AND WHEREFORES

EXAMINING THE END OF A FAILED UNDERTAKING can reveal much about its beginning. Evident in the laments and recriminations that follow failure are the aspirations and ambitions that drove the enterprise in the first place. Such is the case with the Coronado expedition, the first organized European-led penetration, from 1539 to 1542, of what is today northwestern Mexico and the U.S. Southwest. After more than two years in the field, having accomplished a prodigious journey of some 4,000 miles and having become the first European-led party to see the Grand Canyon, the immense bison herds of the Great Plains, and the great variety of people who inhabited those places, the expedition was about to begin a five-month disintegration, a ragged anticlimax of disappointment.

As the first signs of spring appeared in late February or early March 1542, Captain General Francisco Vázquez de Coronado convened a *junta*, or council, of captains, royal officials, and other persons of note among the expeditionary force he led. No contemporary document provides the names of those present in the captain general's rooms in an occupied pueblo beside the Río de Tiguex—the modern Rio Grande in what is now New Mexico. In keeping with common practice of the time, however, the group would certainly have included all the leaders of companies—don Tristán de Luna y Arellano, Diego López, don Rodrigo Maldonado, don Pedro de Tovar, don Diego de Guevara, Hernando de Alvarado, Pablo de Melgosa, Juan de Zaldívar, and Velasco de Barrionuevo—along with the royal *contador*, or accountant, Luis Ramírez de Vargas, and the royal *factor*, or tribute collector, Antonio de Rivero de Espinosa. Other lay persons of rank such as don Alonso Manrique de Lara and don Lope de Urrea would have been present, along with at least the superior of the cadre of

Franciscan friars that accompanied the expedition, fray Juan de Padilla.

The calling of such councils was standard procedure for Spanish-led expeditions of the day when any decision of moment had to be reached and time permitted consultation. And the captain general of this expedition was no autocrat. Essentially the expedition was an imperial town seeking a site for itself. In this respect it was governed like the town it was supposed to become, by a *cabildo,* or town council, of leading citizens.

Certainly the question before this council in the earliest days of spring 1542 was fateful: Should the expedition persist in its search for wealthy oriental states or should it acknowledge that it had been pursuing a phantom and return to Nueva España? Would anything be gained by spending another year in the far north? Or should the expeditionaries reckon up their losses and seek other opportunities?

The captains and *caballeros,* men of noble status, spoke in turn, without dissent at first. Their unanimous judgment was to face about and return south, empty-handed but alive and ready perhaps for more certain ventures. All signed their names to that resolution. Likewise, the rank and file of the expedition, the tailors, shoemakers, meat cutters, scribes, hosiers, and merchants who served as horsemen and footmen, petitioned to return to Nueva España, although they were not included in the council.

As expeditionary Pedro de Castañeda de Nájera remembered it decades later, "they gave their formal opinion, [which was] that they should return to Nueva España since nothing of wealth had been found and there was no settlement in what had been reconnoitered where *repartimientos* could be made to the whole expedition."[1] By *repartimiento,* or *encomienda* (the two words were used interchangeably at the time), Castañeda de Nájera referred to a royal grant of the right to collect tribute from vassals. In 1544 Vázquez de Coronado and his attorney put it this way: "In none of [that great amount of territory] had they seen, talked with, or had reports of civilized people among whom it would be possible to increase His Majesty's royal patrimony."[2] Don Pedro de Tovar testified that the party never found "a land in which it would be possible to settle."[3] The famous Seven Cities of Cíbola, for instance, had turned out to lack "wealth and civilization."[4]

So on or about April 1, 1542, the Coronado expedition vacated the two or three pueblos it had occupied for two winters along the Río de Tiguex and began retracing its route back toward the Ciudad de México, Mexico City, from which it had departed.

Lives of Ease and Honor

For those accustomed to think of European occupation of North America in terms of nineteenth-century homestead pioneers and gold rushers, the council's decision, ratified and enforced by the captain general, may seem puzzling. Although Coronado expedition member Juan Jaramillo, for instance, imagined that the Great Plains were "very productive of every kind of fruit" and Castañeda de Nájera thought that in the mountains of what is now northern New Mexico "there were sources of silver, if they had been looked for," no one on the expedition prospected for precious metals, and no one attempted to cultivate the Great Plains.[5]

It has become a mechanically repeated cliché that Spanish conquistadores suffered from an insatiable lust for gold that trumped every other motive. The sum of available evidence shows otherwise. Generally speaking, raw natural resources such as minerals and arable fertile land held, by themselves, little or no attraction for the Coronado expeditionaries and members of other Spanish-led *entradas* in the Americas during the first half of the sixteenth century. Although unique in many other ways, in this respect the Coronado expedition shared the object of other enterprises of conquest of the day. For the free European men who paid to go on the expedition, one generalized formulation probably covers the most widespread of their ambitions: to secure for themselves and their dependents lives of ease and honor.

How did one do that in sixteenth-century North America? Instead of the array of what are commonly considered resources today, it was the native peoples of the Americas on which the viability, prosperity, and justification of a universal Spanish empire were seen to depend.

Understanding what drove the Coronado expedition and therefore why it was abandoned requires bridging a crucial cultural and temporal gulf. A profound divide exists between sixteenth-century Spanish conquistadores' visions of the "New World" and the corresponding views of the "West" held by eighteenth- and nineteenth-century Anglo-American frontiersmen. In the later, Anglo-American case, as historian Frederick Jackson Turner so insightfully pointed out more than a century ago, it was "an area of free land" that lured westward migration, settlement, and exploitation during the 1700s and 1800s.⁶ By and large, the native peoples of the land were seen as obstacles and impediments to that movement.

For the members of the Coronado expedition and about 130 other *entradas* mounted throughout the Americas during the first half of the 1500s under the authority of the Spanish king, it was American natives themselves, rather than empty land, who constituted the attraction of the hemisphere. Key to comprehending this cultural difference are centuries-old Iberian traditions of conquest, *encomienda*, and tribute, which draw us back even farther into the past before we can proceed forward.

Between A.D. 711 and 722, Islamic Moors under a leader named Tariq ibn Ziyad were invited to come to the aid of one side in a civil war between Christian religious factions in the Visogothic kingdom that had held sway over the Iberian Peninsula for more than two centuries. In the end, the Moors abandoned their role as mercenaries and overran nearly the entire peninsula, defeating the presumptive Christian king Rodrigo and establishing sovereignty through Islamic states. That conquest, in turn, set off a Christian reconquest, or *reconquista*, that was to last sporadically for 770 years. The *reconquista* culminated in the capitulation of the last emir of Granada, Mahomet Abdala, better known as Boabdil, on January 2, 1492.⁷ As had been royal practice earlier during the *reconquista*, immediately in the wake of the fall of the last Islamic state in Iberia the Spanish monarchs granted to the most illustrious of the leaders of the triumph *repartimientos*, or grants of authority over Moorish vassals, on whom the newly installed Spanish lords levied increasingly onerous tribute.⁸ Indeed, it was the right to levy taxes and tribute that constituted the principal benefit of being designated lord of a reconquered territory.

The swelling ranks of semiautonomous Christian overlords finally threatened to block the Spanish monarchs' pretensions to preeminent, peninsula-wide authority. Even as early as 1480 Queen Isabel of Castilla had overseen the issuance of ordinances aimed at limiting the independence of the tribute-collecting nobility. She and her husband, Fernando, king of Aragón, undertook a program to reduce both the size and the power of the Spanish nobility.⁹ It was the monarchs' hope, in the aftermath of Christopher Columbus's revelation to Europe of a "new world" in the west, also in 1492, not to extend the granting of *repartimientos* and *encomiendas* to the "islands and the mainland of the ocean sea," as the Western Hemisphere was known for a time. But the royal treasury and bureaucracy were not nearly large enough to fund and control the extension of Spanish dominion over what eventually proved to be two huge and populous continents.

That extension of sovereignty could be carried out only by the numerous and well-to-do *hidalgo* class, which comprised the range of the privileged from dukes and *marqueses* to petty nobility. And for such labor and expense, *hidalgos* expected reward in the centuries-old *repartimiento* tradition. Despite the monarchs' apprehension, then, from the first, *repartimientos* and *encomiendas* of Native American communities were made to "deserving" Spaniards. Columbus himself began the process in 1497, and Nicolás de Ovando, governor of the island of Española, formalized and made it routine by 1505.¹⁰ An *encomienda*-granting document from Yucatán in 1544 expresses the rationale behind New World *repartimientos*:

> I give in *encomienda* and *repartimiento* to you . . . the town of Taxica . . . with all its lords and *caciques* and nobles, and all the divisions and subject villages of the said town, so that you may use and profit by them in your estates and commerce . . . I give it to you in remuneration for your services and hardships and expenditures, and for the services you have rendered to His Majesty in . . . conquest and pacification.¹¹

As a result of such a grant, a native community was obligated to pay tribute to the king through "its" *encomendero*, who in turn was to provide military protection and religious instruction to all the people of the community. On the islands of the Caribbean, tribute provided to *encomenderos* generally took the form of labor.[12]

When, in 1521, the great Mexica, or Aztec, capital of Tenochtitlan fell to the combined assaults of a thousand or so Europeans and many thousands of native allies led by Hernando Cortés, the victorious conquistadores expected *repartimientos*. Cortés, too, anticipated such recompense and forthwith assigned *repartimientos*, or *encomiendas*, as they now came to be called, to 313 of Tenochtitlan's conquerors. Because the population of the Mexica state (primarily in what is today central Mexico) was very large in 1521—perhaps as many as 3 million people and certainly at least 1 million—*encomiendas* granted to its conquerors averaged thousands of tributaries (adult men) apiece.[13] A well-developed preconquest tradition of in-kind or commodity tribute among the Mexica and their neighbors resulted in the payment of the same type of tribute to Spanish *encomenderos*, in addition to labor. In Nueva España the most common items of in-kind tribute were gold, cotton cloth, and foodstuffs. Tribute, in effect a per capita tax, has been called "the central unique economic feature of Spanish dominion over New World peoples."[14]

Only 18 years after the fall of Tenochtitlan and the granting of *encomiendas* there, the Coronado expedition was planned and organized in the Ciudad de México, which had in the meantime risen from the rubble of the Mexica capital. As historian Robert Himmerich y Valencia has written, although "it is impossible to know exactly what an *entrada* recruiting pitch was like, most surely it held out the promise of *encomiendas* for the participants."[15] Even if the organizers of the Coronado expedition offered no such explicit inducement, its leading participants, as well as many of the rank and file, certainly expected to earn lucrative *encomiendas* in Cíbola, which was said to be even grander than Tenochtitlan.

When the rumors and reports of Cíbola's greatness and wealth proved mistaken, the aspiring *encomenderos* of the expedition felt betrayed. They searched energetically across hundreds of miles of territory for some other indigenous community that could supply valuable commodities in sufficient quantities to underwrite lives of ease and honor. "None of them found anything."¹⁶ With the principal aim of the expedition foreclosed, there was no sensible reason to prolong the search. The captains and *caballeros* spoke one after another in council in support of turning back south, and the expedition started for home.

Eventually, at least 18 members of the Coronado expedition became *encomenderos* anyway, although elsewhere in the Americas, not at Cíbola or anywhere in Tierra Nueva.

Complementary Motives

After the *junta* agreed to abort the expedition, fray Juan de Padilla unexpectedly announced that he and another Franciscan, fray Luis de Úbeda, would remain in the north.¹⁷ Padilla would go to Quivira, far out on the plains, while his confrere would stay at Cicuique (SeeKWEEkay), or Pecos Pueblo, in what is now New Mexico. This, fray Juan said, they would do under license from their provincial, Marcos de Niza, "since his great passion was to convert those people [of Quivira] and bring them to the Faith."¹⁸ Meanwhile, fray Luis proclaimed that "with a chisel and adze that was being left to him he would put up crosses throughout those *pueblos*, or communities of modest size, and would baptize infants he would find on the point of death, in order to send them to heaven."¹⁹

The captain general, though clearly displeased by the assertion of Franciscan independence and undoubtedly concerned for the friars' safety, acquiesced to their separate plans. A herd of sheep was segregated and dispatched for the friars' support. And Vázquez de Coronado and his advisors permitted fray Juan to take with him a Portuguese layman, Andrés de Campo, as well as a black man, a *mestizo* (an offspring of the union of an Indian and a Spaniard), and several Indians from Nueva España.²⁰ These last included two Indian *donados*, or lay assistants, by the names of Sebastián and Lucas, from Zapotlán in today's Jalisco, where fray Juan had been *guardián*, or superior, before the expedition.²¹ As Juan Jaramillo later remembered, "some Indians, including one from my company, a Tarascan called Andrés, also stayed."²² Meanwhile, expeditionaries Melchior Pérez and Juan Jaramillo each provided black slaves to accompany and support fray Luis in his missionary work at Cicuique.

They were a Cristóbal, a second Sebastián, and an unnamed slave of Pérez's, who also had his wife and children with him.²³

Stated most broadly, the aim of these two Franciscans and their small entourages was to bring into the Catholic faith as many American natives as they might be able to. For followers of Saint Francis of Assisi in the early 1500s, the missionary enterprise had a special urgency. Many believed their order to be one of two that, within their lifetimes, were expected to achieve the complete conversion of the world, which would culminate in the second coming of Christ.

Much of the enthusiasm for evangelism among the early New World Franciscans, including fray Juan de Padilla, can be traced to their acceptance of the ideas of the twelfth-century apocalyptic cleric Joachim of Fiore.²⁴ Joachim and his followers preached the imminent end of the world, to be ushered in by the worldwide spread of a reborn Catholicism effected by two new religious orders. Many Franciscans of the early 1500s were sure theirs was one of those two evangelical orders destined to bring about the renewal of the Church and the conversion of the world.²⁵ The Joachimites' view of human history divided it into three great eras: the Age of the Patriarchs (the Old Testament), the Age of the Apostles (the New Testament), and the final era, the Age of the Missionaries, which would culminate in the millennium. For many Franciscans, the beginning of the third age was signaled by the revelation to Europe of unproselytized multitudes in the Western Hemisphere.²⁶

An indication of the influence of Joachimite millenarianism in the early evangelization of Nueva España is that all 16 of the first Franciscan missionaries to Nueva España—including "Los Doce," the first twelve, led by fray Martín de Valencia—were millenarians, as was the first bishop of Mexico, fray Juan de Zumárraga.²⁷ Fray Juan de Padilla's adherence to Joachimite ideals seems all but certain, given his close association with several of Los Doce and the bishop.²⁸ Padilla must have considered his return to Quivira a glorious duty and a fortunate opportunity to hasten the return of Christ.

The members of his small ecclesiastical company were not the only people who voiced a desire to remain in Tierra Nueva once the decision to return south was announced. Others reversed themselves and decided to try to stay, given the friars' resolve. Testifying two years after the end of the expedition, Alonso Sánchez, a cobbler and small merchant who was on the *entrada*, certified that he, "his wife and son, and another 60 persons wanted to stay in that land with fray Juan de Padilla."[29] Castañeda de Nájera amplified that story, writing in the 1560s that a group "requested that the general leave seventy chosen men. They would stay there and hold the land until the viceroy sent them aid or summoned them [to return]." In addition, some of the *caballeros* who had previously put their signatures to the agreement to turn south now changed their minds and even tried to retrieve and destroy the document recording the *junta*'s formal decision.[30] According to Juan Jaramillo, "10 or 12 of us were not party to [abandoning Tierra Nueva], arguing with [the captain general] about it in order to keep him from doing it."[31] These lay members of the expedition who expressed a desire to stay in the north were forbidden to do so and were compelled to retreat southward with the rest of the expedition, minus most of its ecclesiastical contingent.

If Alonso Sánchez and his wife, Francisca de Hozes, were typical of those who sought to remain behind the expedition, then that group was composed of people whose prospects in the Ciudad de México or elsewhere in Nueva España were unpromising. Certainly there were many among the expeditionaries who had been without profitable employment before their departure for the north. As Cristóbal de Oñate put it after reviewing the muster of the expedition, many of those going "were licentious and had no [means] by which to sustain themselves" in the Ciudad de México or elsewhere.[32] When the Sánchez couple mustered into the expedition early in 1540, observers in the Ciudad de México said that Alonso was in debt and had been unsuccessful in his trade. Serván Béjarano, for example, stated that he knew Alonso Sánchez "to be a small merchant, and because he is very short of funds and does not have [anything] with which to sustain himself, he is going to the land to seek a livelihood."[33] Sánchez and his wife had little to look forward to back in the Ciudad de México, where several thousand ambitious Europeans now lived, scrambling after every opportunity.[34] Furthermore, as will be seen later, the Sánchez family faced dunning by creditors back in the viceregal capital. Better, they must have thought, to stay where the husband would have a corner on the crucial trade in footwear to the small group of expeditionaries who proposed to stay in Tierra Nueva. Beyond that, there was still the possibility that a populous and wealthy indigenous community would be found where lives as *encomenderos* would be possible.

Like Sánchez, other members of the expedition pursued their usual occupations or engaged in other economic activities while on the *entrada* and clearly saw the expedition itself as a means of making a livelihood. Among the known active entrepreneurs were Melchior Pérez, Cristóbal de Escobar, and Domingo Martín, all of whom took significant herds of livestock with them, evidently with the intention of selling animals to other members of the expedition.[35] Juan Jiménez, a likely clothing merchant, also made the trip, conducting numerous business transactions along the way.[36] Artisans such as hosier Tomás Blaque, tailors Juan Gómez de Paradinas and Juan Cordero, blacksmith Francisco de Santillana, and pictorial painters Cristóbal de Quesada and Bartolomé Sánchez were almost certain to have plied their trades en route to Cíbola, Tiguex, and Quivira.[37] For all such persons the expedition in its own right was a source of income, and they would have been able to continue to support themselves in any Spanish community of sufficient size that might have been founded in Tierra Nueva.

Holding reasons markedly different from those of European conquistadores and missionaries for making the long trek north were the Mexican Indians. *Indios amigos*, or allies and sometimes servants, in fact made up the largest component of the expedition, totaling perhaps 1,300 to 1,500 persons when the *entrada* began.[38] They came from what is now central and western Mexico and were recruited into the expedition principally as warriors, in groups under their own leadership. *Indios amigos* were a major part of the fighting force of the expedition, and their involvement in combat helps explain the ease with which most of the indigenous communities encountered were subdued or overawed into pro forma submission.[39] The *amigos* were invaluable to the expedition because they came from cultures such as the Mexica and the Tarascan, in which war and its skills had been centrally important for centuries before the Spanish conquest. As historian Inga Clendinnen eloquently wrote: "Mexica society was committed to war, not as an occasional heroic obligation, but chronically ... To be born male in Tenochtitlan was to be designated a warrior ... All were given the opportunity to excel; those who did excel were lavishly rewarded ... 'Success' was measured narrowly by the number and status of enemy warriors taken alive in one-to-one combat."[40] A painted document from Mexico in the 1540s, the Codex Mendoza, provides further details: "Warrior costumes identified the warriors according to rank, [the warriors] rising in higher authority with each rank, by the number of captives they captured in warfare."[41]

This central Mexican warrior tradition and its route to advancement survived the conquest. Although Spanish authorities forcefully put a damper on ritualized warfare between indigenous communities under their control, they also made possible continued achievement for warriors by repeatedly enlisting them as allies in campaigns against native uprisings and still unconquered groups, such as those met by the Coronado expedition. Although the documents detailing recruitment of Indian allies for the Coronado expedition itself are vague, others of the same era suggest strongly that the opportunity for performing feats of war was the overriding motivation for native warriors to sign on. For instance, explicit promises were made to central Mexican Indians in Durango, Mexico, in the 1560s that they would be allowed to keep the prisoners they might take while serving as auxiliaries.[42] The right to take and keep prisoners was crucially important to Mexica religious and military custom, which called for the periodic sacrifice of important war captives. Permission to keep captives for their own uses was probably given to the 1,300 or more *indios amigos* who participated in the Coronado expedition. As a result, those native warriors had a strong incentive for engaging in combat and perhaps even provoking it.

Contemporary documentary evidence suggests that some indigenous leaders, at least, chose to commit their people to participating in the *entrada* in exchange for a cash payment and reduction of their community's tribute obligations. According to an Indian leader called don

Alonso in the Tarascan-Purépecha community of Pátzcuaro in what is now Michoacán, don Luis de Castilla, a close associate of the Spanish viceroy, "told [the leaders] that he wanted to pay for the food and load bearers they had supplied to the people who were going to Tierra Nueva and for that reason he was reducing and ordering that they pay less tribute."[43] Later, some native allies of the Coronado expedition chose to stay at Cíbola and elsewhere in Tierra Nueva. There, unfettered by Spanish strictures on traditional indigenous warfare and other traditional practices, they were likely in ensuing years to have displayed their abilities as warriors in the Pueblo world to their advantage. It is possible that many of them became honored and respected members of their new communities as a result of that military skill, for intertribal warfare was common in Tierra Nueva, and warriors also held an important place in Pueblo societies.[44] Certainly for central Mexican Indians who felt aggrieved or marginalized under Spanish dominance, remaining in the north allowed escape into a purely native environment that offered at least the possibility of restored status and autonomy. It is even remotely possible that some *indios amigos* planned from the beginning of the expedition to desert in order to escape Spanish domination.

Indian allies were not alone in seeking advancement through display of military prowess. European expeditionaries, too, could earn more exalted positions or financial rewards as a consequence of exploits in battle. For elites such as Vázquez de Coronado and other captains and *caballeros*, successful prosecution of the *entrada* could mean prestigious and lucrative offices in the imperial bureaucracy. And not a few persons of all ethnic backgrounds joined the expedition at least partly out of an urge to experience the excitement and adventure of the conquest of the Americas, an undertaking that had been all the talk in both Europe and the New World for two generations.[45]

A Red Herring

Herbert E. Bolton, the mid-twentieth-century biographer of Vázquez de Coronado, wrote that "Coronado made one of the significant expeditions of that remarkable era of the opening of the Western Hemisphere by Europeans . . . To the map of the interior of North America he added Cíbola, Tusayán, the Llanos del Cíbola, and Quivira."⁴⁶

Bolton also credited the Coronado *entrada* with discovery of the Continental Divide, a more accurate assessment of the width of North America than had previously been made, the first written description of the Grand Canyon, and a contribution to the understanding of magnetic declination. Although those few geographical observations do appear in documents deriving from the expedition, such remarks are rare. Almost completely lacking in the documents are descriptions of the landscape, delineations of topography, and precise identifications of the routes traveled. By emphasizing the few instances of geographical comment made in the documents, Bolton conveyed the impression that geographical exploration was a major preoccupation of the expeditionaries. This was an ascription of geographical curiosity to the expedition by a modern historian for whom it was important to show that the *entrada* was not an utter failure. Persistent application by modern historians and others of the label "explorers" to sixteenth-century Spanish expeditionaries has served to euphemize an enterprise that was essentially one of personal aggrandizement and imperial extension of political, economic, and religious hegemony.

Typically, for conquistadores of the first half of the sixteenth century, the service that stood to earn the award of an *encomienda* was to add to the royal dominion a large group of sophisticated and prosperous people. The Coronado expedition's drive was to locate large population centers where valuable commodities were being produced. The expedition explored the country almost exclusively to determine where the people were, how many of them there were, and what they did for a living. The expeditionaries followed guides from one native settlement to another, traveling by long-established routes. They did not blaze trails. And their interest in geographical exploration per se was all but nonexistent. In their own terminology, they were conquistadores, not *exploradores*, or explorers. Their reports do not provide the material for practical road maps. Even with the reports of the Coronado expedition in hand, later travelers from the Ciudad de México to Cíbola would routinely have had to rely on human guides to show the way.

This is not to say that members of the Spanish bureaucracy lacked any interest in geography. A royal cosmographer and the staff of the office of the *piloto mayor*, or chief pilot, assiduously extracted what information they could from expedition reports from the world over. But from expeditionary documents one gets no sense that the participants themselves were animated by a desire to "know" or "reveal" the physical globe. Such intellectual urges were not prominently or frequently expressed by expeditionaries in either word or deed. In fact, many members of the expedition, like other Europeans of the day, still held firmly to fixed and unchallengeable medieval beliefs about the configuration of the world.

Imperial Interest and Composite Motives

The motives outlined so far are those that stirred people to enlist and invest in the Coronado expedition and others of that era. For the imperial administration and the royal court, additional factors justified the encouragement and licensing of *entradas* such as the one led by Francisco Vázquez de Coronado. Carlos I, king of the Spanish realms and Holy Roman Emperor with the title Carlos V, emphasized one particular element of his own motivation on the day in 1520 when he addressed the Cortes of Castilla as emperor-elect:

> From God alone is empire. Nor have I undertaken that charge of such great measure for my own sake. For well was I able to be content with the Spanish empire [*Hispano imperio*] with the Balearics and Sardinia, with the Sicilian kingdom, with a great part of Italy, Germany and France and with another, as I might say, gold bearing world [meaning the Americas] . . . But here befalls a certain fatal necessity concerning matters which urges me to take sail. Furthermore, decision must be taken out of proper respect for religion, whose enemy thus far has grown so that moreover neither the repose of the commonwealth, nor the dignity of Spain nor finally the welfare of my kingdoms are able to tolerate such a threat.[47]

The king and his advisors thus saw themselves engaged in a grand mission to defeat the enemies of the Roman Catholic Church and, as the king's grand chancellor, Mercurino de Gattinara, put it, to bring peace and justice to the world.[48] To establish a universal empire under the dual authority of the Spanish crown and the Roman Catholic Church was the overarching desire. Not only was that consistent with the enrichment of the Empire and the Church, but it actually implied that goal. Imperial justification dovetailed neatly with the ambitions of individuals from king to *criados* (his retainers or household members) and *criados* of *criados*, all the way to the humblest levels of society. So it was that the executors of the estate of expeditionary Juan Jiménez asked that he be granted a papal indulgence because of his participation in a "holy crusade"—his service on the Coronado expedition.[49]

Although the motivations set out here were surely the most potent and prevalent ones to affect those who made up the Coronado expedition, this short list is by no means exhaustive. Nor were expeditionaries necessarily subject to only one motive. Indeed, that was probably rarely the case. Instead, for individuals, as for the expedition as a whole, the inducement of aspirations and the push of necessity combined in complex and shifting configurations to direct them toward Cíbola and beyond.

Aspiring to become a wealthy *encomendero* or a member of the household of such a lord was not at all incompatible with seeking a more prosaic living in the meantime. And the risk and wonder of adventure, along with the display of derring-do in war, could sometimes earn the king's favor and merit the award of an *encomienda*. In addition, the would-be *encomendero*, the expeditionary with the Coronado *entrada*, could at the same time see himself as an agent of the faith, hastening the millennium and the universal authority of the Church.

With a complex web of motives that varied from person to person, then, is where we begin. All the motives outlined here became focused for several thousand people on a single place, the Seven Cities of Cíbola.

CHAPTER 2

Precious Goods of Greater India, China, and Antilia

If most European expeditionaries were urged on by dreams of sumptuous lives as *encomenderos*, then why did the newly "discovered" lands of the Ocean Sea, especially their northern and western reaches, seem to promise such a seigneurial existence? The beginning of an answer comes again from the chronicler and former expeditionary Pedro de Castañeda de Nájera. A repeated theme that sounds throughout his *Relación* is "in what region Greater India lies." That is a crucial issue because Greater India was, according to the chronicler, "what was being sought when the expedition set out to go there."[1]

It was common knowledge among members of the Coronado expedition, as among Europeans of the day at large, that the most opulent populations on earth were to be found in Greater India, China, and Antilia. Since at least the days of the Roman Empire, Iberian elites had been accustomed to acquiring and using luxury goods from the Orient. Those goods included finery such as silks and other elegant fabrics, porcelain, lacquerware, cloisonné, furniture, tapestries, spices, gemstones, pearls, silver, and gold. Asia's "coveted products, such as silks, spices and porcelains, and the commercial monopoly wielded over them by Islamic intermediaries was what motivated European navigators to open up new communication routes which provided direct contact with 'The Indies.'"[2] Pound for pound, silk was for centuries more valuable than any of the precious metals and so provided a powerful incentive for conquest and reconnaissance.[3]

The celebrated book *The Travels*, written by Marco Polo and his collaborator, Rustichello, perennially popular since its appearance around 1300, is flush with details of the richness of the East. For example, the authors spoke of Kublai Khan's capital, Khan-balik (modern Beijing), this way:

> You may take it for a fact that more precious and costly wares are imported into Khan-balik than into any other city in the world. Let me give you particulars. All the treasures that come from India—precious stones, pearls, and other rarities—are brought here. So too are the choicest and costliest products of Cathay itself and every other province . . . It is a fact that every day more than 1,000 cart-loads of silk enter the city; for much cloth of gold and silk is woven here.[4]

Not only was the Far East a place of inconceivable wealth, but it was also a potential field of Christian missionary labor. After all, the great Kublai Khan himself had sent a message to the pope inviting missionaries to China as early as the thirteenth century.[5] For centuries Cathay and Greater India fired the imaginations of ambitious Europeans, ecclesiastic and lay alike.

In the late 1530s, when the Coronado *entrada* was being organized, European cosmographers and cartographers still conceived of the islands and land masses that Columbus had seen nearly 50 years earlier as eastward appendages and the periphery of Asia. Circumnavigation of the globe in 1518–22 had shown the southern Mar del Sur (South Pacific Ocean) to be extremely wide, suggesting to some Europeans that the Americas were continents independent of Asia. Many others, probably the majority, maintained that in their northern reaches Asia and America were one.[6] If Castañeda de Nájera is representative of the Coronado expeditionaries—and in this case he probably is—then they were among the latter group, who believed in a contiguous Amerasia. Writing in the 1560s, the chronicler still held the opinion that "just as this land of Nueva España is a [continuous] landmass with El Peru, so is it also with Greater India or China."[7] He went on to lament that the Coronado expedition had missed its chance at lives of ease for all by setting its course eastward from the Río de Tiguex, rather than westward: "I think that if those mountain ranges where that [Tiguex] river has its headwaters were crossed and [if] the lands from which those people [the Pueblos] originate were entered, magnificent news would probably be obtained. [That is] because, according to the direction, [that land] is the beginning of Greater India, although [in] remote regions."[8]

As historians have previously noted, long-established preconceptions maintained a hold on popular thought in Europe, even in the face of mounting conflicting evidence.[9] The strong medieval conviction that earth's inhabited land was divided into three parts, and only three, Europe, Asia, and Africa—one for each of Noah's sons and his descendants—made acceptance of the concept of an independent continental America extremely difficult.[10] Only slowly and with considerable theological agony did the observations of conquistadores and navigators convincingly redraw the globe. Certainly such a reconfiguration of the earth had not been absorbed into the popular consciousness in Spain or anywhere else in Europe at the time of the Coronado *entrada*. To travel west and north from the Ciudad de México was, for the expeditionaries, to approach the affluent lands of Greater India and China, civilized but non-Christian places where wealthy Indian populations, ripe with tribute goods, awaited their conquerors. Splendid *encomiendas*, they imagined, lay only weeks of travel away in the Orient.

Preconceptions: Antilia, Amazons, and Aztlán

Persistent medieval European notions of world geography also reserved a spot for a place called Antilia in the Ocean Sea to the west of Europe, between there and Greater India. Antilia was thought to be the refuge of seven Catholic bishops who had fled the Moorish invasion of Iberia in the 700s. As recounted in a gloss on the globe prepared by the cartographer Martin Behaim, or Boheim, in 1492: "In A.D. 734, when the whole of Spain had been won by the African heathen, the above island of Antilia, called Seven Cities, was occupied by an archbishop from Oporto, Portugal, with six other bishops, and other Christians, men and women, who had fled thither from Spain by ship, together with their cattle, property and goods. In 1414 a ship from Spain got nearest to it without danger."[11]

In one of a series of raids from North Africa, a Muslim force under Tariq ibn Ziyad had achieved astounding success in the early eighth century, overrunning nearly the entire Iberian Peninsula. Many, indeed, were the Visigothic Christian refugees who abandoned their homes and fled during the Muslim invasion. The remainder of the story of the seven bishops, though, is apparently apocryphal.

Supposedly, each bishop founded a city, and all of these, over the centuries, became extremely prosperous. A nautical chart of 1424 drawn by the Venetian cartographer Zuane Pizzigano even supplied the names of the cities: Asay, Ary, Vra or Ura, Jaysos, Marnlio, Ansuly, and Cyodne.[12] The prospect of rich Christian communities in the direction of, perhaps even near, Asia was an enticing possibility for generations of aspiring overlords and missionaries. Although claimed sightings of Antilia took place earlier, not until 1492 did it seem within reach. On September 25 of that year Columbus's crews thought they sighted an island they had expected to find in accordance with earlier charts. This, they presumed, was Antilia. They were disappointed the following day to find that they had mistaken a cloud bank on the western horizon for a land mass.[13]

The Genoese navigator had in fact set his course to the west at 28 degrees north latitude, precisely in the hope of running into Antilia. Traveling on that latitude, maintained the Florentine physician and cosmographer Paolo dal Pozzo Toscanelli, one would inevitably circle from the Canary Islands to Japan by way of Antilia.[14] As events played out, Columbus landed two and half weeks after sighting the false island on what he thought was the fringe of Asia. En route, he had not located the seven cities. The Portuguese bishops and their flocks were to remain elusive throughout the sixteenth century, until finally they were forgotten or dismissed as mythical. But while the story lived, Antilia was a goal of dozens of journeys on land and sea, including the Coronado *entrada*.[15] A version of the name is still applied to the archipelago that marks the eastern limit of the Caribbean Sea.

Beyond the supposed seven cities of the bishops, on "the right hand of the Indies," lay another fabulous land, an island of amazons, women who lived totally without men. That island, according to the *Sergas de*

Esplandián, a chivalric tale published in 1508, was known as California.¹⁶ Nor were California and Antilia presumed to be alone on the periphery of Greater India. St. Brendan's Isle, Ophir, the land of Gog and Magog, the Terrestrial Paradise, and scores of other exotic and wealthy places were sprinkled across the globe westward from Europe.

Not only European geography posited the existence of marvelous places. Indigenous origin stories from the Valley of Mexico told of another place with a curious numeric similarity to Antilia: the Seven Caves of Aztlán, also called Teocolhuacan and Chicomoztoc. According to a version of the story recorded by the Dominican friar Diego Durán in the 1570s, the Mexica, or Aztecs, and their relatives began migrating southward from the caves "near the region of La Florida" in A.D. 820. "The people erected great and curious buildings in each settlement along the way, so that today remains of these edifices are found in many places where they stayed."¹⁷ When Europeans heard the stories of the Seven Caves of Aztlán, they easily conflated them with the Seven Cities of Antilia and other New World places soon to be heard of that were likewise associated with the number seven.

The presumed existence of such places near Greater India—that is, to the north and west of the Ciudad de México—inspired anticipation of prosperous lives as *encomenderos* among the Coronado expeditionaries.

Relevant Experience in the Indies

When Europeans arrived in what we now know as the Caribbean Basin, the evidence of where they were was equivocal, but to such people, none of whom had ever been to Asia, it was not inconsistent with reports and tales of that luxurious and populous continent. The tropical climate and the vegetation were not out of line with what they thought they knew about Greater India. There were, for instance, in the paraphrased words of Columbus, palm trees "differing from those of Guinea and from ours," along with other trees "beautiful and green and different from ours." There were trees identified as cinnamon and mastic and other "aromatic" plants.¹⁸ On striking the coast of what we now know as Cuba, Columbus and his companions concluded that they were "off Zayto and Quinsay," referring to Zhao'an and Hangzhou in China.[19] The admiral died in 1506 still believing that the lands he had seen and visited from 1492 to 1504 were part of opulent Asia.[20]

Such conclusions were consistent with much contemporary geographical thought and were slow to give way in the face of new evidence. There was indeed much to suggest that the islands and continental land newly revealed to Europe were at least close to Asia and other wealthy places such as the seven cities of the Portuguese bishops. Rumors of teeming, luxurious polities in the oriental mold abounded, some of European origin and others inspired by Native American reports. Many of these rumors launched expeditions, usually unsuccessful, to confirm them.

Some of the reports seemed to be confirmed. For instance, in 1517 native accounts led Francisco Hernández de Córdoba to the Yucatán Peninsula, thought for years afterward to be an island and given the name Isla Rica, the Wealthy Island. There Hernández and his followers entered a large town with towers and pyramids where the people wore cotton clothing. The town was promptly christened El Gran Cairo, revealing the expeditionaries' oriental expectations. Coasting westward, Hernández got a look at "a settlement with up to three thousand [stone] houses with innumerable people" in what is now the Mexican state of Campeche.[21]

Following up on that and other sightings of the protohistoric Maya, less than two years later Hernando Cortés, with a fleet of nine ships, heard about even grander places westward. Pursuing that direction, Cortés and his followers put in at an anchorage they called San Juan de Ulúa on the Gulf Coast of what is now Mexico. Reports from nearby natives spoke of extremely large cities in the interior, where an omnipotent ruler received lavish tribute. In early November 1519 a huge land expedition, composed principally of indigenous warriors in company with Cortés's modest troop of Europeans, arrived at Tenochtitlan, the seat of the Mexica empire. The city occupied an island in Lake Texcoco in the Basin of Mexico, where, wrote one of Cortés's men, "we did not know what to say, or whether what appeared before us was real, for on one side, on the land, there were great cities, and in the lake ever so many more."[22]

Within days Cortés and his followers, now guests of Moctezuma in the island city, uncovered a storeroom of "such a number of jewels and slabs and plates of gold and chalchihuites [semi-precious green stones] and other great riches, that they were quite carried away and did not know what to say about such wealth."[23]

Easily the largest city in the Indies, and certainly among the largest in the world as known to Europeans of the time, Tenochtitlan stood as a stunning promise of lordly futures for those in the service of Emperor Carlos. Although modern estimates of its protohistoric population vary widely, a figure of 200,000 to 300,000 for the city itself seems not excessive.[24] Chances are that none of the Europeans with Cortés had ever been in a larger city or one more sumptuously exotic. According to Francisco López de Gómara, later Cortés's secretary:

> There was no one in all his [Moctezuma's] dominions that did not pay some tribute to the lord of Mexico . . . the owners gave a third of their yearly produce, to wit: dogs, fowl, birds of plumage, rabbits, gold, silver, precious stones, salt, wax and honey, mantles, featherwork, cotton, cacao, maize, chili, sweet potatoes, broad beans, kidney beans, and all kinds of fruit, greenstuff, and cereals, by which they live.[25]

Surely Tenochtitlan would be only the beginning. And indeed, within weeks of the capture of the Mexica capital,

> the king of Michoacán, called the Cazonci, an ancient and natural enemy of the Mexicans [Mexica], and himself a very great lord, sent ambassadors to Cortés . . . Cortés sent Cristóbal de Olid, with 40 horse and 100 Spanish foot, to found a colony at Tzintzuntzan. Cazonci was happy to have them settle there and gave them a quantity of feather and cotton clothing, 5,000 pesos in base gold (mixed with silver), and 1,000 marks of an amalgam of silver and copper.[26]

Entradas sent out by Cortés subsequently took control of populous polities all over what is now Mexico and Mesoamerica. Often in accordance with preconquest records of indigenous tribute systems, Cortés and his lieutenants conferred hundreds of *encomiendas* on themselves, their subordinates, and expeditionaries who had distinguished themselves during the conquests. By 1555 more than 500 persons had been granted *encomiendas* in Nueva España alone.[27]

Meanwhile, in the 1530s, in what we now know as South America, another empire rivaling that of the Mexica had been conquered and distributed for administration by *encomenderos*, that of the Andean Inca. Writing from secondhand information about Cajamarca, one of several population centers in the Inca Empire, Gonzalo Fernández de Oviedo y Valdés reported that "the valley has much level land, all settled in *pueblos* . . . In this [particular] *pueblo* [Cajamarca] there are probably two thousand *vecinos* . . . The plaza that is mentioned is larger than any in Spain . . . Its residences are very well built and each more than two hundred paces long."[28] It was clearly another remarkable place, promising perpetual income to its overlords. Indeed, the greatest treasure ever assembled in the Indies was soon extorted from the Inca's subjects and shared among Spanish conquistadores. As for the longer term, every man who received a share of the ransom at Cajamarca "almost automatically became a large *encomendero* of one of the more important Peruvian cities."[29]

Hearsay and Corroboration about the North

As Spanish sovereignty expanded through the Americas during the first decades of the sixteenth century, the impending discovery of Antilia and an approach to Greater India was a constant background motif. Understandably, Castañeda de Nájera used a discussion of the famous seven cities to open his *Relación* of the Coronado *entrada*, including in the title of the first chapter a specific reference to "how the first settlement of the seven *ciudades* became known."[30] He then explained that ten years before the departure of the Coronado *entrada*, Nuño Beltrán de Guzmán, former president of the Audiencia (high court) of Nueva España, had "mustered nearly four hundred Spaniards and twenty thousand [native] allies from Nueva España" in order to reconnoiter the seven *ciudades*.³¹

As Castañeda de Nájera told the story, Guzmán had with him a native of Oxitipar, now in the eastern part of the Mexican state of San Luis Potosí. This man, known as Tejo, claimed to have made a trip or two far into the interior with his merchant father. They had reached "seven very grand *pueblos* where there were streets of silver workshops," where his father had traded feathers for gold and silver.³²

In pursuit of these seven *pueblos*, Guzmán and his expedition traversed what is today west-central Mexico and trekked northward along the Pacific coastal plain as far as the vicinity of modern Culiacán. Guzmán founded several Spanish *pueblos* and distributed dozens of *encomiendas* to his followers.³³ But for several reasons, including, significantly, the return of Guzmán's rival Hernando Cortés to Mexico from Spain, the expedition in search of Tejo's *pueblos* of silver workers was abandoned. Thus, according to Castañeda de Nájera, "the name of the Seven *Ciudades* and the search for them have endured. [Still] today [the 1560s] they have not been reconnoitered."³⁴

The next news of these marvelous seven *ciudades* came in 1536 with four shipwreck survivors, Álvar Núñez Cabeza de Vaca, Alonso del Castillo Maldonado, Andrés Dorantes, and Esteban de Dorantes. They had been captives of American natives in what is now Texas after a sea disaster had killed most of their hundreds of companions in an expedition led by Pánfilo de Narváez. After years of servile existence among indigenous groups, the four finally fled toward the possibility of Spanish settlements in Nueva Galicia, Guzmán's new jurisdiction.

In the course of what became a much celebrated trek, ending at Culiacán, they met natives who told of "*pueblos* with many people and very large houses," where the people wore "cotton shirts." These towns, they said, lay north of the Cabeza de Vaca party's route.³⁵ The people of the north were supposedly skilled metalworkers, a description that seemed to be confirmed when the shipwreck survivors were given "some small bags of silver" said to have come from the northern *pueblos*.³⁶ Then, according to the survivors' "Joint Report," other natives "gave the Christians [the

Spaniards] a copper bell and some cotton blankets and said [they] came from the north."[37]

Upon their return to Spanish jurisdiction, the four dutifully reported in writing to the viceroy of Nueva España and to the king details of what they had seen and heard during their years crossing the continent. They frequently spoke about the same things, both in public and in private. The result was an overheated atmosphere of anticipation among the Europeans of the viceroyalty—anticipation of another Tenochtitlan, another Peru, even the verge of Greater India. It was widely assumed that the places the survivors had heard of were the same towns told of by Tejo and sought by Guzmán just a few years earlier. Tejo's towns, in turn, were identified with the seven cities of the Portuguese bishops, Antilia.[38] Now there were not just stories but also hard physical evidence in the form of a native-made metal bell and cotton cloth. ■

CHAPTER 3

CÍBOLA, A NAME FOR THE GOAL

AS THE KING'S ALTER EGO, Antonio de Mendoza, viceroy of Nueva España, held the responsibility of determining what should be done about the Cabeza de Vaca party's news. Even with excitement over the reported land of the copper bell, the Tierra Nueva, bubbling through Nueva España, Viceroy Mendoza moved deliberately. Such caution was his habit and policy, as is clear from some advice he gave 14 years later to don Luis de Velasco I, who succeeded him as viceroy. Mendoza wrote to his recently arrived replacement: "If you do not want to make a mistake, do little and do [that] very slowly, since most affairs permit that. Following this [method], you will not be deceived and [people] will not mislead you."[1]

In the case of what to do about Tierra Nueva, Mendoza's actions showed him focused on three preliminaries. First, as a responsible recipient of sensational news, his effort was to learn, in as much detail as possible, what the four survivors had to tell about everything they had seen and heard. He then formed a judgment of the character and reliability of the four reporters. Did they agree with each other in the essentials? Did they seem to be exaggerating or lying? Did their stories jibe with other reports? By taking such time-consuming steps, Mendoza would lessen the chance that he was being deceived or misled. Finally, after making his evaluation, he would decide on a course of action.

So, according to historians George Parker Winship, Arthur Aiton, and Herbert Bolton, when the bearers of news about Tierra Nueva reached the Ciudad de México in late July 1536, the viceroy lodged them in his own home.[2] There they remained for two months, ample opportunity for repeated conversations between them and the viceroy, both individually and as a group. Additionally, Mendoza asked that they prepare

27

a formal written report. He forwarded to the king the resulting document, written by Cabeza de Vaca, Dorantes, and Castillo Maldonado, now usually referred to as the Joint Report. In addition, according to the seventeenth-century historian fray Antonio Tello, Mendoza directed Cabeza de Vaca and Andrés Dorantes "to prepare a map of their journey and the lands they had seen."[3] If such a map was indeed drafted, it has not been seen in centuries and may have been destroyed, discarded, or simply lost.

In general the four survivors' representations, both written and oral, were tantalizing but inconclusive. Evidently Mendoza found Cabeza de Vaca to be "a person who should be relied upon," a credible informant, just as the royal chronicler Gonzalo Fernández de Oviedo y Valdés did later.[4] There was no reason for Mendoza to doubt that Cabeza de Vaca and his companions had heard and seen things that led them to believe in the existence of sizable settlements of "civilized" people far to the north. As the royal *contador*, Rodrigo de Albornoz, understood it, they told of "a very excellent and great land, comprising many settlements."[5] Such reports added considerably to earlier rumors. Determination of their plausibility fulfilled the viceroy's second requisite task. Still, there was no *eyewitness* evidence of the existence of populous towns of metalworkers, cloth weavers, and stonemasons, about whom the survivors told of having heard.

With the reliability of the party of survivors established and what they said they had seen and heard recorded in writing, the third order of business for the viceroy was to settle on what action to take in response to their remarkable news. Whatever Mendoza chose to do, he had to bear in mind that the viceroyalty had many other pressing concerns besides possible distant civilizations. The strength of the evidence was insufficient to demand that all else be put on hold while a full-blown expedition went out to bring distant and perhaps chimerical polities immediately into the Spanish imperial orbit. Nevertheless, some concrete step in that direction had to be taken, particularly because a number of other powerful and ambitious Spaniards in the New World were eager to undertake an expedition to the lands of the north on their own initiative. Among them was the renowned Hernando Cortés, who, being present at the time in

not a huge undertaking: more scouting

the Ciudad de México, had also conferred with the survivors.⁶

As Herbert Bolton put it, "Mendoza proposed to Vaca and Dorantes that [together] they should head a further reconnaissance of the regions they had traversed or had heard of on route."⁷ In Mendoza's own words, he wanted "to send some people to that land in order to learn for certain what it was."⁸ Such an endeavor would have been under Mendoza's own aegis. Assuming that he made such a proposal to the two jointly, as he did later to Dorantes alone, they assuredly rejected it. Cabeza de Vaca bridled at the idea of being only the viceroy's deputy in such a scheme. A little over a year later he turned down a similar offer from Hernando de Soto, which his contemporary Francisco de Villalta explained by saying that Cabeza de Vaca "did not wish to go under another's banner."⁹ He believed his accomplishment in crossing the continent merited reward from the king in the form of his elevation to a high imperial post, perhaps on a par with Mendoza himself.

In October 1536 Cabeza de Vaca and Dorantes, perhaps with partnership in mind, prepared to sail for Spain and the royal court.¹⁰ Afraid that no one would be left in Nueva España who was familiar with the territory crossed and peoples met by the survivors, Mendoza arranged, before Dorantes left the Ciudad de México, to purchase his black Moorish slave Esteban, who had also made the trek. As it turned out, severe storms prevented Cabeza de Vaca and Dorantes' departure, and the two remained in Nueva España until the following spring.

When Mendoza heard that after a second attempt to sail, Dorantes still had not departed, he dispatched urgent messages to the disappointed ocean traveler, asking him to journey back to the Ciudad de México. Dorantes returned. As the viceroy later wrote, "I spoke with him many times because it seemed to me that it could be of much service to Your Majesty to send him with forty or fifty horse[men] to learn the secret of those regions."¹¹ Dorantes eventually and reluctantly agreed to lead such a trip. But then, according to Mendoza, "when I had arranged what was necessary for his journey and had spent a great deal of money for this purpose, the [agreement] came apart, I do not know how, and such an enterprise was not undertaken."¹²

Negotiations with Dorantes had taken some months, beginning in spring 1537. Even as late as December that year it still appeared that Dorantes was about to lead a small expedition northward.¹³ By sometime in 1538, though, the viceroy had settled on a third choice for leader of the reconnaissance to Tierra Nueva, a forty-year-old Savoyard friar and priest named Marcos.

Why Marcos de Niza

It had been obvious to Mendoza that either Cabeza de Vaca or Dorantes would be a suitable leader for the reconnaissance. Their companion Castillo Maldonado, a *caballero* and brother of an *oidor*, or judge, of the first Audiencia of Nueva España, was evidently more interested in urban posts.¹⁴ When circumstances dictated that Mendoza choose an alternate, he consulted the Franciscan provincial and the advisory council of the Province of the Santo Evangelio. He gave their nomination priority over the advice of veteran conquistadores.

The opinion of the Franciscans carried such weight because of a movement then rising toward its peak of power in Spain. After 45 years of Spanish-led activity in the Americas, the royal court, at the urging of ecclesiastics of various orders, found the cumulative record of treatment of the New World's native peoples abysmal. They had suffered massive, violent loss of life, routine theft of property, and chronic abuse of women and laborers. As early as 1511, beginning with an excoriating sermon on the island of Española by Antonio de Montesinos, a crescendo of agitation had been heard at the Spanish court on behalf of limited rights for the indigenous people of the Americas.

By 1537 a former *encomendero* and subsequently a Dominican priest, Bartolomé de las Casas, was successfully lobbying the king and his counselors to severely limit contact between Indians and lay Europeans. He had even advocated, in 1536 or 1537, that "conquest" be undertaken with no force whatsoever, by mendicant friars alone.¹⁵ In that very year Pope Paul III added his sweeping influence on the issue by promulgating a bull titled *Sublimus Deus*, in which he declared that "Indians and other peoples should be converted to the faith of Jesus Christ by preaching the word of

God and by the example of good and holy living."¹⁶ At the same time, Las Casas was beginning an experiment in an area of what is now Guatemala, newly dubbed Vera Paz, through which he hoped to demonstrate the feasibility of converting Indian peoples to the Catholic faith and assimilating them into the Spanish Empire without coercion of military force. His plan was to go to the Indians with only friars; no other Spaniards would be permitted to enter that territory for five years.¹⁷

That the attitudes of the anticoercion movement now dominated the royal bureaucracy is exemplified by Viceroy Mendoza's 1538 statement that "pacification," as he called it, had to be carried out with "the good of the people of the land" always in mind.¹⁸ In addition to their firsthand knowledge of the route to the north, it was assuredly Cabeza de Vaca and Dorantes' record of harmonious relations with the Indian peoples they had met that recommended them as potential leaders of a reconnaissance to those same peoples and beyond. Throughout their odyssey they had adhered to peaceful methods that would have cheered Las Casas. Time and again the Cabeza de Vaca party had been eagerly welcomed into native settlements, and its parting had been the occasion of lament. At the end of the survivors' journey they had even been able to arrange a rapprochement between slave-hunting Europeans and Indians who had fled their homes to escape them.¹⁹

When Cabeza de Vaca and Dorantes decided not to lead the viceroy's proposed reconnaissance, Mendoza turned naturally enough to the ecclesiastics. The Franciscan provincial fray Antonio de Ciudad Rodrigo offered the name of fray Marcos de Niza. The provincial touted Marcos as "wholly virtuous" and learned in theology, and therefore "suitable and competent to make this journey."²⁰ Marcos had been outspoken in his criticism of the especially brutal conquest of Peru, then still under way. He was also a correspondent and supporter of Las Casas's. A version of his account of conquistador abuse of Peruvian natives was appended several years later to the great Dominican's famous indictment of common conquistador practices, *Brevissima relación de la destrucción de las Indias* (A Brief Account of the Devastation of the Indies).²¹

So it was that fray Marcos was nominated. He had also been

recommended by the bishop in the Ciudad de México, fray Juan de Zumárraga.²² In November 1538, the king, responding to Mendoza's request, authorized fray Marcos to make the reconnaissance.²³

The Reconnaissance

The viceroy added firsthand knowledge of the northern lands to fray Marcos's personal resources by sending Dorantes's former slave Esteban with the friar.²⁴ There is some evidence that Mendoza had manumitted Esteban after purchasing him. For example, he was incorporated into the viceroy's personal guard and was never henceforward referred to as a slave.²⁵ Marcos and Esteban were joined by a second Franciscan friar, named Onorato. In the company of the newly appointed *residencia* judge (a judge who investigated administrative performance) for Nueva Galicia, Francisco Vázquez de Coronado, who was then en route to his post, and a cavalcade of horsemen, Marcos, Esteban, and Onorato left the Ciudad de México in November 1538, bound on their reconnaissance.

Unexpected pressing business awaited Vázquez de Coronado in Nueva Galicia, resulting from the death in battle of the governor there, Diego Pérez de la Torre. Thus it was not until early spring 1539 that Vázquez de Coronado, now acting governor of the *provincia*, could escort fray Marcos and his party to their jumping off point, Culiacán, the northernmost Spanish settlement in the jurisdiction. As Marcos later wrote, he "departed from the *villa* [town of moderate size] of San Miguel in the *provincia* of Culiacán on Friday, the seventh day of March in the year one thousand five hundred and thirty-nine," along with a large group of Indians from farther north who had been recruited to accompany the religious band.²⁶

As the party walked northward along the Pacific coastal plain, it was greeted with great cordiality, each new settlement having been prepared by native emissaries going in advance. After only a few days' travel fray Onorato fell ill and had to be left behind. As was typical of Spanish reconnaissance in the New World, fray Marcos, as he continued onward, "always sought to learn about [any] land with many settlements and people [who were] more civilized and intelligent than [was the case] among those whom [he] was encountering."²⁷ On March 23, Dominica de Pasión, two weeks before Easter, the friar and his company, now 40 leagues inland from the sea because the seacoast and the trajectory of travel diverged, reached a native settlement known as Vacapa. There Marcos rested until after Easter.

While Marcos waited to celebrate the mystery of Christ's resurrection and to receive news about the coast from indigenous messengers he had dispatched, he sent Esteban ahead to learn what he could. Esteban was to send messengers back and not get too far in advance of the friar. "If what [was reported] was of moderate importance, he would send me a white cross [the size] of one *palmo* [the width of four fingers]; if it was grand, he would send one two *palmos* [in size]; and if it was something grander and better than Nueva España, he would send me a large cross," wrote the friar later.[28]

According to Marcos's *relación*, "in four days the messengers came from there from Esteban with a very large cross the height of a man." The messengers urged the friar to leave immediately to follow Esteban because the news was extraordinary. With the messengers came a man who conveyed to Marcos that he had been to a marvelous land he called by the name Cíbola, 30 days' travel beyond where Esteban was. Cíbola comprised, according to him, seven *ciudades*, or major settlements, of stone buildings decorated with turquoise.[29] Marcos resisted the temptation of precipitous action and held to his schedule, not leaving Vacapa until the Monday after Easter.[30]

As fray Marcos then traveled northward he received more messengers from Esteban, always bearing larger crosses and repeating the news of large populations of sophisticated people ahead. After three days Marcos reached an indigenous settlement where many people led him to understand that they had been to Cíbola. They communicated "that besides these seven *ciudades*, there are three other *reinos* [states], which are called Marata, Acus, and Totonteac." Furthermore, they conveyed to the friar that "they went to the first *ciudad*, which is called Cíbola, and labored there tilling the land and in other services. For their labor [the people of Cíbola] give them [bison] hides from among those they have there, and turquoises."[31]

Marcos proceeded northward, always receiving similar reports about Cíbola and the other *provincias* (ethnic regions) and *reinos*. At one point he was told that the people of Totonteac wove fabric like that of the friar's own habit, *chamelote*, a blend of silk and camel wool.[32] This was stunning news. Truly, the people to the north sounded like "very civilized people." The most important of the *ciudades* of Cíbola was said to be called Ahacus.[33] At a community probably on the upper waters of the San Pedro River in what is now the state of Arizona, the friar received additional information about the other major polities of the region. Marata was to the southeast. It had apparently once been more heavily settled than it was now in 1539. Totonteac, by contrast, stood evidently at the zenith of its stature, "the grandest [thing] in the world." A third polity, called Acus (AHCOOS), was simply "another very grand *provincia* and *reino*."[34] The name Marata must have stirred the interest of those familiar with the work of the ancient geographer Claudius Ptolemy. On one of his maps appeared the same name, on the Arabian Peninsula.[35]

Both Esteban, through the messengers he sent, and Marcos expressed full credence in the information they received during their separate progress northward. Both asserted "the great veracity of this people . . . , without being mistaken on a single point."[36] The friar was certain he was about to arrive at some marvelous place. As he later wrote, "each day seems like a year to me because of my desire to see Cíbola."[37]

On May 5, 1539, fray Marcos left the final settlement before he would reach Cíbola, which was still 19 days' travel away across an expanse without permanent settlements. With Marcos traveled many Indians from that last occupied native town, including 30 richly attired leaders.[38] Meanwhile, Esteban, about 16 days ahead of the friar with his own native entourage, was about to arrive at the famous seven *ciudades*.[39]

Before Marcos could get there himself, he and his Indian companions were met by Indians who had accompanied Esteban. They were fleeing southward after calamity had overtaken their leader. Breathlessly, they told what had happened. "One day's journey before reaching Cíbola, Esteban sent his gourd [ahead] with messengers in the same way he was always accustomed to send it in advance." When the leaders at Cíbola saw the gourd, one of them "took it in his hands and saw the bells, [and] flung it to the ground with much wrath and anger. And he told the messengers that they must leave immediately. [He said] that he was acquainted with who those people were. [He told] the [messengers] to tell them not to enter the *ciudad*."⁴⁰

Esteban boldly approached the *ciudad* anyway. He was blocked from entering and lodged in a large building outside the community. As Marcos later recounted, one of the black man's Indian companions told what happened then:

> During this whole night they did not give us [anything] to eat or drink. The next day [when] the sun was one lance [high] Esteban left the building, and some of the *principales* with him. Immediately many people came from the *ciudad*. When [Esteban] saw them, he started to flee, and we [did] too. Right away they gave us these arrow wounds and injuries. We fell down and other dead people fell on top of us. We stayed that way until night without daring to stir. We heard great shouts in the *ciudad* and saw many men and women who were on the lookout on the roofs. We saw no more of Esteban; rather we believe they shot him with arrows as they did the rest who were traveling with him. And [we believe no one] escaped except us.⁴¹

The Friar's Report

In his subsequent *relación*, the friar insisted that despite this horrifying news, he and several Indian companions walked on and approached close enough to see the first *ciudad* of Cíbola but did not attempt to enter it.⁴² It seems more plausible that upon hearing the doleful news about Esteban, Marcos turned around and retraced his route to the Río Sonora, Vacapa, Culiacán, and the Ciudad de México.⁴³ Such a course is consistent with the scant information the friar later reported about his supposed dash to Cíbola and back. Certainly Marcos's contemporaries were unanimous in their opinion that he did not in fact see Cíbola until he arrived there with the vanguard of the Coronado expedition a year later, in July 1540.

At that time, Vázquez de Coronado was furious with Marcos and minced no words in saying that the friar "has not spoken the truth in anything he said."[44] Four years later Captain Diego López testified that "it was publicly known and widely held that fray Marcos had not seen things previously that he had pretended to."[45] Marcos himself seems never to have disputed such charges.

By late August 1539 Marcos, accompanied by Vázquez de Coronado, was back in the Ciudad de México.[46] He certified a formal written report of his travel on August 26. It is generally a sober document, although it repeats over and over indigenous claims that Cíbola was an extraordinary place. The friar lent his credibility to those claims. Marcos had been dispatched to verify the existence of the places Cabeza de Vaca and his companions had heard about. Distilled to its fundamental message, his report told the viceroy and the king, "Yes, they do exist, and here are their names, their approximate locations, and what the people there are like."

Marcos's *relación* makes no mention of gold, silver, or other metals at Cíbola. In private, though, the friar may have expanded on or embellished the information from Esteban's messengers and other indigenous informants regarding Cíbola, Marata, Totonteac, and Acus. The uncle of Marcos's barber, for instance, testified later that year that the friar had told his nephew that "the *ciudades* are surrounded by walls and guarded at their gates. [They are] very wealthy, and there were silversmiths. The women were accustomed to wear golden necklaces and the men, belts made of gold."[47] A riot of such claims swept through the viceroyalty. Some may have originated with fray Marcos; others assuredly were the products of rumor. Neither the copper bell brought from the north earlier by Dorantes nor Tejo's story of his father's commerce with silversmiths had been forgotten. As a result, the atmosphere in the Ciudad de México was electric with anticipation. The Seven Cities, it seemed, had been found!

Why Fray Marcos Stretched the Truth

Marcos de Niza, a priest and the provincial, or administrative head, of the Franciscan Order in Nueva España, evidently lied in his *relación* by claiming that he had personally seen the first *ciudad* of Cíbola. In speaking privately he may also have embroidered reports he had been given by natives of the Río Sonora Valley. At the very least, he said nothing, not even in extensive, face-to-face conversations with Viceroy Mendoza and Vázquez de Coronado, to contradict rampant rumors that Cíbola, Marata, Totonteac, and Acus were extremely wealthy places. Many of those rumors were spread and amplified from pulpits by Marcos's fellow priests, whom he made no effort to correct.[48] Those exaggerations and outright lies were to lead to an extravagant expenditure of effort, life, and wealth in an enterprise that would sorely disappoint and hurt its participants and generally harass and harm the native people of Tierra Nueva.

What would lead a churchman, who had taken a vow to live an exemplary life, to practice and condone such deceit? First, Marcos could not, of course, have foreseen the detrimental outcomes of the expedition he was ensuring would take place. Second, he expected to find a wealthy, populous, sophisticated polity even before he left the Ciudad de México, given the information received from Cabeza de Vaca and his companions. The accounts of informants along the way only confirmed what he probably already believed. Third, although he had not himself seen much of what he reported in the *relación*, he had no reason to doubt his Indian informants. As he put it, neither he nor Esteban had "caught the Indians in the least lie."[49]

Fourth, the assertion that he had seen Cíbola from a distance might have seemed to him only a technical untruth. After all, Esteban, the friar's advance eyes and ears, had surely seen it. Marcos himself had seen it for weeks in his mind's eye, in conformance with the vivid and detailed descriptions many declared eyewitnesses had given him as he walked northward through Sonora. His images, though, might have reflected a less than perfect understanding of what his informants tried to convey to him. He and they shared no common language, and plenty of occasion existed for misunderstanding. Sometimes interpreters were available, sometimes not. On at least one occasion Marcos and his informants resorted to pantomime.[50]

Furthermore, what might have seemed to Marcos the slightest fudging of facts was surely justifiable in his mind because of the supreme importance of his mission to convert the people of Cíbola and hasten the return of Christ. Considering the Cíbolans' hostility toward Esteban, getting to their country to bring them to the Holy Faith was going to require the kind of armed support a full-scale reconnaissance and conquest would afford. It seems only human that Marcos might have told and fostered minor untruths in the service of God as he saw it.[51]

CHAPTER 4

License from the King and His Council

Viceroy Mendoza read fray Marcos's report—perhaps even listened while it was dictated—and then forwarded it to the king in Spain. He was not, however, fully persuaded of Cíbola's value. Almost immediately he took two steps typical of his deliberate habit. First, within days he sent a directive to Melchior Díaz, a prominent settler at Culiacán, instructing him to retrace Marcos's route north, in order "to learn whether the report Father fray Marcos brought was in agreement with what he would see."[1] Something about Marcos's *relación* or what he had said in person was unconvincing or worrisome to Mendoza.

Second, to still the public clamor for an immediate expedition, as well as to forestall others from pursuing that option to his discredit, the viceroy announced that an expedition was being planned and that his governor in Nueva Galicia, Francisco Vázquez de Coronado, would lead it. He wrote to Alonso de la Torre, the royal treasurer on the island of Española, in mid-October 1539: "What I have decided at present regarding this is to send as many as two hundred horsemen by land and two *navíos* by sea with as many as a hundred arquebusiers and crossbowmen, and these [*navíos*] also with some religious." At the same time, Rodrigo de Albornoz, the royal *contador* in Nueva España, sent a letter to de la Torre in which he wrote:

> The viceroy is sending Francisco Vázquez de Coronado there [to Tierra Nueva] with three hundred men (two hundred horsemen and one hundred footmen) who are to make an extensive report

39

and provide information about the land. And they are to do what they can easily. [These three hundred are going] together with twelve religious of the Order of Saint Francis, who are going with them in order to bring the [natives] to the knowledge of the true road to our Holy Catholic Faith. Their departure from here [the Ciudad de México] will be in a month and a half.³

Although Mendoza would not hear from them for many months, Melchior Díaz and Juan de Zaldívar, along with some 15 horsemen and an unknown number of *indios amigos*, dutifully left Culiacán on November 17, 1539, bound for Cíbola.⁴ They traveled northward and were well received by the native people of the region, who provided corn for the horses when they had it. Then, when Díaz "had traveled a hundred leagues from Culiacán, he began to find the land cold and experience hard frosts. As he went farther it became even colder until it so happened that some of his Indians froze [to death], from among those they were taking in their company. And two Spaniards survived great risk [of death]. When [Díaz] saw this he decided not to travel farther until winter was over."⁵ The reconnaissance reached the ruined, red-walled pueblo known as Chichilticale in what is now southeastern Arizona and proceeded no farther.

Like Marcos, Díaz and his party did not reach Cíbola. What they learned about it en route, though, was quite different from what the friar had reported. In a letter written by Díaz to the viceroy, probably in late February or early March 1540, he delivered disappointing news about the seven *ciudades*:

> there are seven *lugares* [small settlements]. It is probably a short day's journey from one [*lugar*] to another. [The native informants] call all of them together Cíbola.
>
> They have crudely worked buildings made of stone and mud ... Of the seven *lugares*, three are very large, four [are] not as big. [The informants] indicate, as it seems to me, [that] each *lugar* [is] three crossbow shots square. According to what the Indians say and indicate about the buildings (namely that they are joined) and

their size, and the [number of] people who reside in each building, [the population] must comprise a large multitude.⁶

According to Mendoza, Díaz remarked that there were "many people along the trail, but . . . they are not suited to any other use besides making them Christians," a statement that dismayed the viceroy.⁷ Cíbola, then, did not hold out the prospect of lavish or even comfortable *encomiendas*. Products with European value were in short supply or were nonexistent there. Díaz's judgment from the statements of his informants, some of whom "have been there [in Cíbola] for fifteen and [even] twenty years," was that for laymen Cíbola was nearly worthless.⁸ But by spring 1540, when Mendoza received this dismal assessment, his expedition was already well on its way to Cíbola, almost to Culiacán.

Even without Díaz's disparaging report, in the fall of 1539 the viceroy was not eager to embark on the expensive, labor-draining, and security-threatening enterprise that an expedition of conquest and reconnaissance to Tierra Nueva would be. Mendoza had been at his post as viceroy for not quite four years, following a dozen years of civil strife, recriminations, usurpations of power, and bitter factionalism in Nueva España. It might prove dangerously foolhardy for him to divert attention and resources to a place of questionable value hundreds of leagues from his seat of government.

As if discord and dissention within the European community were not enough to recommend against an expedition, there was also the continuing threat of revolt by African slaves. Several revolts had erupted in recent years, one of which young Vázquez de Coronado had been dispatched to quell only two years previously to the southwest of the Ciudad de México.⁹ As a former *alcalde*, or magistrate, of the city testified in 1545, in the late 1530s it was believed that "the Blacks and Moorish slaves of the Spanish *vecinos* [certified citizens] of this city [of México] and other places had formed a league with the Indians and had determined to kill all the Spaniards."¹⁰ In addition, there was the ever present danger of uprisings among the indigenous populace even without alliance with other disaffected elements. The subjugated native peoples of Nueva España were by no means fully content and pacified. Hostilities flared up often.¹¹ The reduction of defensive manpower that would result from the departure of a major expedition might open the door to unrest, as indeed it probably did in Nueva Galicia in 1540.

A Swarm of Competitors

Notwithstanding such formidable disincentives to mounting an expedition to Tierra Nueva, two powerful factors pushed the viceroy toward that undertaking. The first was the possibility that taking possession of Cíbola and the other *provincias* would add substantially to the royal patrimony and to the viceroy's own prestige and wealth. The second was rivalry. Four other influential and able men were already pressing the king for permission to lead and finance an expedition to the north: Hernando Cortés, Pedro de Alvarado, Nuño Beltrán de Guzmán, and Hernando de Soto.

In the words of the royal accountant, Rodrigo de Albornoz, "concerning the subjugation of [Tierra Nueva], there is a dispute between the lord viceroy, [who] says it pertains to him because he has discovered it, and the *marqués* [Cortés], [who] alleges and declares that he discovered it much earlier."¹² In addition, Cortés presented in court written royal authorization to him for conquests in that region. In 1529 Queen Juana, the emperor's mother and joint sovereign with her son, had conceded to Cortés the right to "reconnoiter, conquer, and settle whatever islands there are in the Mar del Sur that are within Nueva España and all those you may encounter toward the west, provided they are not within territories for which governors have already been provided."¹³

Pressing this claim, Cortés was in the Ciudad de México in fall 1539, poised to launch his own conquest and reconnaissance. Indeed, he had already taken steps in that direction, dispatching four voyages between June 1532 and May 1539 into what is today known as the Gulf of California and even going in person to the peninsula of Baja California in 1535.¹⁴ While fray Marcos was on his long trek at the viceroy's behest, Cortés sent Francisco de Ulloa with a small fleet up the Gulf of California. As Cortés told it in a legal brief in 1540:

When one of the ships which Francisco de Ulloa had taken returned to the port of Santiago de Buena Esperanza, which is in the *provincia* of Colima, he disembarked a sailor so that he might come to me from there to give a report of what had happened during the expedition. Don Rodrigo Maldonado, who (by order of the viceroy) was in that port as a guard for this purpose, apprehended him and tortured him so that he could find out what information he was bringing. When he was unable to extract [anything] from him, he went with horsemen to the port to seize the ship in order to learn [the secrets] from its men. [The ship] was already leaving the port, and they followed it along the coast more than a hundred and twenty leagues.[15]

Such was the vigor with which Mendoza, acting under the king's authority, sought to restrain Cortés's ambition. Although Ulloa sailed and completed his voyage, Cortés was blocked from future thrusts toward Cíbola. In frustration, he sailed for Spain and the royal court in 1540. He died near Sevilla seven years later, never having returned to Nueva España and without success before the king's councils in arguing his claim to the right to mount further expeditions of his own.

Cortés, though, did not offer the only competition to the viceroy's prerogatives regarding reconnaissance and conquest. Hernando de Soto was another of Mendoza's rivals. A veteran of the New World since 1514, in the early 1530s he had been a key figure in the conquest of Peru. The lavish financial rewards he had received put him in a position to sponsor expeditions of his own, and his service record led him to expect a post of high authority in the imperial hierarchy. In 1536 he returned to Spain, seeking to realize that expectation. He was admitted to the prestigious religious-military Order of Santiago but failed in bids to secure the governorships of Quito and Guatemala. In 1537 he was appointed governor of the island of Cuba and granted license to fund and lead an expedition to the North American mainland, known as La Florida. In the late 1530s, before leaving Spain for Cuba, he offered a position in the expedition to Álvar Núñez Cabeza de Vaca, himself ambitious and recently arrived from the New World, where he had rebuffed a similar offer from Mendoza.

Although Cabeza de Vaca also turned down the invitation from the veteran of Peru, he fired the expectations of Soto and his associates with information about cotton-clothed people with turquoise and metals who lived in permanent stone buildings in the interior of the continent.[16] Soto departed for Cuba with a fleet in April 1538 and, after a lengthy layover there, made landfall with a large expeditionary force on the west coast of what is now the state of Florida in May 1539.

Neither he nor members of his *entrada* had further communication with the remainder of the Spanish world until survivors of the group, minus their captain general, who had died in what is now Louisiana, reached Pánuco in Nueva España in 1543.[17] Soto never received news of what fray Marcos had heard about Cíbola, Marata, Totonteac, and Acus. Nevertheless, his representative at the Spanish court, Juan de Barrutia, claimed in April 1540 that Soto was even then "pursuing and seeking this newly discovered land . . . , of which he had received news from the . . . natives."[18] Indeed, after an initial thrust north and east, the trajectory of Soto's expedition was toward the west, in the general direction of Cabeza de Vaca's land of the copper bell. As Barrutia framed his argument before the Consejo de Indias (Council of the Indies), all others, including Viceroy Mendoza, had been warned to stay out of the vaguely bounded territory specified by royal *cédula* (letter of royal order) as the field of Soto's activity.[19]

Engaging frequently in combat with American natives and suffering deprivation and disease, the Soto expedition lost half its number to death, including the governor and captain general himself in 1542. His lieutenant, Luis de Moscoso, who had been with Soto at least since his days in Peru, doggedly kept the remnants of the expedition moving west and southwest. Finally, the increasing unproductiveness of the land of modern east-central Texas forced an end to the attempt to proceed overland. The expedition concluded as it had begun, as a sea voyage, sailing newly built brigantines westward along the northern coast of the Gulf of Mexico.[20]

Meanwhile, Nuño Beltrán de Guzmán, also in Spain, where he had been sent as a prisoner, made a case before the Consejo de Indias that Cíbola and the other *reinos* Marcos had been told about pertained "to the jurisdiction of Nueva Galicia and to himself" as its conqueror and former governor.[21] As part of the proof of this contention, he entered into the case record the report of an expedition made by his nephew Diego de Guzmán in 1533 as far north as the modern Mexican state of Sinaloa.[22] In the 1540s, though, Nuño Beltrán de Guzmán was embroiled in a series of legal cases arising from his governorships of Pánuco and Nueva Galicia and his presidency of the first Audiencia of Nueva España. These kept him in Spain and in custody until his death in 1558.[23]

Perhaps the most serious challenge to Viceroy Mendoza's exclusive right to conquest and reconnaissance within his viceroyalty came from Pedro de Alvarado, *adelantado* (lifetime governor) of Guatemala. Alvarado's long and continuing record of conquest and his active presence on the Pacific coast made him a force to be taken seriously. He had been in the New World for 30 years or more by 1539, had been an important lieutenant of Cortés's during the conquest of Tenochtitlan, and had made Guatemala a jurisdiction under his own administrative authority. In 1536 he had returned to Spain to lay before the Consejo de Indias a proposal to construct a fleet on the Guatemalan coast and sail to the Molucca Islands in the Orient. When he returned to the New World three years later he brought with him a contract from King Carlos that conceded to him exclusive right to make seaborne reconnaissance from Guatemala on the Pacific Ocean toward the west and north over a distance of 1,500 leagues—about 4,000 miles.[24] Because Cíbola was widely thought, on the basis of fray Marcos's reports, to be near the coast, Alvarado saw that potential prize as within the territory covered by his royal contract.

Mendoza, in his plans regarding Cíbola, envisioned a coordinated sea and land *entrada*. The independent plans of Mendoza and Alvarado both involved sea voyages on the Pacific, setting the stage for possible confrontation. In light of the civil war then raging in Peru, which had arisen over just such antagonisms, the king and his counselors issued a series of *cédulas* in July 1540 to forestall such an outcome in Nueva España.[25] Among the provisions of the *cédulas* was recognition of the viceroy's precedence in mounting a reconnaissance of Tierra Nueva. But he was also directed to reach an agreement with Alvarado over the associated sea voyages.

In late November 1540, at Tiripitío in Michoacán, the two concluded and signed a formal partnership agreement under which they would jointly mount a series of reconnaissances. The Coronado expedition, already then in the field, was included among them. The document specified the rights and obligations of each party, including especially how costs and profits would be shared. In general, the future profits were to be split evenly, Mendoza would assume ownership of half of Alvarado's fleet, and expenses would also be shared equally.[26]

Before Alvarado's arm of the venture could get under way, however, the Caxcán people of Nueva Galicia rose up en masse against the *encomenderos* to whom they had been assigned. Alvarado and his men, who were in nearby Colima, were drafted into the Spaniards' defense. Following a rash assault on the *peñol* (rocky crag) of Nochistlán, which the *adelantado* led, he died in July 1541 as a result of a freak accident suffered during retreat from the *peñol*.[27] Alvarado's death put an end to both the partnership and any potential conflict over Cíbola.

Unknown to either Mendoza or Alvarado at the time of his death, in Madrid the Consejo de Indias had definitively settled the multiparty legal wrangling over the right to mount an expedition to Cíbola in favor of the viceroy. The Consejo agreed with its *fiscal*, or court attorney, who urged that it be ordered that "the aforementioned reconnaissance and conquest be continued in Your Highness's name as it has been begun by your viceroy."[28] In the New World the issue had already been decided for all practical purposes by the viceroy's action of launching an expedition fully a year and a half earlier. By the time the Consejo's decision was announced, that expedition was on the Great Plains, on its way to Quivira.

License to Mount an Expedition

What all five contenders before the Consejo, including the viceroy, had sought was royal permission to undertake their proposed enterprises. Although occasional unauthorized *entradas* took place, most potential conquistadores operated in accordance with the procedures laid down by the royal councils. They generally aspired not to independence from the empire but to status and rewards within it. Adherence to established protocols was essential.

One of those protocols had to do with royal license to mount an expedition. Beginning in the 1520s, a series of *cédulas* had been issued to govern reconnaissance and conquest. They specified that "concession of [the right to conduct] reconnaissance is first to be reviewed [by the Consejo de Indias]."[29] The process to be followed in the hope of obtaining an expedition license resembled the modern process of grant application. A statement of intended activities and their geographical scope had to be submitted to the Consejo de Indias, along with a statement about the manpower and financing of the proposed *entrada*. The members of the Consejo assessed the proposal and either approved or denied it. Approval, if given, came in the form of an official document, a *capitulación*, specifying the rights conceded to the successful applicant and the obligations imposed on him.

Only rarely was concession of a license accompanied by an offer of royal financial support for the approved enterprise. As Gonzalo Fernández de Oviedo y Valdés, royal chronicler for the Indies for Carlos I, complained sometime around 1540: "Almost never do their Majesties put their wealth and money into these new expeditions, instead only permits and high-sounding words."[30]

No master plan guided the opening of the Western Hemisphere to Spanish activities. The pattern of expansion of Spanish occupation and exploitation of the New World was not dictated from the royal court but was the result of ad hoc initiatives taken by ambitious private individuals in the New World. The existence of two huge, populous, and previously unknown continents presented the prospect of incredibly rich prizes to be earned in pursuit of what seemed an obviously righteous cause: enlargement of the Spanish Empire and swelling of the congregation of the Catholic Church. One result was a nearly feverish pace of ferreting out prosperous native populations throughout the 1500s, but especially in the first half of the century.

With receipt of the royal license, Mendoza preserved the jurisdictional integrity of the viceroyalty and thereby served the institutional interests of the king, while proposing to enlarge the population of royal subjects. Included in the license were the words, "What you have said you would do seemed excellent to us. That is, with the advice of the *oidores* of that *audiencia* and other persons [who are] concerned with the service of God, Our Lord, and ourselves, that you have resolved to dispatch, at your own expense, up to three hundred footmen and horsemen to conquer the land [of Cíbola] in our name."[31]

The brief *cédula* from which this quotation comes conferred on Mendoza, as a private citizen rather than as viceroy, the right to mount an expedition to Tierra Nueva. It thus was intended that royal funds would not be expended on the enterprise, although any peoples subjugated as a result would become vassals of the Spanish monarchy and would be subject to royal law and obligations to the king, including the payment of tribute and taxes.[32] If all went well, Mendoza and the other leaders of the expedition could expect reward from the Spanish crown in the event that a prize population was added to the royal patrimony. Customarily, such reward involved appointment to administrative posts, usually within the conquered territory, supported by royal salary or the right to collect and use tribute. ■

Chapter 5

Raising a Force and Paying for It

Many were the Europeans and New World natives, too, who, following fray Marcos's news about Cíbola, were ready and even eager to go there. The viceroy determined, though, that a force of about 300 European men-at-arms and 1,500 or so native allies would be both financially feasible and sufficient to bring the Tierra Nueva of Cíbola under the king's dominion. A force of that size was consistent with Spanish expeditionary practice at the time and was also doubtless influenced by Marcos's report of the sizes of the indigenous groups he had seen in the north.

So it was that in mid-November 1539 a man named García Navarro testified in Habana, Cuba, that "the viceroy was openly mounting an expedition to that land, and . . . placards [had been] put up in order to raise a troop." He had heard as much while he was in the Ciudad de México in early October.[1] If recruitment for the expedition to Cíbola was like that for others of the period, it included having one or more *pregoneros*, or criers, walk the streets of the city and announce in a booming voice that 300 or more horsemen and footmen were needed. Perhaps one of those *pregoneros* was the black man named Pedro who later served in that capacity on the Coronado expedition.[2] Such resounding calls were often preceded by the tattoo of a drum and the shrill of a fife.

Raising the necessary men was easy. As Pedro de Castañeda de Nájera later wrote:

> When [Vázquez de Coronado and fray Marcos] had arrived in [the Ciudad de] México and met with don Antonio de Mendoza, it immediately began to be spread abroad that the Seven Ciudades Nuño de Guzmán had searched for had been discovered. And the

49

raising of an armed force and the assembly of people began, in order to go to conquer them. The good viceroy had such influence with the friars of the Order of San Francisco that they made fray Marcos provincial. As a result, the pulpits of that order were full of so many marvels, and such magnificent ones, that in a few days more than three hundred Spaniards were assembled and about eight hundred Indians native to Nueva España.[3]

Castañeda de Nájera, however, was not an eyewitness to the recruitment of the expedition in the Ciudad de México. He was living at the time outside the new Spanish *villa* of Guadalajara, in what is now the Mexican state of Jalisco, and did not join the expedition himself until it passed through Guadalajara early in 1540.[4] Many of the mechanics of recruitment, therefore, were unknown to him.

The means by which participants joined the enterprise were various. Although responses to placards and *pregoneros'* announcements were certainly among them, most expedition members came to it in other ways determined by their social condition. Broadly speaking, the European and African participants in the *entrada* can be separated into two categories: independent actors and subordinates. Independent actors were at liberty to choose to take part in the expedition; they usually were European men of moderate or higher economic status. Viceroy Mendoza termed such people "*hombres libres*," or free men.[5] Wives, children, servants, and slaves of those men typically went on the expedition at the behest or direction of their husbands, fathers, or masters. As subordinates of varying degree, their choices were constrained more than those of the *hombres libres*. Some of these subordinate persons may have participated in the expedition with enthusiasm or played a role in the decisions that led to their participation, but they were not in a position to "enlist" on their own account.

"Enlist," or *alistarse* in Spanish, is an important concept in this context, for to become a full-fledged member of the expedition one had to make a public statement before a notary. It was customary to generate in this way an *alarde*, or muster roll, of those who stood to share in any booty an expedition might seize. In the case of the Coronado *entrada*, the formal muster roll was not prepared in the place where most recruitment took place, the Ciudad de México, but rather in Compostela in Nueva Galicia nearly five months after fray Marcos made his report and the call for enlistment was published.

That muster roll, which survives, furnishes a great deal of information about 287 *hombres libres*, including their names. Knowing their names has led to the location of other documents that shed light, among other things, on the variety of means by which they enlisted. In addition, from other contemporary documentary sources, a minimum of 80 more European men-at-arms are now known to have gone on the expedition whose names do not appear on the February 22, 1540, muster roll.[6]

To consider the varieties of enlistment in the expedition, I begin with the 12 men who served as its captains, or lay leaders—don García López de Cárdenas; Diego Gutiérrez de la Caballería; Diego López, a *regidor*, or councilman, of Sevilla in Spain; don Rodrigo Maldonado; don Tristán de Luna y Arellano; Juan de Zaldívar; Melchior Díaz; don Diego de Guevara; Velasco de Barrionuevo; Francisco de Ovando; Juan Gallego; and Pablo de Melgosa—as well as Francisco Vázquez de Coronado, who was appointed captain general, and Lope de Samaniego, the expedition's *maestre de campo*, or field commander. These men were all either asked to go on the expedition or themselves applied to the viceroy to go. Vázquez de Coronado had come to the New World in Mendoza's company in 1535 and was a rising star in the viceroy's entourage. The rest of the leadership of the expedition was not a random collection of ambitious, adventurous men answering a recruitment poster. They were instead already linked to the organizers of the enterprise or involved in the ongoing conquest of Nueva Galicia and the extension of its jurisdiction.

Among the captains, five were importantly connected to Mendoza or Vázquez de Coronado. García López de Cárdenas was, through his wife, distantly related to the viceroy, who directly ordered him to go on the expedition. He was also linked to don Luis de Castilla, a close associate of Mendoza's and a key behind-the-scenes force in the expedition to Cíbola. Suggesting the closeness of their relationship, López de Cárdenas once granted don Luis his power of attorney.[7] Don Rodrigo Maldonado was brother-in-law of the *duque* del Infantado, Iñigo López de Mendoza, the head of the house of Mendoza, and Velasco de Barrionuevo had served for several years in the viceroy's personal guard.[8] Another close affiliate of don Luis de Castilla's, later linked to Mendoza through his son Carlos de Arellano's marriage, was Tristán de Luna y Arellano.[9] Going on the expedition as royal treasurer as well as to watch over his family's investment was Diego Gutiérrez de la Caballería, uncle of Beatriz de Estrada, Vázquez de Coronado's wife.[10]

In addition to the cadre of Mendoza associates, three captains—Diego López, Melchior Díaz, and Lope de Samaniego—had served with Nuño de Guzmán in the conquest of Nueva Galicia and continued to be active there in positions of importance.[11] Two others, Juan de Zaldívar and don Diego de Guevara, were relatives of Cristóbal de Oñate, a former captain under Guzmán and now lieutenant governor of Nueva Galicia under Vázquez de Coronado.[12] Only two captains, Francisco de Ovando and Pablo de Melgosa, have not yet been linked to either Mendoza or Nueva Galicia before the expedition.

Rank-and-file members of the expedition to Cíbola signed up in several ways. A significant group of 52 men came already attached to captains as members of six preexisting, rudimentary companies. Ten men, for example, mustered under Rodrigo Maldonado: Juan de Torquemada, Francisco Gutiérrez, Sancho Rodríguez, Alonso de Medina, Hernando de Barahona, Leonardo Sánchez, Antón Miguel, Gaspar de Guadalupe, Hernando de Castroverde, and a man named Cepeda.[13] They were likely all *criados*, or retainers and household members, of Maldonado's.

Thirteen of the enlistees had come from Spain with Mendoza's entourage in 1535 and, regardless of rank, can properly be classed as his *criados*. They were Pedro de Ledesma, Diego Hernández, Gonzalo Hernández, Diego López, Sebastián Soto, Hernando de Alarcón, Antonio de Ribero, Gaspar Saldaña, Pedro Cortés, Juan García de Plasencia, a second Diego Hernández, Luis de Quesada, and Diego Núñez.[14] Artilleryman Juan Troyano had also traveled to Nueva España with the viceroy. Witnesses for him later proudly testified to his status as a *criado* and said that the viceroy had provided him with a salary to enable him to participate in the *entrada*, where his skills with artillery and bridge building were considered crucial.¹⁵ Documentary evidence concerning a number of other men strongly suggests that they, too, arrived in Nueva España in the company of the viceroy, but positive proof is lacking. These men and the baker's dozen just listed went on the expedition because of their linkage with the viceroy and were either urged to enlist by him and his staff or themselves asked to go.

Other expeditionaries, too, must be counted as *criados* of the viceroy's, although they did not travel to Nueva España with him. Among them was the painter Cristóbal de Quesada, whom the viceroy sent on the expedition in order "to paint the things of the land."¹⁶ Also having close viceregal links were 25 men who had served in Mendoza's personal guard before leaving on the expedition to Cíbola: Francisco López, Pedro de Salinas, Pero Hernández, Juan Vaca, Pedro de Ortega, Julián de Sámano, Juan de Santovaya, Antonio de Ribero, Juan de Contreras, Pedro de Vargas, Juan Ruiz, Marcos de Ruiz de Rojas, Juan Ruiz de Medina, Alonso López, Juan Vizcayno, Gaspar de Saldaña, Juan Rodríguez, Manuel Hernández, Francisco Gómez, Juan Barbero, Hernán Páez, and Juan de Fioz, along with Velasco de Barrionuevo, Hernando de Alarcón, and the Cepeda mentioned earlier.¹⁷

Criados of Vázquez de Coronado's, such as Hernando de Valle and Alonso de Toro, members of the captain general's household, also went on the expedition.¹⁸ Vázquez de Coronado's close associates have as yet been identified by name in smaller numbers than the viceroy's. Doubtless there were on the expedition many *criados* affiliated with Mendoza, Vázquez de Coronado, the captains, and other leading persons whose connections with them remain to be revealed. Captain Rodrigo Maldonado, for example, described the captain general as having taken "many *criados*."¹⁹ Similarly, *escribano* (secretary) Gerónimo Mercado de Sotomayor, testifying in 1547, stated that García López de Cárdenas also took "many *criados*" on the expedition.²⁰ This was typical of the captains.

Many other men having no such known ties signed up to make the *entrada*, responding to public report and rumor. Often enlisting in twos and threes, these were men linked by blood, place of origin, or life's routines.

There were, for instance, at least seven father-and-son pairs on the expedition,²¹ five pairs of brothers,²² and six sets of cousins.²³ Frequently men enlisted in the expeditionary force with others from their hometown. Some of the groups of compatriots were unusually large. The contingent originally from Guadalcanal and three neighboring towns (Llerena, Azuaga, and Fuente del Arco, all within 20 miles of Guadalcanal) in what is now extreme northern Sevilla province and extreme southern Badajoz province in Spain numbered perhaps as many as 26, a very large group in comparison with those from other, more populous towns.²⁴

A few expeditionaries had been recent inmates of the Ciudad de México jail. They included Juan Bautista de San Vitorés, Juan Navarro, Francisco Martín, Francisco de Espinosa, and three of Mendoza's guardsmen mentioned earlier—Alonso López, Pero Hernández, and Juan de Fioz. These men had all been in jail at or about the time Marcos de Niza returned to the city from his reconnaissance of Cíbola. How they were recruited is unknown, or whether their sentences were shortened in exchange for their agreement to join the expedition. Interestingly, also on the expedition were two jailers from the same prison, Francisco Díaz and Diego de Puelles.²⁵

Other men clearly had had social and commercial dealings with each other before the expedition. Among them was the partnership of Cristóbal de Escobar and Domingo Martín, who together purchased livestock to bring on the expedition.²⁶ Some expeditionaries had known each other for years. Melchior Díaz and Juan de Zaldívar, for instance, had been acquainted since at least 1536 and remained so throughout their lives.²⁷

A broad range of common experiences and backgrounds made for many more friendships among European members of the Coronado expedition than have yet been documented. These people were overwhelmingly from the Spanish kingdom of Castilla, although a number came from the kingdom of Aragón. Within Castilla, the modern areas furnishing the largest numbers of participants were Extremadura, Castilla y León, and Andalucía, in that order. In the first half of the sixteenth century all these *comunidades* (Spanish "states") tended to be poor and rural and lacked economic opportunities for their residents. Expeditionaries from outside Spain came foremost from Portugal, with a scattering from Italy, Germany, France, England, Scotland, Corsica, Greece, and Crete.[28]

Most of the expeditionaries belonged to the same generation, being in their late teens or twenties at the time the *entrada* got under way in late 1539. More than three-quarters (69) of the men for whom age is known (89) were between 13 and 29.[29] One consequence of their relative youth was that they generally were not established socially or politically, did not have large households of their own, and were seeking opportunities for economic security and positions of status in their society.

For some participants in the Coronado expedition, the paths by which they came to join up are known in surprising detail. Alonso Pérez de Bocanegra, a son of *bachiller* (holder of a university degree) Alonso Pérez, was sent by his father from Salamanca "to war because of [his] dissoluteness," probably at the university there.[30] Meanwhile, Pedro de Benavídez and Florián Bermúdez boasted of having traveled voluntarily "two thousand leagues by land to go on the conquest and pacification of Tierra Nueva," starting from Desaguadero in what is now Argentina and passing through Gracias a Dios (in today's Panama) and Honduras.[31]

Ecclesiastical Members

Fray Marcos de Niza, after his return from the north in 1539, had been selected to be provincial of his order in Nueva España and so could have remained in the seat of his province, the Ciudad de México. But he was expected to guide the full-fledged expedition to Cíbola—and he could do no less, being the only European who, according to his own report, had actually covered the entire route to the seven *ciudades* and presumably knew the way. With him were to go four other Franciscans, two priests and two lay brothers, as well as their small entourage of assistants, servants, slaves, and other companions.[32]

From his friend Bishop Juan de Zumárraga's household Marcos selected first a lay brother named fray Luis, from Úbeda, to accompany him. Fray Luis proclaimed that "with a chisel and adze" he would build and set up crosses and would baptize what children he could.[33] It was not until reaching Compostela that fray Marcos rounded out his little company with fray Juan de Padilla, the second most senior member of the religious contingent; fray Antonio de Castilblanco; and an Italian lay brother, fray Daniel. Juan de Padilla was deeply interested in stories of the Seven Cities of Antilia. When the organization of the expedition was announced, he sought out Vázquez de Coronado and asked to join. He had been the *guardián*, or superior, at two *conventos*, or religious houses, in Nueva Galicia before leaving for Cíbola.[34] Of humbler status, fray Daniel embroidered and was said to wear a coat of chain mail under his robe, against his skin, as a means of penitence.[35]

In the end, Luis and Juan de Padilla were to remain behind in Tierra Nueva when the expedition was abandoned, in an effort to preach to the natives of the north. Both were killed and earned the martyr's palm. Little is known about fray Antonio, other than that he served as Vázquez de Coronado's confessor. Historian Fray Angélico Chávez suggested that fray Antonio, unlike Luis and Juan, did not look forward to a mission among the Indians and was thus a reluctant participant in the expedition to Tierra Nueva.[36]

Slaves, Servants, Women, and Children

Much more numerous on the expedition than ecclesiastics were slaves, servants, women, and children. In Spain during the middle decades of the sixteenth century, European men of even modest status were customarily attended by slaves and servants. One of many documented examples among members of the Coronado expedition is Juan Jaramillo. Although he later became a captain, at the time of the expedition he was an undistinguished member of the rank and file. Even so, he had with him at least two black slaves.[37] Other members of the rank and file who are known positively to have had slaves with them on the expedition were Pedro de Benavídes, Miguel de Entrambasaguas, Melchior Pérez, and Juan Troyano.[38] Higher-ranking persons took many more slaves. Francisco Vázquez de Coronado had with him at least seven black slaves, four men and three women. Likewise, García López de Cárdenas took many servants, a muleteer, and black slaves, both male and female.[39] No precise total exists, but in all likelihood the number of servants and slaves equaled or exceeded 368, the number of European men-at-arms on the expedition.

Like any other quasi-military force of the day, the Coronado expedition included wives, children, and other companions. Incontrovertible proof exists only for the presence of four wives who were along: María Maldonado, Francisca de Hozes, and the unnamed Indian wives of Juan Troyano and Lope Caballero.[40] But these four are assuredly far from the total number of free women who participated in the expedition.

Both Francisca de Hozes and María Maldonado were well remembered by former expedition members who later wrote chronicles of the undertaking. Hozes, like her husband, shoemaker and trader Alonso Sánchez, was probably in her forties at the time of the expedition and certainly did not give birth during its course, as Herbert Bolton suggested.[41] Already a mother in 1522, Francisca arrived in the New World that year with her husband and some of their children. An adolescent son accompanied her and Alonso on the Coronado expedition while five to seven other, probably all adult, children remained in the Ciudad de México.[42] Señora Sánchez was the first witness called during the investigation in 1544 of the expedition's treatment of American natives.

Unlike Francisca de Hozes, María Maldonado was quite young when she participated in the expedition to Cíbola, probably in her teens or early twenties, about the same age as her husband, Juan Gómez de Paradinas.[43] Fellow expeditionary Juan Gómez de Salazar remembered 20 years later that María and her husband took *criados* with them on the expedition and that María cared for the ill of the armed force and sewed and mended for them, "as best she could and did many other excellent things."[44]

The two Native American wives came from very different environments. Lope de Caballero's spouse originated in what is now central Mexico, perhaps in the vicinity of Puebla de los Ángeles, where her husband was a *vecino* not long after the expedition to Cíbola. Juan Troyano's wife, on the other hand, was from the Pueblo world of what has become the U.S. Southwest. Just when and under what circumstances her relationship with Troyano came about is unknown. Years afterward Troyano said that God had been pleased to provide him this *compañera*, or companion.[45]

Indios Amigos

From the sixteenth century onward it has been common for historians and other writers about Spanish-led expeditions of conquest in the Americas to portray them as small groups of intrepid European knights arrayed against native populations overwhelmingly superior in number.[46] In this they follow many of the conquistadores themselves, who usually reported their expeditions that way. Yet the actual armed expeditionary forces were almost always much bigger than the core number of European members. Customarily the Europeans were accompanied by huge contingents of recently subjugated indigenous warriors.

In the case of the Coronado expedition, those Indian allies, or *indios amigos*, dwarfed the remainder of the expedition. At least 1,300 natives of central and western Mexico made the trek, although they rarely appear in either sixteenth-century Spanish accounts or modern histories. Nevertheless, at least 800 Indians were recruited for the expedition from the Valley of Mexico and another 500 or so were added as the force moved through what are now the Mexican states of Michoacán, Jalisco, Nayarit, and Sinaloa.[47]

Contemporaneous estimates of the size of the Indian component of the expedition range from 1,300 to 5,000.[48] I use the estimate at the low end of that spectrum because it is provided by more than one independent source, including Serván Béjarano, who was present at the muster in Compostela and stated later that the native contingent numbered "from 1,300 to 2,000 Indians native to this land."[49] The sixteenth-century witnesses agree that no firm count of the *indios amigos* was ever made. Several native leaders later made it clear that the expeditionaries did not all travel by a single road, and further, contingents of indigenous load bearers, or *tamemes*, were employed in succession over relatively short stretches of the route, returning to their homes when their stint was complete. Regardless of the exact figures, all sources agree that the number of *indios amigos* was very large.[50]

Castañeda de Nájera qualified the region of origin of the 800 *indios amigos* from the Valley of Mexico by saying that "they were from Nueva España and the majority from hot lands," perhaps a reference to today's *tierra caliente*, the hot, coastal lowlands.⁵¹ Evidence provided in 1544 by indigenous *principales*, or leaders, through an interpreter gives a much more detailed, if still fragmentary, account. According to Juan Tlecanen, a Mexica leader from Tenochtitlan who had gone on the Coronado expedition, "four hundred and fourteen Indians" from there had been with the expedition.⁵²

Meanwhile, from Tenochtitlan's neighboring community of Tlatelolco came at least six men whose names are known: don Luis de León and don Martín, *principales* at Santiago de Tlatelolco, and Francisco Jiménez, Juan Coavis, Martín Xalacate, and Francisco Yautl.⁵³ Also from the environs of Tenochtitlan was a man "called Andrés" from Coyoacán, who stayed in Quivira with fray Juan de Padilla.⁵⁴ Juan Coavis, a native of Tlatelolco, testified that "eighty Indians from that part" of the island community participated in the *entrada*.⁵⁵

Coming from farther west in what is now Mexico were many expedition participants from the former Tarascan state, now the Mexican state of Michoacán. Two Indian *principales* by the names of don Alonso and Francisco Abuy, from Pátzcuaro, led a native contingent of at least 100 men.⁵⁶ Another man from the same region, named Lucas, participated in the expedition to Tierra Nueva and eventually accompanied fray Juan de Padilla on his ill-fated mission to Quivira.⁵⁷ Also sending *indios amigos* on the expedition were the indigenous communities of Zacayuca and Culiacán, as well as "many other *pueblos*."⁵⁸ Even the less settled Otomí people of Michoacán contributed members to the expedition, led by a *principal* known as don García de Padilla.⁵⁹ In addition, "a great quantity of [Indians] from many [other] *provincias* and *pueblos*" also served during the expedition.⁶⁰

It is often claimed that Tlaxcaltecas, earlier allies of Hernando Cortés, joined the expedition to Cíbola. Documentary evidence to back that claim is slim. Still, it is not unreasonable to suspect that some were present, possibly survivors of Nuño Beltrán de Guzmán's force that effected the initial conquest of Nueva Galicia in the early 1530s, who had settled in the Culiacán area and were picked up there in 1540 by the Coronado expedition.⁶¹ The Tlaxcala Codex, prepared probably in the

1580s, contains a drawing and caption claiming that during the Coronado *entrada* "the Tlaxcaltecas were there in the service of His Majesty and the royal crown of Castilla."[62] However, no contemporaneous information referring to the presence of individual Tlaxcalans on the expedition has yet come to light.

The Codex Aubin, a pictorial manuscript glossed in Nahuatl, records events year by year in the history of Tenochtitlan, the Mexica capital, which became the core of the rebuilt Spanish Ciudad de México. The entry for 1539 depicts *tenochca*, or natives of Tenochtitlan, leaving for "*yancuic tlalpan*," the lands newly discovered by Marcos de Niza. Then the codex records the return of the survivors of this group from the north in 1542, after they joined en route another force of warriors from Tenochtitlan that had been led to Nueva Galicia by Viceroy Mendoza to put an end to the Mixtón War the year before.[63]

Forty years after the end of the Coronado expedition, an *entrada* into New Mexico led by Antonio de Espejo found several of the expedition's *indios amigos* still in the Zuni area. They were "Mexican Indians [that is, from the Valley of Mexico], and also a number from Guadalajara, some of those that Coronado had brought."[64] Espejo listed the names of three of those found at Zuni: Andrés (from Coyoacán), Gaspar (from the Ciudad de México), and Antón (from Guadalajara).[65] Visible in the documents because they went with fray Juan de Padilla on his martyr's mission to Quivira at the end of the Coronado expedition were two Indians whom Juan Jaramillo believed to be "from Zapotlán and around there," one evidently known as Sebastián.[66] The Christian name of one final Indian who participated in the expedition is known. A woman called Luisa, a native of Culiacán, evidently served as an interpreter but fled from Vázquez de Coronado during the return from Cíbola in 1542.[67]

How animosities and potential conflicts between such diverse native groups were dealt with is unknown. Tlaxcaltecas, Tenochcas, and Tarascos, for instance, had been perennial adversaries only a generation before the Coronado expedition. It is difficult to imagine that all the Indian allies marched under a single leadership or even that they traveled and camped en masse. A further puzzle is to what extent, or even whether, the contingents of native allies were under the control of Vázquez de Coronado and his captains. It would not be surprising if the captain general's authority over the native allies was tenuous, perhaps sometimes nonexistent. Testimony from 1546 suggests that *indios amigos* traveled in "companies" of 20 men each but were sometimes shared out among the European expeditionaries, in one case at a rate of 10 Indians per European.[68] It appears that the Indian allies of the expedition may have been organized in several different ways.

Indios amigos were, most significantly, part of the fighting force of the expedition. Their involvement in combat helps explain the ease with which most of the indigenous communities met by the expedition were subdued or overawed into pro forma submission. Some of the Indian allies also occasionally traveled ahead even of the expedition's advance guard, serving as intermediaries and emissaries, as was the case at Cíbola in July 1540.[69] In addition, the *indios amigos* carried supplies, guarded livestock, and constructed shelters. Their active involvement in the expedition was essential to what success it had.

How Native American allies were recruited for the Coronado and other contemporary expeditions has hardly been studied. Two possible methods are recorded in documents dating several decades after the Coronado *entrada*. In Durango an *alcalde mayor* threatened to impose a fine if the "Mexicanos," or Mexican Indians, would not go to "help put down the Chichimecs." In another case, Mexican Indians were promised they would be allowed to keep prisoners they took while serving as auxiliaries.[70] A further possibility is suggested by this example from Sinaloa in 1612: "The captain . . . drafted two thousand Indian warriors from several Christian and allied gentile nations. In exchange for their service the latter asked to be allowed to take enemy scalps with which to dance . . . The captain agreed to their request."[71] Assuredly, these were not the only possible inducements. Documentary evidence specific to the Coronado expedition says only that Lorenzo de Tejada, the *oidor* of the Audiencia of Nueva España, "spoke with the *caciques* of Santiago [and other native communities], telling them that since the Spaniards were going to Tierra Nueva some of the Indians might also want to go of their own free will."

It is also known that at least some of the *indios amigos* were compensated by having their tribute temporarily reduced.[72]

MOST EUROPEAN EXPEDITIONARIES PAID TO GO

Securing promises to participate in the expedition to Cíbola was one thing; making it a reality was another. Anticipated resistance from the indigenous people of Cíbola and its neighboring *reinos* made adequate arms, armor, and munitions a necessity. The expeditionaries, however, carried relatively few items of European arms and armor: dozens of swords, 19 crossbows, 21 arquebuses, a dozen steel helmets, and assorted pieces of body armor. Only a few of the wealthiest participants had anything like a full suit of metal armor. As is shown by the expedition's muster roll and other contemporaneous documents, its war gear was dominated by articles of indigenous make: quilted cotton armor, obsidian-edged weapons such as *macanas* (double-edged swords) and lances, and circular, feather-decorated shields. In this respect, as in so many others, the expedition had a decidedly Mexican Indian appearance. More than 90 percent of the European members of the expedition carried indigenous arms and armor. The corresponding European goods were in short supply.[73]

Not only would the fighting men have to be armed, but also some 2,000 or more people would have to be fed for many months. They would all need clothing, too, replacements for what would wear out with the simple passage of time multiplied by the rough and sometimes hostile conditions to be expected. And there were the incidentals of life beyond the edge of empire: utensils for food preparation and cooking; paper, ink, and other writing supplies to allow production of the mandatory documentary record; wine and wheat flour for wafers, without which saying daily mass was unthinkable; inexpensive but abundant trade and gift goods, seen as crucial for currying the goodwill of natives of the north and purchasing supplemental supplies from them if need be; medicines and unguents with which to treat the inevitable illnesses, wounds, and injuries; musical instruments such as drums, fifes, and bugles; chains and other restraints for common malefactors as well as prisoners taken in war; raw materials and tools to permit fabrication and repair of equipment; and navigational

HUGE INVESTMENT: high expectations

instruments and the printed tables necessary to interpret their readings—perhaps a cross-staff and certainly a compass and a clock or hourglass. All these things and many more had to be acquired before the expedition could begin.

Thousands of objects and containers would then have to be transported over many hundreds of leagues. At least 600 pack horses and mules did part of the job.[74] But the equipage was so massive that human load bearers, Indians known as *tamemes*, were necessary, too. In aggregate the expedition's *tamemes* may have numbered in the thousands.[75] Sometimes even the 550-odd saddle horses of the men-at-arms would have to be pressed into pack service.[76] Horses and mules necessitated even more supplies: corn for feed when possible; horseshoes and horseshoe nails by the thousands; bridles, saddles, cinches, and other tack; and tools of the farrier's trade.

Horses were not the only essential livestock. Beef cattle, sheep, and hogs had to be brought along in herds of thousands. In 1541, more than halfway through the *entrada*, the meat stock was counted and still tallied 500 cattle and 5,000 sheep.[77] Without that stock, the expedition would have been a disaster from the first.

The cost of all the goods, equipment, and food was staggering. Shirley Cushing Flint has estimated conservatively that outfitting the Coronado expedition cost the equivalent of more than 600,000 sixteenth-century silver pesos.[78] To put that in perspective, a laborer in those days could expect to earn about 100 pesos in a year. Put another way, the money spent in mounting the Coronado expedition exceeded half the distributed ransom of the Inca Atahuallpa, considered at the time to have been a fabulous treasure.[79] That expeditionaries were willing to invest so much is an indication of how huge a prize they expected Cíbola to be.

As was true of most Spanish-led expeditions of the sixteenth century, the funds that financed the *entrada* came from the participants themselves. Not a single peso was supposed to come directly from the king.[80] Almost all the European men-at-arms who enlisted for Viceroy Mendoza's expedition invested in the enterprise. Mendoza and the Vázquez de Coronado–Estrada family were initially the largest investors, contributing significant fortunes of about 85,000 and 71,000 silver pesos, respectively. Belatedly, Pedro de Alvarado joined as a third major investor, perhaps putting in as much as 90,000 pesos. Meanwhile, the 12 captains who went on the expedition spent on average 5,500 pesos each, for a total of more than 60,000 silver pesos among them. As for the rank and file, it is estimated that together they spent a minimum of 355,000 silver pesos to participate in the expedition. All those who did invest expected handsome profits from the valuable goods of the people of Cíbola and other *reinos* that would be subject to tribute exactions.[81]

Few members of the expedition possessed large sums of cash. Instead, they operated on credit, often mortgaging various sorts of property or relying on uncollateralized promissory notes. Vázquez de Coronado used his wife, Beatriz de Estrada's, dowry to bankroll his participation in the *entrada*. Her dowry consisted of one-half of the *encomienda* (tribute collection) from the indigenous community of Tlapa, in what is now the state of Guerrero in Mexico.[82] Tlapa was a large *encomienda*, encompassing probably more than 11,000 tribute payers (heads of households) in the late 1530s.[83] Gold was an important resource for Tlapa and a major component of its tribute.[84] The couple placed the *encomienda* in a *censo*, an arrangement under which a religious order paid them an agreed-upon amount in exchange for the right to receive the tribute paid by the Indians of Tlapa for a specified period. Two years after the end of the expedition Vázquez de Coronado was still in debt for more than 10,000 pesos. He had been forced to sell real estate and movable goods but was still unable to extinguish his debt.[85] His was only an extreme example.

Juan de Zaldívar, one of the expedition's captains, returned from Tierra Nueva in debt for 5,000 to 6,000 pesos, money he had spent feeding and outfitting slaves, *criados*, and other members of the expeditionary force.[86] Others for whom documentary proof of indebtedness as a result of the Coronado expedition is available include Juan Gómez de Paradinas, Pedro de Ledesma, Cristóbal de Mayorga, Juan Paniagua, Melchior Pérez, and García Rodríguez.[87] Entering into debt in order to participate in the *entrada* was the rule. Hundreds of persons were eager to encumber themselves to ensure a place in the troop bound for Cíbola. ■

CHAPTER 6

Avoiding Provocation, Demanding Submission

To move an immense throng of people and animals through densely populated Nueva España posed risks of triggering grievances and inflaming animosity among the native people. Occasions for offense were legion. People and animals might trample crops or simply eat them. They might block or otherwise interfere with native traffic on the roads. They might occupy houses or other shelters without leave. They might foul or deplete water supplies. They might create nuisances of noise or odor or refuse. They might pilfer or destroy personal goods. They might swagger and bully. They might violate taboos or profane sacred places, objects, or persons. They might show contempt for native leaders or elders. They might kidnap and rape. They might flirt or tease or poke fun. They might insist on purchasing supplies when the natives' stocks were already short.

Such infringement of local norms and customs could be expected to provoke recalcitrance or violence from the people of the indigenous communities through which the expedition was to pass. The volatility of relations between Europeans and the natives of Nueva España at the time was expressed powerfully in a letter written to the king by Jerónimo López, one of the conquistadores of Tenochtitlan, in 1545:

> The natives of this land are very fond of making disturbances . . . it is clear that they hate all the Spaniards and that they would like to see us all dead and cut into pieces . . . If [a Spaniard] takes anything to eat, even giving a coin in payment, he quickly finds one hundred or a thousand men assembled against the one

Spaniard, who take him and throw him on the ground, tying his hands behind his back, shaving his beard off, and committing ten thousand other offenses against him.¹

Furthermore, given the climate of the day in Spain, outbursts of complaint or more drastic reactions among the Indians would be certain to unleash a cascade of criticism at the royal court against the viceroy and his minions. That criticism, coming from fray Bartolomé de las Casas or other powerful proponents of Indian rights, could end careers and ruin reputations.

As Antonio de Mendoza told his replacement as viceroy, Luis de Velasco, in 1550, "the main thing His Majesty has ordered me has been to charge me with [ensuring] the Christianity and benign treatment of the natives."² It is no wonder, then, that Mendoza sought to minimize the chances that the Coronado expedition would leave grief or anger in its wake as it passed through previously subdued territories, now populated by at least nominal Christians and vassals of the king of Spain. He made arrangements aimed at safeguarding places such as Toluca, Pátzcuaro, and Tonalá on the road west to Compostela.

First, "since it seemed to him that if the expedition departed from [the Ciudad de] México en masse, it would do some injury [as it passed] through the lands of the [native] allies, [the viceroy] decreed that they were to go [separately] to meet in the *ciudad* of Compostela, the seat of government of the Nuevo Reino de Galicia, a hundred and ten leagues from [the Ciudad de] México, in order to start the expedition in an orderly manner from there."³

Second, Mendoza sent people ahead of the expedition, at least in areas under Spanish control, in order to purchase provisions for the force as it passed through. Juan de León Romano, for instance, performed such duty at Ucareo, a native community along the main route from the Ciudad de México westward to Michoacán (the town now known as Pátzcuaro).⁴ To avoid the expedition's having to impress load bearers from native settlements to carry those provisions, the viceroy hired *tamemes* to transport the supplies. To do this he dispatched León Romano, don Luis de Castilla, and perhaps others along the road to Michoacán. The two are said to have paid the bearers "much to their satisfaction," usually after the fact in reduced tribute assessments.⁵

With these arrangements in place, between the last days of November 1539 and mid-February 1540 hundreds of expedition members followed the road from the Ciudad de México to Pátzcuaro and then northwest to Compostela without reported incident. The viceroy, too, made the journey, planning to inspect the united force and send it off from the capital of Nueva Galicia. New Year's Day 1540 (December 25 in those days) found him and his entourage at Pátzcuaro.⁶ On the sixth of January 1540, Mendoza, acting in the name of the king, formally designated Vázquez de Coronado as captain general of the expedition bound for Cíbola, although that decision had been made months earlier.

The document by which the designation was made included the following general statement about how the captain general and the force he was to lead were to behave toward American natives from Michoacán onward:

> In regard to treatment of the native Indians of the lands through which you may travel and [where you may] be, and in regard to what you may have to do and [what agreements you may have] to conclude in [those lands], we order you to observe and fulfill the directive which we have ordered given to the persons who go, as you are going, to reconnoiter and pacify lands and new *provincias* and which you are taking (signed by our viceroy and the secretary, [who have] signed at the end of the document). [You are to adhere to this] word for word, without exceeding or running counter to its substance and form, under [pain of] the penalties referred to in the directive.⁷

Although the text of the directive that Vázquez de Coronado and his subordinates were expected to abide by was not included in the captain general's appointment, it doubtless read much like the admonition delivered a year later by Mendoza to Captain Hernando de Alarcón: "You shall be very careful that the people who go in your company not inflict injury on or [exercise] force against the Indians. They are not to take anything they may possess from them against their will, nor are they to enter their houses without your permission."⁸

Indeed, shortly after the viceroy saw the expedition to Tierra Nueva off from Compostela late in February 1540, Vázquez de Coronado "issued and ordered proclaimed ordinances very beneficial to the natives of the lands to which he was going." As expressed by the captain general and his attorney later, "among those there was one according to which no man-at-arms was to enter an Indian's house or take anything or burn a house without permission from his captain, under penalty of death."⁹ Like this particular order, many other such rules, if not all of them, derived directly from the viceroy's directive, which in turn had its model in royal decrees concerning the benevolent treatment of American natives. Dozens of laws, ordinances, decrees, and commands forbidding arbitrary and abusive treatment of Indians had issued from the courts of successive Spanish monarchs since the early years of the sixteenth century. According to the captain general, "because of a public announcement he had made, no one, neither Spaniard nor Indian, dared to enter the houses of the natives, and the army always took up quarters outside the town[s], in order to avoid the injury that fighting men are accustomed to do."¹⁰

Despite the captain general's issuing a formal code of behavior, hostilities frequently broke out between Indians and expeditionaries. In part this was because the armed force was now in Nueva Galicia, where native animosity was greater and the Spanish grip more recent and more tenuous than in the Mexica and Tarascan heartlands. Conquest, which had been particularly brutal, was fewer than ten years in the past and was patchy at best. North of San Miguel de Culiacán, the most distant Spanish outpost of the Nuevo Reino de Galicia, the Spaniards exerted no hold at all. And disquiet, associated with news and rumors of earlier and continuing violence and slaving by colonists, had spread far beyond the physical reach of Spanish expeditions.

Only a matter of days after Vázquez de Coronado published his ordinances for the benevolent treatment of Indians, the expedition reached the native *provincia* of Chiametla. With the massive force already short of food, the *maestre de campo*, Lope de Samaniego, was sent with a detail to procure what food he could. Samaniego had, in the early 1530s, led the initial conquest of this area himself and evidently was heartily disliked there as a result. The indigenous Chiametlans resisted his party's demands for food. A running skirmish broke out, and Samaniego was fatally shot. As a result, a second foraging party was dispatched. It seized supplies of food and a number of Indian prisoners. Vázquez de Coronado ordered the prisoners "who seemed to be from the area where the *maestre de campo* died" to be hanged.[11] Similar scenes were to unfold throughout the course of the *entrada*.

According to Vázquez de Coronado's claim, "war waged by the aforesaid general and his army during the *entrada* and reconnaissance was fully justified, the Indians having prompted it."[12] In 1544 a series of sworn witnesses supported that view. One former expeditionary, Lorenzo Álvarez, testified that "before war was waged in any place, many exhortations were made in the presence of friars who went on the expedition . . . the natives were given all the assurances . . . [but] those Indians were never willing to accept the pledges. Instead, they made threats and shot arrows, for which reason [the Spaniards] were forced to wage war."[13]

Requerimiento, the Formal Summons

Álvarez's references to "exhortations" and "pledges" derived from the *requerimiento*, a document that had been employed by Spanish-led expeditions in the New World since 1513. Likely prepared at royal request by a renowned legal scholar named Juan López de Palacios Rubios, the *requerimiento* expressed the intentions of expeditionaries and the royal court that stood behind them. It was supposed to be read aloud to natives upon first contact with a group or settlement new to an expedition. If possible, it was to be translated into the native language, on the slight chance that the raft of foreign concepts it contained, including terms of Christian faith and Spanish governance, might be made comprehensible. The *requerimiento* was to serve two major purposes. First, within a European legal framework, it would establish the legitimacy of Spanish political sovereignty over the people to whom it was read. Second, it would afford an opportunity to those native people to submit willingly to the authority of the monarchs of Spain, the Roman pope, and their delegates. Otherwise, that authority was to be imposed upon them.¹⁴

The summons itself was a lengthy document that traced a chain of authority from God to the pope and on to the Spanish sovereign, the expedition's captain general, and finally each reader of the *requerimiento*. Then it offered the indigenous listeners a single future, as vassals of the Spanish king and adherents of the Catholic faith, and two roads to that future: peaceful submission or the compulsion of war. Although the details of the demand must rarely, if ever, have been understood by the indigenous Americans to whom it was read, certainly the insistence of the readers and the intent of the armed men who backed them up were unmistakable. The central demand was phrased this way: "We ask and require . . . that you acknowledge the Church as the ruler and superior of the whole world, and the high priest called Pope, and in his name the king and queen . . . our lords, in his place, as superiors and lords and kings of these islands and this mainland."¹⁵

Despite the starkness of the *requerimiento*'s ultimatum, it was in the long-term interest of aspiring overlords to preserve as many Indian lives as possible. Only live adult male heads of household could be expected to pay full tribute. Aspirations of suzerainty may have served as a counterweight to bloodier motives. While hopes for the future and the mandate to read the *requerimiento* may have restrained some conquistadores, including Vázquez de Coronado, from precipitous attacks on New World natives, only the most naive and parochial Europeans could believe that it truly offered those natives any choice. Inherent in the document, and in the cultural assumptions that underlay it, was the unquestioned presumption that anyone, anywhere, would recognize the superiority of Christian European culture over any other and would readily and immediately abandon his or her own traditions and embrace those of the person reading the *requerimiento*. The absurdity of that presumption did not go unremarked by some sixteenth-century Spaniards. Bartolomé de las Casas, for instance, famously remarked that, upon reading the *requerimiento*, he did not know whether to laugh or cry.¹⁶

Nevertheless, the *requerimiento* salved the consciences of some Europeans who in all sincerity saw it as an element in the compassionate treatment of American natives. And Vázquez de Coronado scrupulously saw that it was read, at Cíbola, at Tusayán, at Tiguex.

The Problem of Food

If use of the *requerimiento* was by and large an empty gesture when it came to the welfare of non-Christian Indians, then other measures were potentially more consequential. Two and a half months after the Coronado expedition departed from Compostela, the viceroy dispatched a parallel, seaborne arm of the *entrada*. Led by Hernando de Alarcón, a one-time captain in Mendoza's personal guard, the little flotilla was to carry provisions, clothing, and equipment to supply the terrestrial expedition.[17] Had a rendezvous between the ships and the land expedition been achieved, a better supplied expedition might have been less likely to impose on local Indians for food and clothing. As will be seen, no such rendezvous occurred, and the expeditionaries spent nearly two years buying, cajoling, and extorting corn and *mantas*, or capes, from the Pueblos of the Rio Grande region. Still, at least part of the motivation for Alarcón's voyage was to minimize the land expedition's demands on native people for supplies.

Nor was that the only such attempt made by the *entrada*'s organizers and leaders. At Eastertime 1540 the 2,000 or so walking and riding expeditionaries reached San Miguel de Culiacán. There the force was reprovisioned by the European settlers, who in turn had levied the supplies from Indians of the area whom they held in *encomienda*. As Vázquez de Coronado prepared to move the expedition north beyond effective Spanish jurisdiction, he "thought that it would be very trying to travel with the entire force, since he had information that there was a shortage of provisions. He instead took the *maestre de campo* don García López [who had replaced Lope de Samaniego after his death] and about 80 horsemen with him to go in advance and reconnoiter, seeing what was there."[18] He also took with him "most of the Indian allies" but left in Culiacán the majority of the horses, which were large consumers of corn.[19] Those left behind, both people and animals, were to follow in two weeks. By making this arrangement the captain general both reduced the likelihood of hunger for his advance guard and significantly decreased the volume of foodstuffs Indians along his route would be expected to supply in the near term.

Having advance knowledge from Melchior Díaz and Juan de Zaldívar, who had made the preliminary reconnaissance recounted in chapter 4, that the crops ahead of the expedition were not yet ripe, Vázquez de Coronado was prudent indeed in his decision to proceed with a reduced force. That was even without taking into account the burden the food requirements of the full expedition would have placed on the native people of Corazones, Señora, and Suya (all in modern Sonora), as well as other, less productive areas. As the captain general later explained in his own defense,

> all the towns there are between Culiacán and the province of Cíbola, through which the accused [Vázquez de Coronado] passed, came out in peace and welcomed him very warmly. Where they had provisions, they provided them. This was because the accused had some individuals from the army go ahead carrying a cross as a sign of peace. And they were to assure [the natives] that the general would do them no harm. Further, the accused gave [the natives] items of trade and things that the viceroy had provided for this purpose. With these they were very satisfied.[20]

Likewise, in fall 1540, when the expedition had taken up winter quarters in Tiguex pueblos along the Rio Grande,

> a number of Spaniards, men-at-arms, and Indian allies complained to the [captain general] that they did not have clothing and were dying of cold. And they asked that he order some clothing to be gathered from the neighboring pueblos, with which they might cover and protect themselves from the cold. Seeing the need that existed, [Vázquez de Coronado] ordered don García López to take trade goods and with them try to purchase, from the pueblo of Chia, some robes, hides, and *mantas* with which to clothe and save the people.[21]

Although accusations were made that expeditionaries repeatedly took both clothing and food from Indians without their consent and without compensation, years afterward the former captain general claimed that only after the expedition left Tierra Nueva did he hear that the Spaniards "took clothing from [the Pueblos'] houses against their will."[22]

Any assessment of how solicitous of Indian welfare the Coronado expedition was hinges on the scale at which the examination is made. Certainly, the expedition's record as a group was not admirable. Equally certainly, some individuals were more concerned with the benevolent treatment of Indians than others. Vázquez de Coronado may belong in the category of the more concerned. But he was also pragmatic. Depending on circumstances, he could be ruthless and could keep himself ignorant of what others under his authority might have done. His pursuit of justice for a Pueblo woman raped by a prominent expedition member, for example, was half-hearted and perfunctory. On the other hand, his compliance with the formal protocols regarding treatment of Indians required by the king and viceroy was worthy of any conscientious functionary. The expedition, however, also included many men, among them at least five captains, who within the previous decade had participated in the bloodbath that had been the conquest of Nueva Galicia.[23]

Generally speaking, the leaders of the expedition to Tierra Nueva knew that gratuitous provocation of the local Indian population was likely in the short term to precipitate violent retaliation and in the longer term to earn censure from higher Spanish authorities.

CHAPTER 7

Almost a Highway

WITHOUT APPARENT PROVOCATION OF THE NATIVES along the route, units of the expedition made their way separately from the Ciudad de México as far as Compostela late in 1539 and early in 1540. Once most of the expeditionaries, though not all of them, had assembled at Compostela, the viceroy conducted the formal review of the force and had a muster roll drafted on February 22, 1540. Each of the 289 European men-at-arms swore "to the best of his knowledge and judgment, [to] obey and fulfill [the king's] directives and [those] of the lord viceroy in his royal name."[1] Mendoza may also have reviewed the large contingent of native allies, but no enumeration of them survives, if indeed a list was ever prepared.

With preparations complete, captaincies assigned, instructions given, and oaths sworn, the expedition departed from Compostela on February 24, its official launch date. For two days the viceroy accompanied the northward-bound throng. Then he turned back to look after other business at Colima. The expedition, traveling by companies, continued on, following a route along western Mexico's Pacific coastal plain to the indigenous community of Chiametla in the southern part of today's state of Sinaloa. There it was met by Captains Melchior Díaz and Juan de Zaldívar, returning from their stymied attempt to reach Cíbola at Mendoza's command, after several winter weeks or months spent at or near the ruined pueblo of Chichilticale. Besides announcing their inability to confirm fray Marcos's report of Cíbola, the two informed Vázquez de Coronado that food would be in short supply north of Culiacán. It was at Chiametla, too, that *maestre de campo* Lope de Samaniego was killed. Don García López de Cárdenas, a member of a prominent Madrid family, was named to take his place, and the expedition moved on.

It reached the eight-and-a-half-year-old Spanish *villa* of San Miguel de Culiacán, in what is now northern Sinaloa, on the day before Easter, March 27, 1540. On the way the force had found it necessary to make "*entradas* in the *tierra de guerra* [land where the natives were hostile to the Spaniards] in order to seize supplies of food."[2] After Easter, with an elaborate mock battle, the expedition ceremonially took possession of Culiacán. About the road to there from Compostela, Juan Jaramillo wrote: "It is a well-known and much-traveled route because in that valley of Culiacán is a *villa* settled by Spaniards."[3]

There the expeditionaries found plentiful provisions. It was also there that the captain general, knowing from Díaz and Zaldívar that scarcity lay ahead, decided to split his force. He would leave most of the Europeans at Culiacán and push on to Cíbola himself with an advance guard.[4] This proved a wise decision, as Vázquez de Coronado himself later wrote to the viceroy: "To judge by what happened, I am certain I have guessed right in not engaging all the combined armed force in this undertaking. [That is] because there have been such great difficulties and such a shortage of foodstuffs."[5]

A hundred and fifty leagues later—about 400 miles—on May 26, the advance guard reached Los Corazones, where almost four years earlier Cabeza de Vaca and his companions had feasted on deer hearts. There, halfway to Cíbola, on what today is called the Río Sonora, the Europeans and Mexican Indians "found more people than in any other part of the land [they] had left behind. And a large quantity of seed [corn], but there [was] no [fresh] corn for eating among them."[6] Because this place "appeared to be well disposed, it was ordered [that] a *villa* be settled here by Spaniards who were coming behind."[7] This *villa* was called San Gerónimo and was subsequently moved northward, first to Señora and then to Suya.

After passing those two populous indigenous communities, both also on the Río Sonora, the advance guard crossed a topographic divide to the north-flowing San Pedro River in what is now the state of Arizona. There, food was even scarcer. Expeditionary Juan Jaramillo, for instance, mentioned only "some roasted maguey stalks and *pitahayas* [cactus fruits]" that were offered as gifts by Indians of primitive appearance.[8] About halfway from Los Corazones to Cíbola the advance guard reached the red-earth pueblo Chichilticale, a landmark they had been told about by Díaz and Zaldívar. According to Castañeda de Nájera, "it grieved everyone to see that the renown of Chichilticale was reduced to a ruined roofless house."⁹

From there until reaching Cíbola, a distance of about 210 more miles, the expeditionaries saw no permanent habitations at all.¹⁰ Such "unsettled" areas, or *despoblados*, were of no more interest to the Europeans than similar areas in the Old World had been to their ancestors. Marco Polo, for example, 300 years before had found unsettled stretches in Asia to be "nothing worthy of mention in our book."¹¹ Not only were unsettled areas intrinsically uninteresting, they were also dangerous. In a *despoblado* there was no chance to procure food from agricultural natives. Despite Vázquez de Coronado's foresight in proceeding from Culiacán with only part of the expedition, his advance guard now suffered severely from hunger. Expeditionary Cristóbal de Escobar remembered years afterward that "more than sixty of our Indian allies had [already] died along the way from hunger, as well as some Spaniards and Blacks."¹² An anonymous member of the expedition reported that "on the seventy-third [day out from Los Corazones] we reached Cíbola, although with extreme difficulty, the loss of many horses, and the death of some Indians."¹³

Despite the hardships of hunger, "the general and his troop crossed the land without opposition, since they found everyone to be at peace because the Indians were familiar with fray Marcos and some of those who had traveled with Captain Melchior Díaz when he and Juan de Zaldívar went to make a reconnaissance."¹⁴ This lack of overt resistance to the advance guard's progress suggests that on the whole it succeeded in not antagonizing the native people it met along the way.

That was about to change. When the force reached the distance of a few leagues from Cíbola, "two or three Indians from that province and principal pueblo came to [the captain general]. And he spoke to them by means of signs, so that they would understand that they did not come to do them harm."¹⁵ Then he "sent [a message] (in His Majesty's name) with some Indians who were natives of Cíbola and who, a day previously, had come voluntarily to the army, to summon the Indians who were in Cíbola."¹⁶

No response came from Cíbola, so the captain general dispatched two Nahuas from among the contingent of Indian allies to venture ahead "carrying a cross in their hands as a sign of peace."17 What happened when the Cíbolans rejected that overture must wait. First, it is important to take a look at the roads and native guides that enabled the expedition to reach Cíbola in the first place.

Roads

Beginning with Marcos de Niza's 1539 reconnaissance and continuing throughout the two and a half years of the Coronado expedition proper, including the advance guard's hungry trek to Cíbola in the spring and early summer of 1540, every contingent of the expedition followed already existent indigenous trails, some of them so heavily used as to deserve the name "highway." Only rarely did the expedition have to modify or detour from those roads. When it did, it was usually because of the requirements of horses and other livestock. The animals required wider, smoother passages than did foot traffic.

The expedition did not randomly explore territory. Indeed, what it did can be described as "exploration" only of the most superficial and rudimentary type. It was the equivalent of a modern "explorer's" traversing the southwestern United States by driving the Interstate highway system from Los Angeles through Phoenix, Albuquerque, Oklahoma City, and Dallas to El Paso. While such a trip might reveal a great deal about the modern Southwest, most of the land, many of its people, and virtually all the region's non-urban resources and activities would never be seen.

The well-trodden roadways used by the Coronado expedition connected centers of population and had already been in use for centuries before 1540. Abundant archaeological evidence shows that a large volume of high-value trade goods was transported along these roads for several hundred years before the Coronado *entrada*. Traders had carried goods such as turquoise and bison hides, procured and processed in the Pueblo region of what is now the U.S. Southwest, to trade with people in the Sonora River valley and other places in what is now northern and northwestern Mexico. Some of those goods, particularly turquoise, were subsequently retraded farther southward, reaching even southern Mesoamerica.[18]

In the opposite direction came marine shells and tropical feathers, especially those of the scarlet macaw. The Pueblos manufactured items of personal adornment from shells obtained in this way from the Mar del Sur (as the Spaniards called the Pacific Ocean and Gulf of California), as well as the Mar del Norte (the Gulf of Mexico). They still use macaw feathers for ceremonial purposes today. These and other goods formed the basis of a regular interregional trade that long before 1540 had given rise to an extensive road network. At the time of the Coronado *entrada*, this north-south route running up the Pacific coast was the major trade pipeline in that sector of North America. As such, it determined the route by which the Coronado expedition, Marcos de Niza, and Nuño Beltrán de Guzmán before them sought to penetrate the continent. Other routes, equally important to native commerce and the Coronado expedition as its travel continued, crossed the continent west to east, linking the Pueblo world with people of the Great Plains and the Pacific Coast. Of course not only goods but also people, news, and ideas flowed along the roads.[19]

As an example of how rapidly and how widely news traveled over the indigenous road network, consider the case of Captain Hernando de Alarcón, who led the sea voyage meant to complement and resupply Vázquez de Coronado's land expedition. He and a group of his companions managed to penetrate the continent by water as far as the lower reaches of the Gila River in what is now southwestern Arizona. Near the limit of its travel, Alarcón's party met an Indian who had recently talked with others who had themselves just returned from Cíbola, almost 400 miles distant. This man's friends had observed the arrival of the main body of the Coronado expedition at Cíbola, a process that took a full day. They described aspects of the expedition in astonishing detail.[20]

Guides and Languages

The Coronado expedition observed and took advantage of these trade and communication routes and employed experienced long-distance travelers along them as guides. The *entrada* was, for all practical purposes, a matter of following guides from one principal town to another by way of these direct and heavily used routes. Such a procedure suited the major motivation of the expedition: it was a wisely chosen method for locating the most populous and therefore most prosperous places, where profitable *encomiendas* might be established. If, on the contrary, the expedition's goal had been to survey the natural resources of the region, particularly mineral resources, or to thoroughly map the geography, then the big-city, interstate-highway-type tour would have been a misguided strategy.

Lacking road maps of Tierra Nueva, the Coronado expeditionaries sought to obtain at each principal town one or more guides to show them the direct route to the next and to steer them correctly at intersections and forks in the intricate network of indigenous roads. Occasionally the guides were asked to locate alternative routes that would more easily accommodate horses and other livestock. Besides traveling on established highways, the expedition was always led by experienced native guides.

Often guides seemed willing, even eager, to conduct the expedition farther along its way. Pintados, or tattooed Indians from the interior of northern Mexico, and Seris from the Gulf of California coast, for instance, insisted on accompanying fray Marcos for well over a hundred miles.[21] The Hopi people of Tusayán "gave [López de Cárdenas] guides in order to continue his travels."[22] On the other hand, the expedition sometimes found it expedient to seize guides by force. The captain general himself later testified that as the advance guard approached Cíbola, he had "ordered don Pedro de Tovar and Melchior Díaz to bring him an Indian from among those who were walking by a lake, in order to get information and an interpreter from them."[23] And on at least one occasion reluctant native guides fled from the expedition, forcing a return to the nearest indigenous settlement to procure more guides.[24]

Because no single person had experience of the great mass of land that comprises what is now northwest Mexico and the American Southwest, the expedition had to rely on a succession of local guides. Those people included a Sonoran refugee from Cíbola, an emissary from Cicuique, and an assimilated captive from Quivira, along with many others. Some of the guides performed services well beyond simply leading the armed party, taking upon themselves the role of emissary or ambassador. The guide about whom we know the most was the man known in Spanish as Bigotes, who reappears later in the story. He traveled ahead of a scouting party led by Hernando de Alvarado, assuring the people at each successive pueblo that they need not be afraid, so that "all [the people] came forth in peace, seeing that men feared throughout all those *provincias* were traveling with Bigotes."[25]

Nahua allies of the expedition, from among the huge corps of Indian warriors, served in a similar capacity, perhaps because of the Europeans' mistaken notion of the close cultural and linguistic affinity among all Native Americans. When the advance guard made its final approach to Cíbola, Vázquez de Coronado sent two Nahuas ahead with a message of peaceful conquest. They returned to tell him that "the pueblo and province were at war and were not willing to come to peace."[26] Several other native guides and emissaries figured importantly in the expedition and are discussed in later chapters.

It was crucial that each guide communicate satisfactorily with members of the expedition. Expedition leaders had to be able to tell their guides what sorts of places they were seeking and needed to feel confident that they were being understood, at least at an elementary level if not in all details. Translation and interpretation were among the expedition's most vital needs. At least rudimentary communication between the expeditionaries and native people—or its lack—was pivotal in all dealings between the two groups. Once the expedition reached what is today Sonora, none of the native languages was known to its European members. Along the route the expedition traveled from Compostela to Quivira and back, no fewer than 17 different indigenous languages were spoken in the early 1540s, as well as numerous dialects of them.[27]

The expeditionaries used two principal methods in their efforts to understand and be understood by Native Americans. The first was to speak through an interpreter or a chain of interpreters. When the advance guard reached Cíbola early in July 1540, it was necessary, according to royal order, to read the *requerimiento* to the native people there. As expeditionary Pedro de Ledesma later recalled, the Indians of Cíbola "were made to understand, with signs and through an interpreter [the Spaniards] had brought from the valley of Corazones, that they were not coming to do them any harm."[28] The interpreter's principal language was likely a Piman dialect or possibly Ópata. Almost certainly there was at least one other native intermediary between him and the Spanish leaders of the expedition.

Not content with an oral translation of the demand for submission at second or third hand, fray Juan de Padilla also "made [the Indians from Cíbola] understand these things by signs."[29] Whether a mutually intelligible sign language was available to the signer and the Cíbolans is unknown. The interpreter employed by fray Juan to convert the message into hand signs was probably an Indian ally of the expedition. Whatever the case, that system of signs could not possibly have accommodated many of the concepts of the *requerimiento*. Yet the use of hand signals and sign language, even with its limited ability to communicate abstract and foreign ideas, served as the Coronado expedition's second most important means of exchanging information with American natives.

Because of the extent and power of Mexica-Aztec influence throughout Mesoamerica in the centuries before European conquest, facility in speaking and understanding their language, Nahuatl, was widespread even beyond the confines of the Mexica state. With European conquest, some of the new overlords, especially missionary friars, sought to perpetuate and even extend the use of Nahuatl. Some friars saw Nahuatl as the potential indigenous lingua franca of the Americas. Nahuatl thus frequently served as one of the bridges between Spanish and the multitude of mutually unintelligible native languages the Coronado expedition encountered. Nahuatl speakers among the expedition's corps of native allies had much more frequent and extended contact with the indigenous people of Tierra Nueva than did the Europeans. That is evident from the fact that a number of people from Tierra Nueva picked up words and phrases of Nahuatl from the expedition. There is no evidence that any of them learned Spanish vocabulary. For example, during the spring of

1541 the guide and interpreter from the Great Plains nicknamed El Turco communicated to European leaders of the expedition "by means of signs and in the Nahuatl language (which he knew slightly)."[30]

The Coronado expedition was neither prepared nor equipped to operate without reliable native assistance. Even more useful than mere guides were persons who could also serve as emissaries—persons who had social, political, commercial, or other relations with residents of the next destination town and could speak its language.

For these very reasons Viceroy Mendoza had purchased the black slave Esteban from Andrés Dorantes and sent him with fray Marcos when he departed northward in 1539. Esteban had previously been to at least some of the places Marcos intended to go. And he seemed to have an extraordinary facility in establishing communication with Native Americans and in gaining their confidence and cooperation. Even from the first, though, Marcos also had with him Indians from Petatlán, Cuchillo, and places farther north, whom he relied on to communicate with natives he met.[31] As he traveled farther north he picked up other guides, Seris from the coast, Pintados from the interior, a man he described as a "*vecino* of Cíbola," and finally a group of "thirty *principales*" from the headwaters of either the Río Sonora or the San Pedro River.[32] Marcos was pleased with his guides. He later wrote that "the Indians have told me [accurately beforehand about] everything I have seen until now. [They] always told me [about] the *pueblos* I would of necessity find along the trail, and their names."[33]

The friar was curious about how they knew so much about distant places such as Cíbola. In what is now Sonora, his indigenous guides communicated to him that "they were accustomed to travel to the *ciudad* of Cíbola in thirty days of travel . . . for turquoises, [bison] hides, and other things and that [the people of Cíbola] have a great quantity of each of those in their *pueblo* . . . They told me that [they traded] for their sweat and their personal service," working seasonally in the fields of the Cíbolans.[34] Marcos saw for himself some of the fruit of that employment, "more than two thousand extremely well dressed [bison] hides . . . [and] a much greater quantity of turquoises and [turquoise] necklaces in this valley than in all the places I had left behind. Everyone says that it comes from the *ciudad* of Cíbola."³⁵ Clearly, the road to Cíbola was in regular use, a fact confirmed by Marcos's own observation as he and his guides proceeded toward his goal. Along the way he saw "old shelters and many signs of fires from the people who traveled to Cíbola along this trail."³⁶

A year later, when Vázquez de Coronado and his advance guard traveled the road to Cíbola, they found much the same situation and again relied on native guides. Those guides proved especially valuable when the advanced guard got beyond the point fray Marcos had reached. It became painfully obvious at Chichilticale that "there was no one who had seen [what lay ahead], except the Indians who had gone with the Black."³⁷ Over and over again during that trek northward and ensuing side trips, whether to Tusayán, the Grand Canyon, the Mar del Sur, or the Tiguex pueblos, the expedition would have been sorely pressed without the guidance provided by natives of the region.³⁸

Even though, or perhaps because, the expeditionaries depended so heavily on indigenous guides, they were ready to see trickery in any inconsistent behavior by those guides. Disagreement between Plains Indian guides later led to a crisis for the expedition and the execution of the guide called El Turco. Spaniards came to the Western Hemisphere already primed with popular stories of treacherous guides, often Turks, so they anticipated and might have projected that possibility onto American natives. The deceptive guide was a staple of the wildly popular chivalric romances of the day in Spain. Many expeditionaries were preconditioned to expect attempts at deception.³⁹

The Coronado expedition was not unique in its reliance on indigenous intermediaries. From Christopher Columbus to George Crook, Europeans and their Euroamerican successors employed native guides, interpreters, scouts, and warriors to advance non-native plans and strategies. Looking at the situation from the other side, American natives, in small but important numbers and in all eras, directly engaged outsiders in diplomacy, trade, and cultural exchange in the hope of shielding themselves and their communities, of improving their condition in a rapidly shifting world, and sometimes of avenging perceived wrongs committed by other native groups. As will be seen in later chapters, the individual Pueblo and Plains

Indian intermediaries who attempted to bridge the cultural divide between Native Americans and the Coronado expedition generally suffered for it.

It was with a combination of necessity and suspicion that Vázquez de Coronado entrusted the expedition to Tierra Nueva to a succession of native guides. Communication with them was rudimentary for the most part, and they operated from unknown but potentially deadly motives. Nevertheless, with few hitches, expeditionaries and guides managed to cross thousands of miles by way of native roads between the largest communities of sedentary Indians in the region. ■

CHAPTER 8

By Sea to Chichilticale

While Vázquez de Coronado and his advance guard made their hungry way northward from Culiacán to Cíbola, another party paralleled them by sea. Dispatched by the viceroy from Colima in May 1540, Captain Hernando de Alarcón was assigned to rendezvous with and resupply the land expedition.[1] His little fleet of three small ships sailed coastwise northward, nosing into every bay and inlet in search of some sign of the expedition. As a result of statements made by fray Marcos, Alarcón and his crews, as well as the viceroy and the captain general, thought that a port could be established at Chichilticale from which the expedition would be contacted and reprovisioned. Instead, unbeknownst to the land expeditionaries and the crews of the fleet, north of Culiacán the coast and the direct road to Chichilticale and Cíbola diverged steadily. A port for Chichilticale proved illusory.

Without Alarcón's having made contact with the captain general, his ships ran aground at the head of what is today known as the Gulf of California. Luckily, they were refloated by the tidal bore that still surges up the gulf with each rising tide. They were now, in late August, about 300 miles west of the route followed by the force on land. Consulting his pilots and crews and calling a council of royal officials and other prominent men, Alarcón found them generally of the opinion that the difficulties of passing onward justified abandoning the voyage and returning to Colima. That course had been followed the previous year by a fleet led by Francisco de Ulloa on behalf of Hernando Cortés.

Although in such situations the master of ships, the first among equals, was "obliged to conform with the majority" or potentially be liable for damages, Alarcón "was still determined that [they] should go farther and continue the journey."² Picking their way through sandy shoals, the three small ships reached the heavy flow of a river they named the Buena Guía, the modern Colorado. Resolved to pursue a rendezvous with the land *entrada*, the captain ordered that two rowed boats be made ready so that he and 20 men could ascend the river. To this point Alarcón had the benefit of the previous experience of one of his pilots, Domingo del Castillo, who had sailed with Ulloa the year before. The Buena Guía, though, was hitherto unknown by Europeans, and contacting Vázquez de Coronado would hinge on information and assistance from the indigenous people who lived along the river's shores.

Rowing and towing the boats and using a sail by turns, the small party laboriously made slow headway upstream, occasionally seeing and then cautiously trading with Indians on land. Traveling in the boats was at least one Indian, a native of points farther south, who was expected to serve as interpreter. To Alarcón's chagrin, for five days none of the Colorado River people recognized the interpreter's language, although, "because they saw he was like them, they held back."³ Both parties briefly laid aside weapons, Alarcón pantomimed and distributed glass beads and items of brightly colored clothing, and Indians inundated the strangers with local foods. But wariness on both sides eventually pushed the groups apart. The European captain anticipated ambush and imminent aggression. With his small force, Alarcón reembarked and proceeded upriver. Eventually he made another attempt at conversation by means of gestures with a fresh group of natives. Indians even took up the tow ropes and hauled the boats upstream. At each stop Alarcón distributed small makeshift crosses, acting out their adoration.

Then, remarkably, on the sixth day the captain realized that "one [Indian] had responded to [the interpreter]."⁴ This suggests that Alarcón's interpreter and his Colorado River interlocutor both spoke Piman dialects.⁵ The representative of the river people acted as though he were a leader, or *principal*, of his group and was perhaps a trader or traveled widely for other reasons. His compatriots did not understand the language of Alarcón's interpreter. The *principal* initiated a lengthy interrogation of Alarcón, through the Spaniard's interpreter, asking who he was, where he had come from, and why he was there. His questions bristled with skepticism.

The captain responded with a claim often put forward by conquistadores of the day. He said he was a son of the sun, which had sent him from very far away to bring peace to the chronically warring peoples of the region. Hernando Cortés, Álvar Núñez Cabeza de Vaca, and Francisco de Ibarra, among others, also elicited the designation "sons of the sun" from indigenous groups they encountered. This may represent an effort to identify the Christian god with what conquistadores commonly interpreted as the chief supernatural being throughout the Native American world, the sun.[6] By and large Alarcón's explanations seemed to allay the Indian's suspicions. In turn, the *principal* provided information about peoples who inhabited the river basin, peoples who spoke as many as 23 languages.[7] Additionally, he acknowledged that he had previously heard about other men with beards, like Alarcón, but very far away. Whether this vague awareness of Europeans reflected the earlier activities of Cortés, Ulloa, and Guzmán to the south or the much more recent passage of the Coronado land expedition to the east is not evident.

Alarcón and his men set out again, frequently running aground in the shallows where the boats were close enough to shore to be towed. Then, seeing people gathered on the opposite bank, they rowed across. This native group also included an elder who could understand the captain's interpreter, once again facilitating detailed interchange of information. Again Alarcón understood that river peoples maintained oral traditions concerning the existence of bearded, white-skinned strangers.

This informative native group was succeeded by other people with whom verbal communication proved impossible. But on went the boats as Alarcón did his best with gestures. The party had now entered "the river [that led, according to the local natives,] to Cíbola," probably the lowest reaches of the modern Gila River.[8] There, another man appeared on shore who could speak with the interpreter. He said that he himself had been to Cíbola, which he described in detail. He even had news of "a black man who wore a beard . . . , wore bells and feathers on his arms and legs," had a dog, and had been killed there—surely Esteban.[9] The man had been killed, according to Alarcón's Colorado River informant, because he had told the Cíbolans that he was an advance man for a heavily armed party behind him.

Another Indian man from a group on shore insisted that other white men were now at Cíbola, men who called themselves Christians and sons of the sun. Excited by this news, Alarcón "conceived the desire to send news of myself to the captain [general]. I talked this over with my men-at-arms, among whom I did not find anyone who was willing to go there, even though I offered them many things on Your Lordship's behalf. Only one Moorish slave volunteered to go, although grudgingly."[10] In the end, not even the Moor set out. Nor were the natives of the riverbank willing to travel to Cíbola with Alarcón or his men, for fear of attack by their neighbors. The captain and his native interlocutor exchanged angry words over this refusal.

Apparently with the idea of replenishing his stock of trade and gift goods, as well as replacing his reluctant boat crews, Alarcón turned around after 15 days and was carried swiftly downstream, about 50 to 60 miles, to the mouth of the Río de Buena Guía, where the three ships and the remainder of his men awaited him. With the desired changes made, the captain once again headed northward. He now learned from natives along the river that the trip to Cíbola would take as much as two months by land, and much longer by keeping to the boats. Despairing of reaching Cíbola at such a great distance, Alarcón decided to abandon the plan to join Vázquez de Coronado. At the place where that decision was made, he "had a very tall cross set up and on it I had lettering engraved to the effect that I had reached that point. I had this done so that if it should happen that any of the general's men reached there, they would have information about me."[11]

Returning to the ships, Alarcón made sail southward. Although he "landed many times and penetrated a long distance inland to see whether we could learn anything about Captain Francisco Vázquez and his company, we obtained no other hint of them than what I had heard [already] on that coast."[12] Repeatedly the ships' crews erected crosses and buried messages as they descended the gulf, in the hope of getting word to the captain general.¹³ At the port of Colima Alarcón delivered a summary report of his five-month voyage to the viceroy's *mayordomo*.

Amity between Alarcón and Colorado River Indians

Viewed from the perspective of relations with indigenous people, the Alarcón voyage stands out dramatically among the several *entradas* made by the Coronado expedition and its subsidiary units. The voyage was notably peaceful; no open hostility is documented between Alarcón and his men and natives of the lower Colorado and Gila Rivers during the nearly two months of its towed and rowed riverine travel. Although there were angry verbal exchanges, a bumping incident, and reports and fears of planned native attacks, the threshold of deadly violence was never crossed by either side.

In contrast, every other episode of extended contact between the expeditionaries and indigenous groups eventually resulted in violent conflict. A telling comparison is provided by the *entrada* led by Captain Melchior Díaz from Los Corazones, to which he had recently returned from Cíbola under Vázquez de Coronado's orders, to the Río de Buena Guía in search of Alarcón and his fleet during the fall of 1540. Departing from San Gerónimo de los Corazones after mid-September, as Alarcón was making his second ascent of the rivers, Díaz reached the Buena Guía (which he called the Río Tizón) after 150 leagues (probably three to four weeks) of travel.

Alarcón had already abandoned the effort to link with the land expedition and had turned back southward. But Díaz did find a message left by Alarcón's party. Chiseled on a tree trunk, it read, "Alarcón reached this point. At the foot of this tree there are letters."¹⁴ With the central aim of his trek now unattainable, Díaz determined to reconnoiter the region. He and his 25 European companions, along with Indian allies of unknown number, encountered and clashed with indigenous groups in the vicinity of the rivers—perhaps some of the same people who had just dealt with Alarcón without warfare. Some of those natives were now angered enough to seek large-scale retaliation against the Díaz party. In Castañeda de Nájera's later telling, the natives "had been trying to arrange to make an assault on our people and had been looking for the suitable occasion."¹⁵

The opportunity came as Díaz and his force attempted to cross the Tizón–Buena Guía on rafts. "The plan was that when part of our people had crossed and part was crossing the river and [another] part was waiting to cross, the [natives] on the rafts would try to drown those they were carrying across. And the remainder of the [native] people would come forth to attack both the groups on land."[16] Díaz caught wind of what was afoot, seized a local Indian, and had him tortured to learn the details of the plan. Once again communication may have been by means of a Piman dialect, although no documentary proof of that exists. The prisoner was executed, and Díaz's men attacked what they took to be an approaching mass of warriors bent on aggression, killing some and routing the rest. It is possible that ultimate disillusion of the natives of the lower Colorado River with Alarcón had primed them for violence against Díaz, who arrived along the river so shortly after Alarcón's departure. Before his departure from the river, the local Indians had caught Alarcón is several lies and exaggerations, including the promise that he would stay with them.

Following Díaz's battle at the river crossing, reconnaissance was cut short when the captain was fatally injured while pursuing a dog that had been harrying sheep being herded by his party. In an attempt to save Díaz's life, his men carried him back toward Los Corazones for 20 excruciating days. He did not live to reach the supply and communication base and was buried along the return route. What remained of his unit traveled the rest of the way back to San Gerónimo "without seeing anything of what they sought."[17] Castañeda de Nájera is not explicit about the objects of Díaz's search. Besides a rendezvous with Alarcón, they surely included the locating of wealthy and populous settlements—universally the goal of Spanish-led reconnaissances through at least the middle of the sixteenth century—as well as discovery of an anchorage from which the expedition to Cíbola could conveniently be reprovisioned.

The relative calm that held between the Alarcón party and the native people it met, in contradistinction to the experience of the remainder of the Coronado expedition, is attributable to a number of circumstances. Most decisive were several practices the captain and his crews followed routinely, some purposeful and others without conscious forethought. Most conspicuous were gestures of nonbelligerence, mandated by the captain and scrupulously repeated by his crews. As Alarcón wrote afterward about an early encounter along the Río de Buena Guía, "I began to make signs of peace. Taking [my] sword and shield, I threw them into the *barca* [which was] beached, stepping my feet onto them, making [the Indians] understand by this and other signs that I did not wish to make war with them, and that they should do the same. Having seized a banner, I lowered it and had the men I had with me also sit down."[18] Alarcón seems to have been a somewhat more autocratic leader than Vázquez de Coronado and succeeded in achieving adherence to his generally peaceful tactics. If Alarcón's own narrative can be believed, his force never expressly threatened and was never seriously threatened by the indigenous people it met. At the least hint of menace, Alarcón and his men withdrew. In his subsequent report he put it this way: "I did not want to engage anyone."[19] Alarcón's first action on encountering indigenous groups was not a confrontational reading of the *requerimiento*, as it was for other units of the Coronado expedition.

The Europeans understood that there was frequent hostility among the Indians of the lower Gila and Colorado Rivers. Still, by and large, individual native groups met by Alarcón reciprocated his demonstrations of nonviolence, piling their weapons and enforcing a ban on carrying arms in the captain's presence. This despite the fact that "there were so many Indians, that if they had wanted to impede our passage, they could have done so, even had we been many more than we were."[20] Such a peaceful outcome required not only a lack of belligerence on the part of the Europeans but also a complementary receptivity to peaceful overtures by the Indians.

For the most part, the Colorado and Gila River natives seem to have viewed Alarcón and his crews as a benign, even salutary, group. They were humans, but of a very different type, who seemed to live on the water and only reluctantly came ashore, retreating in their boats to midstream each night to sleep. They seemed not covetous of the natives' wives, children, or property, and they offered trade on favorable terms. They gave out beads, capes, shirts, and other goods without apparent expectation of payment.²¹ The only reciprocal behavior the gifts required was that the natives kneel each morning with joined hands before a wooden cross. Evidently the Indians had heard about whites before, though without the unsavory reputation that one might expect. And certainly, Alarcón's small group posed no peril.

A little band of noncombative bearers of gifts must have seemed worth encouraging to stay, something several native groups indicated they wanted. And groups sought to reserve exclusively to themselves the benefits the white-skinned water people brought, portraying neighboring groups as warlike, treacherous, and undeserving. For many days they competed to become home to the Alarcón party, even offering the captain positions of honor.

Finally, though, news of other, clearly less peaceful white men in the continent's interior—the main body of the Coronado expedition—and Alarcón's interest in joining them turned the Colorado and Gila River natives' fascination to doubt about the newcomers' ultimate motives. In only a few weeks' time the Indians learned all they cared to know about the seemingly generous river travelers. Their hospitality waned and shifted to tolerance and then barely that. In the end, it may have been only the brevity of the Alarcón party's stay at any given settlement that made for peaceful relations with the Indians. Rarely did the reconnaissance party remain with a native community longer than an afternoon and morning.

A Second Voyage Planned

Almost immediately after Viceroy Mendoza received Alarcón's report, he set plans in motion for a follow-up voyage. Once again the viceroy relied heavily on don Luis de Castilla, who provided one of the ships for the proposed second voyage.²² On the last day of May 1541, only a year after he had begun the first attempt to rendezvous with Vázquez de Coronado, Alarcón received instructions to this effect: "While you are without knowledge of Francisco Vázquez, you shall not devote yourself to anything except searching for him and connecting with him."²³ A concerted and intensive effort was to be made to reach the captain general or his captain Melchior Díaz, who, unknown to the viceroy, had died while attempting to find Alarcón the previous year. If he succeeded in that, Alarcón was to establish a settlement from which regular contact with and resupply of Vázquez de Coronado could be maintained. Furthermore, the viceroy would send merchandise and a merchant with Alarcón, to whom the captain was to give every assistance possible, in order to lay the groundwork for establishing trade with Tierra Nueva.[24]

Before Alarcón could get under way, events scuttled the planned second voyage to the Río de Buena Guía and Río de Cíbola.[25] Within months of the Coronado expedition's departure from Compostela, an *encomendero* to whom Vázquez de Coronado had granted the tribute of Indians at Guaynamota was killed by those Indians.[26] In March of the following year, *encomendero* Miguel de Ibarra attempted to visit the Indians of his *encomiendas* at Suchipila. He found an uprising in progress, with the church and monastery burned and the Indians fortified on several *peñoles*, including one called Mixtón.[27] This marked the beginning of what has become known as the Mixtón War, one of the most serious threats ever to Spanish sovereignty in the viceroyalty of Mexico.

In spring 1541 Cristóbal de Oñate, Vázquez de Coronado's lieutenant governor of Nueva Galicia, where the uprising was centered, dispatched a plea for help to the viceroy in the Ciudad de México. Then Oñate learned that the viceroy's new partner in conquest, Pedro de Alvarado, had his fleet at the port of La Navidad. Oñate sent an urgent request for the *adelantado's* aid. As a result, Alvarado ordered his and Mendoza's men to disembark and deployed them to settlements around Nueva Galicia. Among the men so dispatched in June 1541 were Alarcón and 30 men from his crew, ordered off their ships and assigned to defend Autlán, about 15 leagues inland from the port. The uprising raged throughout the rest of 1541 and into 1542, and Spanish presence in the region hung very much in the balance. By the time Spanish control was reasserted, the decision had been made in Tierra Nueva to abandon the Coronado expedition, and a second voyage by Alarcón thus became unnecessary.

As will be seen later, the Mixtón War was one factor precipitating the return of the Coronado expedition itself. Also contributing importantly to the judgment that continuation of the Coronado *entrada* was impracticable was Alarcón's demonstration of the infeasibility of resupply by sea. The hitherto unrecognized immensity of the continent prohibited the shipment of bulk goods, either inbound supplies or outbound regional products. As an economically marginal region at best, now proven to be without a means of cheap and easy supply, a Spanish Tierra Nueva could not and would not be maintained. ■

CHAPTER 9

INSIDE CÍBOLA

JUST AS INDIANS ON THE COLORADO and Gila Rivers had heard about Europeans before they ever saw them, so, too, had the Ashiwi, the people of Cíbola-Shíwana as they called it, Zuni as it is known today. Cíbola, the name fray Marcos had heard in Sonora, was probably a Pima or Ópata version of Shíwana. Or perhaps it was a rendering of *si:wolo*, the Zuni word for bison, Shíwana's most important commodity as far as the Sonorans were concerned, bison hides standing for the place itself.[1]

The Ashiwi had heard reports of white people and black people, of horses, hogs, chickens, and sheep, of steel and firearms, of mineral lust and slaving, years before Esteban appeared on their borders with his entourage of Sonorans and Sobaipuris. As the late Zuni anthropologist Edmund Ladd put it:

> Traveling traders came to Zuni who spoke strange languages, probably Nahuatl or some other southern language . . . What the long-distance traders were bringing into the Zuni villages was not only material like macaw feathers, bells, seashells, and so forth, but also the news from farther south. That news was not very good because what they were describing was slave raids by Nuño Beltrán de Guzmán and others in the southern Sonora area.[2]

Whether information about Spanish-led activities came to the Ashiwi through long-distance traders or as a cumulative result of shorter "grapevine" exchanges during commercial, social, hunting, or other contacts, it seems inescapable that such information accumulated at Cíbola-Shíwana. Stories and reports certainly began filtering across the hemisphere in 1492, increasing in frequency and detail as Europeans and their associates penetrated deeply and quickly far into both North and South America during the first decades of the sixteenth century. For the Ashiwi, with significant ties to people of the Río Sonora and, through them, to the northwestern fringes of Mesoamerica, it was from that direction that the most voluminous information must have come. The same route had brought word for decades, even centuries, of Mexica, Tarascos, and other Mesoamerican peoples who practiced large-scale ritualized warfare. That the two groups, Old World and Mesoamerican, were sometimes acting in concert by the 1530s and together making thrusts to the northwest must have presented an unsettling prospect to those at Cíbola who heard about it.

The Ashiwi welcomed certain goods from the south and the people who transported them, at least in relatively small numbers and for short periods. Temporary field workers from Sonora were regularly accommodated at Cíbola. For the most part unbeknownst to the Ashiwi, significant elements of their daily lives had originated to the south, in the very heart of Mesoamerica: corn, beans, and the art of agriculture itself, cotton and the manufacture of pottery, and the outline of their rain- and ancestor-centered ideology, featuring elaborately masked and costumed spirit proxies.[3]

Knowledge, rumor, and transfer of cultural practice have never, of course, flowed in only one direction. So it was that upon reaching the native settlements of Sonora, fray Marcos and Esteban had been given detailed descriptions of Cíbola-Shíwana. In all likelihood, people even farther south also possessed scraps of information about the place of terraced houses, the place of bison hides, the place of turquoise in the north. Across territories jealously defended against physical encroachment, information, foodstuffs, raw materials, artisanal products, and their bearers often moved with as little restriction as the weather.

Anticipation of the Expedition's Arrival

Enormous parties of young warriors bent on taking prisoners and booty were altogether another matter. The arrival of Esteban in Cíbola-Shíwana had come as no surprise to the people there. Esteban and his entourage must have been shadowed for days, and runners had carried news back to the Ashiwi war leaders. In more recent times it has been the responsibility of the Priesthood of the Bow at Zuni to keep watch on the trails.⁴ It is likely that this was the case in 1539, too. Thus, suspicion of the feathered black man was strong among the Ashiwi before he ever reached the seven *ciudades*.

As a result, the leaders of Shíwana barred Esteban from entry and "put him in a large building which is outside the *ciudad*."⁵ During the night, a formal council of leaders must have been held in Shíwana. Ladd imagined the outcome of that council, on the basis partly of Zuni oral tradition and partly of traditional Zuni practice: "Remember Guzmán's raids into Sinaloa; killing, slave raids? All of these elements were without doubt computed by the war priest. The only thing that came up was 'slave spy.' So Estevan was killed, unfortunately for Estevan. He was killed not because he was black, not because of his demands, but because of his statement that he was 'leading white men more powerful than himself.'"⁶

An armed party with a reputation for hostility was unwelcome. In the aftermath of Esteban's killing, the Ashiwi sent a message to their contacts at Chichilticale saying that "if Christians came, they were to consider them of no importance and were to kill them, since they were mortal . . . [and] if they did not dare [to kill the Spaniards], they were to send [a messenger] to tell [the people of Cíbola], because they would come to do it right."⁷

When, in summer 1540, the massive, mostly Indian party led by Francisco Vázquez de Coronado reached Chichilticale, the natives of that region did not attempt to kill them. But they did send word north to Cíbola-Shíwana, so the Ashiwi were on the lookout. By the time the vanguard of the expedition got within eight leagues of the first *ciudad* of Cíbola, even they knew their approach was no secret. "It was here [at the Río Bermejo] that the first Indians of that land were seen. They were two, who fled and went to spread the news [of the Spaniards' arrival]," wrote former expeditionary Castañeda de Nájera.⁸ At about the same time "four Indians came out peacefully, saying that they were there because they had been sent to that unsettled place to tell us we were welcome." Those men, in reality reconnoitering the vanguard, understood the critical hunger of the force and said that "on the next day all their people would be coming out along the trail with food."⁹ As expeditionary Pedro de Ledesma later recalled, "the Indians wandered about looking over the army like men who had come to see what people were in the camp and how they were organized."¹⁰ They left and never returned.

Meanwhile, at Hawikku (HAHweekoo), the southwesternmost *ciudad* of Shíwana, "the people of the area had come together there, since it is a *provincia* of seven pueblos, in which there are other pueblos very much larger and stronger than Cíbola."¹¹ Besides concern over the approaching armed force, another motive that would have led the Ashiwi to congregate at that particular time was a ceremonial observance in the active summer series of their annual cycle, *Olo'ikyaikyaka*, which had begun at the solstice, equivalent to about June tenth in the Julian calendar then in use in Europe.¹² With advance warning of the approach of strangers of dangerous repute, surely the ceremonial was speeded up, curtailed, or postponed. Instead, councils must have been held and the steps to be taken by the Ashiwi in response to this intrusion debated.

As a result, all women, young children, and the elderly of both genders were moved to the safety of the Ashiwi's traditional refuge, a pueblo atop Dowa Yalanne (DOHwah YAHlahnay), the steep-walled mesa about a dozen miles northeast of Hawikku.¹³ Hawikku itself was cleared of goods—ritual paraphernalia, jewelry and clothing, tools, prized pigments and pottery—leaving only corn and other stored foodstuffs, which would stop the advance of the vanguard, at least for a while, if it managed to gain entrance.¹⁴ Stones, the traditional, if rudimentary, weapons of the besieged, were stockpiled on roofs. And a trap was set. All the ladders customarily used to scale the blank exterior walls of the pueblo and gain access to the roofs, which were in effect the town's streets, were removed—all but one.

Like Hawikku, the remaining six pueblos—Kechiba:wa, Kwa'ki'na, Kyaki:ma, Mats'a:kya, Halona:wa, and Chalo:wa—were all but depopulated.¹⁵ A congregation of Ashiwi, perhaps numbering several thousand, was now fortified and sequestered on Dowa Yalanne. A force of two hundred or so warriors awaited the strangers' approach at Hawikku. Such concerted and coordinated action suggests practical integration among the Ashiwi of the sixteenth century beyond simple sharing of language and culture. As will be seen later among the Tiguex of the Rio Grande, the concerted action of the several pueblos of Cíbola in July 1540 suggests the existence of some practical political integration of the whole people. Perhaps that defensive unity was made possible by shared religious organization or clan structure that crosscut pueblo boundaries. Whatever the precise nature of that interpueblo mechanism, its existence is difficult to dispute. The Ashiwi acted in concert as the Coronado expedition approached.[16]

The *Provincia* of Cíbola

Even before the prodigious work of Claudius Ptolemy in the second century A.D., European geographical tradition sought to make the world comprehensible as a mosaic of "provinces or regions" and "prefectures." Provinces were thought to be territories inhabited by people who were politically homogeneous and politically distinct from their neighbors. Ptolemy distinguished in Hispania, or Iberia, for instance, three provinces: Baetica, Lusitania, and Tarraconensis.[17] It was second nature for members of the Coronado expedition to see the New World as organized in similar units. They recognized, or thought they recognized, a succession of contiguous *provincias* and *reinos* (provinces and kingdoms), punctuated by unsettled areas (*despoblados*), all the way from Compostela to Quivira.

One of those homogeneous regions of settlement was the *provincia* (sometimes styled a *reino*) of Cíbola, composed of its seven *ciudades* and an undefined surrounding hinterland. As the captain general himself put it: "The seven *ciudades* are seven small towns, all consisting of the [sort of] houses I describe [here]. They are all located within close proximity, within four leagues. All [together] are called the *reino* of Cíbola. Each one has its own name, and no single one is called Cíbola."[18] In accordance with this notion, Vázquez de Coronado expected to meet the "lord" of Cíbola, a European-style head of the presumed polity. He eventually had to admit that "from what I have concluded and understood, none of these towns has one."[19]

Rather, as Castañeda de Nájera later wrote, "there are no lords like [those] throughout Nueva España. [Instead], they are governed by a council of the oldest [individuals]."[20] Edmund Ladd wrote, from the perspective of a Zuni and an anthropologist:

> In general, the whole political system revolved around the religious leaders, who acted as a unit rather than as individuals . . . most Zunis agree that during precontact times, the people were governed by the [Bow Priesthood], acting under the direction of the priestly council . . . Nothing is positively known concerning the origins of the council. However, based in part on traditional knowledge, there was probably a supreme council of [Bow Priests] among the Zunis, instituted by them for their mutual protection when they lived in segregated towns. Their center of activities was probably one of the larger villages, perhaps Hawikuh or Kechipauan.[21]

Underlying the authority of the Bow Priests was an elaborate web of kinship, clans, and religious societies that bound individuals in one pueblo to those in others. This linkage made possible the pan-Cíbola authority of the priests. Such an overarching authority facilitated the eventual consolidation of the Ashiwi into a single town, today known as Zuni, in the 1680s. And in July 1540, it was probably the council that orchestrated the orderly and nearly complete relocation to Dowa Yalanne in the days before the Coronado expedition arrived.

As will be seen later, concerted action by pueblos in other *provincias*, notably Tusayán (Hopi) and Tiguex (Southern Tiwa), suggests that the Spanish concept of *provincia* accurately recorded the existence in the sixteenth century of political institutions with at least limited authority over groups of related pueblos from Tusayán to Cicuique-Pecos. The Pueblo world at the time was not one of 90-odd discrete towns. Rather, larger political units existed and were reflected in the conquerors' nomenclature. *Provincias* and *reinos* were not entirely the projection by foreigners of familiar Old World categories onto an alien world.

As members of the Coronado expedition understood it, between Chichilticale and Cíbola they passed through a wide unsettled area in about 15 days of travel, a distance of some 80 leagues, or about 210 miles.[22] That is not to say that the region was utterly devoid of human presence. But there were no permanently inhabited settlements that fit into the Spanish hierarchical categories of *lugar*, *villa*, *pueblo*, and *ciudad*. Nor were there even isolated *casas* (buildings) similar to Chichilticale. In addition, the *despoblado* was considered to lie beyond the political control of any people who did live in such settlements.

Eight leagues southwest of the first *ciudad* of Cíbola the vanguard struck the Río Bermejo, usually thought to be the modern Little Colorado River.[23] In the opinion of the Europeans, that was where the *provincia* of Cíbola began. "The following day they entered the settled land in good order."[24] Shortly after that they saw the first local natives, probably less than ten miles from Hawikku. From about there onward, vanguard members saw plumes of smoke rising off to the side of their route, which they interpreted, probably rightly, as signals to Hawikku of their approach.[25] In all likelihood the Spaniards and their allies had been observed from cover for days before this by Ashiwi lookouts. Certainly from the Indians' point of view, the outsiders had been within their normal sphere of activity and use long before the expeditionaries themselves recognized the crossing of a boundary.

Information assembled by request of the Zuni Tribe for use in litigation during the 1970s seeking compensation for seizure of land by the United States sheds considerable light on traditional Ashiwi territory. That territory began with the residential core, which was surrounded by a much larger agricultural use area. It was the residential core, located along and adjacent to a 12-mile stretch of the Zuni River, that the Coronado expedition vanguard entered one day beyond the Río Bermejo. Some of the Ashiwi's agricultural fields, though, lay many miles from their pueblos and were farmed from seasonal houses. The agriculture use area made up an extensive territory with an irregular perimeter encompassing irrigable land adjacent to the upper Little Colorado River and several of its tributaries, including the Zuni River.

This territory straddled what is now the boundary between the states of New Mexico and Arizona.²⁶

Beyond this the Ashiwi utilized a far greater domain for other purposes, including collection of sacred, medicinal, and edible plants, hunting, and acquisition of minerals such as clay, pigments, salt, and various stones used for tools and weapons.²⁷ Archaeologist T. J. Ferguson and anthropologist Richard Hart have written, and the modern Zuni people maintain, that "the traditional boundaries of the Zunis were known and understood by members of the tribe (and by members of other, neighboring tribes)." As recently as 160 years ago those boundaries reached as far south as modern Glenwood, New Mexico, west to the San Francisco Peaks in Arizona, east to the Malpais lava flows southwest of Mount Taylor in west-central New Mexico, and north as far as the latitude of the Hopi pueblos.²⁸ By that reckoning, a good part of what the expeditionaries saw as "unsettled" land was in fact part of the Ashiwi homeland.

Naturally, over the centuries preceding the coming of the Coronado expedition, that homeland had not been static. Indeed, the very people known as Ashiwi had not always been identifiable as a discrete group. Both tribal oral traditions and archaeologists agree that Cíbola, as the outsiders saw it in 1540, had existed only since the 1300s, a result of the migration and combining of groups who had most recently lived to the east and southwest of the residential core of Cíbola.²⁹ At roughly the same time, other clusters of settled agricultural communities also arose in the region. About 90 miles to the northwest was Tusayán-Hopi; approximately 60 miles to the east was Acuco-Acoma. Each of these neighboring groups spoke an entirely different language, although they broadly shared cultural, religious, political, and economic patterns of life. They relied on one another for exotic material goods and occasionally took refuge with each other. They influenced each other, copying, adapting, and modifying the others' practices. And from time to time they came into conflict, even prolonged and violent conflict. The boundaries that signaled the transition from one homeland to another shifted across the landscape.

So it was into an indigenous world of vagrant, invisible, and selectively permeable boundaries that the vanguard of the Coronado expedition intruded nearly a month after the summer solstice, in early July 1540 according to the Julian calendar of Europe. The most crucial part of the year for Ashiwi sustenance was under way, not traditionally a season of warfare or raiding. Community attention and effort was instead focused on the nurturance of crops and the indispensable supply of irrigation water. The Ashiwi, however, had no choice but to interrupt that focus, and perhaps their traditional summer solstice ceremonies, and take precautions as an armed force of some 1,000 approached with its own urgent need for food. ■

CHAPTER 10

Refusal to Submit

The Nahua emissaries who had been sent ahead to Cíbola returned to the vanguard with news that "the pueblo and province were at war and were not willing to come to peace."¹ Now aware that the expedition was unlikely to be welcomed at Cíbola, the captain general sent a detachment northeastward, upstream along the Zuni River, to secure a dangerous pass he had heard about from Indians with the vanguard, who had perhaps been with Esteban almost a year earlier.² "That same night the Indians [of Cíbola] came to occupy that pass in order to defend it. When they discovered it was occupied, they attacked our people there," to the eerie sound of conch shell trumpets.³ Vázquez de Coronado later remembered what he had been told about the attack this way: "When a quarter of the second watch was over, Indians struck and shot some horses with arrows. They would have done more harm except that don García [López de Cárdenas, the detachment's leader] was on the alert."⁴ The 20 or 30 Europeans mounted horses and chased off the raiding party of perhaps as many as a hundred men.

With the return of daylight, the captain general brought up the rest of the vanguard. Reunited with López de Cárdenas's detachment, the whole body advanced toward Hawikku. Although they had been forewarned months earlier by Melchior Díaz and Juan de Zaldívar that Cíbola might not be the spectacularly wealthy and populous place reported by fray Marcos, still the first view of Hawikku was a shock. Rather than a dazzling, awe-inspiring city like Tenochtitlan as it had appeared to Cortés's troop 20 years earlier, the first *ciudad* of Cíbola was a "small pueblo crowded together and spilling down a cliff. In Nueva España there are *estancias* [ranch buildings] which from a distance have a better

Fray Marco's guilt

appearance. It is a pueblo with three and four upper stories and with up to two hundred fighting men. The houses are small and not very roomy. They do not have [individual] patios; a single patio serves a neighborhood."⁵ There were no towering pyramids, no spacious causeways, no monumental sculptures, no tens of thousands of inhabitants streaming out to greet the vanguard.

The compact, mud-colored rooms stacked on one another were so different from the expeditionaries' expectations that the men turned furiously on fray Marcos, howling disgust and hurling threats. The friar offered no excuses, no defense. Within days he would flee back to the Ciudad de México with his reputation in shambles, lucky to escape with his life. Remarkably, he seems never even to have protested that he was not entirely to blame for the expeditionaries' dashed hopes. His silence and subsequent unplanned departure from the expedition constituted a tacit confession that he had, in fact, misled everyone connected with the *entrada*. That included the whole range of organizers and participants, from Viceroy Mendoza and Vázquez de Coronado and his wife, Beatriz de Estrada, to the couple Alonso Sánchez and Francisca de Hozes and Martín Caççol, an Indian from México-Tenochtitlan who would soon accompany the disgraced friar on his return to the Ciudad de México.⁶

Even in the midst of a profoundly rude awakening, the specter of starvation drove the captain general and his followers on. More out of habit than desire, they followed the program of conquest dictated by the royal court. At the distance of a crossbow shot from the walls of Hawikku, Vázquez de Coronado "sent don García López, fray Luis, and the scribe Hernando Bermejo with some horsemen to deliver the *requerimiento* that His Majesty had ordered. And they went forward to do so. The [captain general] decided to be there [himself] and, taking some horsemen and trade goods that he carried, he left marching orders for the army and joined don García López and the clerics. [Then] 300 Indians with bows and arrows and round shields approached close to where [Vázquez de Coronado] and the others were. Although they were summoned three times to offer peace and made to understand, through the interpreter who had been sent to speak with them and went to them, they were never willing to come in peace nor to render obedience to His Majesty. Nor did they stop shooting arrows."⁷

The *requerimiento* opened with a brief history of the world from a Spanish Catholic point of view. From God to the pope and on to the monarchs of Spain, it traced the king's right to rule all the peoples living beyond the meridian lying 370 leagues west of the Cape Verde Islands. There followed a formal demand that peoples of the New World submit to the rule of the Spanish king and accept missionaries to teach them the rudiments of the Roman Catholic faith. The text concluded with this ultimatum:

> If, [however,] you do not do [what I ask] or you maliciously delay [doing] it, I assure you that, with the help of God, I will attack you mightily. I will make war [against] you everywhere and in every way I can. And I will subject you to the yoke and obedience of the Church and His Majesty. I will take your wives and children, and I will make them slaves. As such, I will sell and dispose of them as His Majesty will order. I will take your property. I will do all the harm and damage to you that I can, [treating you] as vassals who do not obey and refuse to accept their lord and resist and oppose him.
>
> I declare that the deaths and injuries that occur as a result of this would be your fault and not His Majesty's, nor ours, nor that of these *caballeros* who have come with me.⁸

Hernando Bermejo, the captain general's secretary, dutifully recorded that the summons had been delivered the requisite number of times, and also that the Ashiwi refused to comply. They were not unusual in that respect; there is no known case in which an indigenous group in the Western Hemisphere, without understanding what was being asked of it, acquiesced to the demands of the *requerimiento*. Whether naively conceived to provide natives a legitimate opportunity to consider accepting vassalage to the king or cynically contrived to appease critics of the widespread and gratuitous slaughter of conquest, the *requerimiento* was, as some Spanish critics of the day were quick to point out, a tragic farce.

Defense of Cíbola

The Ashiwi's responses to the *requerimiento*, or the threat that it signified, were several. "The Indians [probably Bow Priests] drew lines in front of [the friar], indicating that the army should not cross them, threw dirt in the air," and "struck fray Luis in his robe with an arrow, which it pleased God did him no harm." Pedro de Ledesma, an expeditionary who was present, testified later that "seeing this, the general attacked them with the whole force, and they lanced up to forty men."[9] Eyewitness accounts reveal distinct phases in the fighting at Hawikku on July 7, 1540 (Julian). It began with what were clearly warning arrow shots from the warriors, aimed close to but not striking the people and animals of the party delivering the *requerimiento*. Spaniards such as Ledesma assumed these were lucky misses, but clearly the arrows were intentionally slightly off target. The expeditionaries' reply was a deadly charge by horsemen wielding lances.

In open terrain such as the unforested floodplain of the Zuni River adjacent to Hawikku, mounted lancers proved to be a fearsome and potent military force throughout most of the Spanish colonial period. The speed and power of the horse, combined with the stout, sharp lance, could be devastating against men on foot in an unobstructed plain. The danger of lancers became obvious to Indians all over the continent with their first experience of mounted men-at-arms. Thereafter, they avoided such unequal encounters. In the world of the Pueblos word spread quickly of the tactics necessary to withstand the Spanish-led force. After this single charge at Hawikku and a similar one a few days later at Tusayán, whenever massed hostilities threatened, Pueblos withdrew to their fortresslike towns or to steep, rugged land and fought from there, or they simply waited their adversaries out.

According to Vázquez de Coronado, he tried to stem the killing at this point, ordering his men to break off the chase. Ladders were let down, and the surviving warriors mounted to the flat rooftops of Hawikku. A brief, tense breathing space followed. What possibilities were held in those minutes we will never know.

With the demonstration of 40 deaths, the captain general offered what to him and his European comrades seemed a generous arrangement. He had the *requerimiento* read yet again: the people of Cíbola would be treated "joyfully and benevolently" if they would "acknowledge the Church as lord and superior of the Universe [and] world, and the Sovereign Pontiff (called the Pope) in its name, and His Majesty in his stead as superior, lord, and king." The flight of arrows that sailed from the roofs of Hawikku in rejoinder was an unequivocal rejection of the offer of peace in exchange for submission. Under the terms of the *requerimiento*, only one option was open to the expeditionaries.

"Because the hunger we were suffering did not permit delay, I dismounted with some of those gentlemen and men-at-arms. And I ordered that the crossbowmen and arquebusiers make an assault and remove [our] enemies from the defensive structures, so that they could not do us injury," wrote Vázquez de Coronado only days afterward.[10] The arquebuses and crossbows were unlimbered and the *versillos*—very small bore cannons that swiveled on a pin inserted into a wooden base—were discharged. Europeans rushed the pueblo. "However, in short order the strings of the crossbowmen's weapons broke, and the arquebusiers accomplished nothing because they were so weak and debilitated that they could hardly stay on their feet."[11]

In any event, arquebuses were heavy, slow to load and fire, and not especially accurate. Crossbows, although powerful and accurate, could not nearly match the speed with which warriors of Cíbola could discharge their arrows and rain stones on the attackers. Unless used in large numbers, which the Coronado expedition did not possess, European weapons of the day were rarely able to overmatch well-fortified and well-prepared American natives such as those of Cíbola.

Someone among the attackers spotted the lone remaining ladder leaning against the pueblo's exterior wall and notified Vázquez de Coronado. Because he was one of the few men who possessed a suit of armor, the captain general may have been a reasonable choice to attempt to mount to the roof by way of the ladder. As he did so, in a seemingly impetuous act of leadership, the defenders sprang an ambush and rained stones down on him, knocking him twice to the ground. The second time, hit in the head, he lost consciousness and might have been killed, had García

López de Cárdenas and Hernando de Alvarado not first shielded him with their own bodies and then carried him away from the fight.[12]

While Vázquez de Coronado lay unconscious in a nearby tent, probably suffering from a relatively mild concussion, the assault resumed.[13] There are no documentary details of the continuing attack and defense. But as Castañeda de Nájera reported, "in less than an hour the pueblo was entered and taken."[14] It is clear from the captain general's own account that it was not European arms—not arquebuses, crossbows, artillery, or horses—that tipped the balance as the sheer walls of the pueblo were assailed. Instead, it was the relative number of fighters on the two sides. Because "most of the Indian allies," perhaps 500 to 800 or more, accompanied the vanguard, the expeditionaries enjoyed a two- or three-to-one numerical advantage over Hawikku's defenders. When the *indios amigos* joined the assault, as they probably did now, that advantage was rendered irresistible by the fact that the bloody ferocity and relish for war of the Tenochca, Tlatelolcas, Tarascos, and other allies of the expeditionary force were matters of common lore even in Cíbola. Such knowledge would have come to Shíwana in bits and pieces over the years with trade and travelers from the Río Sonora and perhaps farther south. In the face of the raging swarm of Europeans and Mexican Indians that was the advance guard in full force, the Ashiwi warriors simply disappeared. They "let themselves down from the other sides" and made their way by numerous routes to the stronghold of Dowa Yalanne.[15]

Empty Possession

The number of Ashiwi left dead is unknown. If the later Spanish claims are approximately accurate, then it was scores at least. Apparently there were wounds but no deaths among the expedition vanguard, including wounds to four captains and an equal number to men from the lower ranks.[16] Casualties among slaves, servants, and Indian allies go unremarked in the surviving documents, so one cannot even guess at the number of casualties among those groups.

When they entered the pueblo, the members of the vanguard found it deserted and stripped of most goods except large quantities of stored food, especially corn. "I think they have turquoise in quantity. By the time I arrived," though, wrote the captain general, "this had disappeared, along with the rest of their possessions, except the corn."[17] Europeans and Mexican Indians alike apparently went on an eating binge. The corn, beans, and other stored food allayed the pangs of hunger for the expeditionaries. But close-up inspection of Hawikku only completed the disillusionment its aspect from a distance had unleashed.

The long-anticipated rich furnishings, clothing, and ornaments, evidence of opulence, were absent. "The walls are made of stone and mud, and some [are] walls of mud alone," wrote a close associate of the captain general's in disgust.[18] The Spaniards renamed the pueblo "Granada" because it was reminiscent of the cramped and impoverished Moorish quarter of that city, called the Albaicín, which was characterized at that time by low adobe buildings.[19] Added to its humble appearance, the first town of Cíbola was small, comprising only "some two hundred houses," according to Vázquez de Coronado.[20] Cíbola was, in fact, no *ciudad* at all, certainly not by Spanish standards of the day. Ultimately, when the total population of the pueblos of Cíbola, Tusayán, Acuco, Tiguex, Tutahaco, Quirix (KeeREESH), Jimena (HeeMENah), Cicuique, Jemez, Aguas Calientes, Yuque Yunque, Chia, and Brava was tallied, Castañeda de Nájera pointed out the harsh reality: "There are *repartimientos* in Nueva España with a greater number of people, and not just one but many."[21] The combination of meager size and lack of valuable commodities meant that supporting 368 Europeans and their households and auxiliaries with tribute from Cíbola, or even from the entirety of Tierra Nueva, was hopelessly impossible. A handful of *encomenderos* might have been maintained in something like the style they felt was their due, but not nearly the whole troop. Not even the debts and expenses of the expedition could be redeemed at Cíbola.

It was these excruciatingly obvious facts that led the captain general to write repeatedly in his first letter to Viceroy Mendoza from Cíbola that "everything the friar had said was found [to be] the opposite."[22] Cíbola was only a jewel made of paste to add to the royal crown. Therefore its reconnaissance and conquest were likely to win only hollow rewards from the king. And the idea of profiting personally from the products of Cíbola would have been laughable if it were not so economically ruinous for most of the expeditionaries. "God knows I would have wished to have better news to write Your Lordship," wrote Vázquez de Coronado, "but I have to tell the truth."²³

The captain general and many other expeditionaries were able, in the space of a few days, to overcome the shock of shattered illusions and carry on. The former enthusiasm for the enterprise was absent, but the sense of duty and honor was strong enough to sustain familiar activities. Vázquez de Coronado told the viceroy that even "if all the wealth and treasure of the world were here, I would not have been able to do more in His Majesty's service and [that of] Your Lordship than I have done in coming to where he has directed me [to come] . . . Nor do I intend to leave here short of death, if it be of service to His Majesty or Your Lordship that it be so."²⁴

Three days after the vanguard occupied Hawikku, a small group of men from the pueblo came to the captain general on the pretext of arranging peaceful relations. Their subsequent actions revealed their true intentions: to scout the Spanish-led force and to retrieve more of their belongings. Vázquez de Coronado harangued them about the benefits of vassalage to the Spanish king, and the ostensible emissaries stayed the night. "But suddenly, on the next day, they packed up their belongings and food and fled to the hills [with] their women and children."²⁵

Eight or ten days after that, the captain general took the initiative, traveling some five leagues to the pueblo of Mats'a:kya (Mahtsahkyah). There he found a few Ashiwi and invited them to bring all the people down from nearby Dowa Yalanne and live peacefully with the expedition, if they wanted to. Days later a third parley was held at Hawikku. "But up to the present," wrote Vázquez de Coronado regretfully on August 3, 1540 (Julian), nearly a month after the occupation of Hawikku, "they are still keeping their wives and children and all the goods they have in their fortified places."²⁶ All seven pueblos of Cíbola had been deserted in favor of the security of Dowa Yalanne. Without the application of deadly force, the Ashiwi could not, as a group, be induced to join their would-be overlords in their pueblos. This situation, with most of the Ashiwi occupying Dowa Yalanne, was to last as long as the expedition was in the region. The two groups, Cíbolans and European-led expeditionaries, remained strictly segregated, with contact limited to occasional visits to the expedition by Bow Priests.

Two Portentous Decisions

A few Ashiwi men, then, singly and in small groups, continued to contact the expedition and even spent extended periods of time with the foreign force at Hawikku. Probably they were keeping tabs on the intruders and studying their weaknesses and vulnerabilities. But they passed themselves off as innocuous old men who brought a few turquoises and tattered pieces of woven fabric to the captain general. They also revealed a little about the Ashiwi, their neighbors, and their surroundings. The captain general asked them to paint him a representation of the local fauna on cloth. Reluctantly, the Ashiwi complied. Vázquez de Coronado judged from the resulting slap-dash image that they were "poor painters."[27] Regardless of their skill or lack of it, the priests evidently provided the bare minimum of information to the expeditionaries, and at least some of it was false or misleading. The captain general suspected as much, writing, "They are not being clear to me . . . I believe they are not telling me the truth, thinking that in any case I would have to leave them soon and turn back from here."[28]

By this means the expeditionaries learned vaguely about other *provincias* called Tusayán, to the northwest, and Tiguex, to the east. Also on the basis of what the Bow Priest spies revealed, supplemented by his own geographical estimates, the captain general was able to conclude that he was "a hundred and fifty leagues away from [the Mar del Sur] and that the one in the north must be much farther away."[29] The implications of the great distance of Cíbola from any possible seaport were profound. Resupply of the expedition by sea would be extremely difficult and time consuming, if not impossible. That would be a great handicap and the source of grave trouble for the expedition the farther it might go on. Pushing farther into the interior of the continent would require reliance primarily on the natives of Tierra Nueva for food and clothing.

Nevertheless, shortly after he wrote his letter to the viceroy, Vázquez de Coronado dispatched Melchior Díaz and Juan Gallego southward with the report to Mendoza and instructions to Tristán de Luna y Arellano at San Gerónimo to bring the bulk of the remainder of the expedition on to Cíbola. Reunited, the full expedition would find out what it could about the peoples and settlements of the rest of Tierra Nueva. These two decisions, to search farther and to call up the remainder of the expedition, were not the captain general's alone but were made in collaboration with a *junta* of leading members of the expedition. In the end, the push of debt awaiting most expeditionaries in the Ciudad de México must have carried great weight in the discussion. Those debts could be extinguished easily only with income from Tierra Nueva, so it behooved the expeditionaries to find whatever of value was there. But the resulting imposition on the Pueblo people doomed any chance there might have been for amicable relations. Also at work in the decision to continue pursuing the expedition's goals essentially unchanged from the original plan was the momentum of the group's resolve. The commitment of time, energy, money, and hope was temporarily difficult to reverse. It would take the better part of two more years to finally wear out that commitment—for most expeditionaries to become reconciled to turning around and going home without the much anticipated prize.

Some expeditionaries doubtless were able to raise their spirits by remembering the tribulations and near failures of other conquistadores such as Hernando Cortés and Francisco Pizarro. Only through all but superhuman perseverance had they and their expeditions finally located and taken control of the teeming and wondrously prosperous *reinos* of the Mexica and the Inca. So the leaders of the Coronado expedition resolved to persevere. In hindsight, it seems easy to see that the decision was a poor one. ■

CHAPTER 11

IN THE WAKE OF DISILLUSIONMENT

NURSING PHYSICAL INJURIES and still smarting from disappointment, the expeditionaries to Tierra Nueva nevertheless held to the formula of conquest and reconnaissance. The captain general "determined, next, to dispatch [parties] throughout the whole environs to obtain information about everything and first to suffer every disaster before abandoning this enterprise."[1] In succession, Pedro de Tovar—with 20 men-at-arms, a friar, and an unknown number of Indian allies and guides—and García López de Cárdenas—with a dozen others—were sent to reconnoiter Tusayán.[2] Like Melchior Díaz, Tovar had been on the northern frontier for nearly a decade before the Coronado expedition and was one of the founders of Culiacán.[3] It is likely that his seasoned skepticism recommended him to Vázquez de Coronado and his advisers as most qualified to put rumors and reports of Tusayán to the test.

Those Ashiwi from whom the captain general could coax information painted a less than alluring picture. Vázquez de Coronado heard from them the name of the place as Tucano and understood that it comprised "seven towns that are far from here and are like these [of Cíbola]."[4] Still, Tovar and his company were dispatched with supplies and a license to reconnoiter for 30 days.

As at Hawikku, the expeditionaries must not have arrived unannounced. The Hopitu, the people of Tusayán (Tucano), "had received word that Cíbola had been overrun by the most ferocious people, who rode animals that ate people."[5] They apparently had been watching the trails. As the Spaniards of Tovar's party told it, though, they were able to sneak up on the first pueblo undetected, "conceal themselves at the base of the cliff below the pueblo," and hear voices from the buildings above.[6] The

Hopi lookouts had done their job stealthily, warning their people to seek the security of their pueblos, which explains why Tovar and his companions saw not a single Hopi along the route from Cíbola, a route routinely walked by native traders and visitors between the two *provincias*, as well as by native farmers tending distant fields.

This first pueblo of Tusayán, perched high on a cliff, was probably Awatovi on Antelope Mesa, now a ruin in northeastern Arizona, which would ordinarily have been the first Hopi pueblo encountered by a party traveling from the Zuni area in the sixteenth century.[7] With the first light of day, Hopi warriors stole down from the mesa and approached the foreigners, blocking their further approach. "There was an opportunity for the interpreters to talk with them and recite the *requerimiento* to them, since they are people of good understanding," wrote Castañeda de Nájera. "After all this, though, they marked out lines, demanding that our people not cross them toward their pueblos, which were some distance away."[8]

Men of Tovar's party, defying the Hopi ban against their entry, stepped unyieldingly across the lines of cornmeal or pollen. One of the Hopis responded by striking a Spanish horse across the nose. The horsemen immediately attacked. Several Hopis were knocked to the ground, but before hostility could escalate, other Hopis rushed from the pueblo, offering gifts and food. A semblance of peace ensued. Tovar and his company accepted what they interpreted as the Hopis' submission, and the Hopis on their part complied minimally with Tovar's requests for information and assistance. The succeeding 300 years were to show that the Hopi people as a whole never welcomed the European presence and held its individual representatives at arm's length.

Faced with this first European intrusion, in August 1540, the Hopis diverted Tovar's attention away from themselves and refocused it on other, distant peoples said to be living on a great river to the west. This was a ploy used repeatedly and successfully by American natives contacted by the Coronado expedition—to laud the wealth and size of distant Indian communities. As enticing as the Hopis' stories were, with the period of his commission running out, Tovar retraced his route to Cíbola, where he passed on the report of large-bodied riverine people west of Tusayán.

Without delay, the captain general dispatched a second reconnaissance to the west from Cíbola, this one under the command of García López de Cárdenas, the expedition's *maestre de campo*. At the same time, he sent Melchior Díaz south to San Gerónimo with the disgraced fray Marcos and messages for the viceroy, carried by Juan Gallego. Díaz, shortly after his arrival at San Gerónimo, set out for the Mar del Sur in search of Alarcón, the journey that would lead to his death.

López de Cárdenas and his company reached Tusayán probably late in August or early in September. There was no reported conflict, but both he and the Hopitu were eager for him to move on. The Hopis supplied guides for the trek westward. They led the modest contingent of expeditionaries through unsettled country to the brink of what today is called the Grand Canyon in north-central Arizona. From the rim they could see the great turbulent river, the Colorado, that had cut the canyon and would, they were told, lead to other native settlements. Attempts to descend the cliffs to the water below were frustrated by the ruggedness, steepness, and depth of the canyon. López and his companions briefly tried to continue westward by first detouring south from the canyon, but lack of water forced them to give up and return to Cíbola. As Castañeda de Nájera summarized the two westward reconnaissance trips: "The pueblos of that *provincia* remained at peace even though they were never visited again. Nor did [the members of the expedition] learn about or try to find other settlements along that route."[9] Their lack of interest in Tusayán confirms yet again that the expeditionaries sought neither empty land nor small, impoverished settlements.

Tusayán was not the only potential prize that seemed to the expeditionaries worth tracking down. Even if he was mistaken about Cíbola and Tusayán, perhaps Marcos was right about places such as Marata, Totonteac, and Acus, places he had reported as *reinos*, entire kingdoms, huge and prosperous. Vázquez de Coronado quizzed the Ashiwi Bow Priest scouts about them. The anonymous writer of the document known as the Relación del Suceso described the process this way: "When an interpreter had been obtained from the natives of Cíbola, they told about what [is] farther on."[10] The captain general reported to the viceroy the disappointing results of the conversations, conducted by means of signs or through the interpreter, commenting first on

> the *reino* of Totonteac, extolled so highly by the father provincial [Marcos], who said that there were such marvelous things and such grandness there. And, [further,] that [the natives] there made *paño*. The Indians say, [instead,] that it is a hot lake, around which there are five or six dwellings. [They] also [say] that there used to be some others, but they have been destroyed during the wars. There is no *reino* of Marata here nor do the Indians have any information about it. The *reino* of Acus is only one small *ciudad* called Acuco, where cotton is harvested.[11]

One by one the conquistadores' aspirations were smothered by the unvarnished reality of modest pueblos whose villagers successfully farmed small areas where the soil was favorable and water relatively abundant in an otherwise austere land. At Acuco—Acoma Pueblo as it is known today—for instance, "they have an abundance of food: corn, beans, and [turkeys like] those of Nueva España."[12] To European eyes and ears, though, Acoma offered little beyond subsistence, nothing easily convertible into European-style wealth.

In their frustration, the expeditionaries suspected lies everywhere. Vázquez de Coronado wrote to the king that the Indians of Cíbola "refuse to tell me the truth about everything, imagining, as I have said, that soon I will have to depart from here."[13] The captain general vacillated between the conviction that the Ashiwi were inflating the truth, exaggerating their stories of wonders farther on, and the belief that they were disguising the actual prosperity of their own land and hiding away its wealth.

A Collapse of Time

Vázquez de Coronado and the other expeditionaries had no way of knowing that at Cíbola they sat on the fringe of what, in the eleventh and twelfth centuries, had been, in modern parlance, the "Chaco interaction sphere," or the "Chaco phenomenon." This "phenomenon" represented a florescence of ancestral Pueblo culture in the greater San Juan River basin, primarily in what is today northwestern New Mexico but spilling over into northeastern Arizona, southwestern Colorado, and southeastern Utah. The Chacoan system was "characterized by construction of large planned towns, the presence of contemporaneous unplanned villages, roads, water-control features, [and] luxury items such as turquoise, copper bells, macaw remains...."[14] Today, as in 1540, only a few hundred yards west of Hawikku, the expeditionaries' "first pueblo of Cíbola," lie the ruins of an even older, Chaco-style building, perhaps the one where Esteban was housed during his brief and fatal acquaintance with the Ashiwi.[15] Other Chacoan ruins are scattered over the modern Zuni Reservation, among them the spectacular Village of the Great Kivas northeast of modern Zuni Pueblo.[16] Elsewhere in the region there were, from the late 900s to the early 1100s, at least 125 contemporaneous or nearly contemporaneous "great pueblos" in the Chacoan tradition. The ruins of those massive buildings still testify to an exquisite architectural sensibility and highly skilled planning and engineering. In their heyday the buildings compared favorably with the constructions of other "high" cultures of pre-Columbian America, the Maya, Mixtec, Olmec, Mexica, Toltec, Tarascan, Inca, and others. Other components of Chacoan culture were equally impressive, including stunning, fine-line ceramic decoration and a web of long, wide, straight-line roads crisscrossing the region.

The impression given by the surviving remnants of the Chaco phenomenon is one of a large, thriving population that readily and routinely expressed itself in a highly developed aesthetic and was dedicated, at least in part, to production of and commerce in luxury goods. By the 1500s that grandeur was principally a thing of memory, although the Ashiwi were descendants and heirs of the Chacoan culture and still were major suppliers of turquoise and bison robes and consumers of exotic shells and feathers. Cíbola was in part a linear descendant, but a lesser shadow, of the Chacoan past.

Cíbola's sixteenth-century reputation in Sonora and elsewhere owed at least as much to that pedigree as to its current achievements. The stories that fray Marcos heard in Sonora and Arizona and dutifully relayed to the viceroy were conditioned by Cíbola's fabled past. They told not so much about what Cíbola was in 1539 but about what it had been centuries before, at the crest of the Chacoan wave. At least that is my sense; it seems a coherent and reasonable possibility, though one impossible to prove.

Similarly, it appears likely that the grapevine talk Marcos heard about Marata and Totonteac referred not to places and peoples literally contemporaneous with the friar. Rather, the "news" was tradition and history of the most stupendous human accomplishments in the region, long collapsed to ruins by Marcos's time but still very much alive and exciting in the tellers' oral repertoires.

Marata was described to Marcos and then by him to the king and viceroy as lying "to the southeast" of the southern San Pedro River valley in modern Arizona.[17] It once had had "many very grand settlements." More recently it had "shrunk to a great extent."[18] The ethnohistorian Carroll Riley has suggested, judging from its description and direction, that Marata was perhaps an "offshoot" of Casas Grandes (Paquimé), now a well-known archaeological site in the Mexican state of Chihuahua, some 150 miles southeast of the San Pedro River where it crosses into the United States.[19] There seems no reason to suppose, however, that the polity reported by Marcos was not Paquimé itself, rather than a satellite.

The career of that once-great community and its regional influence had ended 100 to 150 years before Marcos's trip and the resulting Coronado expedition. But from about A.D. 1200 to 1400 Paquimé had been the largest and most prosperous settlement of the region, linked by roads to dozens of other communities over many thousands of square miles, communities that shared elements of Paquimé culture. Its massive adobe architecture, striking polychrome ceramics, elaborate shell jewelry, ritual ball game, and religious system were common throughout that wide territory. Its name and reputation would have been familiar all over what is now northwestern Mexico and into at least the southern parts of modern New Mexico and Arizona.[20] By 1540, though, the place seems to have been unknown at Cíbola, at least by the name Marcos had been told.

The place known to fray Marcos as Totonteac was likely the settlements of the cultural florescence known today as Hohokam, the remains of which are concentrated along the Salt and Gila Rivers in south-central Arizona, roughly 150 miles northwest of the lower San Pedro River. According to the friar, Totonteac lay "to the west" of the San Pedro.[21] "Totonteac," he wrote, "is much grander and better than all the seven *ciudades*. And [they said] that [Totonteac] comprises so many buildings and people that it has no end."[22] The only known prehistoric settlement area west of the San Pedro River that approached the magnitude and magnificence of that description was that of the Hohokam. The evidence of platform mounds, ball courts, shell jewelry manufacture, and a rich ritual life at large centers of Hohokam population such as Snaketown (south of modern Phoenix, Arizona) make those numerous settlements the most likely—virtually the only—match for Totonteac.[23] The cultural organism known as Hohokam faded about 150 to 200 years before the time of the Coronado expedition. Yet its fame lived on among its neighbors' descendants, so that it was still considered a marvel in the 1530s and 1540s.

We should not be surprised at such longevity of reputation. It happens in our own time. Much of the splendor that draws today's visitors to Rome, for instance, is not that of the modern city but of one defunct for almost two millennia. Members of the Coronado expedition, unlike tourists seeing Rome, had not the slightest inkling that the polities they were seeking—Cíbola, Marata, Totonteac, and later Quivira—no longer existed as living societies and had not for centuries. To have had any chance of gaining such an insight they would have needed means of communicating with American natives that were capable of subtler discrimination than a chain of variously skilled and attuned interpreters allowed. And even then, a general lack of alertness to genuine cultural variation left the notion that people might see past and present in profoundly different ways inaccessible to early modern Europeans such as Vázquez de Coronado, fray Juan de Padilla, and Pedro de Tovar. Instead, they were simply dumbfounded at the consistent disjunction between what Indians told them and what they themselves saw. The expeditionaries grew increasingly frustrated and angry.

That Indian informants from Sonora to Quivira routinely employed tactics of deception, purposely confounding here and now with past and gone, remains a possibility. That explanation would have made sense to most members of the expedition, and on several occasions expeditionaries openly accused their indigenous informants of lying. I suggest, however, that the lack of congruence between native reports and on-the-ground observation by members of the expedition stemmed more from a widespread indigenous sense of time and tradition of oral history that recognized a sweeping simultaneity of all events, whether ascertainable or not by the unaided senses at any given moment. Within such a conception of time, Marata, Totonteac, and Cíbola were as vivid and present as was the captain general trying to understand the stories about them recited by a native authority, either under pressure or of his or her own volition.

The anthropologist M. Jane Young, in attempting to comprehend the relevance of ancient rock art to modern Zunis, formulated this pertinent, concise statement of a typically Zuni notion of time:

> Although [the Zunis] may introduce a myth as having occurred "a long time ago" or "in the beginning," they do not envision the events of the myth as over and done with, situated at a single point in a linear flow of time; instead they perceive them as ever-present, informing the here and now. It is this perspective that accounts for the "presentness" of the beings of myth and folktale in Zuni life... One may say that time for [the Zunis] is reversible; past, present, and future are coexistent.[24]

I suggest that just such a fluidity between "now" and "then" was frequently embedded in reports fray Marcos and the Coronado expeditionaries received from native informants all across Tierra Nueva.

Inhabiting different conceptual worlds when it came to past and present and past-in-the-present, European expeditionaries and American natives were predisposed to misunderstanding. This pitfall plagued communication between the two groups throughout the course of the Coronado *entrada*. Europeans persisted in asking to be told about and shown the most prosperous and populous places in the region. As chance had it, such places had existed not so very long before 1540 in the American Southwest and northwestern Mexico, places that even the Europeans would have judged large and wealthy. Indigenous informants told the expeditionaries about those spectacular places, indicating their continuing existence, and when the expeditionaries investigated further they inevitably felt deceived.

In August 1540, just as the expeditionaries became convinced that Marata, Totonteac, and Acus were figments of imagination or deceit, of no interest to them, a visitor arrived offering a new prospect. And a process that would eventually lead to a dead end of misunderstanding began again.

CHAPTER 12

OVERTURE FROM CICUIQUE

AT ABOUT THE TIME GARCÍA LÓPEZ DE CÁRDENAS and his company departed from Cíbola for Tusayán, an Indian embassy arrived from the east.[1] As expeditionary Pedro de Ledesma reported it, "as many as twenty Indians came to render obedience and to offer themselves as allies. Among them came a *principal*, said to be from a pueblo called Cicuique, to whom [the Spaniards] gave the name Bigotes, and another one they called the *cacique*." The memories of other members of the expedition differed about the number of men in the embassy but agreed on other particulars.[2] Bigotes, so called because of an obvious mustache he sported, and his fellow diplomats had set out on the 70-league walk from Cicuique (now known as Pecos Pueblo) shortly after hearing news of the capture of Cíbola. The people of Cicuique would, as a matter of course, have heard about the killing of Esteban at Hawikku the previous year, and they probably expressed a variety of opinions about whether the Ashiwi had acted properly.

Now, in 1540, at Cicuique, which held itself to be the strongest and was the largest pueblo of the region, councils of elders and religious and political leaders had doubtless been convened to consider the shocking report from Cíbola. The key question was how to react to what might have seemed to them retaliation for the killing of Esteban. The leaders at Cicuique would have put forward many options and posed many queries. In the end, some combination of all their concerns animated the party led by Bigotes. It traveled ostensibly as an ordinary group of traders, entrusted, as always, with the care of relations with the people with whom they would have commerce. In general, the emissaries' demeanor was to be nonbelligerent. They would act unconcerned, certainly unpanicked, by the aggression against Cíbola. They would, though, be all ears and eyes. They would listen to the Pueblo neighbors they met along the way—at Tiguex, at Acoma—and to the Ashiwi themselves at Dowa Yalanne. They would view for themselves the occupiers of Hawikku and talk with them if they could.

They would want to ascertain whether their understanding of the recent events in Cíbola conformed to what they saw and heard now, in person. Did the foreigners have designs on or animosity toward other pueblos? Did the Ashiwi have countermeasures in the works? Should Cicuique consider the newcomers its enemies? What sort of people *were* the attackers from the south? Where exactly did they come from? What did they want? How powerful were they really? Had their assault on Hawikku been worse than the one Cicuique had withstood from Plains bison hunters called Teyas a generation before? Did they plan to stay? Most of these questions would remain unspoken, their answers to be inferred from demeanor and aspect: swaggers or limps; glimmers of greed and lust or the glaze of boredom; refurbishing of war gear or longing for home to the south; impatience or torpor. The foreigners would betray their intentions and their desire and capacity to carry them out.

The embassy from Cicuique used the main trail, by way of Acoma and Mats'a:kya, detouring to Dowa Yalanne to consult with the lion's share of the Cíbolans in their stronghold. As they moved on from Dowa Yalanne, their approach was made known to the new occupiers of Hawikku before they came into sight at a steady, casual pace. Through an interpreter, the visitors conversed with sentinels at the entrance to Hawikku. With no undue delay, the tall, young Bigotes and his laden companions were shown into the presence of Vázquez de Coronado and his close advisers, the captain general probably sitting in a chair on a low dais under an awning in one of the plazas of the pueblo.[3] Bigotes offered gifts, not of the highest quality, to the seated leader: bison hides, leather shields, and leather skullcaps, all, it should be noted, items and raw materials of war. Vázquez de Coronado reciprocated with domestic goods: glass drinking vessels, multicolored glass beads, and brass hawksbells.[4] The symbolism of the unbalanced exchange relaxed the parties marginally.

Still through a series of interpreters, forming a chain of languages (perhaps from Towa to Zunian to Pima or Ópata to Castellano), Bigotes was understood to say that "they had learned that foreign people had come to their land, brave men who hurt those who defended themselves and gave benevolent treatment to those who submitted."⁵ Speaking in reverse order through the interpreters, the captain general gave notice of the asserted rights of the king of Spain and the good intentions of the Catholic Church. Bigotes was asked to render obedience to king and pope. Instead, he replied that "they were coming to be allies of [the Spaniards] and to offer peace."⁶ In the several surviving contemporaneous accounts of this interview at Hawikku, suggestions that Bigotes and his party made a formal submission remain just suggestions. Rodrigo Simón, a rank-and-file member of the expedition, recalled two years after the end of the enterprise that "messengers from the province of Cicuique came in peace to offer obedience to His Majesty and to request support against some pueblos with which they had differences and were at war."⁷ The documentary evidence, coming wholly from the European side, strongly suggests that the arrangement Bigotes had in mind was one not of subordination but of alliance. As Vázquez de Coronado himself put it, "they came in order to know [the Europeans] and to have them as friends."⁸

Relations between the expeditionaries and the representatives from Cicuique were amicable enough during the two or more days they were together. It is unlikely, though, that either party could have spelled out to the other the precise nature of the relationship they inaugurated as a result of that interaction at Cíbola. Both groups, for their various reasons, were evidently satisfied, at least for the time being. Bigotes told about his home pueblo, as well as those that lay between there and Cíbola. He appears to have offered to lead the expedition on a tour of the Pueblo world. And he mentioned that beyond it lay vast plains where bison flourished. One member of Bigotes's party even bore an image of a bison tattooed on his body, by which the expeditionaries deduced that the animal being talked about was a humpbacked cow, perhaps like the ones the Venetian traveler Nicolo di Conti had seen in Asia a hundred years earlier and that Cabeza de Vaca had been told about during his and his companions' travel.⁹

"Within two or three days," testified Vázquez de Coronado later, he told the Indians from Cicuique that "he wanted to send Captain Hernando de Alvarado with horsemen, in order to make his arrival and the reason His Majesty had sent him known to [their] provinces and the neighboring pueblos. Also, he wanted Alvarado to reconnoiter what was farther on."[10] Alvarado and his company of 23 men-at-arms, with a license to travel for 80 days, set off on the back track with the emissaries from Cicuique on August 29, 1540 (Julian). Also in Alvarado's party was an unknown number of Mexican Indian allies, as well as fray Juan de Padilla, just back from Tusayán with Tovar.

The first of the pueblos they encountered was Acuco-Acoma on its sheer-walled mesa, "one of the strongest things that have been seen."[11] Akumeca, people from that pueblo, descended to the valley floor of their own accord, bringing gift goods that they exchanged with the Europeans. As became routine during this escorted tour of the pueblos, Bigotes or one of his companions had arrived in advance of the Alvarado party, assuring that its reception was hospitable and its stay brief. It was evidently Bigotes who set both the pace and the itinerary of the scouting party's circuit. At least some of the Europeans climbed the vertiginous hand- and toe-holds to the pueblo. But according to Alvarado, "its ascent is so difficult that we regretted having climbed up to that place."[12] Neither gifts nor the stone pueblo itself seemed to warrant the effort. And besides, Bigotes was moving on.

Four more days of travel brought the party to today's Rio Grande, which they christened the Río de Nuestra Señora and later called the Río de Tiguex.[13] The unidentified expeditionary who wrote the Relación del Suceso reported, "We found a well-settled river which flows north and south. It probably has seventy pueblos in all, more or less, [counting both] small and large [ones]. Their design [is] like those of Cíbola, except that they are nearly all made of well-built mud walls."[14] As usual, Bigotes or another of the emissaries from Cicuique traveled ahead to the first of the pueblos of Tiguex.

Situated along the wide but relatively shallow Rio Grande in what is now the area encompassing Albuquerque and Bernalillo, New Mexico, the Tiguex pueblos were, as Castañeda de Nájera put it, "at the heart of the pueblos."[15] Perhaps the first Pueblo people to reside in the Rio Grande Valley, the Tiguex had been there more than 500 years and were the envy of some of the later arrivals because of their bountiful and well-watered land, with its generally mild, if erratic, climate and a sheltering rampart of mountains to the east that also offered easy access to wild plants and animals. In the best years, Tiguex farmers were able to grow enough corn and other staples, including beans and squash, to supply the community for seven years.[16] They also cultivated cotton and wore cotton clothing.

The day after the reconnaissance party reached the Rio Grande, according to Alvarado, "the *principales* and people came from twelve pueblos. [They came] in order, those from one [pueblo] behind the other. They walked around our tent playing a flute, and an old man [was] speaking. In this [same] way they came into the tent and presented me with food, *mantas*, and hides they were carrying."[17] These were representatives of all the Tiguex pueblos, summoned by Bigotes. We may never know whether, as he led Alvarado through the pueblos, Bigotes simply offered his Pueblo neighbors prudent advice on how to avoid the intruders' displeasure or, by parading his newly made allies, ambitiously pressured them to follow his lead. Whatever the message Bigotes delivered, nearly the whole *provincia* responded in unison with demonstrations of peaceful intent.

In this manner, as a representative from Cicuique paving the way each time, Bigotes guided the Alvarado party "through the pueblos and provinces and he went ahead, making sure that the Indians of those pueblos came out in peace with clothing and provisions and welcomed [the Spaniards] very well. In particular . . . Bigotes assured that the people of Brava [Taos Pueblo] came out in peace."[18] Rodrigo de Frías, although he had not been a member of Alvarado's company, later testified on the basis of conversation with Alvarado that "all the [people of the] Río de Tiguex, Cicuique, and Brava had come out to him in peace, with the exception of two pueblos where they came forth in war and which he had pacified."[19] Details of the force applied by the Alvarado party have not come to light, but once again we can assume that the Mexican Indian allies were instrumental in suppressing Pueblo resistance. The Tiguex and other Pueblo peoples of the Rio Grande were not enthralled with the idea of having armed strangers thrust upon them. The Pueblos acquiesced to their presence, however, in most cases at the strong urging of Bigotes.

To the intruders, the great river valley offered a favorable appearance after the bare-rock mesas and shrubby vegetation of Cíbola and Acuco. Not only was the valley physically more temperate, but it was also home to many more people than was the territory to either its west or east. It was the great population center of the region in the sixteenth century. Dozens of pueblos dotted the riverbanks, flanked by great swaths of river bottom, lush at this season with stands of corn, cotton, and other crops. The valley was at its best. Alvarado dispatched a letter to the captain general, advising him that Tiguex would be a much more salubrious and comfortable place to spend the approaching winter than would the seven *ciudades*. "The general relaxed more than a little with news that the land was improving."[20]

Despite the rosier outlook, Alvarado's tour of the Rio Grande pueblos revealed that their population, although larger than that of Cíbola, was still much smaller than that which the Europeans had become used to in the Basin of Mexico and the highlands of Peru. Castañeda de Nájera estimated the total population among all the pueblos, including those outside the Rio Grande Valley—Cíbola, Acoma, Jemez, Zia, and Cicuique—at "about twenty thousand men," perhaps a total population of 60,000 to 100,000.[21] This compared with an estimated minimum of 5 million people in central Mexico at the time of conquest in 1520–21 and 4 million in what is today Peru.[22] The disparity between those areas and Tierra Nueva was so great and so obvious that it provoked Castañeda de Nájera's remark about there being many "*repartimientos* in Nueva España with a greater number of people."[23]

Alvarado's tour of the pueblos ended at Cicuique, Bigotes's home pueblo in the pine-forested upper Pecos River valley. The reconnaissance party probably received its heartiest welcome at Cicuique. The captain and his companions had seen what Bigotes wanted them to see and met whom he wanted them to meet. Conversely, they did not see what Bigotes hid or neglected to show them. This helps explain why the expedition never, during its two years in Tierra Nueva, visited such places as the Tompiro pueblos in the Tularosa Basin of New Mexico and was unaware of the turquoise mines near modern Cerrillos, which the Pueblo people had exploited for centuries. It does not necessarily make Bigotes a devious or calculating guide. It does demonstrate, at a minimum, the degree to which this expedition, like others throughout the hemisphere, was dependent on its guides and often at their mercy, a fact that must have been apparent to the guides themselves.

The party of emissaries and their newfound allies rested at Cicuique for several days. The impressive stone-walled hollow rectangle of hundreds of residential apartments must have swarmed with activity, for the harvest season was beginning. Food seemed limitless, and the party of Europeans and Mexican Indians was doubtless feasted more than once. Alvarado had discussions with Bigotes about joining him in an assault on another nearby pueblo. Then, "when Hernando de Alvarado wanted to continue on his course in the direction the general had ordered, the Indian called Bigotes asked him for permission to stay behind in his house because he was worn out and had been guiding [the Spaniards] for forty or fifty days."[24]

Although he might indeed have been drained by his unrelenting role as diplomat, that was Bigotes's office by both affinity and selection. It was his concern to regulate the political balance in the Pueblo world to the advantage of Cicuique. The pueblo's burgeoning population, relatively speaking (about 2,000, as inferred from Castañeda de Nájera's guess),[25] argued for expansion from the Pecos River valley into the Rio Grande. The people of Cicuique had their eyes set on one of the Tiguex pueblos. Bigotes had, with Alvarado's unwitting help, been working to further that goal. The bison plains and the nomads who inhabited them were of little moment in insinuating Cicuique into Tiguex. Thus, to lead Alvarado there would be a wasteful diversion, if consolidation of the position of Cicuique as dominant among the pueblos was the point. So Bigotes protested his exhaustion and offered in his stead "two guides, to whom [the Spaniards] gave the names Turco and Ysopete" (EesohPEHtay).[26] Both were natives of the Great Plains, El Turco from Haraee and Ysopete from Quivira.

Alvarado accepted the offer, and with new guides the reconnaissance party began ~~its tour of the~~ bison plains. The author of the Relación del Suceso, who was one of the Europeans with Alvarado, wrote that "at the beginning of [the plains] he found a small river which flows to the southeast. After four days' journey he found the [bison], which are the most extraordinary kind of animal that has been seen or read [about]. He followed this river a hundred leagues, each day finding more [bison]. We availed ourselves of them [for meat], although at first [it was] at the horses' peril, until we had experience. There is such a quantity [of bison] that I do not know what I might compare [them] to, except the fish in the sea. [I say this] because . . . there were so many [bison] that many times we were traveling right through the middle of them."[27]

The river the Alvarado party followed was probably the modern Canadian, flowing across east-central New Mexico and into the Texas Panhandle, although there is a slight chance that it was the Pecos. The group's attention was focused at first almost wholly on the bison. That remained the typical reaction of European and Anglo-American travelers for the next 300 years when they first encountered the immense bison herds of the Great Plains. Initially, the Spaniards spent a great deal of time chasing and killing some of the seemingly infinite number of great, shaggy, hump-backed beasts, which they called "wild cattle." It took days for the fascination to fade. During that time the Alvarado party, and later the entire expedition, became familiar with the bison's appearance and behavior—so much so that even 20 years afterward Castañeda de Nájera could pen this vivid account:

> There was not a horse that looked [the bison] in the face that did not flee from their gaze. [That is] because they have a wide and short face. From eye to eye [it is] two *palmos* across the forehead. The eyes [are] protuberant from the side [of the head], so that when they are running in flight they [can] see whoever is chasing them. They have very large beards, as billy goats [have]. When they run away they carry the head low, the beard dragging across the ground. From the middle of the body to the rear, they are

narrow-waisted [with] very fine, dense, and short hair, like ewes. From the waist forward the hair [is] very long in the manner of a raging lion. [It has] a great hump, larger than [that] of a camel. The horns [are] short and stout; they are exposed [only] a little above the hair. About May they shed their hair from the middle of the body to the rear in a fleece, which turns them into veritable lions. In order to get rid of their hair, they rub against the few small trees there are in some small ravines. There they scrape themselves until they cast off the fleece, as a snake [does] its skin. They have [a] short tail and a small brush at the end. They carry it high when they run, in the way a scorpion [does]. It is something to see that when they are young calves, they are bright red and like our cattle. With time and age they change in color and [other] features."[28]

In the midst of Alvarado's slow, distracted progress through the bison, his principal guide, the plains native he knew as El Turco, revealed electrifying news. As the artilleryman Juan Troyano later told it: "One day while they were making their reconnaissance, the Indian called Turco said, by means of signs and in the Nahuatl language (which he knew slightly), that he was not familiar with the land towards the direction [they were then going], but that he would lead in another direction, towards which he pointed. He would lead them there because in that direction there were very large settlements and also gold, silver, and painted pictures."[29] This was the first news anyone on the expedition had had of another *provincia*, far out on the plains, known as Quivira.

By means of signs and through Nahua interpreters—some of the Mexican Indian allies—Alvarado asked for more particulars. El Turco animatedly expanded his description to a spellbound audience, making it known that "in his land there was a river in a plain which was two leagues wide. There were fish as large as horses there. And [there were] a great many exceedingly large canoes with more than twenty rowers on each side, which also carried sails. The lords traveled on the poop, seated beneath awnings. On the prow [there was] a large eagle of gold. He said further that the lord of that land slept during siesta under a great tree, on which a great number of small golden bells hung. In the breeze they gave him pleasure. Further, he said that generally everyone's common serving dishes were worked silver."³⁰ This sounded exactly like the sort of place most expeditionaries dreamed of: a large population center where people practiced the arts and occupations known to European civilization, including metal working. It was a thrilling possibility revealed by a native of that very region, who indicated further that back at Cicuique there was tangible proof of what he said.

"Among the things that he said was that in the pueblo of Cicuique there were a bracelet and other items of gold that he had brought from Quivira. The Indian called Bigotes had ordered them hidden."³¹ The guide added that the Spaniards "should not tell Bigotes what he had said because they would kill him."³² In a moment, interest in bison was eclipsed. Because the term of Alvarado's commission would not allow him to go all the way to Quivira, he decided to cut the reconnaissance short and return without delay to Cicuique. There he would examine the jewelry El Turco had described and would send a message to the captain general about this remarkable development. "Such and so many were the things that [El Turco] said about riches of gold and silver that there were in his land that [Alvarado's company] did not diligently pursue the search for [bison] beyond seeing a few. Then they returned in order to give the general the magnificent news."³³

The small reconnaissance party rushed westward, making a halt at Cicuique to talk with Bigotes and see the golden jewelry. The surviving contemporaneous documents provide inconsistent and conflicting information about the sequence of events there. The artilleryman Juan Troyano was one of the members of the Alvarado party and thus may provide more accurate evidence than Castañeda de Nájera, Vázquez de Coronado, and others who had only secondhand knowledge. According to Troyano, Alvarado did not immediately confront Bigotes about Quivira and the jewelry, although he may have insinuated and asked leading questions.

Instead, he complied with Bigotes's request that his men join a force of warriors from Cicuique that was headed for a place known as Nanapagua,³⁴ "with which they were at war." For that purpose the people of Cicuique "assembled three hundred men ... among whom went the *cacique*, Bigotes, and El Turco." Two days out from Cicuique, El Turco disappeared. Alvarado demanded that Bigotes and the *cacique* produce the erstwhile guide. When El Turco still did not appear, Alvarado seized the two native leaders and restrained them in chains and collars, whereupon El Turco materialized. This second heavy-handed act on Alvarado's part—the first being his coercion of submission by two of the Rio Grande pueblos already related—set the stage for much of what was to come.

Eager to get to the bottom of the story about Quivira, Alvarado and fray Juan de Padilla immediately grilled Bigotes, the *cacique*, El Turco, and Ysopete. Presented with El Turco's assertions about the armbands or bracelets from Quivira, both Bigotes and the *cacique* responded by insisting that the plains native was lying, while El Turco held firm, supported by Ysopete. At Alvarado's insistence, the raid on Nanapagua was abandoned. He had El Turco and Ysopete put in chains, too, and removed all four captives to Tiguex, hoping for a resolution there.[35]

Information from contemporaneous documentary sources is contradictory about further questioning of the prisoners conducted at Tiguex. Juan Troyano, still claiming to have been an eyewitness, testified in 1544 that when Alvarado reached Tiguex, he found the captain general there. When "Francisco Vázquez," Troyano stated, "saw that some Indians said one thing and the others another, he ordered [the expeditionaries] to set dogs on Bigotes in order that he might testify to the truth of what El Turco and Ysopete were saying."[36] The captain general, on the other hand, denied not only that he had ordered dogs to be set on the two *principales* but also that he had any knowledge at the time that such an extreme interrogation method had been used. He swore that "[long] afterwards, when they had come to this province [Nueva Galicia], he learned that because [Bigotes] denied what [Alvarado and] don Pedro de Tovar asked him and because he was not willing to confess, don Pedro told him to tell the truth or else 'that dog that was wandering loose would bite him.' Seeing that he chose not to confess, don Pedro called the dog and it bit [Bigotes]."[37]

Like most other witnesses deposed during the 1544 investigation, Vázquez de Coronado's head groom, Juan de Contreras, contradicted the captain general's version of events, agreeing in most particulars with Juan Troyano. Contreras also swore that "Hernando de Alvarado, with Francisco Vázquez present and by his order, set dogs on them three times. This witness saw that they were bitten and injured severely, as he was present when this occurred."[38] Expeditionary Rodrigo de Frías testified that after the dog attack, "Bigotes was not well and had an arm and a leg crippled."[39] Whoever gave the order, the setting on of dogs was both a personal injury and a further source of Pueblo grievance against the Coronado expedition.

When, even after the dog attacks, Bigotes and the *cacique* maintained that El Turco was lying, they were held prisoner in the Spanish camp. According to expeditionary Cristóbal de Escobar, during their imprisonment "the [people] of the province of Cicuique sent to beg for their return," an event the captain general denied ever happened.[40] In any case, the people of Cicuique were incensed by what they saw as a shameless affront to their hospitality. "Because the Indians of Cicuique went about half ready to revolt," testified Juan Troyano, "and were hostile, in order to calm them, after a certain time [the Spaniards] sent Bigotes there. He never returned."[41] That is the last the surviving documents reveal about the young leader and diplomat from Cicuique. If he continued to hold an important position within his pueblo, he never again engaged with the strangers from the south.

Despite Captain Juan de Zaldívar's claim to the contrary, the armbands or bracelets were never found, and the expeditionaries were unable to learn more about them.[42] El Turco persisted in his claims and was held under close guard to prevent his disappearing again. Vázquez de Coronado and the other leading members of the expedition, in council, resolved to travel in search of Quivira, come spring. ■

CHAPTER 13

The Heart of the Land of Flat-Roofed Towns

ALVARADO'S FAVORABLE MESSAGE to the captain general about Tiguex had been opportune. The leaders of the expedition had already decided to bring most of the remainder of the expedition to Tierra Nueva from the Río Sonora Valley. Thus the expedition was committed to spending at least one winter in Tierra Nueva. That influx of hundreds of additional people and thousands of livestock would overwhelm the resources of Cíbola, just as they had already taxed those of San Gerónimo. Pasture for cattle, horses, and sheep was a particular worry. Juan Jaramillo had complained that Cíbola was "a somewhat sandy land and not well covered by pasture."¹ It was crucial that an area be located that could sustain the huge expedition group. Tusayán had proved as incapable of that task as Cíbola. Now, with word of a much more populous and abundant region, embracing dozens of pueblos and watered by a great river, the expedition's leaders relaxed.

With September already well advanced, providing winter housing was another urgent need. Accordingly, "at that time the general had sent don García López de Cárdenas to Tiguex with a troop to prepare quarters, in order to take the expedition there to spend the winter."² When the *maestre de campo* and his contingent of Europeans and Mexican Indians reached the Río de Tiguex–Rio Grande in the vicinity of modern Albuquerque, New Mexico, they found a comparatively lush environment with riverside grass and hundreds and hundreds of acres of ripened corn in the ample floodplain. There were large forests for firewood, although they were on mountain slopes several miles from the river along which the many native settlements clustered. López de Cárdenas and his party were received cordially, still benefiting from Bigotes's diplomacy. Rather than passing on, though, as Alvarado had recently done, the field commander and his followers clearly intended to take up residence in the midst of the Tiguex pueblos. In the unlikely event that the people of Tiguex had felt no misgivings about the Alvarado party, they certainly did now about the López company, which they knew to be only a fragment of the large expedition then poised at Cíbola.

Indeed, by the time the *maestre de campo* left Cíbola for the Rio Grande, Tristán de Luna y Arellano had led the train of the expedition across the 150 leagues from San Gerónimo to Hawikku. The decision to overwinter among the Tiguex was sealed. In preparation for transfer of the entire expedition from Cíbola to the Rio Grande, López de Cárdenas "wanted to build straw huts, but the winter was so harsh that it was not possible to maintain the people there. The *maestre de campo* asked the Indians to provide quarters for him in the pueblo where they were, after which the Indians left it."³ Another contemporaneous version of these events paints a picture of heavier-handed action by López de Cárdenas: "Since it was important that the natives see, I mean give up, a place where the Spaniards would be lodged, they were forced to abandon one pueblo and were given shelter in the other pueblos of their friends. They did not take [with them] more than their persons and clothing."⁴

This latter account is given credence by large numbers of crossbow dart points and lead balls found in recent decades in the vicinity of Santiago Pueblo, which is presumed to have been this pueblo. Many of the lead balls had been flattened by impact against the walls of the pueblo.⁵ A violent expulsion of the residents, consistent with these objects, helps to explain the abiding anger of a Tiguex man whom the Spaniards called Juan Alemán. He was one of the leaders of this first abandoned pueblo, known in the sixteenth-century documents as Coofor (Cohonfor), and he would attempt to kill López de Cárdenas later in the winter.

Both in his ouster of the residents of Coofor and in his failed attempt to put up thatched shelters nearby, López de Cárdenas raised the ire of the Tiguex. For construction of shelters the *maestre de campo* and his party evidently used cornstalks left in the Pueblo fields after harvest.

Further, they turned their horses and other livestock into the harvested fields to graze. What López de Cárdenas did not guess was that the Tiguex commonly kept those cornstalks as winter fuel, sources of wood being at some distance from the pueblos. The *maestre de campo*'s appropriation of dry cornstalks was viewed as blatant theft of a valuable resource, the first of many to follow.⁶ So even before the full expeditionary force reached the Rio Grande, the Tiguex held several grievances against the newcomers.

Once López de Cárdenas was established in Coofor, the captain general departed from Cíbola to join him, taking a southerly route to Tiguex by way of a cluster of allied pueblos known to him as Tutahaco. These pueblos were part of what is known today as the southern Tiwa region, from Albuquerque south to the confluence of the Rio Grande and the Rio Puerco.⁷ Winter was fast approaching; snow was already on the mountains bordering Vázquez de Coronado's route. Cold temperatures prevailed in the high country. Up and down the Rio Grande, stands of golden-leaved cottonwoods signaled the turn of season, even as warm afternoons succeeded each other. It had been a wet year in this semidesert, and that trend would continue.⁸ Hundreds and hundreds of native farmers were bringing in the last of the crops. Ears of corn and rings of squash were spread to dry on every rooftop, where children shooed away birds and other potential animal threats to the food supply.

Along almost 175 miles of the river's course, from modern Taos south to today's Socorro, similar scenes were repeated. By Castañeda de Nájera's count, there were about 50 pueblos on the immediate banks and adjacent terraces of the river and another 23 away from the river, from Tusayán-Hopi in the west to Cicuique-Pecos in the east.⁹ A rough estimate, based on a guess by Castañeda de Nájera, projects a total population in the Pueblo world in 1540 of around 80,000.¹⁰

In the river valley, where the expedition was now reassembling by units, the pueblos were massive, adobe, and often multistory communal residential blocks. Public plaza areas frequently occupied the vacant spaces between blocks. Flat roofs were work spaces and served as streets as well. There were no ground-level doors; rather, roof hatchways led by ladders down into generally dim rooms. Smoke from cooking and heating fires exited by the same hatches. Except in cold weather, people did much of their work outdoors. Thus, when the parties of the Coronado expedition arrived in the valley one after another, Pueblo men at least were much in evidence, traveling to and fro, from fields, from the nearby towering mountains, and between pueblos. As at Cíbola, women were probably generally kept out of the strangers' sight. It was a busy place at its busiest season.

The neighbors of the Tiguex, too, had had a bountiful year. All the Pueblos of the Rio Grande shared a common way of life, founded on irrigated farming and at the mercy of the weather. There were rivalries from time to time between the Tiguex, Quirix, Tewa, Tano, and Towa peoples over access to cropland and water and periodic abandonment and reestablishment of settlements. But all in all, a dynamic equilibrium had prevailed for several centuries. At any point in time, each group held use of a specific territory, known and generally respected by its neighbors, embracing several settlements and extensive floodplain land. Within each of these *provincias*, as the Spaniards called them, the people shared a common language and culture and maintained a loose political bond. They each could and did act occasionally in concert, as units. Tiguex itself is generally considered to have comprised 12 pueblos in 1540, although estimates by members of the expedition range from 12 to 20.[11]

Since the Quirix, or Keres, people, the Tiguex's neighbors to the north and west, arrived from the San Juan River basin in the 1300s, there had been no further large-scale immigration into the valley. Thus, all the Pueblo groups were made uneasy by the influx of strangers from the south in fall 1540. Like the Towa people of Cicuique-Pecos, some groups linked themselves briefly to the expedition against their neighbors. Vázquez de Coronado even testified that the people of Cicuique "were enemies of the people of Tiguex."[12] But in the end, when violence broke out between the expedition and the Tiguex, although some pueblos were ostensibly neutral, none entered into active league with the European-African-Mexican force. They paid lip service to friendship with the expedition but provided sanctuary to the Tiguex when the time came. By the end of the winter that was now beginning, general agreement would exist among the Pueblos that departure of the Coronado expedition would be good riddance.

East of the Pueblo world for a distance of 300 miles or so lived semi-nomadic people whose primary livelihood came from bison. They harvested bison for hides, meat, blood, bones, sinews, and other parts. According to Indians from the pueblos, these plains peoples were called Querechos and Teyas. By and large they maintained symbiotic relations with the Pueblos, regularly trading bison products for pottery, corn, and other agricultural products. Bands of Teyas even spent the winters just outside several of the pueblos, including Cicuique, with which they may have had a formal peace pact. Even intermarriage was not uncommon. From time to time violence erupted, too. At the time the Coronado expedition entered the Pueblo world, memories were still alive of a concerted attack by Teyas that had left several pueblos desolated in what is today the Galisteo Basin, northeast of Tiguex.[13] The Teyas had struck, plundered, and then returned to their usual territory in the plains.

In Tiguex itself, Coofor, the first pueblo occupied by the expedition, sat next to the Rio Grande, on its west side, just across the river from the southern neighborhoods of today's town of Bernalillo, New Mexico.[14] It was "in the center of the mountain chain, in the most level and spacious [part] of it."[15] Vázquez de Coronado took up quarters there just weeks before the severest winter in many years descended on the region. By the time Tristán de Luna y Arellano brought the van of the expedition from Cíbola, heavy snow was a daily occurrence. As Castañeda de Nájera told it, "during the ten days the expedition expended [in going to Tiguex] it did not stop snowing in the late afternoons and almost every night, so that in order to establish quarters wherever they reached, they had to pry up a *codo* [equal to the length of a human forearm] of snow and more."[16]

The people with Luna y Arellano must have been greatly relieved to get indoors at Coofor and out of the harsh weather. The Europeans probably were warmed by fires kindled in newly built fireplaces, an innovation brought by the expedition unknown before in Pueblo architecture. And they were heartened by the hope that spring would carry them to a long-anticipated land of prosperity. The talk was about Quivira and the

Indians from there whom Hernando de Alvarado now had under guard in Coofor.

Meanwhile, the *indios amigos* settled into flimsier, makeshift shelters located on the sandy slope about a quarter of a mile farther from the river. Excavated very slightly into the ground, the irregularly shaped structures were erected on frames of light poles.[17] For people accustomed to far warmer climates, these *jacal* buildings (with walls of upright plastered poles) and *ramadas* (roofed, open-air spaces) proved inadequate in the harsh winter weather. The consequent suffering of the allies contributed to escalating demands on the Tiguex people for warm clothing, which in turn fueled violence.

Most of the Tiguex owners and, until recently, occupants of Coofor, after their expulsion by the expeditionaries, had crowded with their neighbors into two nearby pueblos. The closer of the two, called by the Spaniards Pueblo de la Alameda, sat less than a mile and half from Coofor on the opposite, or east, side of the Río de Tiguex. Those who did not find space there were scattered among the other Tiguex pueblos. As they faced their home pueblo across the river in deepening winter, resentment among the Tiguex intensified. Provocation was not long in coming.

CHAPTER 14

Vassalage Denied

Among the Tiguex there was a leader, the *principal* introduced briefly in the preceding chapter, whom the Spaniards of the Coronado expedition called Juan Alemán, "after a Juan Alemán who was in [the Ciudad de] México, whom they said he resembled."¹ He was also known as Juan Emán, Juan Loman, and Jumena. His Tiwa name, or part of it, may have been Xauian (ShahwEEon).² Like other residents of Coofor, he is not referred to by name in the documentary accounts of Bigotes's diplomatic efforts on behalf of Alvarado or of López de Cárdenas's expulsion of the residents of that pueblo. Xauian was, nevertheless, among those affected by both the initial encounter and the subsequent eviction, and he probably was party to whatever parley preceded the expeditionaries' exercise of force to clear the pueblo.

Whether he was opposed to accommodation with the expeditionaries from the first is unknown. But the torture of Bigotes and the *cacique*, with whom he probably had frequent contact as his counterparts at Cicuique, must have angered him. As Castañeda de Nájera wrote in understatement, "the [people of] Tiguex did not have a positive opinion about this imprisonment."³ Xauian must certainly have been among the speakers in council on the subject of the abuse of his neighbors. By the time the captain general authorized an attempt to requisition *mantas* from the Tiguex people, Alemán-Xauian's response to the request was as icy as the weather.

The expeditionaries' lack of cold-season clothing, originally expected to be supplied by ship, turned perilous when temperatures suddenly plunged to life-threatening lows. They had little choice but to approach the people they had just put out of their homes with a request for hundreds of garments. So imperative was the need that requests promptly became

145

demands. First to be summoned and confronted with the demand was Juan Alemán-Xauian, "who was already well acquainted and had had much conversation with [Vázquez de Coronado]." He was asked "to furnish him three hundred pieces of clothing or more."[4]

The *principal* replied that it "was not for him to do, but rather for the governors, and that, above all, it was necessary to engage in consultation and to distribute [the burden] among the pueblos. Further, [he said] that it was necessary to make the request individually to each pueblo." He made no offer to intercede even at the pueblo where he himself was a refugee. So the captain general directed that "certain men chosen from among those who were with him were to go to make the request. Since the pueblos numbered twelve, some [men] were to go on one side of the river and the others on the other." Among the requisition parties were Hernando de la Cadena, Cristóbal de Mayorga, and Alonso de Sayavedra.[5]

Even if the captain general's intent had been to comply as much as possible with Tiguex protocols, the actual execution of the plan unfolded otherwise. When one of the collectors

> arrived at [a] pueblo and immediately made the request to [the leaders], they had to deliver [the clothes right away] because [the expeditionary] had to have time to go on. In this situation, they had no more time than to take off their outer fur robes and hand them over until the number they were asked for was reached. The collectors gave *mantas* and robes to some of the men-at-arms who went there [to Tiguex], who, if [the clothes] were not just so and they saw an Indian with another, better one, they exchanged with him without having greater respect and without ascertaining the rank of the [man] they were despoiling. So that [the Indians] were not a little angry over this.[6]

The expeditionaries' accounts of their sojourn among the Tiguex recite a litany of impositions heaped on the Pueblo people, impositions aggravated by fear, cupidity, lust, and arrogance. While the men were appropriating *mantas*, for instance, at least one of them attacked a Pueblo woman sexually, and other attacks are implied. A delegation from Pueblo del Arenal, where many of Coofor's former residents now lived, went to the captain general asking that he make good his promise to punish transgressors among his people. Instead, a cruel farce ensued, during which a rapist, presumably Juan Villegas, brother of one of the councilmen of the Ciudad de México, changed clothes and in this way avoided identification, although his unmistakable peach-colored horse was readily identified by the husband of the violated woman.

Finally, the repeated provocative acts by expeditionaries passed endurance for the Tiguex: expulsion from their homes, destruction of their winter fuel, torture of honored representatives of their neighbors, forced requisition of their food and clothing, rapes of women, and possibly the picking of fights by Mexican Indian allies. The Tiguex struck back. "They had risen in revolt," testified Juan Troyano, "because the Spaniards' horses were eating their planted fields and because the Christians occupied their houses and demanded *mantas* and other things from them."[7]

"The uprising happened one night . . . [and the Indians] killed 50 or 60 horses and pack animals."[8] In addition they "clubbed and killed four or five Nahua Indians [Mexican Indian allies]" who had been guarding the herds.[9] Overnight, all but three of the Tiguex pueblos were abandoned. According to the author of the Relación del Suceso, "the [places which took up arms] were twelve pueblos which were located together," making up the *provincia* of Tiguex.[10] Meanwhile, the people of the neighboring *provincia* of Quirix remained in their homes and pursued peaceful relations with the expedition. As at Cíbola and Tusayán, such concerted action on the part of each group of villages strongly suggests the existence of political institutions among the Tiguex and the Quirix, respectively, that exercised some interpueblo authority and coordination, especially when it came to defense.[11] The precise nature of those institutions and the extent and limits of their authority are unknown.

With horses and mules missing and Indian guards dead, *maestre de campo* López de Cárdenas was sent out to learn how things stood throughout Tiguex and whether the attack had been an isolated incident or signaled a general uprising. What he found was "the pueblos closed by palisades. [There was] a great shout inside, [where they were] fighting the horses (as in a bullring) and shooting them with arrows. [They were] all up in arms."¹² Vázquez de Coronado "assembled the officials, clerics, and captains who came in the company, in order to consult with them as to whether he should make war against [the Indians] or whether they should let them be and move on forward. [Expeditionary Domingo Martín] saw that everyone agreed that he should make war on them and not leave any place in revolt."¹³

In keeping with royal mandate, the captain general then dispatched Captain Diego López to Pueblo del Arenal to read the *requerimiento* and demand submission to the king of Spain without further hostility. What had become a familiar routine to both expeditionaries and their Pueblo audience ensued. The lengthy document was read aloud in Spanish, followed by efforts to make it understood in the local language and by means of signs. The reply from Arenal, perhaps delivered by Juan Alemán–Xauian, was that "they were not familiar with His Majesty nor did they wish to be his subjects or serve him or any other Christian."¹⁴ López returned to Coofor with that news, which triggered the sanctioning of an attack on Arenal led by García López de Cárdenas, the *maestre de campo*. López de Cárdenas later justified the assault, saying that it was made "to spare other pueblos greater harm . . . in order that the expedition might be carried out more peacefully."¹⁵

After a day and a half of fighting, smoky fires lighted in ground floor rooms of the pueblo by the Mexican Indian allies led the defenders to surrender Arenal. What happened next was later a matter of legal dispute. The *maestre de campo* claimed that while he was occupied elsewhere during the heat of the battle, "he heard a great commotion outside the pueblo and went to see what it was; and [he] found that the soldiers had some of these Indians in a tent . . . He saw that the soldiers were lancing and killing them. He saw that others had been cast into the fires, tied, and that some were burned, stabbed, and others dead."¹⁶

Almost all other expeditionaries who testified about this event in later years told a different story, one in which López de Cárdenas played a much less benign role. For example, artilleryman Juan Troyano swore that when the Indians saw that they were sorely pressed, some of them made a cross, displayed it through the windows, and declared that they would come out in peace. In this way 60 Indians came out. As they came [the Spaniards] put them in the tent of don García López. And they killed others.

When [the Spaniards] saw that no more [Indians] were coming out, they took the Indians who were in the tent and brought some posts that were in the camp. Setting the posts in the ground, they began tying some of [the Indians] to posts in order to burn them. Then [the Indians] who remained in the tent rose up in the tent itself [against the Spaniards]. Therefore, the Christians killed some of them by lancing and stabbing them and the rest they burned alive tied to the posts. [The witness said] that it appeared to him that those [Indians] whom they burned numbered between forty and fifty.

[The witness also said] he saw that before the burning El Turco and Ysopete were brought from the camp where Francisco Vázquez was, in order that they might witness the burning. He does not know who brought them nor by whose order it was done. He said that García López, as maestre de campo, was the one who ordered the stakes set up and the Indians burned. None [of the Indians] remained alive. He does not know whether Francisco Vázquez ordered [García López to do what he did] or not.[17]

No one disputed that the killing and burning happened. The only issues in contention were whether the actions of the expeditionaries were justifiable, whether a promise of clemency had been reneged upon, and whether the *maestre de campo* had been present and ordered the burnings. The devastation of the Pueblo del Arenal was the same either way, and so was the resulting animosity of the rest of the *provincia* of Tiguex and the wariness of the Tiwas' neighbors. The Tiguex were now concentrated in two especially strong pueblos.

As the fighting at Arenal came to an end, the main body of the expedition reached Santiago-Coofor from Cíbola, and winter clamped down in earnest. With 2,000 members of the expedition seeking shelter from the unusual and persistent cold and snow, it is likely that they occupied, in addition to Coofor, the now vacant Arenal, as well as at least one other Tiguex pueblo, possibly Alameda. Such a parceling out of units would still have kept the expeditionaries all within a radius of two miles. There is documentary proof that the expedition occupied more than one pueblo the following winter, so it seems only natural that it did so during the winter of 1540–41 as well.[18]

The final rupture in relations between the Tiguex and the expedition left the Spanish-led force without ready suppliers of clothing and additional food. So Vázquez de Coronado turned to the next nearest people, the Quirix-Keres who lived at Chia, or Zia, Pueblo, some 15 miles northwest of Coofor along the Jemez River, a tributary of the Rio Grande. No documentary evidence exists about whether the expeditionaries applied coercive force to Chia or whether leaders from there offered to aid them voluntarily. In any case, according to the captain general, he "ordered don García López to take trade goods and with them try to purchase, from the pueblo of Chia, some robes, hides, and mantas with which to clothe and save the people . . . [and the Indians] from the pueblo of Chia came to the camp and talked with [Vázquez de Coronado]. And they brought him poultry and other supplies and offered him assistance."[19]

In an attempt to mollify the people of Cicuique, whose leaders Bigotes and the *cacique* were still held prisoner in the expedition's camp, the captain general made a trip there, restoring the *cacique* to his home. The effect of that gesture on the bitterness toward the expedition among the Towa people of Cicuique was minimal. They brushed off Vázquez de Coronado's request to them for fighters to help pacify the Tiguex and remained hostile for the remainder of the expedition's stay in Tierra Nueva.

"Within five or six days after [López de Cárdenas] had returned to Alcanfor [Coofor], as he has stated, the general ordered him to go out again with more people to summon the other people of the province of Tiguex to peace, and if they refused to submit peacefully, to wage war on them."[20] At a very strong pueblo known to the expeditionaries as Moho— one of the two remaining where the Tiguex had sought sanctuary—López de Cárdenas appealed for a conference with the spokesman Xauian–Juan Alemán.²¹ Moho, like the pueblo on Dowa Yalanne in the Cíbola area, was likely a traditional refuge from attack, a place of difficult access and stout construction.

> Even though they were at war, they [the defenders of Moho] ended up talking to him. They told [López de Cárdenas] that if he wanted to talk with them, he should dismount, and they [would] come to him to talk peace. [They also said] that the horsemen should go off to one side, and they would have their people move away. [Then] Juan Alemán and another captain from the pueblo came to him.
>
> It was done just as they requested. [López de Cárdenas] was close to them, and they said that since they were not carrying weapons, he should remove his. With the desire he had to bring them to peace, don García López did so, in order to give them more assurance. When he reached them, Juan Alemán came forward to embrace him. As he did that, the two [others] who came with him withdrew two small clubs they were secretly carrying behind their backs and struck him on the helmet, two such [powerful] blows that they nearly stunned him. Two men-at-arms on horseback were nearby (since they had refused to withdraw even though they were ordered to) and attacked with such speed that they snatched him from [the Indians'] grasp.²²

That violent response at Moho and rejection of the *requerimiento* at another fortified pueblo seemed to leave the captain general and his council no option besides force. The *maestre de campo* was directed to lay siege to Moho and compel the people there to submit. An initial attack on the pueblo was repulsed. The Indians at Moho "had had many days to prepare themselves, they threw so many stones onto our people that they knocked many [of them] to the ground, and they wounded about a hundred men with arrows. Afterwards several died from [their wounds]."²³ For two months or more the expeditionaries surrounded this pueblo "on a height," making desultory thrusts against the town walls and keeping a lookout for possible flight, all the while occupying large pavilion tents in the cold and snow of the early weeks of 1541.²⁴

If, as seems likely, Moho was situated on Santa Ana Mesa overlooking modern San Felipe, it was rendered nearly invincible by the sheer basalt cliffs that form the mesa's perimeter. With a supply of corn and other dried foods stored there, the pueblo could have withstood the expedition's occasional assaults almost indefinitely, except for one crucial element: lack of a perennial water supply. The Tiguex of Moho, perched above the river's floodplain, could view its flow of water only a quarter of a mile away. But hundreds of vertical feet of basalt, the old lava flow on which the pueblo stood, separated them from the river's associated underground flow. They were forced to rely on rainwater and melting snow. Everyone was using as little water as possible. Things got so desperate that the refugees at Moho decided to dig a well through the basalt in search of water. That project met an unfortunate end when the shaft collapsed, killing "thirty persons."²⁵

Finally, despite frequent snowfall that replenished supplies of water, thirst drove the Tiguex defenders of Moho to desperation. Two weeks after turning over a hundred women and children to the custody of the expedition, in order to reduce the drain on their water,

> [the Indians] decided to leave [the pueblo], and so they did. Taking the women in the middle [of the group], they came forth during the quarter just before daybreak. Forty horsemen were keeping watch during that quarter, and they gave the call to arms. The [men-at-arms] in don Rodrigo Maldonado's camp attacked [the Indians]. The enemies knocked one Spaniard and one horse down dead and wounded others. But [the men-at-arms] happened to break through and work slaughter among them until, [when] [the Indians] were withdrawing, [the men-at-arms] attacked them in the river, which was flowing rapidly and was extremely cold. Since the troop from the *real* arrived very soon, those [Indians] who escaped death or injury were few.²⁶

The death toll from the siege and failed escape was at least 200 Tiguex men, as well as dozens from the expedition.²⁷ Many other people from Moho were captured and distributed among the expeditionaries as servants. Whether or not Alemán-Xauian died at Moho is uncertain, but no further mention of him appears in surviving documents of the expedition, suggesting that he did.

Meanwhile, another Tiguex pueblo was subdued by a force led by Captains Diego de Guevara and Juan de Zaldívar. That made a total of three. As summarized in later testimony by expeditionary Rodrigo de Frías, "one was called Pueblo de la Cruz, another was called Pueblo de la Alameda, and the last was called Pueblo del Cerco. After having taken possession, [the expeditionaries] burned the wood from the pueblos and demolished some houses. [The Spaniards] found another three or four pueblos abandoned, and the people had fled. They burned the wood from them also and tore down some houses."²⁸ As a result, "none of the twelve pueblos of Tiguex... was [re]settled during the entire time the expedition was there, despite the assurance [the Indians] were given."²⁹ The whole *provincia* remained depopulated, stalked by parties of Pueblo warriors who made it dangerous for individual expeditionaries or small groups of them to be abroad. Only the pueblo of Chia was on friendly terms with the armed force that kept the region in turmoil all winter.

As the first quarter of 1541 came to a close, frigid weather finally released its grip. The Rio Grande, which had been frozen for almost four months, began to thaw.³⁰ The leadership of the expedition now considered it safe to leave the Pueblo world and take the entire party to Quivira, led by El Turco.

CHAPTER 15

TO THE FARTHEST EDGE

ANTICIPATION RAN HIGH AMONG THE EXPEDITIONARIES as departure from Tiguex began a week after Easter 1541. It was late April in the Julian calendar when the approximately 2,000 people and 7,000 head of livestock set off. No one wanted to be left behind, although that possibility had been discussed in council.[1] Despite general enthusiasm for the trip to Quivira, "already there were some among the members of the expedition [who were] suspicious of El Turco."[2] Even Vázquez de Coronado revealed that because the reports of Quivira were "from Indians and mostly by signs, I did not give them credence until I could see it with my own eyes (their report seeming very exaggerated to me)."[3] The misgivings, though, were eclipsed by widespread optimism. After all, great civilized kingdoms were said to lie over the eastern horizon.

The first leg of the journey, to Cicuique—already well known now to many of the expeditionaries—took just four days. There, in a belated act of diplomacy, the Spaniards released Bigotes. He does not reappear in the documentary record of the expedition. Whether or not his role as broker and shaper of interpueblo relations continued cannot be guessed. Nor can we be sure whether his release gained the expedition any goodwill. Several pieces of evidence suggest not. Juan Troyano testified that even after the restoration of Bigotes, the people of Cicuique "refused to welcome them or furnish provisions."[4] A few months later, as the captain general returned toward the Rio Grande from Quivira, the people of the pueblo "came forth prepared for war."[5]

This apparent lack of diplomatic success did not divert the expeditionaries from their goal of reaching Quivira. Onward they went for four or five days of travel, guided probably by people from the pueblo, to a practicable crossing of the Río de Cicuique, the modern Pecos River. They found it in flood with unusually heavy spring snowmelt.[6] In order to get all the people and animals of the expedition, especially the sheep, safely across, the party built a bridge—most likely a floating bridge, a type commonly used by other Spanish-led expeditions of the period.[7] Constructing and then crossing the structure consumed four days.[8] Once across the dangerous current, El Turco led the expedition eastward through plains for eight days, until the first bison were sighted. The curiosity of heavy, short-horned "cattle" and the congestion they caused slowed the force to a crawl for several days.

During that time the Quivira-bound expeditionaries ran across an encampment of the semi-nomadic bison hunters called Querechos. By a use of signs so masterful that "it seemed as if they were talking," according to Castañeda de Nájera, these people seemed to confirm El Turco's report of an immense river heavily settled by builders of huge canoes.[9] The captain general, writing only months after the event, gave a very different version. "These [Querechos]," he wrote, "did not know how to give me a report about the land to which the guides were taking me or the route by which they wished to lead me."[10]

The two groups, bison hunters and expeditionaries, camped side by side overnight. In the morning the Querecho band struck its hide tents, or tipis, loaded them and their other chattel and supplies onto dog-drawn travois,[11] and headed off in the direction opposite that of the expedition's course.[12] This mutual avoidance by El Turco and the Querechos suggests that there was no love lost between the Caddoan-speaking proto-Wichita and Pawnee (represented by El Turco, Ysopete, and Xabe, a boy from the Quivira region who had also been living at Cicuique) and the Apachean-speaking Querechos.

For two more days the expedition met Querecho bands amid the bison. At about this time El Turco began steering the expedition southeastward, in the direction of what the Spaniards called La Florida, onto "a level and wide land ... more than four hundred leagues in width."[13] This was what is today known as the American Great Plains, specifically that portion of the plains called the Llano Estacado of the Texas Panhandle and South Plains of Texas. Although the land was extremely flat, travel was difficult, always pushing through the seemingly limitless bison herds. The expedition came across many small ponds of water, but invariably these had been fouled by bison, "so bad [that they] contained more mud than water."[14]

With little prelude, dissension broke out between El Turco and his fellow guide, Ysopete. This second guide made a spectacle of his disagreement with El Turco over the new, southeasterly course. "He dropped [to the ground] in the path, indicating to them to cut off his head so that he would not have to go that way, and [indicating] that it was not our route either."[15] Confronted by such radical disparity of opinion between the guides, Vázquez de Coronado and his council decided to dispatch two parties traveling at double time toward the east in an effort to locate a place El Turco called Haya.[16] The first detachment returned without success, but the second ran into an Indian encampment situated in a great *barranca*, or canyon, on the eastern margin of the Llano Estacado. It was Ascension Day, June 26, 1541, under the Julian calendar.[17]

A messenger sent by don Rodrigo Maldonado, leader of the successful reconnaissance, quickly reached the main body of the expedition, which was trailing close behind. The whole force assembled in the *barranca* not far from the native settlement. The Europeans understood that these tattooed people were called Teyas.[18] Unlike their enemies the Querechos days before, they were definitely familiar with Quivira and could speak with El Turco, suggesting that they, too, spoke a Caddoan language.[19] This particular Teya band, at another of its traditional campsites hundreds of miles south, "closer to Nueva España," had, years before, been visited by Cabeza de Vaca and his fellow survivors of the Narváez expedition.[20] Apparently expecting a blessing of their goods such as Dorantes, Cabeza de Vaca, Esteban, and Castillo had bestowed five years earlier, they displayed to the expeditionaries a great mound of cured bison hides. The newcomers took the disclosure as a gift to them and promptly divided up the hides among themselves, as weeping Teyas looked on.[21]

About three o'clock that afternoon, according to the eighteenth-century historian Matías de la Mota y Padilla, while the expeditionaries were still setting up camp and stashing away the hides, a powerful thunderstorm struck, something not at all unusual for the South Plains during the summer.²² With tents only partly erected and some horses perhaps still packed, "a whirling storm arose with the strongest of winds and hail. In a brief while such a huge number of hailstones came down, as large as small bowls and larger and as dense as rain, that in one place they covered the ground [to a depth of] two and three *palmos* and more."²³ The onslaught of hail ripped tents, smashed pottery, stampeded livestock, and bruised people. Supplies were strewn around the camp and beaten and trampled into the muddy ground. That circumstance enabled archaeologists to locate and identify this spot during the 1990s. Known today as the Jimmy Owens Site, it lies about 35 miles northeast of modern Lubbock, Texas.²⁴ With some effort the runaway horses, hemmed in by the steep walls of the canyon, were rounded up, and the battered expedition spent the night under whatever shelter it could improvise.

According to the Europeans' temporary Teya neighbors, Quivira lay at least 40 days' travel to the north and was not nearly as prosperous or populous as in El Turco's telling. With that news, the captain general called the prominent members of the expedition to a council to discuss its precarious situation and its next move. Because the expedition was short of supplies and had now been thrashed by violent weather, the outcome of the meeting was "by unanimous agreement, that the general would go [on] in search of Quivira with thirty horsemen and half a dozen footmen and that don Tristán de Arellano would return to Tiguex with all [the rest of] the expedition."²⁵

As usual for any unit of the expeditionary force, the Quivira party must have included a contingent of Mexican Indians, although none is mentioned in the relevant portions of the surviving documents. The entire expedition proceeded to another large *barranca*, where the parting of ways took place. This second great *barranca* probably lay to the north of the one where the hailstorm had hit. It was possibly today's Palo Duro Canyon, another of the Texas Panhandle's Caprock canyons, or one of its tributary canyons. Those designated to return to the Rio Grande would remain for a while in the second *barranca*, resting and laying in a supply of bison meat and robes against the next winter.

At the insistence of the expeditionaries, the Teyas furnished guides for those going on to Quivira, which indicates that Ysopete, now that unit's chief pilot, did not know his way home from there. But the Teya guides fled after only a few days, so Captain Diego López, *maestre de campo* of the detachment bound for Quivira, returned to the second *barranca* to obtain others. Once again the Teyas complied with the request, and López returned to the detachment. For about a month the Quivira party made its slow way north, still always among bison. On the feast of San Pedro y San Pablo, June 29, 1541, Vázquez de Coronado and his party struck a large, east-flowing river, the modern Arkansas in the state of Kansas. They turned to follow the river downstream for about a week before finally reaching Quivira.

Once more the expeditionaries were disappointed. As the captain general put it, although the guides had "told me that I would not finish seeing it all in two months, in [Quivira] and all the rest [of the *provincias*] I saw and learned about there are not more than twenty-five *pueblos* consisting of houses made of thatch."[26] The Teyas' description proved more accurate than the Quiviran guides' promises. "The people were few and settlement sparse and of little use in increasing the royal patrimony."[27] The Quivirans themselves were "nearly the [same] sort and [have nearly the same] dress as the Teyas," again suggesting that the groups were culturally related and may even have both been Caddoan speaking.[28] In the Europeans' eyes, they were "as uncivilized as all those I have seen and passed until now."[29]

If it was any consolation, the captain general "was welcomed peacefully because of the guides he took."[30] Ysopete and El Turco allayed at least most of the anxiety that arrival of the Europeans and Mexican Indians must have occasioned for the Quivirans. The expeditionaries' interest was briefly piqued because "the lord wore a copper medallion [suspended] from his neck, [which] he esteemed more than a little."[31] But during the entire two and half years of travel to and throughout Tierra Nueva, the members of the expedition did not see "any other metal in these places except that [piece], some small copper bells . . . , and a very small [piece] of metal that appears [to be] gold."[32]

El Turco, who had accompanied the detachment to Quivira under close guard, continued to insist that "the towns where the gold and riches were still lay ahead."³³ The expeditionaries doggedly chased the chimera of that wealthy and populous polity. In the pursuit, Vázquez de Coronado and his companions "spent twenty-five days" in Quivira, trying to learn what might lie farther on.³⁴ They even dispatched a letter to the "lord of Arahey," which they understood to be a kingdom toward the east. The Europeans had concluded that this lord "was a Christian from the shipwrecked fleets bound for La Florida."³⁵ With great disappointment and even disgust, Juan Jaramillo, who was with Vázquez de Coronado in Quivira, later wrote that this lord "came with about 200 men. They were all naked and [had] bows. I do not know what things [they wore] on their heads, and their genitals [were] barely covered."³⁶

The Quivirans and members of the expedition were wary of each other from the beginning. The expeditionaries soon detected, or thought they saw, signs of treachery. According to Melchior Pérez, El Turco "had made a pact with [the Indians] of Quivira, telling them that because the horses were weak and worn out, [the Spaniards] would not be able to do them any harm with the horses, so that one night they would set upon the Spaniards."³⁷ Juan Jaramillo wrote that "El Turco summoned and called together the entire populace in order to attack and kill us one night. We became aware of it and it put us on guard."³⁸ And Gaspar de Saldaña testified that while the expeditionaries were in Quivira, El Turco watched horses running and commented that without corn they would be useless. "A large horse belonging to [Hernando de] Alvarado went there and an Indian commented about how large the horse was. El Turco said, 'titley,' which means 'kill it.'"³⁹

Such open hostility could not be ignored. Some of the expeditionaries had already demanded that El Turco be killed in punishment for his misguidance.⁴⁰ Now the threat he seemed to pose led to swift action. Vázquez de Coronado "ordered the *maestre de campo* to administer justice, once he had investigated what has been said. He also ordered him to ask El Turco why [he] had entered into that conspiracy and why he had led [the Spaniards] deceitfully so as to become lost."⁴¹

Maestre de campo Diego López and Captain Juan de Zaldívar, who had previously urged El Turco's execution, oversaw a brief interrogation of the former guide. His chief accuser was his rival, Ysopete, who "gave evidence that El Turco was telling [the Indians of Quivira] not to bring the Christians or their horses anything to eat, because then they would die. Ysopete reported that conspiracy to [Juan Troyano] and to others who knew how to speak his language somewhat. And he knew some of the Nahuatl language."[42] After questioning that almost certainly included torture, as was not uncommon in that day, "the Indian Turco himself acknowledged this, through the translation of Ysopete and by clear signs." So testified Juan de Zaldívar three years later.[43] The captain general's groom, Juan de Contreras, was present at the formalities when, "without waiting for further talk or counter arguments, a soldier whom they said was Pérez . . . by order of Diego López and Zaldívar, who were present, put a cord around the Indian's neck from behind and tightened it with a stick. That strangled him and then they buried him next to the tent."[44]

El Turco's death did not put an end to the expeditionaries' anxieties. The Quivirans might still attack and overwhelm the relatively small detachment. In addition, it was now late August in the Julian calendar. The turn to colder weather would soon be upon them. Vázquez de Coronado consequently convened a council to consider the options. "It seemed to all of us, who were in agreement," wrote Juan Jaramillo, "that since [the captain general] had left the armed force and we were there [in Quivira], his grace should return in search of them."[45] With that decision made, Vázquez de Coronado and his companions turned back toward the Rio de Tiguex–Rio Grande, led by Quiviran guides by a route much shorter than that of the outbound journey, without the great detour to the south. Ysopete, as he had requested, was left behind in Quivira.

TRUE OR FALSE?

The claims and counterclaims asserting the authenticity or speciousness of the golden armbands and their source in Quivira entailed multiple misstatements, misdirections, misunderstandings, lies, half-truths, and wishful thinking. The Spaniards of the Coronado expedition were never able to sort them all out. Nearly 470 years later, with even less of the tangle of verbal evidence available for scrutiny, it may seem a hopeless task. But it is worth the effort to unravel as much of the tangle as possible because of what the episode of the jewelry reveals about the people it affected. Fortunately, we have some advantages that sixteenth-century expeditionaries and American natives did not have.

The snarl of assertions and denials is most easily dealt with by pulling out the loosest strands first. To begin with, as has already been seen, a group of settlements did exist in the early 1540s that at least some people knew by the name Quivira. It was the home of proto-Wichita Indians east of the hundredth meridian in modern central Kansas, in an area of North America where dryland agriculture was and is usually feasible.

So a place by that name existed, but it did not match the descriptions the expeditionaries understood from El Turco's signs and fragmentary Nahuatl. A large river indeed ran not far from the Kansas location, but it was not nearly as grand as the one El Turco described. It lacked giant canoes and monstrous fish. But surely most disappointingly absent from the actual Quivira were the hallmarks of civilization, according to Europeans of the day: woven fabrics; permanent, preferably stone or brick homes; writing; metal industries; formal streets and roads; glazed ceramics; and a strictly hierarchical political system. Many of these had been implicit in the gestural pictures painted by El Turco.

As Carroll Riley and historians John L. Kessell and Mildred Mott Wedel, as well as others, have pointed out over the last 30 years and more, the place portrayed by the Quiviran guide bears a striking resemblance to what we now know about the land of protohistoric mound-building cultures of the Mississippi River basin.[46] Even while members of the Coronado expedition were suffering disillusionment in Quivira, other expeditionaries under the leadership of Hernando de Soto were seeing the lower Mississippi River and the mega-canoes El Turco had described. A member of the Soto expedition known only as the "*hidalgo* from Elvas" wrote this about his first experience of the natives of the Mississippi:

> the cacique came with two hundred canoes full of Indians
> ... the warriors were standing from prow to stern with their
> bows and arrows in their hands. The canoe in which the cacique
> came had an awning spread in the stern and he [the cacique]
> was seated under the canopy ... The chief [of each canoe] from
> his position under the canopy, controlled and gave orders to
> the other men ... they had the appearance of a beautiful fleet
> of galleys.[47]

In addition, the *hidalgo* from Elvas recorded the abundance of very large fish in the Mississippi River (the Espíritu Santo, as he called it), including a "fish which the Indians brought, sometimes reaching the size of a hog and called 'pexe pereo.'"[48] This fish and several others the *hidalgo* referred to are startlingly similar to the "fish as large as horses" that El Turco had told the Coronado expeditionaries about. El Turco's story and the Soto expedition's observations along the lower Mississippi seem to match with respect to a major river, enormous fish, and great canoes.

There was, however, little gold, if any, among the protohistoric Mississippian peoples of the lower river and what is now the southeastern United States. The Soto expedition saw almost none, and none has been recovered archaeologically. Mildred Wedel has suggested, reasonably, that El Turco, being unfamiliar with gold, was referring instead to the one yellow metal he did know, copper.[49] The Soto expedition saw almost no copper, either—only a single piece—among the southern mound builders. Twice they were told about copper mines and metal working an unspecified distance to the north of where they traveled.[50]

As it happens, modern archaeology has revealed that 200 years before the Coronado and Soto expeditions, copper had been an important commodity among mound builders of the middle Mississippi Valley and the Ohio River drainage.[51] Those people had evidently obtained it through trade with others living around the Great Lakes, where locals mined the soft, shiny metal. For instance, a quantity of sheet copper was recovered from an elite burial at the Cahokia site in the environs of modern St. Louis, Missouri, along with "bushels" of sheet mica, the appearance of which

El Turco could have confused with silver.⁵² Also at Cahokia were the same great river, gargantuan fish, and multi-man canoes.

This conjunction of features suggests the possibility that the city that inspired El Turco's account was, rather than a sixteenth-century Native American city, one that had long been deserted but that in its prime had been a spectacular human achievement. With their multiple pyramid mounds and massive earthen platforms, Cahokia and its neighbors would indeed have been reminiscent of Tenochtitlan. Both places might have been known to El Turco through oral tradition and might thus have been vivid in his mind's eye. Had it still existed as a viable community in the 1540s, Cahokia would have been the kind of place that was so attractive to the would-be overlords of the Coronado expedition.

If El Turco told traditional stories of Cahokia or its neighbors to Alvarado, Vázquez de Coronado, and other members of the expedition to Tierra Nueva, then once again they misinterpreted lore of the past as news of the present, just as they had done regarding Marata and Totonteac. Under this suggestion, El Turco's incompletely executed intention could have been to be truthful in his description of lands far to the east.

Jewelry

When we consider the story of golden (or copper) jewelry said to have been at Cicuique, however, it is difficult not to conclude that either El Turco and Ysopete or Bigotes and the *cacique* were lying. Why El Turco might have felt compelled to gratuitously dress up his description of Quivira with a false tale of jewelry he had once possessed is difficult to fathom. Certainly he had already gotten Alvarado's attention without that added detail. Besides, the expeditionaries could check the story with relative ease, which presented the very real possibility that El Turco would be discredited if he were lying. Because of that, it seems most plausible that El Turco's story about the armband-bracelet was essentially accurate.

As El Turco had anticipated, Bigotes and the *cacique* were far from pleased with the Plains Indian's revelation and were forced to deny the existence of the jewelry. Perhaps the copper band or chain, which must have been what he described, held some important and esoteric ritual significance. Or it might have been a token of diplomatic obligation or privilege vis-à-vis the people of Quivira that could not be surrendered or even displayed to the wrong people. The Coronado expeditionaries understood El Turco to tell them that the people of Quivira were in fact "friends of Bigotes."[53] That special relationship might have involved privileged information and emblematic paraphernalia such as the armband. Thus, Bigotes and El Turco might have been involved in diplomacy between the Pueblo world and the plains tribes.

El Turco must have guessed that telling the expeditionaries about the armband-bracelet was likely to cause trouble for Bigotes and the *cacique*. Yet he did so anyway, which seems an extreme action for one said to be a "brother" (*hermano*)—probably a ritual kinsman—of Bigotes.[54]

Elsewhere, and more commonly, El Turco is said to have been Bigotes's slave (*esclavo*).[55] As Carroll Riley once wrote, though, "what the word 'slave' meant to the Pecos people is anyone's guess, but very likely not what it meant to the Spaniards."[56] The enslavement of adult males was unusual among the Pueblos. In an indigenous pattern described by historian James Brooks, defeated men would die, whereas "their spouses and children were assimilated through marriage and adoption into victorious Indian families."[57] This suggests that El Turco's status might have been more complicated than the term "slave" conveys.

The uses of the two terms, "brother" and "slave," can be reconciled if it is supposed that El Turco's status was that of a reciprocal hostage, a living pledge of abstinence from hostility, sent by his people to Cicuique. Presumably, a corresponding honored hostage was sent from Cicuique to Haraee.[58] Such an arrangement would have been familiar to Europeans of the day because "voluntary" reciprocal hostages were not at all uncommon in medieval and early modern Europe as a means of securing an accord. In this view, diplomatic guarantee brought El Turco to Cicuique as a long-term resident forbidden to leave without express permission. That made him both a captive of sorts and an honorary member of the Pueblo community.[59]

That some such arrangement accounted for El Turco's presence in and lack of free movement from Cicuique is suggested by the contemporaneous report that he and Bigotes (sometimes confusingly called a *cacique*) had been in Quivira together and that Bigotes had acquired the armband there himself. According to an expeditionary and close associate of the captain general's, Domingo Martín, "the Indian called Turco gave an account of a wealthy land and said that the *cacique* and Ysopete had brought some gold bracelets and other valuable jewelry from there."[60] This could be a description of a trading venture, but it is also consistent with the kind of diplomatic outcome suggested here.

My provisional conclusion is that the "voluntary" hostage El Turco was truthful in saying that Bigotes had a metal armband that had originated in Quivira. Further, Bigotes felt he could not reveal the jewelry and therefore was forced to deny, falsely, that he knew anything about it.

But that is not the end of the enigmas surrounding the episode of the bracelet. Why did El Turco bother to inform Alvarado about the jewelry, even assuming it actually existed, when that revelation was sure to put Bigotes in a predicament? How tight a predicament, El Turco probably could not have imagined, but at best it would create unpleasantness for his "brother." Did El Turco harbor rancor over his enforced absence from Quivira? Had friction developed, or redeveloped, between the plains native and his Pueblo "hosts"? In any case, divulging the existence of the armband to members of the Coronado expedition was a hostile act toward Bigotes, unless it was a thoughtless act committed in a rush of exuberance. The latter seems unlikely, because El Turco remained so staunch in his assertion that Bigotes had the jewelry, a further affront each time he repeated the claim.

We will probably never know the precise reasons behind El Turco's slap at Bigotes. But it has implications for modern historians' and archaeologists' explanations of El Turco's subsequent "misguidance" of the expedition. Some scholars, notably Herbert Bolton, have seen in that "misguidance" evidence of conspiracy between El Turco and Bigotes.[61] Carroll Riley has called it the "Pecos Plot."[62] But El Turco's stubborn assertions had done great harm to Bigotes: months in captivity, subjection to torture, the highest disrespect. A league between the two, entered into while they were held in solitary confinement, seems improbable in the extreme. It would have been a cabal of two thoroughly estranged men.

Plots and Conspiracies

The expeditionaries who left documentary records are in unanimous agreement that El Turco twice conspired with other Indians to annihilate all or part of the force. First, members of the expedition were convinced that El Turco had led them away from Quivira and any other settlements for many days, far out onto the plains where corn and other cultivated foods were unobtainable. As Vázquez de Coronado and others on the expedition thought, El Turco "did it by the advice and order of the natives of these *provincias*"—Tiguex, Cicuique, and perhaps others.⁶³ In other words, El Turco had been put up to leading the expedition astray by Bigotes and the cacique of Cicuique.

Second, El Turco himself was seen as the instigator of a plot to withhold food from the detachment that traveled to Quivira, with the idea that the Quivirans would then fall on the weakened men and slaughter them. El Turco took both these actions, according to his European critics and judges, so that the expeditionaries and their livestock, especially their horses, would weaken and die, "so that they would not go to his land to subjugate his parents, relatives, and forebears. [That was] because it was a worthier thing for him to die, so that his relatives would not be subjects of the Christians."⁶⁴

martyr

The Spanish documentary evidence deserves closer scrutiny, because the evidence for these two alleged instances of conspiracy came by means of signs from El Turco in response to torture and from Ysopete, his avowed foe.

Even if El Turco was leading the expedition to Quivira without deceit, rather than luring it to the middle of nowhere as he was accused, he likely would have gone by way of the Teya summer homeland. That is because the Teyas were friends and perhaps distant relatives of his people. The Querechos, on the other hand, who in summer occupied the western and northern fringes of the Llano Estacado, were hostile to both the Teyas and the Quivirans. In effect, the Querechos constituted a blockade to travel across the plains by Caddoan speakers, including El Turco, Ysopete, and Xabe. The longer route by way of the Teyas was the safer route.⁶⁵

There is another explanation involving benign intent that could explain El Turco's seemingly sinister route into the South Plains rather than one aimed directly at Quivira. As briefly mentioned earlier, several scholars, including especially Mildred Wedel, have suggested that El Turco was in fact leading the expedition to the lower Mississippi River valley, which would have made a southeasterly course of travel eminently sensible.

If either of these possibilities was in fact the case and El Turco did not mislead the expedition, as seems at least plausible (I myself lean toward the possibility of his heading for Quivira but detouring around the Querechos), then there is no need to posit the existence of a conspiracy between El Turco and the leaders of Cicuique. There was nothing to conspire about. The conspiracy would have been a figment of European imaginations, the consequence of excessive distrust of guides. Such distrust was the natural outcome of a longstanding Iberian storytelling tradition of evil, lying guides.⁶⁶ In this light, the so-called Pecos Plot may have been simply the projection of European expectations onto a situation the expeditionaries did not understand, with an assist from Ysopete's malicious intent. El Turco did not appreciate the gravity of his choice either to pursue a roundabout route or to lead the expedition to a destination other than his homeland's neighbor, Quivira.

Equally questionable is the existence of a conspiracy between El Turco and the people of Quivira to attack Vázquez de Coronado's detachment there. Crucially, motivation is lacking—or at least none can be perceived in the Spanish documentary record. According to the surviving documents, while in Quivira the expedition did not engage in battle with the native people. There is no evidence that it extorted food or other goods from the Quivirans. Neither were Quiviran women seized or native shelters occupied by force. Why, then, would the people of Quivira have felt aggrieved or offended enough to resort to the chancy option of attack?⁶⁷

Furthermore, virtually all evidence of a conspiracy between El Turco and the Quivirans was provided by a hostile witness, Ysopete. Juan Troyano later testified that "because of what Ysopete said, Francisco Vázquez, in the presence of this witness, ordered Juan de Zaldívar to apply a garrote to kill El Turco."[68] Without either a convincing motive or an impartial accuser, it seems unwise simply to accept the conspiracy accusation as true, as the expeditionaries did. Lacking the ability to communicate fully with the expeditionaries, El Turco fell victim to the animosity of his compatriot Ysopete, who exploited his position as both guide and interpreter.

Although it cannot be shown with certainty that the conspiracies alleged against El Turco never occurred, it would be imprudent to conclude without further proof that they did. As at other points in the course of the Coronado *entrada*, miscommunication and lack of communication were likely determining factors in this episode.

Chapter 16

What Was Seen and What Was Not

When Vázquez de Coronado and his detachment at Quivira faced about and headed back toward the Río de Tiguex in early fall 1541, the expedition's reconnaissance of Tierra Nueva was essentially over. While the Quivira party was on the plains, Tristán de Luna y Arellano had led the lion's share of the expedition back to Tiguex. From there, units from the expedition had made several short trips during the summer within the greater Río de Tiguex–Rio Grande Valley. Captain Velasco de Barrionuevo went north. He and his small detachment visited the Tewa-speaking pueblos near the junction of the Rio Grande and the Chama River, including Yuque Yunque, the pueblo later known as San Juan. There the expeditionaries saw many jars "full of choice shiny metal."[1] That observation apparently caused no sensation at the time, but, as will be seen later, it may have played a role in the choice of San Juan–Yuque Yunque as the first capital of the Spanish colony of Nuevo México when it was established in 1598.

Proceeding farther north, Barrionuevo's detachment revisited "Valladolid," or Taos Pueblo, which had been reconnoitered the previous year by Hernando de Alvarado and his company, shepherded by Bigotes. Beyond these tours of northern Rio Grande pueblos, the expedition made no more forays of reconnaissance. Rather, the expeditionaries under Luna y Arellano's command, after their return to Tiguex from the second *barranca*, occupied themselves with foraging food supplies and refitting lodgings, with, understandably, some anxiety about the coming winter. Evidently, the people of Tiguex successfully remained disengaged from the expedition as they, too, worked to stock up.

Just as Pedro de Castañeda de Nájera did in his narrative of the expedition, I take a break here from linear progression to assess what the

171

reconnaissance of the Coronado expedition revealed. In Castañeda de Nájera's narrative, this intermission, occupying Part 2 of the manuscript, was inserted to offer a candid appraisal of the populations of Señora, Cíbola, Tusayán, Tiguex, the buffalo plains, and Quivira as seen by an aspiring *encomendero*. Repeatedly, Castañeda de Nájera described those lands as having been too sparsely populated and their inhabitants too much consumed with bare subsistence to support the kind of tributary settlement envisioned by most sixteenth-century conquistadores.[2] He cataloged the characteristics of each major unit of population encountered by the expedition that recommended for or against its full incorporation into the Spanish orbit. Further, he highlighted those behaviors upon which a justification of conquest could be hung. In all these ways his report is very similar to those of Vázquez de Coronado, Alarcón, Jaramillo, and the author of the Relación del Suceso.

My focus here is on what these appraisals disclose about the expeditionaries themselves, as well as what can be deduced from their descriptions about the native peoples of Tierra Nueva. In addition to the settlements the expeditionaries saw and considered for possible colonization, I point out the peoples and landscapes they did *not* see and why they did not. What was missed or overlooked, and why, throws light on the motives and methods of the Coronado expedition and those of its indigenous guides.

Assessment of Tierra Nueva

From Culiacán to Petatlán and up the Sonora River valley as far as Suya, the expedition moved along well-beaten trails from one relatively populous settlement to the next, not far distant. Usually the numerous towns were spaced along many, relatively short river valleys. Although the populations were large, they did not offer conditions favorable for the establishment of *encomiendas*. In the first place, the people lived in impermanent structures roofed and walled with cane mats—in the Europeans' view, a sign of impoverishment. More importantly, the expeditionaries saw no signs that the indigenous communities produced commodities of high value to Europeans: no fine fabrics, no dyes, no spices, no precious metals, no gems other than turquoise that had been obtained from Cíbola. The people were all of that "same level."³ The expeditionaries heard reports of others of the same sort both to east and west of the road to Cíbola. The whole region gave the expeditionaries little hope of prosperous lives as tribute collectors. But in the event that a decision was made to conquer these "poor" peoples, despite their unpromising aspect, that action could be justified because, as the Spaniards saw it, many of them were "flagrant homosexuals." Indeed, many Native American societies, including those of the Sonora Valley and the Pueblos of the Rio Grande region, permitted openly homosexual behavior and even recognized a valuable role for homosexuals in their communities. Such a way of life was intolerable to Spanish Catholic expeditionaries.⁴

From the standpoint of attractiveness for colonization, the people the expeditionaries saw next, between Suya and Chichilticale, were even less satisfactory than those farther south. They were "the most uncivilized people of those that had been seen until then."⁵ Beyond there, some 20 leagues north of Chichilticale, even semipermanent settlements disappeared. As Vázquez de Coronado put it, "not a single Indian was found" until the expedition got to within four days' travel of Cíbola.⁶

The vaunted seven *ciudades* of Cíbola proved bitterly disillusioning, notwithstanding that Cíbola, on a European scale of civilized societies, clearly ranked above every other place the expeditionaries had seen since leaving Culiacán. But not even stone buildings, cotton clothing, bison hides, "turquoises, though not in the quantity [the reports] said," and "excellent granular salt that they bring from a lake one day's journey from here" could compensate in Old World eyes for Cíbola's small population.⁷ Had it been a hundred times larger, perhaps tribute in cotton fabrics and turquoise would have made for viable *encomiendas* for hundreds of expeditionaries. The few thousand Ashiwi, though, could not realistically support even a single *encomendero*.⁸

Cíbola salt might have been a profitable item of trade in a Spanish colonial network had there been a substantial market nearby or had transportation been easy and cheap. But neither of those conditions held. Nor was turquoise prized enough in the Spanish world to make it worth transporting over the long and hazardous route to the Ciudad de México and on to Europe. Turquoise was far less prized than emeralds, rubies, diamonds, pearls, and many other precious and semiprecious stones. As for bison hides, they were much too heavy and too little in demand during the first half of the sixteenth century to have much commercial value. As will be seen later, that was about to change so significantly that Juan Jaramillo, looking back in the 1560s, could see bison hides as the most valuable resource of Tierra Nueva.

Eastward from Cíbola was Acuco-Acoma, a *provincia* consisting of "only one small *ciudad* . . . where cotton is harvested."⁹ If Cíbola failed to inspire prospective *encomenderos*, then Acuco did even less. Tiguex and its neighboring *provincias* presented the densest concentration of people the expeditionaries were to see during their entire reconnaissance. Still, the people of the region numbered only in the tens of thousands. That population fell far short of the hundreds of thousands of inhabitants in communities in the Basin of Mexico and the equally populous cities of Asia. As a result, Tiguex, the greatest aggregation of people then living in what has become the American Southwest, did not suit the Europeans' plans.

The people of Tiguex lived primarily by farming, producing an abundance of corn. As members of the Coronado expedition were aware, corn was generally plentiful throughout temperate and subtropical America, where it was the most important staple food. Almost everyone grew it. Thus, it was not a sought-after and high-value trade item in the European scheme of things. The Tiguex, like the Ashiwi, did have "turquoises, of which there are a great many in that land," but again this was an abundance of petty merchandise.¹⁰ Throughout the middle Rio Grande Valley, the Tiguex and their neighbors produced "pottery glazed with lead and jars of consummate workmanship and very many shapes."¹¹ Such heavy, bulky goods, however, would be of little value in central Mexico or Spain, where, in any case, artisans already made beautiful ceramics.

Most telling is Castañeda de Nájera's remark that the Tiguex "are not people who have *tianguez* [markets]."¹² In other words, they were not great producers of trade commodities. Immense daily markets were one of the marvels that had thrilled Hernando Cortés and his followers in Tenochtitlan 20 years before, because they foretold lucrative futures for conquistadores based on *encomienda* tribute to be paid in a host of commodities. As I pointed out earlier, theirs was an ambition of long standing fueled by accounts of Asia such as Marco Polo's *Travels*, recently republished in Spain. Polo and his coauthor rhapsodized again and again about the myriad cities of Asia, such as Tabriz, now in Iran, where the people "live by trade and industry; for cloth of gold and silk is woven here in great quantity and of great value. The city is so favorably situated that it is a market for merchandise from India and Baghdad, from Mosul and Hormuz."[13]

Redeeming features of the Tiguex, in the view of Castañeda de Nájera, were that "there is no homosexuality among them, nor do they eat human flesh or sacrifice it."[14] Leaving aside whether these observations were accurate, they suggested to the expeditionaries an ease with which the Tiguex might be incorporated into a world of European-Christian sensibilities, a prospect of particular gratification to missionary friars and priests. But for lay members of the Coronado expedition, the lack of any substantial financial foundation upon which to erect a colonial structure was pivotal. The Tiguex, like all their antecedents back along the roads from Culiacán, seemed unlikely prospects for absorption into the imperial scheme.

As unsuitable for a tribute-based colony as it was, Tiguex still was the high water mark of possibility for the expedition. The peoples of the plains, the Querechos, Teyas, Quivirans, and people of Haraee, offered even less to ambitious Europeans. Their roaming mode of existence, reliance on hunting, and paucity of possessions ruled out their contributing much, if anything, to the "royal patrimony" or to the wealth and status of the king's minions. Their lack of permanent homes and their scant clothing marked the native people of the plains as uncivilized by European standards and therefore unsuited to life in Spanish society.

Stories persisted of large, sophisticated polities farther east of Quivira, but what the expeditionaries had seen as far as Quivira was unpromising. A pattern had developed, one of hopes fired and then dashed by the reality of societies focused on subsistence and little else. What value Tierra Nueva had, as envisioned by Castañeda de Nájera with 20 years' hindsight, arose from its service as a jumping off point for reconnaissance toward the west, toward Greater India.[15]

Assessment by Indian Allies

Almost all the written records created as a result of the Coronado expedition expressed or were founded upon European aspirations, ideals, and points of view. Yet two-thirds to three-fourths of those who participated in the expedition were not Europeans or even natives of the Old World. They were the American natives who traveled north, in large measure willingly, as adjuncts of the Spanish-led *entrada*. When they left their homes in the south, they, too, had expectations of what Tierra Nueva would be and how it would affect their lives. Are those expectations and their realization or frustration preserved today?

Direct evidence does not exist; no accounts of Tierra Nueva set down by or on behalf of indigenous members of the expedition have yet been located. But that does not leave historians without recourse. A few documents survive from the Coronado *entrada* and contemporaneous events involving natives of central and western Mexico that were composed by indigenous participants in the events themselves. They permit one to make judicious deductions and inferences about the indigenous Coronado expeditionaries.

There is, for instance, a nearly contemporaneous record of the departure from and return to the Ciudad de México of a group of Tenochca—the native people of Tenochtitlan—of unknown size that made up a portion of the Coronado expedition's corps of *indios amigos*.[16] Part of the significance of this pictorial manuscript, a summary history of the Tenochca known today as the Codex Aubin, is that it demonstrates the prominence that participation in the expedition held in Tenochca memory. The expedition was a major occurrence, on a par with the death of the Tenochca's principal leader.

Whether they considered participation in the *entrada* as service to be proud of, as a dismal disappointment, or as something else altogether is not immediately apparent from the entries in the codex devoted to the *entrada*. But the expedition to Tierra Nueva is linked in the codex with another event involving Tenochca warriors just a year and a half later, which strongly suggests that both events were seen as meritorious, as sources of pride, and as opportunities for royal reward. The entry for 1539 includes a prominent reference to the departure of a party of Tenochca with the Coronado expedition. The only event recorded for 1541 is the participation of Tenochca as allies of Viceroy Mendoza in the Mixtón War: "At this time [the Tenochca] conquered the people of Xochipillan."¹⁷ The subsequent entry in the codex, for 1542, records the return to the Ciudad de México of both parties of Tenochca, together. Pride in the two instances of service to the Spanish viceroy, and expectation of reward and preferment as a result, surely dominated the reasons for their inclusion in the historical codex.

The Tenochca leaders and their people, then, participated in the expedition in large measure to solidify or advance the leaders' and the community's status and position in the evolving Spanish colonial order. That is precisely how the principal leader of a native contingent expressed the result of his having led his people into battle after battle during the Mixtón War. He quoted Viceroy Mendoza as having told him at the conclusion of the fighting, "I hold you in high regard and have great affection for you because you have been here at the end of the battle, and I must concede to you everything you may want. And I must honor and favor [your] community. Thus, you, don Francisco, shall be governor, *alguacil*, and *corregidor*."¹⁸ In the same way, many Tenochca and other indigenous participants undoubtedly viewed the expedition to Tierra Nueva in a favorable light.

Some of the *indios amigos* had cause for exulting in their success in one-on-one combat while in Tierra Nueva. Whether their opponents were deemed sufficiently lofty in status to gain for the expedition's allies any elevation in warrior status is uncertain, but probably they were. And some of the Indian allies, notably the relatively small number who remained behind the expedition to live in Tierra Nueva, saw the Pueblo world as an attractive and genial home.¹⁹

What Was Not Seen

Those native allies of the Coronado expedition who stayed in Cíbola, Tiguex, and other places in Tierra Nueva must have soon discovered how little they had known, as members of the expedition, about their prospective new homes. As for the non-native expeditionaries, large and glaring gaps remained in their knowledge of the region they traversed, too. That was in part because the expedition's travel and its resulting field of vision were restricted to the communities and the main-traveled routes to and along which it was guided. By no means did the expedition exhaustively cover the terrain of Tierra Nueva, a fact the expeditionaries themselves acknowledged. Castañeda de Nájera, for example, when writing about the Great Plains, commented that "it may be that [the plains] were crossed somewhat transversely or obliquely, from which cause it appears that there is greater extent of land than if [they] were crossed through the middle."[20]

In addition, the expedition almost always depended on the cooperation of indigenous guides and interpreters. Otherwise, it was blind and deaf and not about to wander aimlessly off. When guides chose to ignore or bypass or conceal communities or features, the expeditionaries never suspected they existed. None of the surviving contemporaneous documents indicates, for instance, that the expedition visited, saw, or even heard about the Tompiro-Salinas pueblos that then flourished in the Estancia and northern Tularosa Basins, east of the Rio Grande and southeast of Tiguex.[21] This ignorance meant that the expeditionaries were also unaware of the series of salt lakes in the Estancia Basin, which the Pueblos had exploited for centuries and which were to be recognized as a major resource once a Spanish colony was successfully established in New Mexico. Further, although members of the expedition inquired of various native people about Totonteac and Marata—places extolled by Marcos de Niza's informants—they apparently made no physical attempt to verify the existence of those allegedly populous and prosperous communities after their guides told them that neither place matched the friar's report.

Given the frequent attention paid to turquoise in fray Marcos de Niza's *relación* and the mention it received in other documents of the expedition, it is surprising that the expeditionaries had no knowledge of the turquoise mines that were then being worked by the Pueblos in the Cerrillos Hills east of the Rio Grande, at the northern edge of the Galisteo Basin. This was true despite repeated traffic by expeditionaries back and forth across the basin, almost within eyesight of the mines. Similarly, the newcomers were in the dark about the locations of sources of lead from which the Pueblos extracted material used in glazing ceramics.[22] This pattern of ignorance of mineral resources suggests a concerted, coordinated, and successful effort by Pueblo people of various linguistic and political affiliations to keep such information from members of the Coronado expedition.

Besides these cases of intentionally produced ignorance, the expeditionaries suffered the accidental myopia typical of travelers who visit a place only once. They easily transformed the conditions they observed briefly into what they presumed were the prevailing norms for Tierra Nueva. The two extraordinarily harsh winters the expedition endured in Tiguex provoked the exaggerated statement by the author of the Relación del Suceso that "the reason for these [Tiguex] pueblos being this type of settlement is, I believe, the great cold."[23] With experience of the weather in other years, the writer could just as easily have written that the pueblos were built to protect their residents from the searing heat. But for members of the Coronado expedition, Tiguex was forever a land of extreme cold, a perception of which the Tiguex themselves probably had no interest in disabusing them.

In much the same way, the expeditionaries experienced Tierra Nueva during a lengthy spell of greatly above-normal precipitation. They had no way of knowing that the opposite extreme, prolonged and severe drought, was equally likely. Indeed, had the *entrada* been attempted during one of the region's most extreme droughts, the party likely would never have reached Cíbola and the rest of interior Tierra Nueva, for lack of water and forage.

The hostility that characterized most extended relations between the expeditionaries and native communities caused the Indians to flee their homes for more distant and secure refuges. The expeditionaries, consequently, found themselves isolated and had minimal contact with the Pueblos and other indigenous peoples of Tierra Nueva. What contact they did have was often violent or took place in carefully controlled interchanges with messengers and emissaries. Therefore, central aspects of Pueblo life such as religious ceremonies and trade with neighbors and distant partners went unwitnessed by and remained utterly unknown to the newcomers. Not a single description exists in the surviving documentary record of the Coronado expedition of the Pueblos' busy annual cycle of masked dances or of the conspicuous, elaborately costumed dancers themselves. Evidently, members of the expedition did not see them. Nor is any mention made of foreign traders, either singly or in parties, visiting the pueblos or transporting goods to and from the Rio Grande region, where the expedition was in residence for more than 12 full months.

The contemporaneous documents offer a few descriptions of aspects of American native life and culture gained through the expeditionaries' brief glimpses. For example, there are physical descriptions of Pueblo kivas, or *estufas,* as they are called in the documents.[24] But the documents provide no insights into the important, year-round activities that took place in those special spaces, suggesting that the expeditionaries' experience of kivas came from observation of abandoned pueblos, supplemented by shreds of information from Pueblo captives. Similarly, a detailed description by Castañeda de Nájera of corn grinding among the Pueblos may well derive from observation of captives who were put to work preparing food for the expeditionaries, rather than from familiarity with fully functioning Pueblo communities.[25] This seems particularly likely in that other common, traditionally female tasks such as pottery making and masculine activities such as weaving are not described at all, probably because in their limited contact with Pueblos the expeditionaries never witnessed pottery being made or cloth being woven.

In short, members of the expedition had only a narrow and restricted view of the land of Tierra Nueva and, most importantly, of the people who inhabited it, the king's potential vassals. Expeditionaries' attitudes toward and decisions about the people of the region were circumscribed by the physical limits of what they saw, by what their guides and other members of the native communities permitted them to see, and by the boundaries of their own interests and curiosity. What they saw and did not see while in Tierra Nueva was profoundly influenced by their focus on the possible existence of large, sophisticated societies that were thought to be producers of commodities typical of Asia.

Likewise, American Natives

Such tunnel vision, of course, is part of the human condition and not a disability peculiar to sixteenth-century Europeans. The indigenous people of Tierra Nueva were subject to a similarly truncated view of the expeditionaries. The Coronado expedition presented to them an anomalous, artificially unbalanced society made up predominantly of young men. To all appearances, it was a community almost devoid of elders, a community incapable of reproducing itself, lacking as it did a sufficient number of women and including very few young children, especially girls. As a consequence, the expedition seemed to be without any but the most rudimentary domesticity. It looked to be a group incapable of feeding itself, except with meat, bent on forcing its way across the continent for unfathomable reasons.

The more constructive aspects of Old World cultures were almost completely hidden from the Indians of Tierra Nueva in what they saw of the Coronado expedition. Even the Franciscan priests and friars accompanying the expedition made little benign impression on the native population, having little opportunity for contact with indigenous people other than as auxiliary support to the armed majority of the expedition. The expedition seemed a malevolent force to be hidden from, chased away, or, if one dared, enlisted briefly in one's own cause.

One effect of such a view was that Pueblo and other native groups rejected and destroyed elements of expeditionary culture and material, even when they might have been of use and value in the Indian world. Horses, for example, were killed rather than employed for transportation or as pack animals. There is no evidence—historical, archaeological, or in traditional native accounts—that at this time Indians took advantage of the docility and manageability of sheep, goats, and cattle, either. They were simply slaughtered immediately for food or destroyed as an enemy's possessions.

Partial knowledge on all sides of the constellation of Old World natives and natives of Tierra Nueva made for a signal case of what James Lockhart has rightly called "double mistaken identity."[26] Probably no other outcome was realistically possible. The parties were immediately polarized, with little reason to exchange much information about each other or to allow each other to acquire such knowledge independently. In the absence of more peaceful contact of long duration, both sides, from Old World and New, were doomed to opaqueness to each other.

Report to the Viceroy

Such incomplete knowledge was hopelessly deficient for governing relations between Indian people and Old World natives. It was adequate, nonetheless, for answering the narrow question, "Did there exist in Tierra Nueva large civilized polities that produced goods of high value to Europeans?" When he reached Tiguex after the long round-trip to Quivira, Vázquez de Coronado immediately set about answering that question formally for the king.

As he wrote to Carlos I, "I returned to this *provincia* [Tiguex] to look after the safety of the company I [had] sent [back] to it and to make a report to Your Majesty about what that land is."[27] After a year and a half on the march, this was his summation: "The best [place] I have found is this Río de Tiguex on which I am [now] located. The settlements along it are not [such] as to allow [Spaniards] to settle [here]."[28]

By October 20 the letter was finished and dispatched south by courier.[29] It confirmed the pessimistic promise of the captain general's letter from Cíbola a little more than a year earlier. Even in the best part of Tierra Nueva there were no people through whom "God, Our Lord, might be served and Your Majesty's royal patrimony might be enlarged."[30] ■

CHAPTER 17

Disintegration and Withdrawal

Evidently by prearrangement, as the end of September 1541 approached, the *maestre de campo* Tristán de Luna y Arellano expected the imminent return of Vázquez de Coronado and his Quivira company. Their homecoming would lead them by way of Cicuique. The people there were still seething from the expedition's ill treatment of their leaders the year before, and the returnees' passage from Quivira might elicit an attack from the pueblo. To forestall that possibility, Luna y Arellano, with some 40 men-at-arms, proceeded to Cicuique.

As anticipated, warriors came out to confront the expeditionaries. A four-day skirmish followed, during which several Pueblo leaders were killed. One wonders whether Bigotes and the *cacique* were in the fight and among the casualties. With the people of Cicuique bottled up in their pueblo, Luna y Arellano and his company waited nearby for the arrival of the captain general and his companions.[1]

It was not long afterward that messengers from the Quivira company arrived. Vázquez de Coronado was on his way, only a few days behind the messengers, and he appeared in due time. His reunion with Luna y Arellano's company and, several days later, with the remainder of the expedition at Coofor was cause for both discouragement and renewed optimism. Quivira itself had not fulfilled its promise, but there was word of other possibilities farther east. After a second winter along the Rio Grande, the captain general vowed, he would lead the entire troop back to Quivira and beyond. That would be an easier task than it had been in 1541 because the route to Quivira was now well known. There would be no great detour toward La Florida this time.[2]

The young plains native named Xabe, the companion of El Turco

183

who had been sent back to Coofor from the *barranca* with the mass of the expeditionaries, fueled hope for 1542. When he "understood that [the general's company] had found nothing, he became sad and dumbfounded, insisting, in such a way that he convinced many [people], that [the result of the general's trip] was such because the general had not penetrated the land farther into the interior."³ Many of the expeditionaries were persuaded by Xabe's unambiguous adherence to his stories. The great cities of India and Cathay still lay ahead. After all, the natives who followed the bison were Turkomans, or very much like them, were they not?

Once the captain general was back in Coofor, he took up the task of writing to the king and viceroy a regularly scheduled letter to report on what had transpired since his last letter in April. It is obvious from this letter of October 1541 that he still seethed over what he and the other expeditionaries saw as Marcos de Niza's deception. He wrote: "Since I reached the *provincia* of Cíbola (to which the viceroy of Nueva España sent me in Your Majesty's name) and saw that there were none of the things fray Marcos [had] told about, I have endeavored to reconnoiter this land [for] two hundred leagues and more around Cíbola."⁴ He described the people of the plains as unsuitable to support a Spanish town. Even the reports of what lay farther on were not enticing. He wrote: "[The report] I was able to obtain is that there was no gold or other metal in that whole land. The rest they gave me reports about are nothing but small *pueblos*. And in many of them [the people] do not plant crops, nor do they have houses, except [shelters] made of hides and grass straw."⁵ The captain general nevertheless gave no indication that he would give up the search.

Vázquez de Coronado's appraisal of Tierra Nueva would later be augmented and seconded by his *maestre de campo* García López de Cárdenas, who, instead of retracing the course to Quivira in the spring with the expedition, would be returning to the Ciudad de México and from there to Spain. A message had arrived by courier for López de Cárdenas informing him that his elder brother and head of the family had died, leaving to him a considerable patrimony. He would journey to Madrid to assume control over the family's noble estate. López de Cárdenas was doubly excused from further duty as field commander because he had also dislocated his shoulder in a fall that summer on the plains. The injury had not healed well, and it incapacitated him for the rest of his life. While at home in Spain, López de Cárdenas would meet personally with the king to give him a first-person report of events of the expedition.

The message for the *maestre de campo* arrived shortly after Vázquez de Coronado reached Coofor in September. It came with Pedro de Tovar and a company of men he was bringing from San Gerónimo, the expedition's supply base on the Río Sonora. Tovar had expected to arrive earlier and to find Coofor vacant because the expedition would have moved on to Quivira. When weather and supplies permitted, he had expected to follow the others onto the plains, guided by crosses they were to have left behind. Now, he and his reinforcements would have to winter over at Coofor or one of the other vacant Tiguex pueblos, awaiting, with their expeditionary companions, traveling weather come spring 1542.

A Second Hostile Winter

While the expedition had been absent from the Rio Grande Valley, "some pueblos had . . . been resettled, [but] they were immediately again abandoned out of fear" when the expedition unexpectedly returned.[6] The Tiguex people had also planted some of their fields, and the expeditionaries now appropriated the crops for their use. As expedition member Cristóbal de Escobar testified in 1544, "some of the same pueblos that [the Spaniards] had burned and laid waste to had been repaired and [the Spaniards] gutted them again, both to make use of the wood and to get the corn and [other] supplies [the Indians] had left buried there."[7]

Even so, delegations from the expedition were dispatched to confer with whatever Tiguex people they could find, in order to lure them back, presumably as sources of food and clothing for the expedition or to satisfy royal mandates concerning benign treatment of natives. None would return. They rebuffed the overtures of the occupiers and despoilers of their homes. More than that, they attacked expeditionaries when they found them alone or at a distance from their quarters. As a result, the winter of 1541–42, though it lacked the full-scale warfare of the previous winter, was filled with tension and animosity on both sides. Because they feared traveling any distance to obtain fuel wood, the expeditionaries continued to demolish the empty pueblos, scavenging them for rafters and roofing material to burn.⁸

Once again the winter weather was fiercely cold and snowy.⁹ The supply of bison meat and bison hides that the expeditionaries had stocked during their weeks of hunting at the *barranca* in the plains, combined with caches of Pueblo corn they were able to pilfer, meant that their second winter in Tiguex was less stringent than the first. But they had other problems besides the continuing hostility of their Pueblo neighbors and a scarcity of food and clothing. Infectious disease swept through the occupied pueblos, perhaps carried by reinforcements or couriers from San Gerónimo and points farther south, where contemporaneous documents show the sickness was already running rampant. "In the province of Tiguex," Vázquez de Coronado's attorney later maintained, "the horses were dying and the soldiers were falling sick."¹⁰ The malady has not been identified, but it was lethal for a number of the expeditionaries, including a man named Juan Jiménez and his close friend Jorge Báez, both of whom succumbed in the early months of 1542.¹¹

Although he seems to have avoided contracting the illness that was circulating through the expedition, the captain general was brought close to death as a result of a freak accident during this period. "What happened," remembered Castañeda de Nájera years later, "was that on one day of celebration the general went out to enjoy himself on horseback, as he was in the habit of doing. He was on a strong horse, and his *criados* had put on a new cinch which, with the passage of time, must have been rotten. While [the general was] racing side by side with Captain don Rodrigo Maldonado it burst in the midst of the race. [The general] ended up falling to the side don Rodrigo was on, and he ran over [Vázquez de Coronado]. The horse ended up striking him in the head with its hoof."¹² As had happened after the head injury at Cíbola in 1540, the captain general suffered a period of unconsciousness. Recuperation lasted much longer this time, and his recovery was even less certain.¹³

Uprising at Suya

In the midst of this swarm of difficulties for the expedition, momentous news arrived from San Gerónimo, now at its third location, an area of indigenous settlement in the Sonora Valley known as Suya. García López de Cárdenas, en route home to Spain, had reached the supply base only to find it deserted and laid waste. The Indians of the region, in what is now extreme northern Sonora, had effectively blocked the route south. Unwilling to attempt to slip through hostile territory of unknown length, and duty-bound to inform Vázquez de Coronado of the dangerous turn of events in Suya, López de Cárdenas and his companions hastily retraced their route to Coofor. There, the captain general was slowly regaining his health.

When the former *maestre de campo* delivered his report to the bedridden Vázquez de Coronado, he "was so affected by it that he fell ill again."[14] Few details were then available, but it appeared that all the residents of San Gerónimo, as well as their horses and other livestock, had been killed. Only months later were the expeditionaries able to piece together an account of what had happened. The 1544 testimony of expedition member Melchior Pérez offers a typical version of the fateful events in Suya. "The reason that those Indians rebelled," swore Pérez, "was that a [man named Diego de] Alcaraz, who was a captain, committed many outrages against them, taking provisions against their will and seizing their wives and daughters in order to have sexual relations with them. For this reason they rose up, rebelled, and killed Alcaraz and other Spaniards."[15] Alcaraz had been left in charge of San Gerónimo when Melchior Díaz left, under orders, on his fatal attempt to rendezvous with Hernando de Alarcón and his ships in 1540.

It turned out that not all the residents of San Gerónimo had been killed. Some had escaped during the Indians' attack, and others had mutinied and fled south before the uprising. It was from some of those survivors that Castañeda de Nájera must later have gleaned the details of fighting at the supply base, which he committed to paper in the 1560s:

> Diego de Alcaraz, who had stayed [in San Gerónimo] with a few sick people, could not maintain himself there, even though he wanted to. [That is] because of danger from the deadly poison

the natives are accustomed to prepare in that area. [The natives], sensing the Spaniards' weakness, no longer allowed themselves to be treated as they used to be . . . One night [the Spaniards] unexpectedly saw fires, which were not usual or customary. This caused them to double the guard. But because during the whole night they noticed nothing [else], they became careless at dawn. Their enemies entered the *pueblo* so silently that they were not seen until they were going about killing and robbing.[16]

As indicated by the captain general's relapse after hearing of the apparent annihilation of San Gerónimo, the shock of that news was powerful at Coofor. There were personal losses for many, including Vázquez de Coronado himself. Among the 30 to 60 Europeans who had evidently been killed was the uncle of the captain general's wife, Diego Gutiérrez de la Caballería, who had served as the expedition's treasurer.[17] Other expeditionaries lost friends, relatives, business partners, and other associates.

The news of the fate of the expedition members left at San Gerónimo also held immediate and dire ramifications for the entire enterprise. With that supply base gone, the chance of obtaining additional food, clothing, and ammunition from Nueva España was foreclosed. Prospects for the expedition in the coming year were bleak, given the likely impossibility of acquiring corn and other agricultural commodities from the people of Tiguex or their neighbors. The expedition had managed to scrounge enough food in 1541, but without waging all-out war against the Pueblos, securing sufficient stores for the coming year would be a hopeless task. From the moment of the destruction of San Gerónimo and the slaughter and scattering of its defenders, the Coronado expedition was untenable.

The Mixtón War

Adding a formula for catastrophe to the already perilous position of the expedition was the great conflagration of the Mixtón War, hundreds of miles south of Suya in Nueva Galicia. The Indians of the *barrancas* and *peñoles* of interior Nueva Galicia, known as Caxcanes, had been nominally brought under Spanish colonial rule in the early 1530s. There followed years of skirmishes between them and their supposed European overlords. Then, in 1541, the natives of the whole Caxcán region rose up against the interlopers. Some people blamed the departure of the Coronado expedition for setting off the violence, and indeed, the removal of a significant number of fighting men from the region as participants in the expedition might well have opened an opportunity for the uprising.

At first, Lieutenant Governor Cristóbal de Oñate and many of the other colonists failed to appreciate the scale of the uprising. Oñate dispatched very small armed parties to bring what were thought to be minor renegade bands to heel. Instead, the tens of thousands of raging Caxcanes mauled the little punitive squadrons, killing many men-at-arms. The Caxcanes even besieged the new city of Guadalajara. Pedro de Alvarado, about to launch a fleet in accordance with the partnership he had entered into the year before with the viceroy, was petitioned for help. He complied, taking the crews from his ships and posting guard companies along his route as he proceeded to Guadalajara. He seemed certain that he and his men would make short shrift of the uprising. When they reached the Caxcán stronghold of Peñol de Nochistlán, though, they found resistance so fierce that they were forced to retreat. As Alvarado's shattered company retraced the road to Guadalajara in late June 1541, a disastrous accident befell the *adelantado*. A horse upslope from him lost its footing and rolled downhill, crushing Alvarado. He lived for only a few days.

Notified of the disaster by fast courier, Viceroy Mendoza determined to go against the Caxcanes himself, with massive force. Spanish presence in all of Nueva Galicia was at peril. If the Spaniards were expelled from that province, the Caxcanes' success might inspire other uprisings elsewhere, producing who could say what consequences for Nueva España as a whole. In January 1542, Mendoza, with a troop of some 500 Europeans and 10,000 Indian allies from central Mexico, left the viceregal capital with the plan of engaging the Caxcán strongholds methodically, one after another.[18] That campaign and its successful outcome, after months of fighting, were completely unknown to the members of the Coronado expedition at the time López de Cárdenas returned to Coofor with word of the demise of

San Gerónimo. The expeditionaries undoubtedly were aware, though, of the Alvarado debacle at Nochistlán, about which they would have heard the preceding fall.

A Dilemma

In tandem, the reports about San Gerónimo and Nochistlán were dire. They meant that the Coronado expedition was stranded many hundreds of miles from possible relief, and aid in any form was unlikely to arrive in the near term. Added to that, Vázquez de Coronado was still governor of Nueva Galicia, which was now threatened with extinction. His duties were divided. He was responsible to all the expedition's investors, including his wife's family, for prosecuting the *entrada* in Tierra Nueva, yet he was also under obligation to the Spanish king to defend the province of his governorship.

Likewise, many other expeditionaries were pulled in two directions. On the one hand, a chance, however shrinking, of establishing manorial lives in Tierra Nueva remained. On the other, relatives and friends, as well as *encomiendas* and other livelihoods for some, were in danger in Nueva Galicia. To persevere in a hostile and so far disappointing Tierra Nueva or to counter the Caxcán uprising by returning en masse to Nueva Galicia—that was the question that confronted the members of the Coronado expedition in the early months of 1542.

The majority of expeditionaries supported a return south. The captain general received a petition to that effect from the men-at-arms. And the captains and other prominent members of the expedition "gave their formal opinion, [which was] that they should return to Nueva España since nothing of wealth had been found and there was no settlement in what had been reconnoitered where *repartimientos* could be made to the whole expedition."[19] Vázquez de Coronado shared this opinion.

But the group was not unanimous. People whose prospects in Nueva España were dim, such as the peddler Alonso Sánchez, his wife, Francisca de Hozes, and their son, demanded that they be allowed to stay at Coofor and await possible reinforcements and resupply. Hozes and Sánchez faced only debt if they returned to the Ciudad de México. They evidently preferred to take the chance that a marvelously teeming and wealthy place would yet appear than to be plunged into immediate poverty if they left Tierra Nueva. Rumors circulated among their faction of 60 or so that the captain general was swayed by strictly personal motives to abandon the expedition. He longed for his wife, they said. Then too, according to the disgruntled expeditionaries, he feared the realization of an astrologer's prediction that he would "suffer a fall from which he could not recover. This mental image of his death gave him the desire to go back to where he had a wife and children, to die."[20]

The captain general insisted that the expedition remain together and not fragment into vulnerable smaller components. Those who desired to remain in Tierra Nueva still pressed their point. Finally, according to Francisca de Hozes's later testimony, Vázquez de Coronado "confined [her husband and others] and threatened them with the gallows because they wanted to stay."[21]

Another group, the Franciscan friars, was beyond the captain general's control. Their fervent aspiration to convert all the natives of Tierra Nueva or be martyred in the attempt was undiminished by the long odds against their success at conversion or by warfare along the road back to their ecclesiastical superiors in the Ciudad de México. Fray Juan de Padilla and fray Luis de Úbeda simply announced that they would stay among the Indians of Tierra Nueva whether the lay expedition did or not. As authority for their decision, they adduced the directive and permission of their provincial, Marcos de Niza. Vázquez de Coronado tried to dissuade them from their resolve, but they would not be deterred. Reluctantly, the captain general acceded to their unilateral plan.

The End of the Expedition

About the first of April 1542, in the Julian calendar, the expeditionaries packed up their remaining goods, equipment, and provisions, loaded them onto horses and mules, vacated Coofor and the other pueblos they had been living in, and turned their backs on the Rio Grande Valley and the entire Pueblo world. A week or so later they were in Cíbola for the last time. When they left there, heading south, "for two or three days' journey the natives [of Cíbola] never stopped following the expedition, behind the rear guard, in order to pick up a little of the baggage or a few servants... This was learned from some [of the servants] who refused to go with [the people of Cíbola] but were constantly urged and begged by them [to go with them]. Even so, they persuaded a few people, and [there were] others who had remained of their own free will."²² Of the *indios amigos*, as many as 200 may have stayed at Cíbola and other pueblos.²³ About 40 years later, several Indian men who had participated in the Coronado expedition were found still living at Hawikku in Cíbola, and there may have been others, suggesting that a sizable group had remained behind in 1542.²⁴

Loss of Indian allies was only the beginning of the attrition the expedition suffered as it made its way back to Nueva España. "During the ten days it took to reach Cíbola more than thirty [of the horses] died. [That is] because there was not a day when two or three or more did not die. And after that, until [the expedition] reached Culiacán, a great many of them died, which was something that had not happened during the entire [rest of] the journey."²⁵ What was affecting the horses is uncertain, but the sequence of deaths suggests a disease rather than poisonous forage. At this point, it is impossible to say whether the equine disease was related to the malady that had killed Juan Jiménez and other expeditionaries at Coofor and was about to kill his friend Jorge Báez. Evidently, the disease ran its course before many more days.

Once again the expedition crossed the 15-day unsettled area between Cíbola and Chichilticale, following the same route as on the northbound *entrada*. That route had been used by individuals and units from the expedition a number of times during the previous two years in the course of communication between Coofor and San Gerónimo in its various locations. Then, two days' travel south of Chichilticale, the withdrawing force met a northbound company under the leadership of Juan Gallego, who had been sent to the viceroy from Cíbola nearly two years earlier, in August 1540. He and his companions had just rampaged their way up the Río Sonora Valley, riding at breakneck speed and taking native settlements by surprise, "killing, laying waste, and setting fire."²⁶

Gallego's company was shocked and angered to find the expedition pulling out of Tierra Nueva. It forced a halt for consideration of "establishing a settlement somewhere around there until a report of what was happening was delivered to the viceroy."[27] According to Castañeda de Nájera, though, the rank-and-file members of the expedition were so set on returning south that nothing came of Gallego's agitation. With the addition of Gallego's small force, the entire expedition headed back into the area he had just savaged.

Unsurprisingly, the people of Suya and Señora-Sonora had been aroused by the recent passage of the Gallego company. They repeatedly attacked the southbound expedition. Expeditionary Alonso Sánchez testified later that "on the way back he saw that those towns and provinces had erupted in war."[28] His wife, Francisca de Hozes, added that the natives of the Sonora area "would have killed don García López de Cárdenas [with whom she and Alonso were now traveling] and those who went with him, if they had not turned back and gotten reinforcements from another captain who was coming close behind."[29] At Corazones, however, things were calm. At a stop in Batuco, not mentioned on the northbound trip, "Indian allies from the valley of Los Corazones came to the camp in order to see the general, like [the] friends they always were."[30] Because of the expedition's large size, it traversed the *tierra de guerra*, or land of war, relatively unscathed.

When the expedition reached Culiacán, it was back in Vázquez de Coronado's own jurisdiction. The indigenous population was at peace for the time being. Some expeditionaries had shown disaffection with the captain general before they reached this outpost of Spanish control. Now, what control he had previously exercised over the force evaporated. People of all stations and all ethnicities began dropping out. Among at least 15 men who remained at Culiacán was the eventual chronicler Castañeda de Nájera.[31] The rest of the way, "the general traveled along, everywhere leaving people who refused to follow him."[32]

Although he was reportedly still in poor health, the captain general stopped off at Compostela, the capital of his governorship of Nueva Galicia, where he and Juan de Zaldívar led an armed party to put down a native uprising nearby. Perhaps he exaggerated his incapacity resulting from the head injuries suffered in Tierra Nueva, playing it up when it suited him, as Castañeda de Nájera claimed. Vázquez de Coronado arrived in the Ciudad de México "with fewer than a hundred men," counting only the European men-at-arms.[33] There he met face to face with Antonio de Mendoza, who himself had just returned from Nueva Galicia after putting a bloody end to the Mixtón War. According to Castañeda de Nájera, the captain general "was not well received" by the viceroy.[34] The two remained friends, however, a relationship later recognized and taken advantage of by the *cabildo*, or city council, of the Ciudad de México.

Vázquez de Coronado made a formal report of the course and outcome of the expedition, presumably in writing, although no such document has been seen in modern times. ■

CHAPTER 18

UPSHOT

It is difficult to see the Coronado expedition as anything but a failure for its participants, and none of the expeditionaries themselves saw it otherwise at the time. Nor can it be convincingly portrayed as other than a disaster for nearly all the native people with whom it interacted. Equally certain, occasional individuals benefited, thrived, and found their lives improved in the environment of the expedition and its contacts with Native American societies.

Rarely were the goals and aspirations that drove the expeditionaries achieved. To begin with, and most importantly, the large, prosperous, "civilized" communities that were the expedition's strongest magnet simply never materialized. Many rumors and stories circulated that such places existed, beginning with fray Marcos de Niza's written report and oral statements. There was Cíbola, of course, the expedition's original destination. But it was not alone, so the reports went; there were also Marata, Totonteac, Tusayán, Acus, Tiguex, and finally Quivira. Each in turn was revealed to be tiny in comparison with the expeditionaries' expectations. Nor did any of them produce the kinds of high-value goods that would have made Spanish settlement worth the effort. To be satisfactory, one or more of those storied places would have had to be populated by hundreds of thousands, even millions, of artisans producing silks or other luxury fabrics, spices, exquisite porcelains, rare dyes, gemstones or pearls, wrought silver or gold, or other exotic, undreamed-of wares.

With respect to Quivira, the writer of the Relación del Suceso phrased his appraisal of its mirage this way: "From some Indians who were found at this pueblo of Cicuique, Francisco Vázquez obtained a report which, if it were true, was [about] the richest thing that has been found in the

195

Indias... Afterwards it appeared certain, however, to have been the devil who was speaking."¹

In October 1541, Vázquez de Coronado himself summed up what he had seen: "The best [place] I have found is this Río de Tiguex on which I am [now] located. The settlements along it are not [such] as to allow [Spaniards] to settle [here]."² In addition to Tiguex's relatively small population—certainly fewer than 10,000 people—it was much too far from any ocean port to make trade in its heavy, petty products such as corn and cotton *mantas* practicable. Castañeda de Nájera's assessment of all of Tierra Nueva was unvarnished: "Nothing of wealth had been found and there was no settlement in what had been reconnoitered where *repartimientos* could be made to the whole expedition."³ It was as simple as that. Lives of ease and honor would be impossible in that cold northern land of scant settlement and subsistence livelihoods augmented with trade in correspondingly cheap goods.

The Franciscan friars fared no better than the lay expeditionaries in fulfilling their dreams. While with the full expedition, they were told of and occasionally saw natives of Tierra Nueva, but the friars almost never had access to those people in order to bring them into the Christian fold. Repeatedly, the indigenous people of Tierra Nueva employed the defensive tactic of flight. They vacated their homes, leaving them for the time being to the expedition, and fortified themselves in rugged country and on nearly impregnable mesas. They waited out the newcomers, and eventually the newcomers left. As a consequence, the few Pueblos and even fewer Ópatas baptized by the friars came from among prisoners taken in battle. There was no opportunity to raise crosses and chapels in the plazas of pueblos. There were no great open-air sermons or burgeoning catechism classes. There was only a relative handful of converts, and their fidelity to the faith was always in doubt because of the compulsion they were under as captives.

The two friars who stayed behind in Tierra Nueva may have made no converts but did earn the palm of martyrdom, for both were killed within months, if not weeks. Only slight documentary evidence exists concerning their deaths. Castañeda de Nájera reported that the people of

Quivira "killed the friar [Juan de Padilla] because he wanted to go to the *provincia* of the Guas who were their enemies."⁴ Fray Luis simply vanished and was assumed to have been killed by people from Cicuique, who had little reason for sympathy with a former member of the expedition. If the arrival of God's kingdom on earth depended on the success of fray Juan and fray Luis's conversion work, then it would have to wait. The millennium was not yet.

From the imperial vantage of the Spanish royal court, the results of the Coronado expedition were meager. Some knowledge of the land mass of the Indies had been gained, however imprecise it may have been and however much it was subsequently distorted and confused in Europe. It was apparent after the Coronado and Soto expeditions that in the latitudes where they had traveled, the land was thousands of miles across. In that vast extent there seemed to be no society of the opulence and size of the Mexica and Inca states. And even if Asia were geographically continuous with Cíbola, it was still a long way distant.

Disappointing though this negative information may have been, it was largely beyond the control of the expeditionaries. Or was it? If they had just turned left rather than right from the Río Grande, as Castañeda de Nájera was later to suggest, would they soon have entered Greater India? Did they do all they could to find that out? The answer to that question was clearly "no." Perhaps worse yet was the fact that the expedition had even failed to establish an advance base from which exploration toward the Orient could more easily be carried out. The expeditionaries had settled none of the land they had seen and traversed. Therefore, they had not conquered. As the Spanish saying of the time went, "*no poblar es no conquistar*"—not to settle is not to conquer. Cortés's former secretary López de Gómara wrote that "he who does not populate does not conquer, and if there is no conquest, the aborigines cannot be Christianized; therefore, the goal of conquest should be to populate."⁵

Less obvious to Spanish authorities was that the return of the Tierra Nueva expedition in 1542 swelled the Spanish population of the Culiacán area. There, the discouraged expeditionaries were attracted by indications of ores of precious metals that had been located while they were in Tierra

Nueva. Certainly, many former expeditionaries were now less sanguine about the possibilities of tribute in ready-made, sumptuous goods and more receptive to ideas of laborious and chancy extraction of raw materials. Among those who settled at Culiacán were the future chronicler Pedro de Castañeda de Nájera and at least 14 other former expeditionaries. This did much to reverse the trend that Vázquez de Coronado had lamented as governor when he found in 1538 that Culiacán was being abandoned.⁶

As for the lay members of the expedition who went along prepared to ply their habitual trades or who invested in goods and livestock to sell to their fellow expeditionaries, they, too, profited little. Melchior Pérez, for example, explained almost ten years later:

> I took on the expedition more than a thousand head of livestock (pigs, sheep, and rams) and seven horses (four of which cost eight hundred *pesos de minas* and the rest, ninety *pesos*). [I took] two *ladino* Blacks (for one of whom four hundred gold *pesos* were offered to me). [And I took] many other attendants (both men-at-arms and servants) and other things necessary for war . . . *Maestre de campo* don García López took the livestock from me in order to feed the expeditionary force at Culiacán (because it lacked [food]). And the Blacks fled from me in the *tierra de guerra*, where they were never seen again . . . as a result of having spent all [this] I ended up in debt for more than five hundred *pesos*.⁷

Beyond the disappointed tradesmen and entrepreneurs who had hoped to make a living or turn a profit from the expedition, nearly every one of the 368 known European men-at-arms had anticipated recouping and even earning a gain on the investment he had made in outfitting and supplying himself for the enterprise. That proved impossible. The little tribute extracted from the people of Cíbola and Tiguex, as well as the goods such as bison hides and provisions such as corn commandeered along the expedition's route, was consumed in subsistence. There was no surplus to share out among the enlisted expeditionaries, most of whom had borrowed the funds they had expended in preparation for the journey.

Again and again during the years following return of the expedition to Nueva España, its former members petitioned the king for recompense of their service, citing the impoverishment into which the expedition had thrown them. Juan Gómez de Paradinas, who had served as the expedition's *alguacil mayor*, or chief constable, lamented almost 20 years later that he had become indebted because of expenditures resulting from the expedition and had been poor since his return to the Ciudad de México.[8] Former expeditionary Domingo Martín claimed in 1543 that he and "the rest" had "returned very much worn out and in debt."[9] Even the captain general was not exempt. He testified in 1553 that "on [the expedition] I spent more than fifty thousand *castellanos* of my own wealth, for much of which I was left in debt and am [so now]."[10] Another huge loser was Antonio de Mendoza. Burned badly, he was not eager to take more such risks. After the return of the Coronado expedition and the dispatch in October 1542 of an ocean voyage to the Orient[11]—part of the multipronged project Mendoza had agreed to with Pedro de Alvarado before the latter's death—the viceroy never again undertook sponsorship of a major expedition. Instead, he turned his energies and resources increasingly to more prosaic economic development within Nueva España.

Generally speaking, the responses to the former expeditionaries' petitions to the royal court for compensation fell short of what they hoped for. Melchior Pérez evidently never received the reward he desired.[12] Cristóbal de Escobar, for whom Domingo Martín testified in 1543, remained in straitened circumstances despite the royal grant of a coat of arms and a minor governmental position.[13] And Vázquez de Coronado died in 1554 without having been satisfied in his claim that "I ought to be further rewarded because of the way I served Your Highness during the aforementioned expedition (as has been stated), because of what I spent from my own wealth in your royal service, because of the rest of the services I have performed for Your Highness, because I am (as indeed I am) a well-known *caballero hidalgo*, and [further] because my ancestors have truly served Your Highness."[14] These examples are typical of the fates of expeditionaries' applications for preferment or recompense after the event.

Any aura of adventure the idea of the *entrada* held for expeditionaries-to-be in the Ciudad de México, Compostela, Guadalajara, and Culiacán in late 1539 and early 1540 had faded by spring 1542. The reality of months of open hostility and suspicion of misdirection by guides and informants, combined with the disheartening results of long and arduous travel, made the expedition an event to get beyond, to push into the past. "The men-at-arms . . . refused to stay" and "consented to nothing except returning to Nueva España," recalled Castañeda de Nájera.[15] Only years later did the expedition become something to brag or reminisce about.

This is not to say that none of the former expeditionaries prospered in the years following the *entrada* or was able to parlay his service during the expedition into an advanced position in society. Alonso Pérez de Bocanegra, who had been a well-to-do member of Tristán de Luna y Arellano's company during the expedition, became a *regidor*, or city councilman, of the Ciudad de México.[16] Rodrigo de Paz Maldonado, an unassigned horseman at the time of the muster in Compostela, moved to Quito, Ecuador, after the end of the expedition, where he was granted an *encomienda*.[17] The chronicler Juan Jaramillo, undistinguished during the expedition to Tierra Nueva, returned to the Ciudad de México and became a respected captain.[18] Perhaps most spectacularly, Juan de Zaldívar became very wealthy, maintaining, in his own estimation, "one of the most important households in the province" of Nueva Galicia.[19]

Altogether less certain is whether warriors among the *indios amigos* who accompanied the expedition achieved results to their satisfaction. If they had hoped to position themselves with privilege in a new Spanish-led society in Tierra Nueva, then attainment of that goal was surely frustrated. If, as I have suggested, their dominant motive for participating in the expedition was to perform feats of combat, then they certainly found ample opportunity during the two years in Tierra Nueva. The Indian allies fought in every skirmish, assault, siege, and engagement of any other kind that is recounted in the documentary record of the expedition. It is also possible that they sought out other opportunities in which more familiarly ritualized one-on-one fighting was possible. Such contests between individual peers might have been arranged extracurricularly—that is, without the knowledge or approval of the Spanish leadership of the expedition.

Although this summary is speculative, it underscores how little still is known about the indigenous members of the expedition, their aspirations, their behavior, and even their fates, except for the few who chose to remain in Tierra Nueva. Of the latter group, some at least successfully integrated into Pueblo societies. They seem to have imparted to their adopted communities some of their knowledge and practices. For example, almost 60 years after the Coronado expedition, some Pueblos showed a rudimentary familiarity with the Nahuatl language.[20] The most likely source was former *indios amigos* left behind by the expedition in 1542. The Mexican Indian adoptees, though, seem to have had no dramatic effect on the Pueblo world.

After the Expedition in Tierra Nueva

Among the indigenous people of Sonora, Cíbola, and the Río Grande, the effect of the expedition was often calamitous. Castañeda de Nájera reported more than 400 Indians killed by the expeditionaries as the direct result of combat at Cíbola and the Tiguex pueblos.[21] In addition, hundreds of others likely died from cold and starvation resulting from expulsion from their homes during the frightful winter of 1540–41. In excess of 10 percent of the Tiguex population likely perished. The documents provide no way to gauge the number of Indian casualties in the Sonora area, but there were many. In both Sonora and New Mexico, the dead undoubtedly included community leaders. Among the Pueblos, people such as Juan Alemán and Bigotes, who held key positions, are likely to have died, leaving voids in their respective communities not easily filled. The psychological trauma of heavy population loss, too, has to have been severe in both areas. Added to that in Tiguex was the desolation of all of the Pueblo towns, which the expeditionaries had ripped apart and robbed of structural wood and cached food and clothing.

Nevertheless, there were native people who benefited from the general havoc wreaked by the expedition. The strength of political opponents of Juan Alemán and Bigotes, as well as of their counterparts at Cíbola, likely surged with the demise of those leaders. In the years following the expedition, people from Chia-Zia Pueblo and their linguistic brethren from the other Keres pueblos evidently moved into territory at the junction of the Jemez River and the Rio Grande that had previously been used by Tiguex people. This is shown by the appearance, after 1542, of what came to be called San Felipe Pueblo near where the Tiguex refuge of Moho likely had been. When the next Spanish expedition, led by fray Agustín Rodríguez, arrived in New Mexico in 1581, it encountered in the vicinity of the confluence of the Rio Grande and the Jemez River five permanently inhabited Keres pueblos, where in 1540 there had been none except Chia, upstream along the Jemez.[22]

Southward on the expedition's route from Chichilticale, native people died not only from warfare but also from devastation of a different sort. Anthropologist Daniel Reff has made a convincing case for the eruption of infectious disease in the Sonora River valley in the wake of and perhaps during the Coronado expedition. It will be remembered that many of the expeditionaries left there under the leadership of Diego de Alcaraz were ill. The documents do not reveal the nature or name of the sickness, but if Reff is correct, it may have been smallpox, measles, or influenza. Whatever the precise infection, records of Jesuit missionaries from the late sixteenth and seventeenth centuries refer repeatedly to outbreaks of epidemic disease, probably the continuation of cycles of illness that had begun with the Ópatas' earliest contacts with Europeans. The communities in which the Coronado expedition had attempted to found its peripatetic supply base, San Gerónimo, were abandoned by 1700. As a result, the Río Sonora Valley probably experienced the worst devastation of any native settlement area contacted by the expedition.[23]

Although Corazones, Señora, and Suya were ravaged by diseases that may have come with members of the Coronado expedition, it seems from both documentary and archaeological evidence that none of the more northerly native societies visited by the expedition was equally affected. As in the case of the lack of success in religious conversion, the explanation may lie in the relatively small amount of actual person-to-person contact between the expeditionaries and the people of Cíbola, Tiguex, and

Cicuique. The sick of the expedition were confined to their quarters, from which all the Pueblos had been expelled. In that sense, the expulsion may have spared the lives of hundreds or even thousands of natives of the Rio Grande region.[24]

Both American natives and European expeditionaries gained knowledge of the other during the expedition's sojourn in Tierra Nueva. Primarily this seems to have resulted in wariness and distrust. The news carried back to Nueva España that the peoples of Tierra Nueva presented dim prospects for colonization based on tribute helped postpone for a full 40 years the Europeans' next entrance into the Pueblo world. It was even longer before the Río Sonora Valley saw Europeans again in any significant number. In the Rio Grande Valley this hiatus of Spanish activity delayed the appearance and calamity of unfamiliar diseases. That disaster did finally strike, but not until the seventeenth century, after permanent colonization opened regular communication with the great disease reservoir of central Mexico.[25]

CHAPTER 19

ONE OF A HUNDRED AND THIRTY

SO FAR I HAVE FOLLOWED IN DETAIL the events of the Coronado expedition, correlating the people and environments of the time with their modern counterparts, piecing together evidence of the expeditionaries' motivations, attitudes, and actions, as well as those of the native people of Tierra Nueva, and tracing many of the outcomes of the *entrada*. All this is enlightening from a regional standpoint for those of us who live in the American Southwest and northwestern Mexico. The stories lend new significance to places in the landscape and provide insights into enduring social, political, and economic circumstances in which we find ourselves as multiethnic societies. Similarly, we can view the Coronado expedition as strictly confined to its temporal duration of almost 36 months between 1539 and 1542—as utterly unique and with little relevance for other times.

From a broader, human perspective, reconstruction of the lives of past people and places provides opportunities for comparison and contrast with events and behaviors in other places throughout history. We can stand far off from the expedition and see it as a timeless example of human behavior, like Greek tragedies and other portrayals of people in seemingly generic predicaments. Such comparisons can be fruitful and instructive; they can even help guide our choices in the future. In many of its aspects the Coronado expedition can be seen as timeless.

Between these two vantages—the strictly regional and the sweepingly universal—one can focus on the expedition in a way that is informative about an epoch, that of the expansion of Europe into what, for Europeans, was an undreamed of new opportunity. For Spaniards, this expansion had its apogee in the sixteenth century. In such a hemispheric perspective, the Coronado expedition is representative of Spanish imperial ventures in the so-called New World. At the same time, it presents a singular case study within the range of those undertakings.

I spend this chapter in that middle ground, looking at the expedition as part of an epoch of conquest in the Western Hemisphere and placing it in the context of sixteenth-century Spanish-led conquest and reconnaissance and the corresponding responses of Native Americans. At the outset I must underscore that the Coronado expedition was not the special case it sometimes appears to have been when viewed through the narrow peephole of the history of the United States. It is not uncommon for those educated in the United States to be aware of the early Spanish colonial period in the Americas through only a handful of events: the conquest of Mexico by an expedition under Hernando Cortés, the conquest of the Incas by Francisco Pizarro and his companions, and the fleeting passage of three conquistadores—Juan Ponce de León, Hernando de Soto, and Francisco Vázquez de Coronado—through territory that is now part of the United States.

These five episodes, though, made up only a fraction of the multiform endeavor that was undertaken in the Western Hemisphere under Spanish direction during the 1500s. Between 1492 and 1598, Europeans under Spanish leadership, joined by enormous numbers of allied American natives and supported by many African slaves, conducted more than 130 major expeditions of conquest and reconnaissance in what are now the United States, Mexico, Central America, and South America.[1] During the three years when the Coronado expedition was under way, at least 13 other large expeditions were in the field elsewhere in the hemisphere. The historian Samuel Elliott Morison once wrote, regarding Spanish sea voyages of reconnaissance to and within the New World, that "had we flown over the Caribbean and the Spanish Main in any one of those years, we would have flushed Spanish ships every two or three hundred miles."[2] A similar situation held on land. Sizable parties crisscrossed the hemisphere on foot and horseback; it was not even unheard of for expeditions to bump into each other, despite the vastness of the continents.

Table 19.1 summarizes the 14 known major expeditions made between 1539 and 1542, classified by modern macro-region.[3] Others have undoubtedly

Table 19.1. Major Spanish Expeditions in the Americas, 1539–1542

Period	Leader	Area	Number of Europeans	Indian Allies
Present-day United States				
1539–43	Hernando de Soto	Southeastern U.S.	600	No
1539–42	Francisco Vázquez de Coronado	Southwestern U.S., northwestern Mexico	370	Yes
1542	Juan Rodríguez Cabrillo	Alta and Baja California Coast	250	No
Present-day Mexico				
1539	Francisco de Ulloa	Gulf of California	100±	No[a]
1539–42	Francisco Vázquez de Coronado	Northwestern Mexico, southwestern U.S.	370	Yes
1540–42	Francisco de Montejo	Campeche, Yucatán	300	Yes
1542	Juan Rodríguez Cabrillo	Alta and Baja California	250	No
Present-day Central America				
1539	Alonso Calero	Panamá, Nicaragua	40–50	No
1539–40	Hernán Sánchez de Badajoz	Costa Rican coast	70	No
Present-day South America				
1537–42	Domingo Martínez de Irala	Río de la Plata, Paraguay	90	Yes
1540	Jerónimo Lebrón	Colombia	300	Yes
1540–43	Gonzalo Pizarro	Peru, Ecuador	200+	Yes
1541–43	Francisco de Orellana	Amazonia	54	No
1540–47	Pedro de Valdivia	Chile	200	Yes
1542–43	Alonso Luis de Lugo	Colombia	200	Yes
1542–44	Álvar Núñez Cabeza de Vaca	Río de la Plata, Paraguay	400	Yes

[a]One interpreter.

escaped notice. Each of the 130-plus sixteenth-century expeditions and each of the 13 expeditions contemporaneous with the Coronado *entrada* was unique in many ways—in its precise personnel make-up, in its internal politics, in the exact environmental and social circumstances it faced, in its equipment and supplies, and, significantly, in the specific indigenous groups it encountered. But underlying that variation was a host of broadly shared attitudes, goals, expectations, and strategies that gave a distinct uniformity to the whole century-long enterprise of conquest and reconnaissance.

Encomiendas

All the 13 ventures simultaneous with the Coronado expedition were stimulated by comparable aims. Without exception they sought, first and foremost, populous native societies with developed industries yielding valuable products that could be tapped by means of the *encomiendas* that were to be granted to the expeditionaries. All pursued indigenous reports of sources of processed, "oriental-type" goods, including objects of precious metal, gemstones, pearls, exotic fabrics, spices, and dyes.

For the expedition led by Hernando de Soto, the target was the very same as that for the Coronado expedition: the large settlements of Tierra Nueva reported by Cabeza de Vaca, Dorantes, Castillo, and Esteban, with their presumed fabrics, gems, and precious metals.[4] Like Vázquez de Coronado, Soto intended to establish a Spanish town, in the vicinity of which the Indians could be "bestowed" in *encomienda* on the expedition's members.[5] Governor Soto and his 600 expeditionaries took aim at Tierra Nueva from the northeastern coast of the Gulf of Mexico.

The sea voyage of Francisco de Ulloa, too, was targeted at Tierra Nueva.[6] Had Ulloa and his crews been able to locate the prosperous settlements thought to be there, then tribute based on indigenous industries would have been expected by those on the voyage.

Initially focused on trade was the coastal voyage of Juan Rodríguez Cabrillo. He planned first to establish a town at a suitable location, contingent on profitable trade with the natives. That was to be followed by distribution of *encomiendas*, once "the land [was] pacified."[7] Cabrillo was also incidentally charged with seeking information about the Coronado expedition, which was still in the field when it departed. Further, it was hoped that Cabrillo and his companions might rendezvous with the trans-Pacific voyage of Ruy López de Villalobos.

On the southern continent, Gonzalo Pizarro's goal was similar. *Encomiendas* were thought to await his expeditionaries in "settled country" where "cinnamon existed," in a native polity ruled by El Dorado, a man who reportedly coated himself with gold for ritual occasions.[8] An offshoot of Pizarro's *entrada*, the expedition of Francisco de Orellana, traveled down the Amazon River ostensibly in search of food. But according to the expeditionaries, the irresistible current of the Marañón River carried them away to the Amazon and then to the Atlantic Ocean. En route they saw and heard about "innumerable islands settled by and full of people," including a kingdom of rich and powerful women, the amazons. Orellana subsequently lost his life in an attempt to find and take control (through *encomiendas*) of those amazon polities.[9]

For the expedition led by Francisco de Montejo the younger, like earlier efforts by his father of the same name, in the same area, it was hope of tribute in "gold and precious stones" that drove the lay conquest of Yucatán. At its interim conclusion, the town of Mérida was founded, and *encomiendas* were distributed there to the successful conquerors.[10] Meanwhile, Álvar Núñez Cabeza de Vaca, whose reports had triggered the Coronado, Soto, and Ulloa *entradas*, had been conceded the governorship of Río de la Plata in South America. His biographer David Howard wrote of Cabeza de Vaca that "he was not obsessed by precious metals ... Wealth, [though,] was necessary to carry out his policies," which were to incorporate the indigenous people of the region into the Spanish sphere.[11] He sought to open a route into interior Paraguay in order to "reconnoiter its settlements" and tap into its wealth by distributing *encomiendas*.[12] More blatantly searching for plunder and tribute in the form of goods made from precious metals, to be appropriated by *encomenderos*, was Cabeza de Vaca's predecessor, Domingo Martínez de Irala.

The two 1539–42 expeditions in what is now Colombia, those of Jerónimo Lebrón and Alonso Luis de Lugo, were lured by wealthy populations that had just recently been located in the region of future Bogotá. Salt, cotton cloth, emeralds, and objects of gold had been found there, all potential tribute items. Additionally, both expeditions carried merchandise to sell to other conquistadors who had preceded them into the region. Ultimately, Luis de Lugo parceled out *encomiendas*, which his own followers and earlier arrivals had been clamoring for.¹³

In Central America the situation was similar. Exaggerated stories of gold industries associated with large population centers stimulated the initial reconnaissance of Panama and Costa Rica. With the establishment of the first successful gold mines in Peru in the late 1530s, the need for supplies and transportation of bullion led to the expeditions of Alonso Calero and Hernán Sánchez de Badajoz. Had they located a navigable water route across the Central American isthmus, as they hoped, they and their followers would have established *encomiendas* based on Indian labor to provision Peru and transport remittances of precious metals back to the mother country.¹⁴ Hoping to tap more directly into indigenous production of precious metals in Chile, Pedro de Valdivia founded two towns and rewarded his followers with *encomiendas*, in accordance with everyone's desire.¹⁵

Although the 14 expeditions of 1539–42 varied in the commodities their members foresaw as the basis of future tribute, nearly all these conquistadores hoped to conclude their *entradas* by living comfortably as *encomenderos* or in *encomendero* households in new Spanish towns situated near the sources of tribute: large, sophisticated indigenous populations. Even before *encomiendas* were established, the demands made by the expeditions on local native peoples for food, clothing, shelter, and women were of similar magnitude and focus.

Dependence on Indigenous Roads, Guides, and Allies

To locate and take control of the indigenous societies that produced goods that could support *encomiendas*, European expeditionaries depended on native roads, guides, and allies. All 9 of the 14 expeditions of 1539–42 that took place entirely on land followed or attempted to follow indigenous roads and used Indian guides. All but one were supported by large contingents of previously subdued native warriors, typically larger by far than the European contingents.

The sole exception to the use of Indian allies by land expeditions was the Soto expedition, which nevertheless seized Indian men and women in the course of its progress, compelling the men to serve singly as guides and the women in groups as load bearers. The results of the decision not to incorporate allied Indian warriors into the expedition were from the beginning catastrophic. The Soto expedition found itself almost continuously in violent conflict with natives of what is now the U.S. Southeast from the time it landed in Florida until it departed from the mouth of the Mississippi River almost four years later. Nearly half the men-at-arms died. A major contributor to this disaster for the expeditionaries was that over and over again the Europeans confronted indigenous forces far outnumbering them, often by a factor of 20 to 1.

None of the rest of the land-based expeditions was so badly mismatched numerically, because each included a significant component of allied indigenous warriors who served both to intimidate resident natives and to fight against them when necessary. The presence of Indian warriors is often difficult to discern in the documentary records of the expeditions. The European conquistadores, for and by whom most of the contemporaneous documents were prepared, understandably touted their own accomplishments to the exclusion of contributions by native allies. Nevertheless, occasional documentary mention of *indios amigos* is sometimes sufficient to allow estimation of the sizes of allied warrior corps, which were always large. For example, the Cabeza de Vaca expedition in Paraguay included at least 1,200 Indian allies and sometimes perhaps as many as 2,600, who substantially outmanned the 400 Europeans.[16] The numbers of *indios amigos* included in the Lebrón and Luis de Lugo expeditions in Colombia were recorded more vaguely as "hundreds of Indians" and "many Indian servants," respectively.[17] As Francisco de Montejo the younger began the *entrada* in 1541 toward what was to become Mérida in Yucatán, his force of 300 Europeans was dwarfed by "a large number of Indian auxiliaries. Most of these allied warriors were from friendly Maya *cacicazgos*, but apparently there were also among them Nahua from the

Adelantado's Mexican *encomienda* of Atzcapotzalco, which lay close to the City of Mexico."[18]

Very rarely, surviving European documents acknowledge the crucial role played by allied Native Americans in the survival and accomplishments of the *entradas*. Pedro de Valdivia, writing to the king of Spain from Chile in 1545, called his Anaconcilla allies "our life-blood."[19] At about the same time, historian Pedro de Cieza de León, recording his observations and judgments in Peru, summarized the importance of *indios amigos* to Spanish-led expeditions throughout the hemisphere by saying that without large numbers of indigenous servants and allies, "in no way, form, or manner could any expedition have been undertaken."[20]

What for hundreds of years have been trumpeted as nearly miraculous victories by "small" parties of European conquistadores seem far less astonishing when the large forces of native allies who routinely fought alongside the Europeans are counted. For generations, a majority of historians and others of European descent has failed to critically examine conquistadores' claims that their encounters with Native Americans were invariably numerically lopsided, to the Europeans' disadvantage. Pulitzer Prize–winning author Jared Diamond, for example, followed many of his predecessors in posing a perennial question about European "conquest" that was based on erroneous information: "When Pizarro and Atahuallpa met at Cajamarca [Peru, in 1532], why did Pizarro capture Atahuallpa and kill so many of his followers, instead of Atahuallpa's vastly more numerous forces capturing and killing Pizarro? After all, Pizarro had only 62 soldiers mounted on horses along with 106 foot soldiers, while Atahuallpa commanded an army of about 80,000."[21]

In fact Francisco Pizarro and his 168 men-at-arms were joined in the attack on Atahuallpa by an unknown number of slaves and servants from the Old World and, most decisively, by a throng of indigenous men and women from Tumbez, Piura, and other native communities that had previously submitted to Pizarro. They served not only as "guides and to help carry their baggage and for other purposes" but also as warriors.[22] Given the Tumbezinos' participation as warriors in concert with the expeditionaries earlier at Puná and Piura, it appears unlikely that they did not also take part in the fighting at Cajamarca, which resulted in Atahuallpa's capture.²³

Reliance on large contingents of recently subjugated non-Christian warriors was a standard tactic of Spanish-led expeditions throughout the Western Hemisphere, as it had been for generations earlier on the Iberian Peninsula. During the final *reconquista* of Granada from the Moors at the end of the fifteenth century, Boabdil, one of two rival Moorish emirs, was defeated in battle and captured by Castilian forces. He agreed to terms under which he "pledged himself to become a vassal of the Spaniard, accepted a two-year truce, and promised to engage in war against his father, in which he would receive Spanish help."²⁴ Similarly, previously defeated Guanche (indigenous Isleño) warriors repeatedly fought in tandem with Spanish forces against other Guanches throughout the Spanish occupation of the Canary Islands in the 1490s.²⁵

All too often in the past, Hernando Cortés has been mistakenly credited with originating the tactic of exploiting rivalries among native groups and incorporating vanquished enemies into his own force. The idea is often presented as if it came to him as an inspiration.²⁶ Rather, he was an adept practitioner of a venerable Iberian tradition.

Aside from the Soto expedition, only the five 1539-42 *entradas* that traveled by ocean and river (the voyages of Ulloa, Orellana, Calero, Sánchez de Badajoz, and Cabrillo) failed to follow that tradition. Presumably this was only for lack of space on the boats and ships. They all did try to take advantage of indigenous interpreters to gain access to the native societies they met. In this they were notably unsuccessful.

Again with the exception of the maritime expeditions, the expeditions of 1539-42 followed native routes from settlement to settlement, rarely finding it necessary to blaze their own trails. Some of the routes were so well trod as to be named roads. Cabeza de Vaca and his fellow survivors, three years before the Coronado *entrada*, had followed what they understood was called the "maize road" through what is now northern Mexico.²⁷ In the 1540s, in Paraguay, Cabeza de Vaca tried, with greater difficulty, to follow "a little frequented path" with the help of a native guide who had not traveled it in a number of years.²⁸ In Colombia it was the Indians' "salt trail" that Lebrón and Luis de Lugo attempted to follow.²⁹ The *hidalgo* of Elvas, a member of the Soto expedition, indicated how crucial indigenous trails were when he wrote that "[the Christians] did not dare to turn aside from the paths."³⁰ The experience of Gonzalo Pizarro and his expedition, who wandered unable to find any path or road, exemplifies the reliance of all land expeditions on indigenous routes. Without a preexisting road, the Pizarro company could not find food, resorted to eating horses and dogs, and suffered many deaths from hunger.³¹

Lack of Success

Whether they resulted from attempts to reconnoiter unsettled regions or from hostile encounters with native people, extreme suffering and death often afflicted the 1539–42 expeditions. Alonso Luis de Lugo "lost about one hundred [of his 200 European] men and three-fourths of the horses and beasts of burden."³² The Soto expedition, most disastrous of all during this four-year period, suffered the deaths of almost half the approximately 600 men who landed in Florida.³³ On the same scale, the Gonzalo Pizarro expedition in Ecuador lost 130 of the 230 European men who began it.³⁴

Even when those dire outcomes were avoided, as in the case of the Coronado expedition, the *entradas* experienced a general lack of success in that they rarely located the large, sophisticated societies they sought. Their members founded only a few Spanish towns, assigned *encomiendas* only in exceptional cases, and by and large failed to recoup their financial investments.

Like the expedition led by Francisco Vázquez de Coronado, all 13 contemporaneous ones were financed privately, usually entirely by the expeditionaries themselves. Most commonly, expedition members took on significant debt to pay for their outfitting and that of their retainers, slaves, and servants. Because so few indigenous producers of oriental-type commodities were found anywhere in the Americas, the expeditionaries seldom had any source of ready wealth to tap into and so no way to extinguish, within a reasonable time, the debts they had incurred. In reference to the Ulloa voyage of 1539, López de Gómara wrote that Ulloa "was on the journey a whole year and brought back no news of any good land.

The noise [of cracking them] was more than the nuts."³⁵ That last sentence is apropos of nearly all the other 1539–42 expeditions. For instance, Álvar Núñez Cabeza de Vaca's brief tenure as governor at Asunción in Paraguay and the expedition he led from there were great money losers. He later attempted, apparently unsuccessfully, to recover his losses, which he claimed amounted to 100,000 *castellanos*.³⁶

The surviving documentary record of the period is replete with lamentations by former expeditionaries over the financial ruin that resulted from their stints as conquistadores. Although some of the complaints were exaggerated and others formulaic, abundant evidence attests that most expeditionaries suffered severe financial setbacks, some lasting for many years, in the aftermath of their journeys. Pedro de Valdivia wrote in 1545, "I owe for all that was spent a hundred and ten thousand pesos."³⁷ Jerónimo de Lebrón departed from Colombia angrily after only six months, his claim to the governorship having been rejected and having grossed only 12,000 pesos in sales of goods, a paltry return for the leader of such an ambitious enterprise.³⁸

Only 4 of the 14 *entradas* resulted in the establishment of long-lasting Spanish settlements: the Montejo expedition, with the founding of Mérida, Yucatán; the Lebrón and Luis de Lugo expeditions, which reinvigorated Santa Fé de Bogotá, Colombia; and the Valdivia expedition, with the founding of Santiago de Chile. Of these three cities, Bogotá alone was situated among Indians who produced readily marketable commodities, items made of gold. A number of former expeditionaries became extremely wealthy in central Colombia as a consequence. At the other two cities, Indians were assigned to expeditionaries in *encomienda,* as they were at Bogotá, but the resulting tribute proved meager. European settlers at Mérida and Santiago were perpetually disgruntled, and it was difficult to maintain the two communities. Valdivia himself later wrote: "Since this land had so evil a fame, as I have said, I had much toil to [re]strain the men I brought to it, and I commanded them by dint of the strong arms of friendly soldiers who chose to come along with me."³⁹ In Yucatán, "the *repartimientos* having been completed, some of the Spaniards were not satisfied with the *encomiendas* they were given, and declared they were of little value and that they wished to leave the land ... because there was no gold or silver in it."⁴⁰ Those who stayed established themselves more modestly on the basis of tribute in cotton fabrics, wax, and honey.⁴¹

The establishment of Spanish settlements at Mérida, Bogotá, and Santiago had not come easily, nor on the first attempt. In all three cases, expeditions prior to those of Montejo, Lebrón, Luis de Lugo, and Valdivia had paved the way for them, much as later happened in New Mexico. Following the Coronado expedition, four further unsuccessful *entradas* took place over a period of 60 years before Juan de Oñate led the colonizing effort that stayed.

Because so few of the expeditions resulted in long-term Spanish presence among newly located native groups, the friars who routinely participated in the *entradas* found little opportunity for religious conversion. Even in the case of the permanent colonial settlements of Mérida, Bogotá, and Santiago, conversion of the neighboring natives was a long, drawn-out, and uneven process. Although friars quickly recognized as nominal Christians thousands of Mayan-, Chibcha-, and Mapuche-speaking Indians, thorough acceptance of Christian ideology was spotty at best. Among the most widely known examples of ostensible conversion masking the persistence of indigenous religious beliefs and practices were the revelations in Yucatán in the early 1560s. There, Franciscan friars discovered widespread reverence of native deities by their Maya charges nearly 20 years after their supposed full and complete conversion to Christianity.⁴² Their religious superiors frequently suggested that the friars were accommodating their behavior to Indian norms at least as much as their flocks were adopting Christian mores and practices.⁴³

How American Natives Fared

Generally speaking, native groups of the Americas resisted efforts by sixteenth-century Spanish-led expeditions to take control of them. In this they were often successful, especially during their first confrontational contacts with Europeans. Because so few of the 1539–42 expeditions managed to establish permanent colonial footholds among indigenous societies, the tactics of native resistance and avoidance seem to have been effective, at least in the short term. If any one defensive tactic stands out as most commonly employed by Indians of many groups throughout the Americas in the sixteenth century when confronted by large European forces, it is withdrawal to rugged or thickly forested terrain. Repeatedly the written records of expeditionaries report finding native settlements empty and recently abandoned. Rodrigo Álvarez's statement about Yucatán is typical: "Many pueblos were deserted and [their people] were scattered among the bush and the milpas."[44]

Only with clear numerical superiority, or in the absence of other alternatives, did indigenous fighters risk open engagement with large Spanish-led expeditions. When they resorted to massed armed conflict, native groups often paid heavy prices in deaths and injuries. The *hidalgo* of Elvas, of the Soto expedition, reported that at least 2,871 Indians from what is now the southeastern United States died as a result of combat with the Soto expeditionaries, although most of the deaths—some 2,500—resulted from a single "accidental" fire at the Indian town of Mavilla.[45] Likewise, at Tiho-Mérida in Yucatán, during fighting with the Montejo expedition, "many Indians died . . . There was a great butchery. There remained heaps of dead Indians . . . [and] the natives who remained alive fled away forever."[46] The results of fighting were much the same in Chile, where Valdivia reported that a large, though unspecified, number of Indians died in fighting.[47]

Casualties were not confined only to Indians native to the areas contacted by Spanish-led expeditions. The expeditionaries' *indios amigos*, too, suffered numerous deaths and injuries in battle with other natives. In Chile Valdivia reported that Mapuches were "killing daily at our house-doors our Anaconcillas [Valdivia's Indian allies]."[48] In Yucatán the native leader Ah Macan Pech recalled that "for six months this suffering was endured by my lords accompanying the principal men [Francisco Montejo and his companions]" in the conquest of their neighbors.[49]

Despite losses, many Indian allies achieved ends they had hoped for in joining the Spaniards. We must assume that some of them improved their status within their communities as a result of accomplishments in war. Such feats included the taking of native slaves, as was reported of the

Guaraní allies of Cabeza de Vaca in Paraguay.⁵⁰ Some, we know, gained preferment within the nascent Spanish colonial society for having aided in the conquest of other indigenous peoples. For instance, in Yucatán, individual Maya elites who cooperated with Montejo and served as allied warriors, such as Ah Macan Pech, were rewarded with the status of *hidalgo* in the Spanish community and were exempted from paying tribute.⁵¹

From routine use of the *requerimiento* to justify its actions to anticipation of comfortable lives for its members based on tribute in oriental-type goods; from reliance on indigenous guides and indigenous roads to frequent recourse to attack on native settlements; and from profound lack of success in founding settlements to deep disappointment of religious goals, the Coronado expedition closely resembled its contemporaries elsewhere in the Americas. ∎

CHAPTER 20

Discontinuity at Mid-Century

IN THE DECADE OR SO FOLLOWING THE CORONADO EXPEDITION, a series of course changes took place in Nueva España and in the Spanish Empire as a whole that significantly affected the enterprise of conquest and reconnaissance. Both lay and religious motives driving the extension of Spanish sovereignty shifted markedly. In each realm an idealism succumbed to mounting contrary experience and a generational shift among aspiring European overlords and missionaries. The results of a swarm of rapid changes were fully evident in the Spanish Americas by the middle of the 1550s. In some details they mirrored the passing of Spain's brief and spotty excursion into the Renaissance. In others they represented independent developments contingent upon the expansion of geographical knowledge, the devastation of introduced disease, and the simple passage of time.

First to come was news in the middle 1540s that the Mar del Sur, or Pacific Ocean, was thousands of miles across, even at the latitude of Nueva España. As we have seen, Viceroy Mendoza and Pedro de Alvarado had contracted a voyage across the Mar del Sur as part of their agreement of November 1540.[1] With Alvarado a casualty of the Mixtón War, Mendoza carried through on their plan for a voyage to the Orient in 1542, enlisting his relative Ruy López de Villalobos as leader.[2] Although López de Villalobos died in the Philippines, news of the ocean crossing he had led eventually reached Spain and, belatedly, Nueva España with survivors of his crew. For many it was disheartening news.

More than 40 years earlier, a small fleet under Ferdinand Magellan had first crossed the tropical Pacific in three and a half months in late 1520 and early 1521.[3] One item of knowledge Spaniards had gained from that trip was that in the southern and equatorial latitudes, the American Indies lay a great distance from the Asian Indies—well over 10,000 miles by Magellan's route. Now, in the 1540s, it was clear that from Nueva España to the Philippines the distance was still at least 8,000 miles. That revelation, together with the fact that Cabrillo's aborted voyage up the North American west coast had not reached people of Asian appearance and culture, suggested that the two Indies were distinct, separated by a vast though perhaps northwardly narrowing ocean.

It would be almost another two centuries before Europeans received conclusive proof that Asia and the Americas were not linked.[4] Nevertheless, the findings of the crews of Cabrillo and López de Villalobos pointed in that direction.[5] It began to appear decidedly less likely that expeditions anywhere in the Americas would ever run into truly oriental societies. Whatever wealth was to be had from American Indians would be native to their lands. Even after the Villalobos crossing, many Europeans, including former member of the Coronado expedition Pedro de Castañeda de Nájera, continued to hold that America and Asia were one. But increasingly, those with New World experience thought otherwise. Seeking Chinese silks and Moluccan spices in either North or South America looked more and more like a wild-goose chase.

By the 1550s, corroboratory evidence for that conclusion had been mounting in the Americas for 60 years. By the time 1555 arrived, at least 103 of the 130 major sixteenth-century, Spanish-led expeditions in the Western Hemisphere had already taken place. Among them, they had revealed only a handful of indigenous societies that produced precious oriental-style goods. And they had covered, either directly or through reports from native informants, a significant share of the land masses of North and South America. Although the immensity of the interiors of both continents had barely been probed, native stories of pearls, gold, silver, gemstones, fabrics, dyes, and spices were growing scanty and repetitious. Fewer and fewer private individuals were thus willing to underwrite expeditions that seemed less and less likely to yield valuable booty and tribute.

ENCOMENDEROS BRIDLED
AND AN ALTERNATIVE SOURCE OF WEALTH

In conjunction with the decreasing likelihood that Columbus had opened a shortcut from Europe to the wealth of the Asian Indies, the institution of *encomienda*, as a way to levy the products of vassals of the Spanish king, came under heavy assault during the middle decades of the 1500s. The onslaught, waged by the Spanish monarchs and abetted by late-coming Europeans to the Americas, had begun with Fernando and Isabel, the erstwhile backers of Columbus. When the queen learned that Columbus was selling New World natives as slaves, she promptly notified him and all others that no one but the monarchs could exercise such control over the lives of her vassals. As the historian Lesley Byrd Simpson wrote in his classic book on the *encomienda* more than 70 years ago, Queen Isabel, as sovereign of Castile, was moved to action by "Columbus's assumption of sovereignty."[6]

This remained the grievance of kings and queens against their *encomendero* subjects—namely, that the *encomenderos* were arrogating to themselves powers and resources that pertained to the monarchs and no one else. Although the Catholic sovereigns permitted extension of the Castilian system of *encomienda* to the Americas as a means of financing the expansion of their domains, they and their successors worked diligently to limit and finally to terminate the power and independence of a growing *encomendero* class. By 1515, the outspoken Dominican friar Bartolomé de las Casas was calling for complete suppression of the *encomienda* system. Instead, for the time being, the king's councils only tinkered with the laws that governed the rights and duties of *encomenderos*.[7]

While the Coronado expedition was in Tierra Nueva, though, a sweeping reform of the *encomienda* system was enacted under the name of King Carlos I. Promulgated in November 1542 as "The New Laws of the Indies for the Good Treatment and Preservation of the Indians," the ordinances called for the abolition of all *encomiendas* upon the deaths of the current holders. The pertinent section reads: "We ordain and command that from henceforward no Viceroy, Governor, Audiencia, discoverer, or any other person have power to allot Indians in *encomienda* by new provision, or by means of resignation, donation, sale, or any other form or manner, neither by vacancy nor inheritance, but that the person dying who held the said Indians, they revert to our Royal Crown."[8]

Although implementation of the New Laws was postponed because of the violent reactions, both actual and threatened, of New World *encomenderos*, the handwriting was on the wall. *Encomiendas* would not for long be a means by which most expeditionaries could establish themselves and their heirs in situations of relative ease. Although the tradition of *encomienda* hung on in attenuated form in frontier areas of the Americas and Philippines well into the eighteenth century, the number of *encomenderos* began to shrink by the 1560s.

The promised extinction of *encomiendas* might alone have been enough to strike the image of independent, tribute-collecting overlords of Indians from expeditionaries' lists of sought-after rewards. But the disaster that had befallen the native peoples during the decade before 1550 rendered that dream untenable regardless of royal action. The epidemic of *cocolitzli*—typhus or another disease—that hit central Mexico between 1545 and 1548 was "the most devastating of all."[9] At least half of all indigenous people died in the affected areas, including the Valley of Mexico, Michoacán, Nueva Galicia, and perhaps, as Daniel Reff has suggested, San Miguel de Culiacán and Zacatecas.[10] The native people of Peru and northwestern South America experienced similar demographic catastrophes.[11] Such massive fatality was debilitating for the ravaged societies. Even people who survived disease were often reduced to the barest subsistence and suffered major social disjunctions. As a result, many groups were simply incapable of generating the tribute goods or supplying the labor that *encomenderos* typically demanded. In an emptier, post-disease world, most *encomiendas* became impractical.

By the strangest of coincidences, just as tribute collection waned as a viable way to make a handsome living, Europeans in the Americas were able to turn to the management of silver mines. In 1546, in the midst of the great *cocolitzli* epidemic, a Zacateco Indian showed a party led by Juan de Tolosa ore that proved to be extraordinarily rich in silver at the site of what was to become the city of Zacatecas, on the eastern flank of the Sierra

Madre Occidental on Nueva España's far northern fringe. By the next year a settlement of miners occupied the site, and in 1548 they struck three tremendous veins.[12] By the mid-1550s Zacatecas had become a rough city of several thousand inhabitants, one of the largest Spanish settlements in Nueva España at the time.[13]

Nor was Zacatecas alone as a silver magnet for ambitious Europeans. Just a year before Tolosa's discovery at the Cerro de la Bufa at Zacatecas, the Cerro Rico had been discovered at Potosí in what is now Bolivia.[14] On both continents these strikes were followed by many others in subsequent years as conquistadores gave way to mining entrepreneurs and others in trades that supported and lived off of the burgeoning mining industry. The interests and aspirations of ambitious Europeans shifted from an essentially medieval appropriation of extant indigenous products to locating and developing mineral and other natural resources little exploited previously by native populations.

The later decades of the sixteenth century witnessed the mounting of occasional large expeditions, but the number of such enterprises was far exceeded by smaller, shorter-range mineral prospecting trips. Indian warriors continued to be enlisted to support and defend mining and related operations, but increasingly the Europeans' need and demand was for Indian men to do the underground work in mines and to perform the myriad menial tasks associated with refining and transporting silver. The motives that drove many lay Europeans in the Americas were transformed during the middle decades of the sixteenth century.

Millennium Postponed

Friars of the mendicant, missionary orders experienced a sea change in their drive to convert the natives of the Americas at roughly the same time. In part, the reasons for this shift were some of the same ones that contributed to the redirection of lay interests. Beginning with the last years of the 1540s and continuing for three decades, a string of events overtook the millenarian Franciscans, whose vision of the imminent coming of the Kingdom of God had spurred a frenetic effort to find and convert all the native peoples of the Americas.

Decisive were the sudden and widespread deaths of so many Indian people in the ferocious epidemics that hit both Nueva España and Peru in the late 1540s. The shock of a death rate of perhaps one-third was profound, for the native people themselves and for the friars who were working to bring them into the Catholic Church. The avalanche of deaths destroyed the optimism of many missionaries. As the historian John Phelan put it, the demographic collapse "shattered the dream of terrestrial paradise."[15] In addition, some friars saw the deaths as a divine message that their single-minded, urgent project of conversion was misguided.

To that horrific blow was added the passing of the generation of millenarian Franciscans themselves. By the early years of the 1550s, only two of the original 12 Franciscans to have journeyed to Nueva España (Los Doce) remained alive—fray Juan de Ribas and fray Toribio de Benavente.[16] The successors to the millenarian missionaries were more often friars who looked with disfavor on the old apocalyptic school of evangelism.[17] A millenarian himself and great advocate of missionary work among the Indians of Nueva España, its first bishop, fray Juan de Zumárraga, had died in 1548, to be replaced by the Dominican Alonso de Montúfar, who had a very different vision of the ecclesiastical mission in the Americas, one less focused on the conversion of Indians.[18] Yet another blow to Franciscan millenarianism was the transfer in 1550 of Antonio de Mendoza to the viceroyalty of Peru, where he died shortly afterward. Mendoza, like his friend Zumárraga, had encouraged the massive effort of evangelization among the indigenous people of Nueva España, undertaken especially by Franciscans.[19]

Part of the transformation of the sixteenth-century Franciscan clergy of Nueva España was its progressive secularization and creolization. For instance, fray Francisco de Rivera, commissary general of Nueva España from 1552 until 1573, deliberately solicited candidates for the priesthood who had been born in Nueva España—that is, who were creoles. When he retired to Spain he left behind more than a hundred newly professed creole Franciscan clerics.[20] Creole priests increasingly reflected the prevailing lay views of the colony, which had never thrown much support behind the notion that the return of Christ hinged on converting Indians. Nor did the lay population give much credit to the millenarian creed that the apocalypse was imminent.

As the indigenous population declined precipitously and the European, Euro-American, and *mestizo* populations grew, the number of secular priests (that is, priests not pledged to monastic, often evangelical, vows) grew. Through parish churches they ministered to the Hispanic and Hispanicized populace and had little or no interest in seeking out and converting "heathens." The visions that had impelled friars such as Marcos de Niza dimmed. Those visions did not disappear, but after mid-century they were only rarely capable of generating the fervor and funding or motivating the enlistment that large expeditions of conquest and reconnaissance required. By the final third of the century the few remaining millenarian Franciscans and their sympathizers were marginal to the thrust of Spanish colonial life.

Counter-Reformation

Such changes within the ecclesiastical ranks harmonized with the religious preoccupations of the royal court after 1556. In that year the ailing Carlos I abdicated the throne in favor of his son, who on accession became Felipe II.[21] The new king shared the spirit of the Counter-Reformation, outlined in part in the pronouncements of the Council of Trent, which had been meeting sporadically since 1545.[22] The menaces of Protestantism, real and imagined, consumed much of Felipe's attention and energy. During his reign, enforcement of religious orthodoxy intensified in the Spanish world. This was not to the complete exclusion of missionary work in Spain's overseas possessions. But there was no question that many in the royal court saw the Protestant states of northern Europe as a mounting challenge to Spanish Catholic hegemony and a peril to the world order they viewed as sanctioned by God. Extirpation of the "heretical" faith became an obsession of Felipe's lengthy reign.

Religious indoctrination of the Native American population, which appeared to be shrinking away in any case, took a distant second place to the struggle against Protestantism. That contest between Christian faiths siphoned ecclesiastical enthusiasm away from missionary work. What had seemed the imminent triumph of God's one and true church at the beginning of the sixteenth century was replaced by a titanic struggle for the existence of Catholicism only 50 years later. What had been the most powerful religious motive for prospective ecclesiastical expeditionaries—an ebullient confidence in the imminence of Christ's return to earth—had atrophied by the mid- to late 1550s, overshadowed by more mundane ecclesiastical careers.

To be sure, great missionary efforts were still to come, such as those of Francisco Eusebio Kino in northwest Mexico in the late seventeenth century and Junípero Serra in California in the eighteenth. But there was to be a decades-long drop in missionary fervor after the middle of the sixteenth century. The resurgence of evangelism among unconverted American peoples in the 1600s owed little to the millenarianism of the first half of the 1500s.

In light of the economic, demographic, and religious discontinuities in Nueva España at mid-century, the fall-off thereafter in numbers of expeditions of conquest and reconnaissance is not surprising. By 1573, when Felipe II promulgated the "Ordinances concerning New Discoveries," the royal mood was one of strictly curtailing expeditions, which from then on were to be called enterprises of "pacification" rather than of "conquest."[23] Freelance expeditions were strictly outlawed and forcibly suppressed, and a formal application process was instituted for prospective leaders of expeditions. During the second half of the sixteenth century only about 30 major expeditions took place, a decline of 70 percent or so from the previous 50 years.[24]

CHAPTER 21

Enduring Life of Rumor

Even if noticeably fewer and less ambitious Spanish expeditions took place in the second half of the sixteenth century than in the first, expeditions of conquest and reconnaissance continued to be mounted. They penetrated into parts of the Americas that had been leaped over during the original scramble for oriental-type goods, and they were launched from the effective limits of Spanish control. Or they probed for a second and third time peoples and places that had previously been deemed unworthy of exploitation. Tierra Nueva fell into this last category.

Some historians have suggested that after the end of the Coronado expedition, memory of it was quickly lost, so that when Francisco Sánchez Chamuscado and fray Agustín Rodríguez led the next realized attempt at colonization to reach the Rio Grande pueblos, in 1581, it was as if the pueblos had never before been seen by Europeans.[1] The documentary evidence indicates otherwise. Both among the former expeditionaries and their immediate associates and in a wider literate world, the knowledge and repute of Tierra Nueva continued to circulate. The northern land remained a subject of conversation and source of speculation for many years, and stories about it helped inspire further expeditions. As Pedro de Castañeda de Nájera wrote in the early 1560s, acquaintances of his in Culiacán and its environs had "often taken the opportunity to importune me very earnestly, begging me not infrequently to elucidate and clarify for them some uncertainty they had concerning specific things they had heard from the common people about things and events that occurred during the expedition to Cíbola or Tierra Nueva."[2]

Likewise, in the indigenous communities that had supplied *indios amigos* for the expedition, the *entrada* remained a vivid part of local history.

For the years 1168 through 1552, the entries in the Tlaxcalan annal known as the Codex Aubin are generally confined to only one or two major events. One of the events for the year 1539 is the departure of Tenochca for Tierra Nueva with the Coronado expedition. Participation in the *entrada* stood out in the people's memory.³

Much closer to the time of the events of the expedition, in 1543 Francisco Tello de Sandoval began a four-year *visita*, or judicial inspection, of all the officials of Nueva España. The 108 people he called as *de oficio* witnesses (the equivalent of prosecution witnesses today) readily recalled the Coronado expedition and the place called Cíbola. They also generally remembered that the expedition had resulted in financial loss for its members, especially Viceroy Mendoza.⁴ It was a happening that, in the phrase of the day, was "*público e notorio*," widely and commonly known.

But the Coronado *entrada* also found much wider and longer-lasting fame. In 1556 in Venice, Giovanni Battista Ramusio published Italian translations of a series of documents arising from the expedition, and the place names of Tierra Nueva and its indigenous peoples were exposed to an avid readership throughout Europe and its colonies.⁵ Ramusio inflated the contents of some of those documents with his own, apparently gratuitous, additions. In the Italian version of fray Marcos de Niza's *Relación*, for example, he inserted several references to precious metals that are missing from the copies signed by Marcos himself. He seems to have added wholesale this lengthy passage:

> [Cíbola] exceeds twenty thousand households. The people are nearly white. They go about clothed and sleep on beds. They have bows as weapons. They possess many emeralds and other jewels, though they do not prize them, but rather only turquoise. With this [stone] they decorate the walls at the doors to their houses, their clothing, and their drinking cups. It is spent like money in all that country. They dress in cotton and [bison] hides. This [cotton] is more valued and desirable to wear. They use drinking cups made of gold and silver, since they have no other metal.

They employ [these metals] more often and in greater quantity than [they do] in Peru. They buy [the precious metals] from the *provincia* of the tattooed people, with turquoise. They know [the metals] are mined there in great quantity.[6]

So it was that 14 years after it had been repeatedly denounced by Vázquez de Coronado, an exaggerated version of Marcos's *relación* was given an undeserved and magnified credibility with Ramusio's publication. Even though it was published along with the captain general's bitter denunciation of the friar and his claims, Marcos's words glowed and shimmered for readers throughout Europe and its colonies, many of whom had no knowledge of the expedition's inglorious end. At about the same time, Hernando Cortés's secretary, Francisco López de Gómara, published a brief account of the Coronado *entrada* in his *Historia de la conquista de México*. Although it did not include the embellishments of Ramusio's translations, neither did it disclose the losses that had resulted. Other published accounts of the people and places of Tierra Nueva from the middle decades of the sixteenth century include one by Bartolomé de las Casas. So impressive were the native settlements there, according to the imaginings of the famous Dominican, that whoever saw the seven *ciudades* would think he was looking at "cities of Spain."[7] All in all, the published accounts of the immediate post-expedition period were as glowing as the general public expectation had been in 1539.

Published maps of the period also assured the long, if often wildly incorrect, remembrance of the places and peoples visited by the Coronado expedition. Probably the best known example of popular cartographic knowledge of the last half of the sixteenth century, Abraham Ortelius's atlas of the world (1570), confidently displayed Cíbola, Quivira, Acus, Tiguex, and Totonteac as medieval European cities, displaced radically to the west of their actual locations.[8] It was all but impossible for even a curious public to obtain accurate accounts of the *entrada* and its results.

Return to Tierra Nueva

To officials of the Audiencia of Nueva España, information about Tierra Nueva was available from unpublished sources, the service records and petitions for preferment submitted by former members of the expedition. It may have been information from such documents that first piqued the interest of Alonso de Zorita, an *oidor*, or judge, of the Audiencia. From as early as 1556 he was active in organizing an expedition that he proposed would accomplish what Vázquez de Coronado had left undone. Zorita evidently was acquainted with don Luis de Quesada, a former member of the Coronado expedition, who must have shared details about that enterprise with the *oidor*, which surely enhanced the rosy picture painted by nostalgic conquistadores.

In his plan for Tierra Nueva, Zorita had an ecclesiastical partner, fray Jacinto (Cyndos) de San Francisco. Cyndos had made a trip to the Zacatecas area in 1559 in company with the Indian *donado*, or lay brother, named Lucas who had been a companion of fray Juan de Padilla's during the Coronado *entrada*. Lucas had escaped southward after fray Juan was killed. Undoubtedly, it was from Lucas that the friar learned many of the particulars of Tierra Nueva about which he became so enthusiastic.[9]

During their planning, Zorita and fray Cyndos put out a call for information from other former members of the Coronado expedition concerning Tierra Nueva and routes by which it was accessible.[10] Among the responses, Zorita seems to have received two written reports (and perhaps others). Those two have served since then as important sources of information about Cíbola and its neighboring polities: Pedro de Castañeda de Nájera's *Relación* and the narrative prepared nearly simultaneously by Juan Jaramillo. Both were addressed to an unidentified illustrious personage, most likely Zorita.[11] Castañeda de Nájera conjectured about Tierra Nueva in a way bound to interest Europeans, who, in the 1560s, were increasingly fascinated by ores of precious metals. He wrote that at Yuque Yunque on the Rio Grande (today's San Juan Pueblo), members of the Coronado expedition had seen jars of shiny metal, suggesting, incorrectly as it turned out, the nearby presence of silver.[12]

On the basis of the sum of information they were able to assemble, between 1558 and 1562 the judge and the friar together made a series of proposals to the king and his Consejo de Indias to mount a new expedition of 100 Spaniards and at least 20 Franciscan friars to return to the land of the Chichimecas. From there, they insisted, access could be gained, as Zorita put it in 1561, to "the Tierra Nueva to which Francisco Vázquez Coronado went, and to Nuevo México . . . *provincias* . . . heavily populated by people, very productive, and showing strong indications of sources of gold and silver."[13] The Zorita-Cyndos expedition, though, never came about. A successful competing proposal was submitted by Francisco de Ybarra, who in 1562 became governor of the new province of Nueva Vizcaya.[14] Subsequently, Zorita fell seriously ill and returned to Spain in 1566, none of his proposals having been approved.[15]

Combined with the reports of Tierra Nueva by eyewitnesses and the fanciful embellishments of those who had only heard or read second- and thirdhand grapevine stories about it was speculation over the place from which the Mexica-Aztecs had migrated to the Basin of Mexico. That supposed place of origin, Aztlán, was said to be somewhere toward the north of the Ciudad de México, perhaps very far north. Tales of Aztlán, presumed to be a place rich in mineral resources, were easily conflated with the tales of Topira and Cíbola. Thus, when the Ybarra *entrada* was launched, there was much anticipation that what had eluded the Coronado expedition would now be found. Aiming first at Topira in modern Sinaloa, Ybarra and his force were sorely disappointed not to find "lands to their liking."[16] The Ybarra party retraced the path of the Coronado *entrada* from Topira up the Río Sonora Valley and then veered northeast, reaching the storied ruins of Paquimé, or Casas Grandes, likely the Coronado expedition's Marata. Thereafter, Ybarra abandoned his effort to reconnoiter and conquer what was by now being called Nuevo México.[17]

A Spanish Colony

Officially sanctioned enterprises of reconnaissance and conquest toward the far north were held in abeyance for 20 years after the Ybarra *entrada*, but the stories of a prosperous Tierra Nueva persisted. To a greater or lesser extent, common knowledge and opinion about what the Coronado expeditionaries had done and seen, replete with distortions and wishful thinking, helped motivate five expeditions into Tierra Nueva during the final two decades of the sixteenth century. The first four of those were no more successful than the Coronado expedition had been in taking control of the region and its people.[18]

The influence of the Coronado *entrada* was more direct and decisive in determining the course of the expedition that culminated in the successful absorption of the world of the Rio Grande Pueblos into the Spanish realm in 1598. The leader and instigator of that undertaking, Juan de Oñate, and at least two of his important subordinates, Juan and Vicente de Zaldívar, were all close relatives of participants in and supporters of the Coronado expedition. They brought to their planning for colonization family traditions about the Pueblo world and firsthand reports of its potential resources.

The Zaldívar brothers must have heard stories about the Coronado expedition in the home of their father, Vicente de Zaldívar, the elder brother of Captain Juan de Zaldívar of the 1539–42 *entrada*. They were also cousins of Juan de Oñate and nephews of his father, Cristóbal de Oñate, who had been Vázquez de Coronado's lieutenant governor in Nueva Galicia and appears to have been a supporter and perhaps a financial backer of the governor's Tierra Nueva enterprise. Furthermore, Juan de Oñate's secretary, Juan Gutiérrez Bocanegra, was probably a relative, perhaps a grandson, of Diego Gutiérrez de la Caballería, the uncle of Beatriz de Estrada who had served as treasurer of the Coronado expedition.[19] Juan Gutiérrez would have been familiar with family traditions about the 1539–42 *entrada*.

In January 1598, Oñate, the Zaldívars, Gutiérrez, and 127 other men-at-arms, plus families and servants, set out from the Santa Bárbara area of what is now north-central Mexico. Following the Río Conchos, which had served as the conduit of entrance to New Mexico for two of the expeditions of the 1580s, the Chamuscado-Rodríguez and Espejo expeditions, the Oñate party angled cross-country to the Rio Grande a score of miles downstream from modern El Paso, Texas. After a ceremony of submission and vassalage at Santo Domingo Pueblo on July 7, 1598, in which a number of Pueblo leaders participated, Oñate and his colonists pushed on to Ohke, or San Juan Pueblo, the Yuque Yunque of the Coronado expedition, which was clearly their intended destination. The reasons behind the choice of Ohke for the first Spanish settlement in New Mexico are not made clear in the surviving documents. One factor almost certainly was reports given by members of the Coronado expedition of possible silver in that area, similar to the one made by Castañeda de Nájera. After arriving at Ohke, Oñate eagerly toured the Rio Grande region, examining pueblos and taking ore samples. Although he did not find the expected quantities of silver, his Spanish settlement at Ohke, christened San Juan, took root and remained the capital of the province for nearly a decade.[20]

Rumors Continue

In the 1560s, Juan Jaramillo had been able to point only to bison hides as a potentially lucrative item of commerce that could be developed in Tierra Nueva. These would help meet a need for durable leather bags for carrying ore in the mines of Mexico and Peru.[21] Gone was any mention of the possibility of gold and silver. But hopes and erroneous first impressions die hard.

Despite the mounting number of financial failures, stories of incredible wealth associated with *entradas* throughout the hemisphere lived on. Indeed, they continue to this day. In many places in the Southwest, tales of "Coronado's gold," often said to be buried or stashed in one of numerous caves, still have hearty supporters and dedicated aficionados. Over the years I have heard from a number of these people, each sure he is on the verge of finding the presumed treasure. As in the past, those who continue to pursue the "seven cities" or the "gold of the seven cities" generally base their beliefs on word of mouth, which may have its ultimate source in stories that circulated in the Ciudad de México in fall 1539, after fray Marcos's return from Tierra Nueva, as preparations were under way for a grand expedition. Or it might have originated in the enhanced accounts published by Ramusio, which were translated from Ramusio's Italian into English and became popular in the English-speaking world in the early years of the seventeenth century.[22] The documentary record that is strictly contemporaneous with the *entrada* recounts unambiguously that the Coronado expedition returned south in 1542 without having seen the least sign of silver or gold, pearls or emeralds, silk or camel hair, vibrant dyes or piquant spices.

Tales of Europeans among the Indians

It is difficult to specify with precision what ideas about Europeans became current among indigenous peoples as a result of contact with or reports about the Coronado expedition. Several things, at least, seem to have been widely held in native communities after passage of the *entrada*. First, Indians became familiar with the Europeans' nearly obsessive need to prepare written records. The surge of events would curiously stop while formal pronouncements such as the *requerimiento* were made and certified in writing. Second, European reverence for the symbol of the cross and its efficacy for Indians as a shield against the intruders quickly became clear to native people, and knowledge of it diffused great distances beyond where the expedition had passed. Even during the expedition, natives sometimes greeted the Europeans with displays of crosses, probably because of the spread of information along indigenous networks in advance of the expedition itself. This prior knowledge of the cross was particularly apparent during the Alarcón voyage.

Third, Europeans' reliance on livestock and the advantages and liabilities it entailed became common knowledge among widely spread indigenous groups within months of the expedition. As a result, Indians often sought refuge in rugged, steep terrain that was difficult of access on horseback. Fourth, European actions repeatedly confirmed earlier reports of conquistadores' brutality. Even far from Señora, Cíbola, Tiguex, and Quivira, the Coronado expedition was known for "killing many native Indians."[23] That belligerence reinforced a frequent native strategy of flight and abandonment of homes in the face of threatened European attack. And finally, Europeans must have seemed laughably gullible when it came to concerted efforts to fool them about wealth that lay ahead.

Like Europeans, American natives were likely to overgeneralize about members of the opposite group, so that stereotypical images of conquistadores sometimes prevented flexibility of reaction to them. Certainly, a general wariness of Europeans was common among indigenous communities after the passage of the Coronado expedition. For American natives, as for Europeans, initial impressions of the other proved persistent and slow to shift. ■

Chapter 22

Violence, Expected but Not Sought

In the months following its end, accounts of the Coronado expedition drew negative attention from powerful groups in Spain. The first was composed of vociferous critics of the means by which Catholicism and nascent Spanish mercantilism were being disseminated in the Western Hemisphere. Those critics were primarily members of the mendicant religious orders, animated by eloquent and persuasive priests and friars such as Antonio de Montesinos, Francisco de Vitoria, and Bartolomé de las Casas.

The ecclesiastics, in turn, roused an even more powerful group, the Spanish monarchs and their principal advisors. Almost since the first claim of Spanish sovereignty over the Western Hemisphere was made, the monarchs and their counselors recognized an obligation to protect the indigenous people of the Americas from possible abuse by the monarchs' own European subjects. Thus, in 1495 Queen Isabel and King Fernando, reluctant to authorize the capture and selling of slaves by Columbus, called for a commission to decide whether Indians could be sold as slaves at all.[1]

That was only the beginning. Over the next five decades Isabel and Fernando and after them their grandson, Carlos I, promulgated three comprehensive legal codes regarding the "benevolent treatment of Indians." The first of those, known as the Laws of Burgos, was issued in 1512 and promptly expanded the following year.[2] The royal conscience had been aroused by a series of sermons and critical polemics delivered in Cuba in 1511 and then in Spain by the Dominican priest Antonio de Montesinos. He had railed against *encomenderos* in his parish in Cuba, threatening to excommunicate them because so many Indians were being worked to death and grossly abused under their supposed tutelage.[3] The resulting laws addressed the issues the priest had raised, specifically the kinds and amount of labor that could be exacted from American natives held in *encomienda*; a requirement that *encomenderos* provide adequate food, lodging, clothing, and religious instruction to their charges; and a prohibition against corporal punishment of Indians except by designated justices.

The Laws of Burgos had only limited success in ameliorating the conditions under which tribute-paying American natives lived. By 1526, after ten years of rule by Carlos I, it seemed necessary to draft a new code. In that year another set of "Ordinances concerning the Benevolent Treatment of Indians" was drafted. It, too, focused on "excessive and immoderate labor" demanded by *encomenderos*, which was said to have resulted in the depopulation of entire towns and regions in the Western Hemisphere. The 1526 ordinances referred for the first time specifically to Nueva España, which had come into being as a Spanish colonial entity since the promulgation of the Laws of Burgos. In addition, they made explicit reference to royal subjects and "conquistadores" who, with appropriate license, might go to "reconnoiter, settle, or trade," requiring that such expeditionaries be accompanied by ecclesiastics and that they read the *requerimiento* to natives of whom they intended to take control.[4]

In the decade and a half following publication of the 1526 ordinances, an unmatched proponent of Native American rights came to prominence in Spain—fray Bartolomé de las Casas. Las Casas "insisted more strongly than any other writer of his century on free and willing conversion."[5] Like nearly all his Spanish contemporaries, he assumed that Indians ought to be converted and that, given examples of devout Christian living, they would naturally and necessarily request instruction in the Catholic faith. Yet las Casas and his many comrades abhorred what they viewed as rampant pillage, rape, and murder of Indians by conquistadores and other lay Europeans of all social levels. Las Casas lobbied tirelessly for stronger laws that would separate Indians and Europeans and leave extension of royal sovereignty strictly to the religious orders. Falling short of that goal, he was nevertheless able to push through the royal bureaucracy a set of

"New Laws of the Indies for the Good Treatment and Preservation of the Indians," issued in 1542.

The New Laws, as they are commonly known, threatened harsh penalties for anyone who, for example, brought "Indians [out of a land he has reconnoitered], except three or four as interpreters."[6] The lengthy set of ordinances laid groundwork intended to end the *encomienda* system and charged government officials and the citizenry at large to take special and perpetual care to preserve and protect the Indians of the Americas. The royal courts were enjoined to "enquire continually into the excesses and ill treatment which are or shall be done to [the Indians] by governors or private persons."[7]

Just as the New Laws were about to be published in Spain, letters reached the royal court voicing weighty complaints about what was claimed to be the Coronado expedition's inhumane and wantonly destructive use of violence against the Indians of Tierra Nueva. Who wrote the letters is unknown, but they found their way promptly to the highest levels of royal power. By 1543, with the attention that had been focused for the past several years on the subject of treatment of natives, the king, his court, and the Consejo de Indias were all sensitive to any suggestion of abuse. Carlos I and his advisors were not about to let pass behavior that seemed to fly directly in the face of the new legal code. Under the king's name, Lorenzo de Tejada, who had been an *oidor* of the Audiencia of Nueva España since 1538, was commissioned in September 1543 to conduct a *pesquisa secreta*, an investigation in closed session, into the matter.[8]

Because Tejada fell ill, the *pesquisa* did not get under way until summer 1544. By the end of that year the *oidor* had taken testimony from 14 *de oficio* witnesses, and by early 1545 Vázquez de Coronado and his attorney, Pedro Ruiz de Haro, had sought out and recorded testimony from at least seven rebuttal, or *de parte*, witnesses. With that, the investigation was complete and was referred to the Audiencia for a decision in the case. The *fiscal*, or prosecutor, for the Audiencia lodged six specific charges of criminal malfeasance and negligence against the former captain general. Those were (1) that Vázquez de Coronado had wantonly ordered the execution of Indians at Chiametla; (2) that he had failed to leave a competent and law-abiding subordinate in his stead at San Gerónimo; (3) that he had, without legitimate provocation, waged war against the Indians of Cíbola; (4) that he had precipitated an uprising of the people of Tiguex by illegally setting dogs on Bigotes and the *cacique*; (5) that he had ordered the execution of El Turco without reason and in secret; and (6) that he had failed to settle Tierra Nueva and forcibly blocked others from doing so.⁹

Without explaining their action in detail, on February 19, 1546, Viceroy Mendoza and the four *oidores* of the Audiencia issued their judgment in the case of mistreatment of Indians in Tierra Nueva, at least as far as Francisco Vázquez de Coronado was concerned. In one short paragraph they announced that the fiscal had not substantiated his complaint, whereas the accused had disproved responsibility for all offenses with which he was charged. They also enjoined the fiscal from pursuing the case against the former captain general any farther. The witnesses called in the case had generally agreed that Indians had been abused and mistreated during the expedition, but the judges believed they could not fault Vázquez de Coronado, who claimed he had not been present when violence against Indians had occurred and had not authorized such abuse. It bears underscoring that the witnesses repeatedly contradicted the captain general's claims of innocence and that the viceroy, who shared responsibility for the expedition, sat in judgment of his choice as captain general and helped exonerate him.

Cristóbal de Benavente, the *fiscal*, was not without a further target. He had previously recommended that Vázquez de Coronado's former *maestre de campo* García López de Cárdenas be punished for his role in the deaths of Indians of Tierra Nueva. Because Ramírez de Cárdenas, as he was now known, had returned to Spain to take up his patrimony, his case was heard before the Consejo de Indias there, rather than by the Audiencia in the Ciudad de México. In December 1549 the Consejo rendered its verdict, holding the former *maestre de campo* accountable on all charges leveled by its *fiscal*. The sentence imposed by the Consejo was a fine of 800 ducats and 30 months of service to the king at Orán, North Africa, at the guilty party's own expense. Through a series of legal appeals, by the end of 1551

Ramírez de Cárdenas and his attorney had succeeded in having the sentence reduced to a 200-ducat fine and 12 months of service at Vélez Málaga, where he had property.[10] The punishment was largely symbolic for what were generally agreed to be horrendous crimes against American natives. No one else was charged or tried.

Neither the king nor the viceroy was displeased with the outcome. The high profile case had kept the king's announced hard line against abuse of Indians before the public consciousness. At the same time, Vázquez de Coronado and, by extension, Viceroy Mendoza had been shielded from blame. Mendoza's reputation and tenure in office were highly important to Carlos I, and both were preserved.

For years Hernando Cortés and his supporters had sought to have don Antonio recalled and a new viceroy more sympathetic to the Cortés faction installed in his place. News of the Coronado expedition's mistreatment of indigenous people added ammunition to the Cortés arsenal. His adherents were yet another influential group in Spain that latched onto that news and sought to turn it against royal officials. In part, they succeeded. The king authorized a general *visita*, or judicial review, of all royal office holders in Nueva España.

For four years, from 1543 through 1546, a *visitador*, or investigating judge, Francisco Tello de Sandoval, a member of the Consejo de Indias, traversed Nueva España listening to complaints and taking testimony on a long list of issues, including mistreatment of Indians by those who had participated in the Coronado expedition. But as in the case of the *pesquisa*, few penalties were imposed on royal officials as a result of the *visita*. The viceroy, after deluging Tello de Sandoval with thousands of folios of testimony from hundreds of witnesses in his favor, avoided even serious reprimand. The *visita* proved to be Cortés's last assault against Mendoza. He died in Spain a year after the *visita* drew to an ignominious close with the recall of the *visitador*, now that don Antonio's brother, don Luis Hurtado de Mendoza, the Marqués de Mondéjar, had assumed the presidency of the Consejo de Indias in 1546.[11]

No former member of the Coronado expedition was subjected to the full force of the existing legal code governing treatment of Indians.

Yet almost all the expedition's contemporaries who were familiar with its details agreed that the group had done unwarranted violence to American natives and had repeatedly ignored their rights as recognized under the Spanish royal judicial standards of the day. In that respect, Spaniards at the time commonly thought of the expedition as a shameful example of Christian conduct.

Without Personal Blame

Both Tejada's *pesquisa* and the *visita* conducted by Tello de Sandoval were politically motivated and manipulated, which renders the accuracy of their findings uncertain. Without attempting either to retry members of the Coronado expedition or to assign individual responsibility, I briefly reexamine the surviving evidence of violence between the expedition and native residents of Tierra Nueva. My particular concern is why the violence took place and whether individuals or groups worked either to foment or to suppress it. I consider first the instances in which violence erupted during the course of the *entrada* and then those in which it appears to have been avoided or minimized.

Two categories of violence can usefully be distinguished in the documentary record of the Coronado expedition: violence targeted at entire communities and violence directed toward individuals. At times, however, the two are not easily discriminated, especially from the standpoint of individual targets of either sort of violence.

Violence against communities, group-on-group violence, was expressed during the Coronado *entrada* as various forms of war: war of conquest, defensive war, ceremonial war, and war of pillage and forced levy of supplies, equipment, and persons. The attack on Cíbola in July 1540, the brief assault on Tusayán a month or so later, and the expulsion of residents from Coofor another month after that were major events of war of conquest conducted by the expedition. Their goal was permanent submission by indigenous populations to Spanish political and religious authority. That goal, in turn, entailed pressure for wholesale alteration of the behavior and cultural bases of native societies. In all three 1540 cases, Indians responded with stratagems calculated to avoid submission to the will of the expeditionaries, including defensive war, flight, feigned capitulation, and gift giving. In none of the three instances was submission achieved that was satisfactory to the European expeditionaries.

In the case of Tiguex, following the rapid, feigned capitulation of the Pueblos and a short peaceful interlude, the war of conquest resumed when the entire Indian *provincia* rose up, unequivocally rejecting Spanish control. The ensuing Tiguex War included the assault on Pueblo del Arenal, the burning of defenders of Arenal, and the siege of Moho. Some of the dismantling of Tiguex pueblos was also part of the violence of conquest, being an element of conquest strategy.

Within or alongside war of conquest, the expedition's *indios amigos* might well have engaged in ritual warfare with Pueblo warriors. Documentary evidence for ritualized conflict during the *entrada* does not exist, but it would be consistent with the traditional practices of many of the Indian allies. The main goals of such conflict were to perform feats that would merit improvement of social status and gain supernatural aid. Accomplishments of this type included defeating peers in combat and capturing high-status prisoners or emblems. If such warfare took place in Tierra Nueva, which seems not unlikely, then it would have been encouraged or staged by the contending parties and might have been conducted beyond the observation of the European expeditionaries.

Both in the Río Sonora Valley and at Tiguex the expeditionaries launched war of pillage and forced levy to compel indigenous communities to provide food, clothing, shelter, and women. Included in this type of war were also the removal of firewood from pueblos in Tiguex and the pillaging of stored food in abandoned pueblos during the winters of 1540–41 and 1541–42. In response to such assaults, the Indian groups fought defensive war, offered partial compliance with levies, and argued their inability to comply. In most cases, war of pillage and forced levy was probably indistinguishable from war of conquest to the natives of Tierra Nueva, because they seemed equally directed toward the imposition of outside will on native societies.

All these types of group-against-group violence practiced by the expedition had their root cause in the Spaniards' pervasive and largely unquestioned belief in the superiority of Spanish society over all others and its right and duty to compel universal conformity with its most cherished principles. Collective assurance of a divinely sanctioned mission, coupled with the personal motives outlined early in this book, unleashed a powerful energy for conquest. That energy, when confronted by the reluctance and resistance of American natives, yielded violence in many forms. The violence committed against Indians of Tierra Nueva was consonant with attitudes and beliefs widely, though not universally, held within Spanish society of the day. It was neither an extreme aberration nor an everyday occurrence, but the attitudes from which it sprang were among those with greatest currency at the time.

The leaders of the Coronado expedition, from Viceroy Antonio de Mendoza to Francisco Vázquez de Coronado and his captains, were in that mainstream of belief. They did not, in general, seek violence, but they did expect it as a frequent accompaniment to extension of the king's temporal sovereignty and the spiritual authority of the Church. At least some members of the expedition thought of it as an enterprise of war from its inception and saw themselves as departing for war when they left the land already under Spanish political authority.[12]

Indigenous responses to the expedition's violence and threats of violence were primarily intended to deflect, defend against, or dodge possible harm. Such steps taken by natives of Tierra Nueva included abandonment of their homes, efforts at diplomacy, and the purchase of peace through limited compliance with demands for food and clothing. Once harm had occurred, though, the natives added to their repertoire of responses revenge and retaliation, as is evidenced by the killing of Lope de Samaniego at Chiametla early in the expedition, the slaughter of horses and their Mexican Indian guards at Tiguex in winter 1540, the attempt to kill García López de Cárdenas at the pueblo of Moho early in 1541, and the devastation of the outpost of San Gerónimo in 1542. In addition, Indians of Tierra Nueva attempted on occasion to play on the consciences of expeditionaries and even to appeal to the Europeans' own formal legal system, as in the case of the appeal to Vázquez de Coronado to punish the man who raped the woman at Pueblo del Arenal in fall 1540.

Shifting the struggle against expeditionary violence to the Spanish legal system placed issues in the arena of individual-on-individual violence, with which Vázquez de Coronado was likely more comfortable than with assessing the legitimacy of conquest. He could not be expected to scrutinize the justifications for that enterprise, but enforcing the criminal code was another matter. Indeed, both the viceroy and the captain general made a special point of prohibiting violent acts such as murder, theft, and rape against individual Indians, acts that were then, as now, considered criminal. The ordinances regarding treatment of Native Americans issued by Vázquez de Coronado, at Mendoza's direction, at the outset of the expedition were all aimed at suppressing such felonies. As it developed, Vázquez de Coronado compiled an uneven record of enforcement of those ordinances. He failed to press investigation of the rape of the Tiguex woman and evidently turned a blind eye to the seizure of Tiguex men's winter clothing. He did, however, punish *indios amigos* who stole goods from Indian homes in Sonora on the way north in 1540.

Enforcement of criminal law by the expeditionaries was not always to Indians' advantage. It resulted not only occasionally in protection of indigenous residents of Tierra Nueva but also in judicial violence against them. The best known examples of this are the torture of Bigotes and the *cacique* and the execution of El Turco. Once in the power of the expeditionaries, these native leaders were subject to normal Spanish judicial procedures, including torture to extract testimony in officially sanctioned inquiries and punishment for lying to the investigating authorities.

Nevertheless, persons both from the expedition and from resident native groups sometimes sought to reduce the potential for and amount of violence. At Cíbola, for instance, Vázquez de Coronado ordered a halt to an assault of mounted lancers, checking what would have been a general slaughter. The decision by the expedition's leadership to besiege Moho rather than continue all-out assault can also be seen as an effort to limit the violence suffered by the Tiguex defenders of the pueblo and its expeditionary attackers. Also at Moho, don Lope de Urrea, a member of Vázquez de Coronado's personal retinue, talked residents of the besieged pueblo into sending some women and children to safety. For that proposal to succeed as it did, it was necessary that leaders on the Pueblo side, too, sought to reduce the effects of impending violence. Furthermore, at the beginning of the *entrada*, Viceroy Mendoza went to great effort and some expense to forestall the possibility of forced levy of supplies at the Indian towns through which the expedition was to pass.

One of the best known examples of efforts by members of the expedition to avoid violence is the behavior of the Alarcón party. Only one minor incident marred the otherwise peaceful course of its river voyage. The small size of Alarcón's crew might have pushed its members in the direction of nonaggressive contact with Colorado and Gila River peoples. It might also have been that Alarcón and the leaders under him favored a fundamentally less belligerent absorption of Native Americans into the Spanish sphere than did most of their peers. The existing evidence does not permit a firm decision on this point.

The northward passage of Esteban de Dorantes in 1539 provides yet another instance of avoidance of violence. Again, that outcome required complementary, reciprocal efforts by the Moor and members of indigenous communities he met along his route. Only at Cíbola was such complementary effort not forthcoming, with fatal consequences for Esteban.

Exercise of Judgment

Violent acts have frequently taken center stage in this book, because violence and disappointment were important themes throughout the history of the Coronado expedition. The expedition was not unusual in this regard, either in comparison with other, similar sixteenth-century enterprises or in comparison with attempts at conquest undertaken at other times of human history. Neither the Coronado expedition nor other Spanish-led expeditions of conquest and reconnaissance of the period were significantly more violent than conquest in other places and at other times.

Certainly by today's standards, though, much of the violence inflicted by the Coronado expedition while in Tierra Nueva must be seen as reprehensible, imitation of which ought not to be encouraged by failing to criticize it. The underlying program of sixteenth-century Spanish conquest of the Western Hemisphere was to impose a government and a religion on peoples who did not, on their own, seek to change the organizing principles of their societies. Carried out with no matter what benign intentions, that program flagrantly denied the equality of humanity between the conquerors and the conquered, the most basic of human rights. The understanding that ensuring that equality is fundamental to harmony among peoples is now embodied in the first article of the United Nations' Universal Declaration of Human Rights, which reads, "All human beings are born free and equal in dignity and rights. They are endowed with reason and conscience and should act towards one another in a spirit of brotherhood."[13] That statement is the outcome of a sequence of thought and debate stretching back at least to Bartolomé de las Casas and like-minded Spanish critics of sixteenth-century conquistadores.

Today, most historians eschew the triumphalist and chauvinistic ethnic boosterism that flavored even the work of some great historians of the past. If the aim of historical research and writing is to increase understanding of the breadth and depth of past human behavior and reveal it as a guide for future actions, then partisan, nationalistic, or chauvinistic glorification, promotion, and justification are to be avoided as much as possible. Sanitized history only misleads the very people it is meant to aggrandize, by falsely assuring victors that their triumphs were inevitable and their missteps inconsequential, that they are on the leading edge of the ordained trajectory of human destiny.

In part, what has engaged me so strongly in studying the Coronado expedition has been the recurrent, eerie echo of elements of the expedition's motivations, practices, and experiences in the histories of the United States and other modern and otherwise enlightened nations. In some of the acts of the Coronado expedition we are confronted with the basest of human drives, all too easy to succumb to. May their story heighten our resolve to do better. In other behaviors of the expeditionaries we can take pride as fellow humans. May they inspire our emulation. ■

Maps

Map 1. Nueva España and Tierra Nueva in 1539

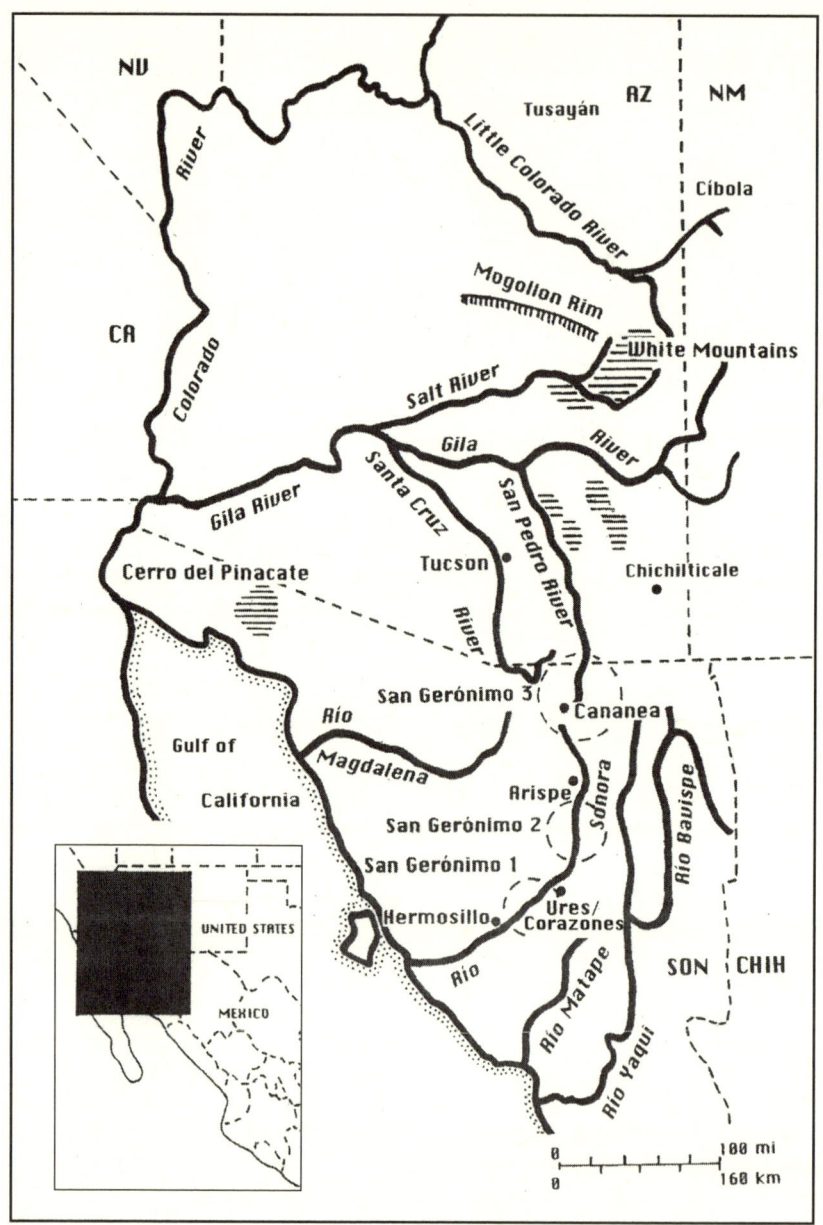

Map 2. Señora to Cíbola

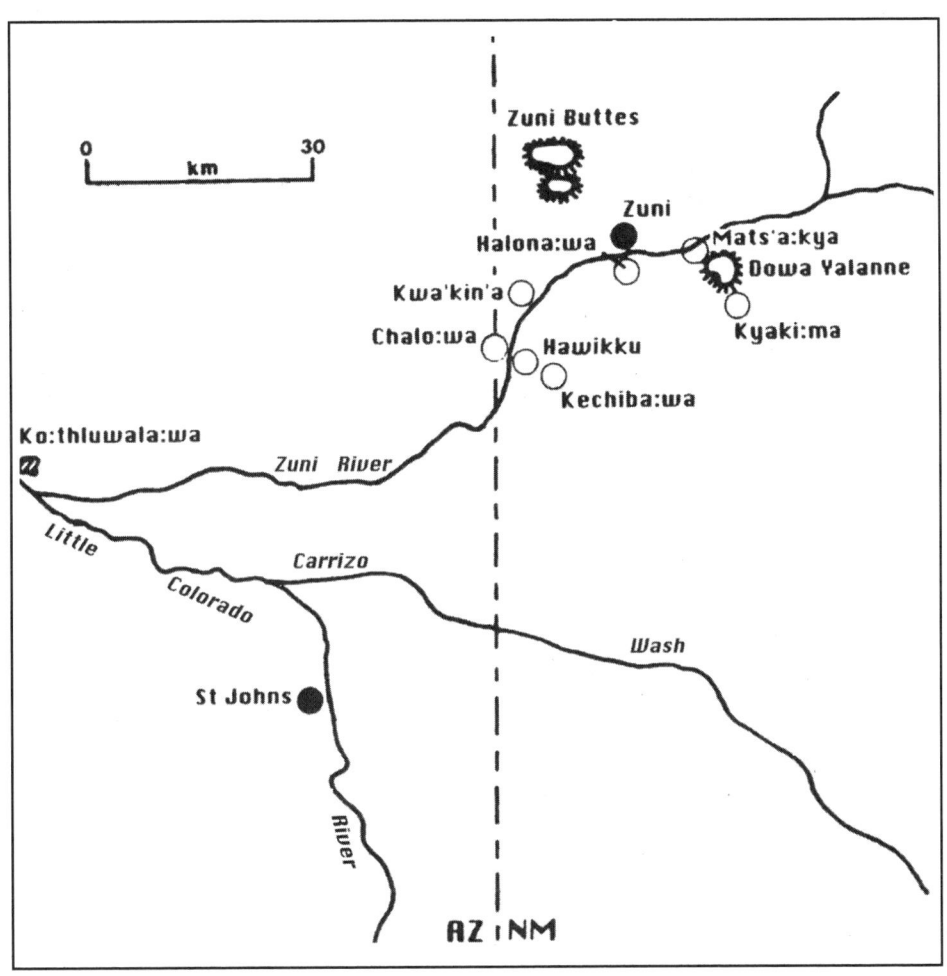

Map 3. Cíbola in 1540

254 ■ Maps

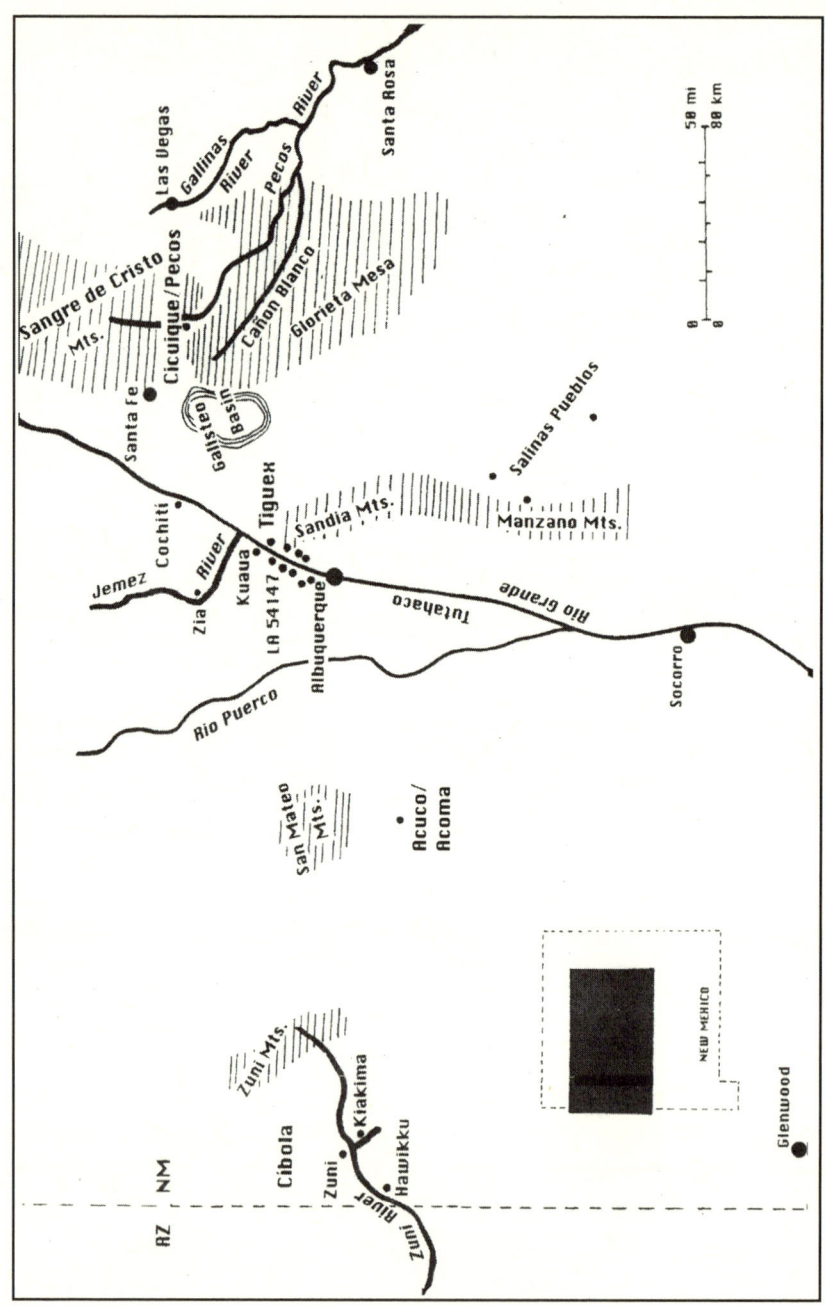

Map 4. Cíbola to Cicuique

MAPS ■ 255

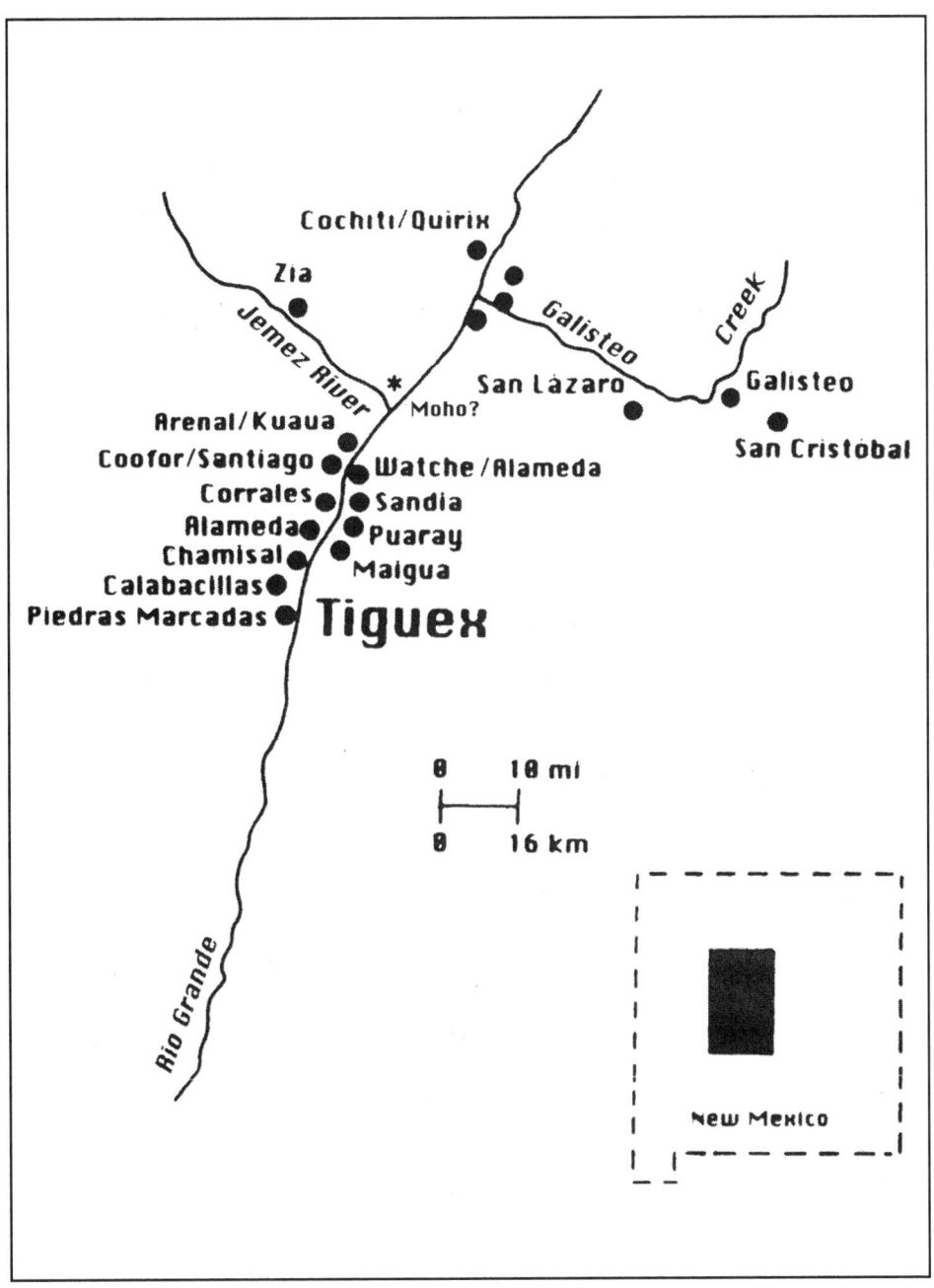

Map 5. Tiguex, 1540–1542

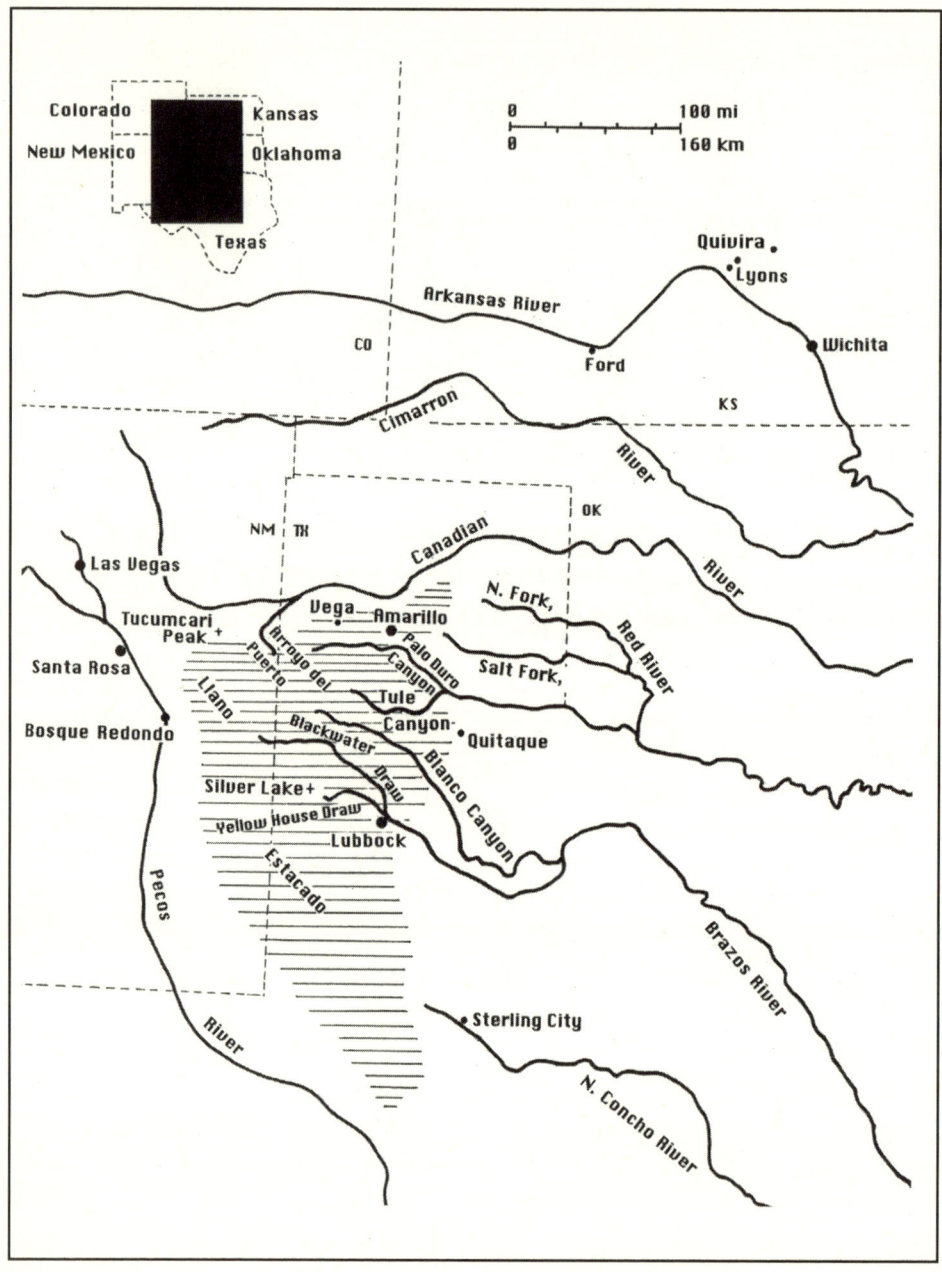

Map 6. Pecos River to Quivira

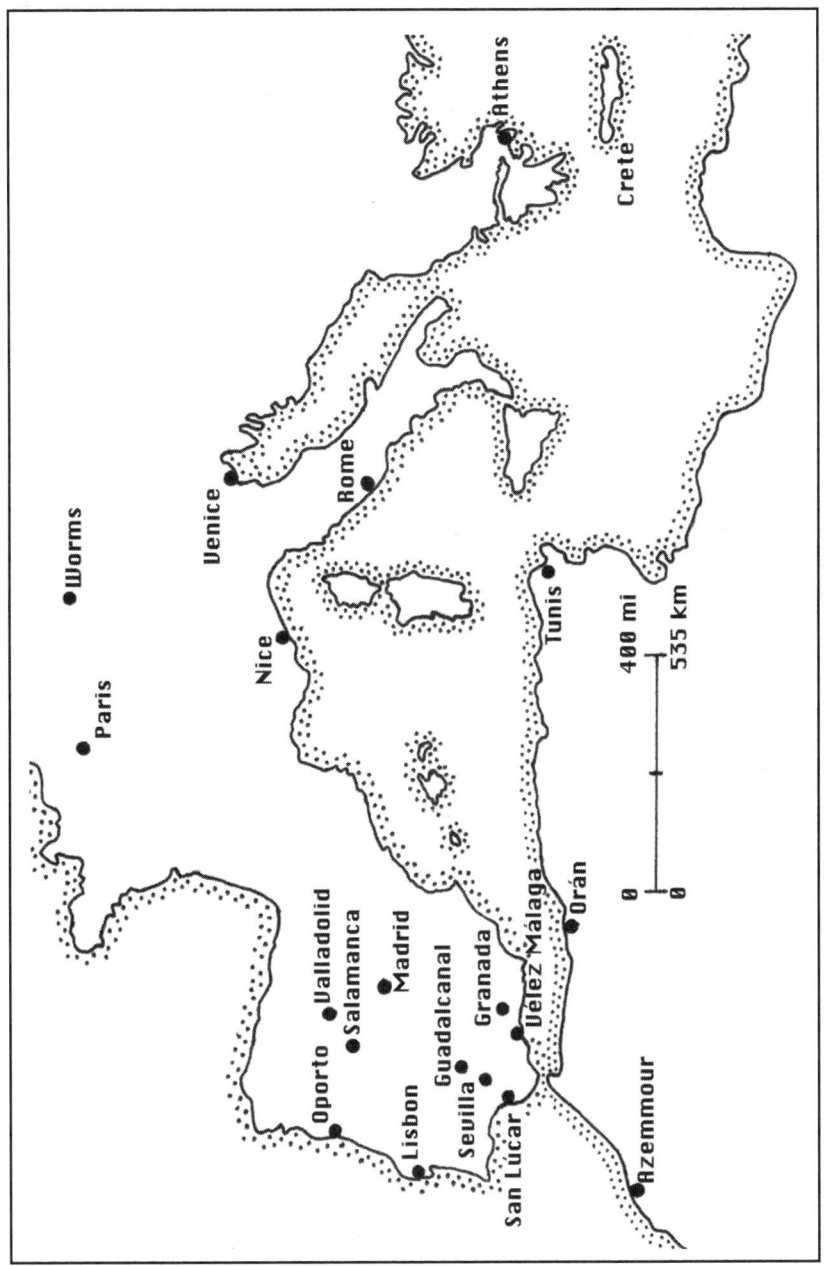

Map 7. Southern Europe and North Africa

Appendices

APPENDIX 1

Major Spanish-Led Expeditions in the Western Hemisphere, 1492–1598, by Date, Leader, and Area

1492–93.	Cristóbal Colón, Caribbean
1493–96.	Cristóbal Colón, Hispaniola, Puerto Rico, Cuba
1498–1500.	Cristóbal Colón, Trinidad, Tierra Firme
1499–1500.	Alonso de Ojeda and Juan de la Cosa, northern coast of South America
1499–1500.	Peralonso Niño and Cristóbal Guerra, Pearl Coast of South America
1499–1500.	Vicente Yañez Pinzón, northern Brazil
1499–1500.	Diego de Lepe, Morison, Brazilian coast
1500–1501.	Alonso Vélez de Mendoza, Luis Guerra, and Antón Guerra, northern Brazil
1500–1502.	Rodrigo de Bastidas, Darién
1501.	Cristóbal Guerra, southern Caribbean islands
1502–4.	Cristóbal Colón, Jamaica, Central America, Tierra Firme
1502–4.	Vicente Yañez Pinzón, northern Brazil
1502.	Alonso de Ojeda, northern coast of South America
1504–6.	Juan de la Cosa, northern coast of South America
1504–6.	Cristóbal Guerra, Luis Guerra, and Monroy, Pearl Coast and Darién
1505.	Vicente Yañez Pinzón and Juan de Solís, Central America, Tierra Firme
1505.	Juan Bermúdez, Bermuda, Hispaniola
1508.	Alonso de Ojeda, Cartagena
1508.	Diego de Nicuesa, Panama, Costa Rica

1508–9.	Vicente Yañez Pinzón and Juan Díaz de Solís, Caribbean coast, Tierra Firme
1513.	Vasco Núñez de Balboa, Pacific coast of Panama
1513.	Juan Ponce de León, Bahamas, Florida, Yucatán
1515–16.	Juan Díaz de Solís, Brazil, Río de la Plata
1515–16.	Gaspar de Espinosa, Panama
1515–16.	Jerónimo de Valenzuela, Panama
1517.	Francisco Hernández de Córdoba, Gulf of Mexico, Yucatán
1518.	Juan de Grijalba, Cozumel, Yucatán, Vera Cruz
1518–19.	Alonso Álvarez de Pineda, northern Gulf of Mexico coast
1519.	Hernán Ponce de León and Juan de Castañeda, Gulfs of Osa and Nicoya
1519–22.	Fernando Magallanes and Juan Sebastián del Cano, Río de la Plata, Patagonia, Strait of Magellan
1519–21.	Hernando Cortés, Campeche, Cempoala, Tlaxcala, Tenochtitlan
1521.	Juan Ponce de León, Florida
1521.	Álvarez Chico, Ciudad de México to Alima
1522.	Pascual de Andagoya, west coast of Panama
1522.	Andrés Niño, Central American coast
1522–23.	Gil González Dávila, Costa Rica
1522–24.	Pedro de Alvarado, Tehuantepec, Guatemala
1522–25.	Cristóbal de Olid, Zacatula, Colima, Nicaragua
1523–25.	Francisco Fernández de Córdoba, Costa Rica, Panama, Nicaragua, Guatemala
1523.	Luis Marín, Tabasco, Campeche
1523.	Francisco Cortés, Colima to Tepic
1523.	Gonzalo de Sandoval, Zacatula to Colima
1524–25.	Estevâo Gomes, Atlantic coast of North America
1524–25.	Aleixo García, Paraguay, Bolivia
1524–25.	Francisco Pizarro, northwest coast of South America
1524–26.	Hernando Cortés, Honduras
1525.	Pedro de Quejo, Florida to Delaware Bay

1525.	Diego García de Moguer, Río de la Plata, Paraná, Paraguay
1525–28.	Francisco García Jofre de Loaysa, Brazil, Strait of Magellan
1526.	Rodrigo de Bastidas, Santa Marta
1526.	Lucas Vázquez de Ayllón, South Carolina and Georgia
1526.	Pedro de Alvarado, Guatemala, Nicaragua
1526–28.	Francisco Pizarro, northwest coast of South America, Túmbez
1527.	Juan Martínez de Ampiés, Santa Ana de Coro
1527–28.	Diego de Mazariegos, Chiapas
1527–35.	Francisco de Montejo the elder, Yucatán, Campeche
1528–36.	Pánfilo de Narváez and Álvar Núñez Cabeza de Vaca, Florida, Texas, Coahuila, Chihuahua, Sonora, Sinaloa
1529.	Ambrosio Alfinger, Lago de Venezuela
1529.	Martín Estete, Isthmus of Panama
1529.	Juan de Panes and Juan Téllez, Veragua
1529–32.	Nuño Beltrán de Guzmán, Nueva Galicia
1530.	Gonzalo López, eastern Durango or western Coahuila, explored Culiacán-Humaya-Tamazula river system
1530–32.	Diego de Ordás, Marañón, Paria
1530–35.	Francisco Pizarro, Inca Peru
1531.	Pedro de Lerma, Río Magdalena, Venezuela
1531.	Ambrosio Alfinger, Colombia
1532–35.	Hernando Cortés, Baja California
1532–33.	Francisco de Viana, Juan de Céspedes, and Juan de San Martín, Río Magdalena, Colombia
ca. 1532.	Juan de Ayolas, Paraguay
1533.	Diego de Guzmán, Sinaloa, Sonora
1533.	Pedro de Heredia, Darién
1533–39.	Sebastián de Belálcazar, Ecuador, Colombia
1534–35.	Pedro de Alvarado, Peru
1535.	Gerónimo Gortal, Orinoco River
1535.	Georg von Speyer, Orinoco River
1535.	Lope Montalvo de Lugo, Colombia

1535–37.	Diego de Almagro, Bolivia, Chile
1535–37.	Pedro de Mendoza, Río de la Plata
1535–39.	Nikalaus Federmann, Venezuela, Colombia
1536.	Juan de Ayolas, Río Paraná and Río Paraguay
1536–37.	Gonzalo Jiménez de Quesada, Venezuela
1537.	Juan de Salazar, Asunción
1537.	Francisco de Montejo the elder, Guatemala, Chiapas
1537–42.	Domingo Martínez de Irala, Río de la Plata, Paraguay
1539.	Francisco de Ulloa, Gulf of California
1539.	Alonso Calero, Panama, Nicaragua
1539.	Hernán Sánchez de Badajoz, Panama
1539–43.	Hernando de Soto and Luis de Moscoso, southeastern United States
1539–42.	Francisco Vázquez de Coronado, northwestern Mexico and southwestern United States
1540.	Jerónimo Lebrón, Colombia
1540.	Hernán Sánchez de Badajoz, Atlantic coast of Costa Rica
1540–42.	Francisco de Montejo the younger, Campeche, Mérida
1540–43.	Gonzalo Pizarro, Peru, Ecuador
1541–43.	Francisco de Orellana, Amazon
1540–47.	Pedro de Valdivia, Chile
1542–43.	Juan Rodríguez Cabrillo, California coast
1542–43.	Alonso Luis de Lugo, Colombia
1542–44.	Álvar Núñez Cabeza de Vaca, Río de la Plata, Paraguay
1543–44.	Diego de Gutiérrez, Costa Rica, Nicaragua
1543.	Álvar Núñez Cabeza de Vaca, Paraguay
1544–56.	Domingo Martínez de Irala, Paraguay, Bolivia
1546.	Juan de Tolosa, Zacatecas
1551–52.	Hernán Pérez de Bocanegra, Gran Chichimeca
1552.	Francisco de Herrera, Gran Chichimeca
1552.	Ginés Vázquez de Mercado, Durango, Chihuahua
1553.	Gonzalo Hernández de Rojas, Gran Chichimeca

Major Spanish-Led Expeditions   265

1558–59.	Francisco Vázquez, Panama
1558–61.	García Hurtado de Mendoza, Chile
1560.	Juan de Estrada Ravago, Costa Rica, Nicaragua
1560–61.	Pedro de Ursúa and Lope de Aguirre, Amazon
1561.	Pedro de Ahumada Sámano, Gran Chichimeca
1561.	Juan de Cavallón, Costa Rica
1561–63.	Juan de Cavallón, interior of Costa Rica
1562–64.	Juan Vázquez de Coronado, central valley of Costa Rica
1563–75.	Francisco de Ibarra and Miguel de Ibarra, Chiametla, Culiacán, Sinaloa, Sonora, Chihuahua
1565–66.	Pedro Menéndez de Avilés, Florida, South Carolina
1566–67.	Juan Pardo, South Carolina, North Carolina
1567.	Rodrigo del Río de Losa, Indé, Durango
1567.	Alonso de Castilla, Gran Chichimeca
1567–68.	Juan Pardo, South Carolina, North Carolina
1568–75.	Perafán de Rivera, Costa Rica
1569.	Juan Torres de Lagunas, Gran Chichimeca
1569.	Francisco Cano, Gran Chichimeca
1573.	Francisco de Puga, Huasteca-Zacatecas
1580.	Juan de Garay, Buenos Aires
1581.	Fray Agustín Rodríguez and Francisco Sánchez Chamuscado, New Mexico
1582–83.	Antonio de Espejo, New Mexico
1583.	Luis de Carvajal, Nuevo León
1585–92.	Miguel Caldera, Gran Chichimeca
1590–91.	Gaspar Castaño de Sosa, New Mexico
1591.	Juan de Morlete, New Mexico
1598.	Juan de Oñate, New Mexico

Appendix 2

Chronological Context of the Coronado Entrada,

A.D. 700–1609

700–711.	Conquest of the Iberian Peninsula by Moorish armies under Tariq ibn Ziyad
734.	Supposed founding of the Seven Cities of Antilia
1150s.	Abandonment of Chaco Canyon in present-day New Mexico
1248.	Christian reconquest of Sevilla from the Moors
1298–99.	*The Travels* written by Marco Polo in collaboration with Rustichello
1345.	Foundation of Tenochtitlan by the Mexica
1350s.	Abandonment of Cahokia in present-day Missouri
1420s.	Abandonment of the Hohokam area in present-day Arizona
1450s.	Abandonment of Paquimé in present-day northern Mexico
1453.	Fall of Constantinople to the Ottoman Turks
1469.	De facto unification of Spain with the marriage of Isabel of Castilla and Fernando of Aragón
1478–93.	Conquest of Gran Canaria, Tenerife, and La Palma in the Canary Islands
1492.	Spanish reconquest of Granada; expulsion of the Jews from Spain; landfall in the Indies by Columbus
1494.	Suleiman I becomes sultan of the Ottoman Empire
1509.	Henry VIII becomes king of England
1511.	Sermons regarding Indian rights by Montesinos in Cuba
1515.	François I becomes king of France
1516.	Carlos I becomes king of Spain

APPENDIX 2

1517.	Martin Luther posts his 95 theses
1519.	Leonardo da Vinci dies; Carlos I becomes Carlos V, Holy Roman Emperor
1519–21.	Conquest of Tenochtitlan by conquistadores under Cortés; founding of the Ciudad de México on the ruins
1519–22.	First crossing of the Pacific Ocean and circumnavigation of the globe by Europeans under Magellan and del Cano
1528.	Beginning of the Narváez expedition to La Florida
1529–32.	Conquest of Nueva Galicia by conquistadores under Guzmán
1535.	Antonio de Mendoza installed as first viceroy of Nueva España
1536.	Cabeza de Vaca, Dorantes, Castillo, and Esteban reach Culiacán; death of Desiderius Erasmus
1538–39.	Trek of fray Marcos de Niza and Esteban de Dorantes to Cíbola
1539.	Departure of Coronado expedition from the Ciudad de México
1540.	Muster of the Coronado expedition at Compostela, February; capture of Cíbola, July; attempt to descend into the Grand Canyon, August; Alarcón gives up attempt to rendezvous with the land expedition, August; expedition takes up winter quarters in Tiguex
1540–41.	Tiguex War
1541.	Coronado expeditionaries reach Quivira
1541–42.	Mixtón War
1542.	Return of the Coronado expedition to Mexico; publication of the New Laws; ships under López de Villalobos cross the central Pacific
1542–43.	Voyage up the coast of the Californias under Rodríguez Cabrillo
1543.	*Pesquisa secreta* of the Coronado expedition's treatment of Indians
1545.	Discovery of silver at Cerro Rico, Potosí, Lower Peru
1545–48.	*Cocolitzli* epidemic in Mexico
1545–63.	Council of Trent
1546.	Silver discovered at Zacatecas, Mexico
1547.	Henry VIII dies and is succeeded by Edward VI; Henri II becomes king of France; Miguel de Cervantes Saavedra is born
1548.	Death of Bishop Zumárraga
1549.	López de Cárdenas convicted of abuse of Indians in Tierra Nueva
1550.	Viceroy Mendoza transferred to Peru

1556.	Abdication of Carlos I; accession of Felipe II as king of Spain; publication of Italian translations of documents from the Coronado expedition by Ramusio
1557.	First bankruptcy of the Spanish monarchy
1558.	Elizabeth I becomes queen of England
1558–62.	Proposals from Zorita and fray Cyndos to return to Tierra Nueva
1564.	Ibarra expedition reaches Paquimé; Manila galleon trade begins
1565.	Founding of St. Augustine in La Florida
1566.	Revolt against Spanish rule in the Netherlands
1571.	Spanish defeat of the Ottoman fleet at Lepanto
1580.	Disaster strikes the Spanish armada
1582.	Gregorian calendar instituted in Spain and its dependencies
1598.	Permanent Spanish settlement of New Mexico under Juan de Oñate; death of Felipe II
1602–3.	Voyage up the west coast of North America under Vizcaíno
1607.	Founding of Jamestown in the Virginias
1609.	Founding of Santa Fe in New Mexico

Abbreviations Used in the Notes and References

AGI. Archivo General de Indias, Sevilla

AGN. Archivo de la Nación, Ciudad de México

AHN. Archivo Histórico Nacional, Madrid

BNM. Biblioteca Nacional, Madrid

Castañeda de Nájera. Castañeda de Nájera's Narrative, 1560s [copy, 1596], NYPL-R, no. 63, transcribed and translated as Document 28 in *Documents*, 384–493.

Documents. Richard Flint and Shirley Cushing Flint, trans. and eds., *Documents of the Coronado Expedition, 1539–1542: They Were Not Familiar with His Majesty, nor Did They Wish to Be His Subjects* (Dallas: Southern Methodist University Press, 2005)

Great Cruelties. Richard Flint, *Great Cruelties Have Been Reported: The 1544 Investigation of the Coronado Expedition* (Dallas: Southern Methodist University Press, 2002)

NYPL-R. New York Public Library, Rich Collection

UCB, Ban. University of California, Berkeley, Bancroft Library

UTA, Ben. University of Texas, Austin, Nettie Lee Benson Latin American Collection

Notes

Chapter 1: Whys and Wherefores

1. Castañeda de Nájera, fol. 130v (*Documents*, 426, 483).

2. AGI, Patronato, 216, R.2, Investigation concerning Nuño de Chávez, 1566, fol. 10r, published in *Great Cruelties*, 358, 379.

3. Ibid., fol. 33v (*Great Cruelties*, 422, 429).

4. Ibid., fol. 33r (*Great Cruelties*, 421, 428).

5. AGI, Patronato, 20, N.5, R.8, Juan Jaramillo's Narrative, 1560s, fol. 4v, transcribed and translated as Document 30 in *Documents*, 517, 523; Castañeda de Nájera, fol. 91v (*Documents*, 412, 468).

6. Frederick Jackson Turner, *History, Frontier, and Section: Three Essays* (Albuquerque: University of New Mexico Press, 1993), 59.

7. Julio Caro Baroja, *Los Moriscos del reino de Granada* (Madrid: Ediciones Istmo, 1991), 40.

8. Ibid., 42, 55.

9. Peggy K. Liss, *Isabel the Queen: Life and Times* (Oxford: Oxford University Press, 1992), 184–85.

10. Peter Bakewell, *A History of Latin America: Empires and Sequels, 1450–1930* (Oxford: Blackwell, 1997), 79–80.

11. Archivo Colonial de Guatemala, Grant from Francisco de Montejo to Antonio de Guevara, 1544, translated by Lesley Byrd Simpson in *The Encomienda in New Spain: The Beginning of Spanish Mexico* (Berkeley: University of California Press, 1966), 203–4.

12. Robert Himmerich y Valencia has pointed out that this was because natives of the Caribbean were already accustomed to providing labor tribute to their native leaders. Robert Himmerich y Valencia, *The Encomenderos of New Spain, 1521–1555* (Austin: University of Texas Press, 1991), 10.

13. Charles Gibson, *The Aztecs under Spanish Rule: A History of the Indians of the Valley of Mexico, 1519–1810* (Stanford, Calif.: Stanford University Press, 1964), 5; Himmerich y Valencia, *Encomenderos*, 13.

14. Patricia Seed, *Ceremonies of Possession in Europe's Conquest of the New World, 1492–1640* (Cambridge: Cambridge University Press, 1995), 83.

15. Himmerich y Valencia, *Encomenderos*, 11.

16. García Rodríguez, in AGI, Justicia, 1021, N.2, Pieza 2, Report Extracted from the Affidavit Prepared for don García Ramírez de Cárdenas [1540s], fol. 5v, published in *Great Cruelties*, 446, 456.

17. Herbert Bolton alluded with some misgiving to late-sixteenth-century accounts of a third friar who stayed behind when the Coronado expedition returned south, a fray Juan de la Cruz. Fray Angelico Chavez later argued persuasively that no such person accompanied the expedition. Instead, the scant information that exists about fray Juan actually applies to fray Luis de Úbeda. Herbert E. Bolton, *Coronado: Knight of Pueblos and Plains* (Albuquerque: University of New Mexico Press, 1949), 338–39; Fray Angelico Chavez, *Coronado's Friars* (Washington, D.C.: Academy of American Franciscan History, 1968), 32–36.

18. Castañeda de Nájera, fol. 136r (*Documents*, 427, 485).

19. Juan Jaramillo's Narrative, fol. 5r (*Documents*, 517, 524).

20. Castañeda de Nájera, fol. 136v (*Documents*, 427, 485).

21. Juan Jaramillo's Narrative, fol. 5v (*Documents*, 517, 524); Fray Antonio Tello, *Libro segundo de la Crónica miscelánea, en que se trata de la conquista espiritual y temporal de la santa provincia de Xalisco en el nuevo reino de la Galicia y Nueva Vizcaya y descubrimiento del Nuevo México* (Guadalajara, México: La Republica Literaria, 1891; reprint, México, D.F.: Editorial Porrúa, 1997), 485.

22. Juan Jaramillo's Narrative, fol. 5v (*Documents*, 517, 524).

23. Ibid., fols. 5r, 5v (*Documents*, 517, 524).

24. Delno C. West, "Medieval Ideas of Apocalyptic Mission and the Early Franciscans in Mexico," *The Americas* 45 (January 1989): 294.

25. Ibid., 295.

26. John L. Phelan, *The Millennial Kingdom of the Franciscans in the New World*, 2nd ed. (Berkeley: University of California Press, 1970), 44–58.

27. Robert Ricard, *The Spiritual Conquest of Mexico: An Essay on the Apostolate and the Evangelizing Methods of the Mendicant Orders in New Spain, 1523–1572*, translated by Lesley Byrd Simpson (Berkeley: University of California Press, 1966), 21; Phelan, *Millennial Kingdom*, 46.

28. As indicated by his co-signing several letters with fray Juan de Zumárraga, fray Martín de Valencia, and others of the original twelve. Chávez, *Coronado's Friars*, 14–23. On the sheerest speculation, Fray Angelico Chavez portrayed Juan de Padilla as obsessed with seeking the legendary Seven Cities of Antilia, Christian enclaves thought to be somewhere in the New World. Ibid., 14–27. Nothing in the documentary evidence indicates that the story of the Seven Cities held any more weight for fray Juan than it did for the rest of the expeditionaries.

29. AGI, Justicia, 267, N.3, Proceso of Francisco Vázquez de Coronado, fol. 14v, published in *Great Cruelties*, 65, 74.

30. Castañeda de Nájera, fol. 131r (*Documents*, 426, 483).

31. Juan Jaramillo's Narrative, fol. 5r (*Documents*, 517, 524).

32. AGI, Patronato, 21, N.2, R.3, Hearing on Depopulation Charges, February 26, 1540, fol. 5r, transcribed and translated as Document 14 in *Documents*, 178, 184. The identities of only four persons who sought to stay behind the expedition in Tierra Nueva are certain: Sánchez, Hozes, their son, and Juan Jaramillo. Whether they are representative of the group of potential settlers is impossible to say with confidence.

33. Ibid., fol. 4v (*Documents*, 178, 183).

34. Hugh Thomas has offered what he calls a conservative estimate of 150,000 Europeans who immigrated to all of Nueva España by 1550. A significant portion of them resided in the Ciudad de México. Hugh Thomas, *Conquest: Montezuma, Cortés, and the Fall of Old Mexico* (New York: Simon and Schuster, 1993), 593.

35. UCB, Ban., M-M 1714, Melchior Pérez's Petition for Preferment, 1551, transcribed and translated as Document 32 in *Documents*, 533–53; AGI, México, 204, N.14, Cristóbal de Escobar's Proof of Service, 1543, transcribed and translated as Document 33 in *Documents*, 554–80.

36. AGI, Contratación, 5575, N.24, Disposal of the Juan Jiménez Estate, 1542 [copy, 1550], transcribed and translated as Document 27 in *Documents*, 326–77.

37. AGI, Justicia, 270, Pieza 4, Residencia of Gerónimo de Medina, 1546; Proceso of Francisco Vázquez de Coronado, fol. 14v (*Great Cruelties*, 78, 83); Disposal of the Juan Jiménez Estate (*Documents*, 326–77); AGI, Patronato, 79, N.3, R.2, Proof of Service of Francisco de Santillana, Mérida, 1594; AGI, México, 1064, L.1\1, Reports of the Conquistadores and Settlers of the Ciudad de México, ca. 1547, fol. 270r; AGI, Contratación, 199, N.23, Goods of the Deceased, Bartolomé Sánchez, 1561.

38. Arthur S. Aiton and Agapito Rey, "Coronado's Testimony in the Viceroy Mendoza *Residencia*," *New Mexico Historical Review* 12 (July 1937): 314.

39. Richard Flint, "What's Missing from This Picture? The *Alarde*, or Muster Roll, of the Coronado Expedition," in Richard Flint and Shirley Cushing Flint, eds., *The Coronado Expedition from the Distance of 460 Years* (Albuquerque: University of New Mexico Press, 2003), 57–80.

40. Inga Clendinnen, *Aztecs: An Interpretation* (Cambridge: Cambridge University Press, 1991), 111–13.

41. Frances F. Berdan and Patricia Rieff Anawalt, eds., *The Essential Codex Mendoza* (Berkeley: University of California Press, 1997), 132.

42. "Memorial of the Indians concerning Their Services, ca. 1563," in Robert H. Barlow and George T. Smisor, eds. and trans., *Nombre de Dios, Durango: Two*

Documents in Nahuatl concerning Its Foundation (Sacramento, Calif.: House of Tlaloc, 1943), 31.

43. AGI, Justicia, 258, Pieza 1, Administrative Review of the Viceroy and *Oidores* . . . Conducted by Tello de Sandoval, 1546, fol. 623r.

44. Polly Schaafsma, *Warrior, Shield, and Star: Imagery and Ideology of Pueblo Warfare* (Santa Fe, N.M.: Western Edge Press, 2000), 3–7.

45. In much the same way, the sixteenth-century mariner Juan de Escalante de Mendoza said of a group of Spanish sailors of the day that they were "restless individuals who possessed a certain education, but whose temperament led them to seek out the risk and adventure of a military life." Pablo E. Pérez-Mallaína, *Spain's Men of the Sea: Daily Life on the Indies Fleets in the Sixteenth Century*, trans. Carla Rahn Phillips (Baltimore, Md.: Johns Hopkins University Press, 1998), 30.

46. Bolton, *Coronado*, 395–96.

47. "The Address of Charles, King of the Romans, to the Spanish Cortes, Immediately before His Departure," translated in John M. Headley, *The Emperor and His Chancellor: A Study in the Imperial Chancellery under Gattinara* (Cambridge: Cambridge University Press, 1983), 11.

48. Headley, *Emperor and His Chancellor*, 10.

49. Disposal of the Juan Jiménez estate, fol. 11r (*Documents*, 338, 361).

Chapter 2: Precious Goods of Greater India, China, and Antilia

1. Castañeda de Nájera, fol. 144r (*Documents*, 430, 488).

2. Carmen García Ormaechea y Quero, "The Far East," in *Art and Culture around 1492* (Sevilla: Sociedad Estatal para la Exposición Universal Sevilla 92, 1992), 44.

3. See Morris Rossabi, "The Silk Trade in China and Central Asia," in James C. Y. Watt and Anne E. Wardwell, eds., *When Silk Was Gold: Central Asian and Chinese Textiles* (New York: Metropolitan Museum of Art, 1997), 7–19.

4. Marco Polo, *The Travels of Marco Polo*, ed. and trans. Ronald Latham (New York: Penguin, 1958), 130.

5. Ibid., 36.

6. For a visual summary of learned thought about the relationship of Asia to America, see David Woodward, "The Renaissance Geographic and Cartographic Background to the First Century of Greater Southwest Discovery and Cartography," in Dennis Reinhartz and Gerald D. Saxon, eds., *The Mapping of the Entradas into the Greater Southwest* (Norman: University of Oklahoma Press, 1998), 5–7.

7. Castañeda de Nájera, fol. 96r (*Documents*, 414, 470).

8. Ibid., fol. 116v.

9. See, for example, Woodward, "Renaissance Geographic and Cartographic Background," 4.

10. Ibid., 11.

11. Translation in Samuel Eliot Morison, *The European Discovery of America: The Northern Voyages, 1492–1616* (New York: Oxford University Press, 1974), 99.

12. Morison, *Northern Voyages*, 100. The chart is reproduced in color in Gavin Menzies, *1421: The Year China Discovered America* (New York: Harper Collins, 2002), opposite 297.

13. Oliver Dunn and James E. Kelley Jr., trans. and eds., *The Diario of Christopher Columbus's First Voyage to America, 1492–1493* (Norman: University of Oklahoma Press, 1989), 40–45.

14. Samuel Eliot Morison, *The European Discovery of America: The Southern Voyages, 1492–1616* (New York: Oxford University Press, 1974), 30, 54; Dunn and Kelley, *Diario*, 28–41. Twenty-eight degrees is approximately the latitude of Gomera in the Canaries and the Ryukyu Islands at the southern end of the Japanese archipelago.

15. Enrique de Gandía, *Historia crítica de los mitos de la conquista americana* (Buenos Aires: Juan Roldán, 1929), 8.

16. Garci Rodríguez de Montalvo, *Las sergas de Esplandián* (Zaragosa: Casa de Simon de Portonariis, 1587; facsimile, Madrid: Ediciones Doce Calles, 1998), 100v.

17. Diego Durán, *The History of the Indies of New Spain*, trans. and ed. Doris Heyden (Norman: University of Oklahoma Press, 1994), 10–12; Bernardino de Sahagún, *Primeros Memoriales*, trans. Thelma D. Sullivan (Norman: University of Oklahoma Press, 1997), 221–22.

18. Dunn and Kelley, *Diario*, 116, 117, 131, 135.

19. Ibid., 129; Robert H. Fuson, trans. and ed., *The Log of Christopher Columbus* (Camden, Me.: International Marine Publishing, 1992), 100.

20. Morison, *Southern Voyages*, 263–67.

21. Gonzalo Fernández de Oviedo [y Valdéz], *Historia general y natural de las Indias*, ed. Juan Pérez de Tudela Bueso, 5 vols. (Madrid: Ediciones Atlas, 1992), 2: 114, 147; Thomas, *Conquest*, 92, author's translation.

22. Bernal Díaz del Castillo, *The Discovery and Conquest of Mexico*, trans. and ed. A. P. Maudslay (New York: Farrar, Straus and Cudahy, 1956), 196.

23. Ibid., 226.

24. A thorough review of population estimates for Tenochtitlan appears in Thomas, *Conquest*, 609–14. Thomas himself, finding all the wide-ranging estimates suspect, settled for the statement that Tenochtitlan was the "largest city on the American continent."

25. Francisco López de Gómara, *Cortés: The Life of the Conqueror by His Secretary*, trans. and ed. Lesley Byrd Simpson (Berkeley: University of California Press, 1964), 154.

26. Ibid., 298.

27. Himmerich y Valencia, *Encomenderos*.

28. Oviedo y Valdés, *Historia general*, 5: 50, author's translation.

29. James Lockhart, *The Men of Cajamarca: A Social and Biographical Study of the First Conquerors of Peru* (Austin: University of Texas Press, 1972), 60.

30. Castañeda de Nájera, fol. 7r (*Documents*, 386, 437).

31. Ibid., fol. 8r (*Documents*, 386, 437).

32. Ibid., fol. 7v (*Documents*, 386, 437).

33. Tello, *Crónica miscelánea*, 70–252.

34. Castañeda de Nájera, fol. 9v (*Documents*, 387, 438).

35. Álvar Núñez Cabeza de Vaca, *Naufragios y comentarios con dos cartas*, 9th ed. (México, D.F.: Espasa-Calpe Mexicana, 1985), 92, author's translation.

36. Ibid., 81, author's translation.

37. Oviedo y Valdéz, *Historia general*, 4: 307, author's translation.

38. Jane MacLaren Walsh, "Myth and Imagination in the American Story: The Coronado Expedition, 1540–1542" (Ph.D. diss., Catholic University of America, 1993), 54.

Chapter 3: Cíbola, a Name for the Goal

1. BNM, MS 3042, Relación de Antonio de Mendoza a Luis de Velasco al término de su Gobierno. Sin fecha. c. 1550 ó 1551, transcribed as Documento Número 5 in Lewis Hanke, ed., *México: Los virreyes españoles en América durante el gobierno de la Casa de Austria*, 5 vols. (Madrid: Ediciones Atlas, 1976), 1: 55. Author's translation.

2. George Parker Winship, ed. and trans., *The Coronado Expedition, 1540–1542*, Fourteenth Annual Report of the Bureau of American Ethnology, 1892–1893, Part 1 (Washington, D.C.: Smithsonian Institution, 1896; reprint, Chicago: Rio Grande Press, 1964), 16; Arthur S. Aiton, *Antonio de Mendoza: First Viceroy of New Spain* (Durham, N.C.: Duke University Press, 1927), 119; Bolton, *Coronado*, 13.

3. Tello, *Crónica miscelánea*, 229.

4. Gonzalo Fernández de Oviedo y Valdés, chapter 7 of Book 35 of the *Historia general y natural de las Indias*, as translated in Alex D. Krieger, ed., *We Came Naked and Barefoot: The Journey of Cabeza de Vaca across North America* (Austin: University of Texas Press, 2002), 295.

5. Biblioteca Real, Madrid, II/3042, Gonzalo Fernández de Oviedo y Valdés, *Historia general y natural de las Indias*, tercera parte, libro XL, capítulo I, 1547, Letters from Antonio de Mendoza and Rodrigo de Albornoz, October 18, 1539, transcribed and translated as Document 7 in *Documents*, 89–94.

6. Baltasar de Obregón, *Historia de los descubrimientos antiguos y modernos de la Nueva España, escrita por el conquistador en el año de 1584*, ed. Mariano Cuevas (México, D.F.: Editorial Porrúa, 1988), 13.

7. Bolton, *Coronado*, 15. I have been unable to verify Bolton's inference documentarily, but it seems consistent with the viceroy's known behavior.

8. AGI, Patronato, 184, R.27, Letter of Mendoza to the King, December 10, 1537.

9. Carta de Francisco de Villalta, June 22, 1556, quoted in translation in David A. Howard, *Conquistador in Chains: Cabeza de Vaca and the Indians of the Americas* (Tuscaloosa: University of Alabama Press, 1997), 33.

10. Álvar Núñez Cabeza de Vaca, "Account of the Disasters (*Relación de los Naufragios*)," in Krieger, *Naked and Barefoot*, 237.

11. Giovanni Battista Ramusio, *Terzo volumen delle navigationi et viaggi*, 1556, Letter of the Viceroy to the King, 1539, fol. 355r, transcribed and translated as Document 4 in *Documents*, 47–48, 49.

12. Ibid.

13. Letter of Mendoza to the King, December 10, 1537, fol. 14v.

14. Rolena Adorno and Patrick Charles Pautz, *Álvar Núñez Cabeza de Vaca: His Account, His Life, and the Expedition of Pánfilo de Narváez*. 3 vols. (Lincoln: University of Nebraska Press, 1999), 2: 422–27.

15. Bartolomé de las Casas, *Del único modo de atraer a todos los pueblos a la verdadera religión* (México, D.F.: Fondo de Cultura Económica, 1942).

16. Lewis Hanke, "Pope Paul III and the American Indians," *Harvard Theological Review* 30 (1937): 71–73.

17. Lewis Hanke, "Introducción," in las Casas, *Único modo*, 47.

18. AGI, Patronato 20, N.5, R.10, The Viceroy's Instructions to fray Marcos de Niza, November 1538, fol. 1v, transcribed and translated as Document 6 in *Documents*, 66, 79.

19. Cabeza de Vaca, "Account of the Disasters," 233–35.

20. Certification by fray Antonio de Ciudad Rodrigo, in AGI, Patronato 20, N.5, R.10, Narrative Account by fray Marcos de Niza, fol. 2r, transcribed and translated as Document 6 in *Documents*, 67, 79–80.

21. Bartolomé de las Casas, *The Devastation of the Indies: A Brief Account*, trans. Herma Briffault (Baltimore, Md.: Johns Hopkins University Press, 1992), 115–18.

22. Fray Juan de Zumárraga, Carta a un ecleciástico desconocido, April 1537, published in Mariano Cuevas, ed., *Documentos inéditos del siglo XVI para la historia de México* (México, D.F.: Museo Nacional de Arqueología, Historia y Etnología, 1914), 83–84.

23. AGI, México, 1088, L.3, Royal *Cédula,* Valladolid, November 22, 1538, fols. 1r–1v.

24. AGI, Guadalajara, 5, R.1, N.6, Letter of Vázquez de Coronado to the King, July 15, 1539, fol. 2v, transcribed and translated as Document 3 in *Documents*, 40, 43; Letter of Mendoza to the King, December 10, 1537, fol. 14v.

25. AGI, Justicia, 259, Pieza 2, Visita of don Antonio de Mendoza, 1546, Roster of the Viceroy's Personal Guard, fols. 49r–51v.

26. Narrative Account by fray Marcos de Niza, fol. 2r (*Documents*, 67, 80).

27. Viceroy's Instructions to fray Marcos de Niza, fol. 2v (*Documents*, 68, 80–81).

28. Narrative Account by fray Marcos de Niza, fol. 3r (*Documents*, 68, 81).

29. Ibid., fol. 3r (*Documents*, 69, 81).

30. Ibid., fol. 3v (*Documents*, 69, 82).

31. Ibid. (*Documents*, 70, 82).

32. Ibid., fol. 4v (*Documents*, 71, 83).

33. Ibid., fol. 5r (*Documents*, 72, 84).

34. Ibid.

35. Claudius Ptolemy, *The Geography*, trans. and ed. Edward Luther Stevenson (New York: Dover, 1991), 26–27.

36. Narrative Account by fray Marcos de Niza, fol. 5v (*Documents*, 73, 85).

37. Ibid.

38. Ibid.

39. *Documents*, 630, Document 6, n. 148.

40. Narrative Account by fray Marcos de Niza, fol. 6r (*Documents*, 74, 85).

41. Ibid., fol. 6v (*Documents*, 75, 86).

42. Ibid., fol. 7r (*Documents*, 75, 87).

43. For decades there has been sometimes heated scholarly debate over whether fray Marcos lied on this point. See, for example, Henry R. Wagner, "Fr. Marcos

de Niza," *New Mexico Historical Review* 9 (April 1934): 184–227; Carl O. Sauer, "The Credibility of the Fray Marcos Account," *New Mexico Historical Review* 16 (April 1941): 233–43; Lansing B. Bloom, "Was Fray Marcos a Liar?" *New Mexico Historical Review* 16 (April 1941): 244–46; Cleve Hallenbeck, *The Journey of Fray Marcos de Niza* (Dallas: Southern Methodist University Press, 1949, reprint 1987); William K. Hartmann, "Pathfinder for Coronado: Reevaluating the Mysterious Journey of Marcos de Niza," in Richard Flint and Shirley Cushing Flint, eds., *The Coronado Expedition to Tierra Nueva: The 1540–1542 Route across the Southwest* (Niwot, Colo.: University Press of Colorado, 1997), 73–101; William K. Hartmann and Richard Flint, "Before the Coronado Expedition: Who Knew What and When Did They Know It?" in Flint and Flint, *Coronado Expedition from the Distance of 460 Years*, 20–41.

44. Ramusio, *Navigationi et viaggi*, Vázquez de Coronado's Letter to the Viceroy, August 3, 1540, fol. 361r, transcribed and translated as Document 19 in *Documents*, 258, 266.

45. Investigation concerning Nuño de Chávez, fol. 24v (*Great Cruelties*, 396, 403).

46. Narrative Account by fray Marcos de Niza, fol. 2r (*Documents*, 67, 80).

47. AGI, Patronato, 21, N.2, R.4, Testimony of Witnesses in Havana regarding fray Marcos's Discoveries, November 1539, fol. 69r, transcribed and translated as Document 8 in *Documents*, 100, 104.

48. Castañeda de Nájera, fol. 16r (*Documents*, 389, 440).

49. Narrative Account by fray Marcos de Niza, fol. 5v (*Documents*, 73, 85).

50. Ibid., 4v (*Documents*, 71, 83).

51. A. Grove Day and others advanced the theory that Marcos lied in collusion with Viceroy Mendoza in order to help mount an expedition to a place the viceroy already knew would disappoint the aspirations of those who were to participate in it. This theory is hardly credible, for Mendoza himself was to suffer a huge financial loss in that event. A. Grove Day, *Coronado's Quest: The Discovery of the Southwestern States* (Berkeley: University of California Press, 1940), 331–33 n. 22.

Chapter 4: License from the King and His Council

1. AGI, Patronato, 184, R.31, The Viceroy's Letter to the King, April 17, 1540, fol. 1r, transcribed and translated as Document 17 in *Documents*, 235, 239.

2. Oviedo y Valdés, *Historia general*, Letters from Antonio de Mendoza and Rodrigo de Albornoz, fols. 22r–22v (*Documents*, 91, 93).

3. Ibid., fol. 23r (*Documents*, 92, 94).

4. Viceroy's Letter to the King, April 17, 1540, fols. 1r–1v (*Documents*, 235, 239).

5. Ibid., fol. 1v (*Documents*, 235, 239).

6. Ibid., fols. 1v–2v, in *Documents*, 236–37, 240. *Lugar* refers to a much smaller community than a *ciudad*—to a hamlet rather than a city. The maximum length of a crossbow shot has been determined by tests of actual medieval weapons to be 370 to 380 yards. "Point-blank" range, determined by the same means, was 65 to 70 yards. Reference here seems to be to a figure nearer the lower end of these extremes. Ralph Payne-Galway, *The Crossbow, Mediaeval and Modern, Military and Sporting: Its Construction, History, and Management* (London: Holland Press, 1903, reprint 1995), 21.

7. Viceroy's Letter to the King, April 17, 1540, fol. 3r (*Documents*, 238, 241).

8. Ibid., fol. 2v (*Documents*, 238, 241).

9. Letter of Mendoza to the King, December 10, 1537, fol. 11v.

10. AGI, Justicia, 269, Pieza 4, Visita of Luis de la Torre, Testimony of Juan Jaramillo, 1545, fol. 5r.

11. As William Taylor put it so succinctly, there was a "need for repeated acts of repression long after the first encounters." William B. Taylor, "Santiago's Horse: Christianity and Colonial Indian Resistance in the Heartland of New Spain," in William B. Taylor and Franklin Pease G. Y., eds., *Violence, Resistance, and Survival in the Americas: Native Americans and the Legacy of Conquest* (Washington, D.C.: Smithsonian Institution Press, 1994), 154.

12. Oviedo y Valdés, *Historia general*, Letters from Antonio de Mendoza and Rodrigo de Albornoz, fol. 23r (*Documents*, 92, 94).

13. José Luis Martínez, ed. *Documentos cortesianos*, 4 vols. (México, D.F.: Universidad Nacional Autónoma de México, 1992), 3: 78.

14. López de Gómara, *Cortés*, 397–404.

15. AGI, Patronato, 21, N.2, R.4\2, Hernando Cortés's Brief to Carlos V concerning the Injuries Done to Him by the Viceroy of Nueva España, June 25, 1540, fol. 4v, transcribed and translated as Document 18 in *Documents*, 245, 249.

16. Charles Hudson, *Knights of Spain, Warriors of the Sun: Hernando de Soto and the South's Ancient Chiefdoms* (Athens, Ga.: University of Georgia Press, 1997), 40–46.

17. Ibid., 50, 65.

18. AGI, Patronato, 21, N.2, R.4, Litigation of the Marqués del Valle, Nuño de Guzmán and the adelantados Soto and Alvarado concerning reconnaissance of Tierra Nueva, 1541, published in Joaquín F. Pacheco, Francisco de Cárdenas, and Luis Torres de Mendoza, eds., *Colección de documentos inéditos relativos al descubrimiento, conquista y organización de las antiguas posesiones españoles de América y Oceania*, series 1, 42 vols. (Madrid: José María Pérez, 1864–1884), 15: 364.

19. Ibid., 366.

20. Hudson, *Knights of Spain*, 364, 398–403.

21. Pacheco, Cárdenas, and Torres de Mendoza, *Colección de documentos inéditos*, 15: 312.

22. Ibid., 15: 325–38.

23. Donald E. Chipman, *Nuño de Guzmán and the Province of Pánuco in New Spain, 1518–1533* (Glendale, Calif.: Arthur H. Clark, 1967), 280–81.

24. Harry Kelsey, *Juan Rodríguez Cabrillo* (San Marino, Calif.: Huntington Library, 1998), 47, 51, 62, 70; Aiton, *Mendoza*, 122.

25. AGN, Hospital de Jesús, 123, Expediente 31, *Cédula* of July 10, 1540; published in Martínez, *Documentos cortesianos*, 4: 216–19.

26. AGI, Patronato, 21, N.3, R.2, Formation of Company between Mendoza and Pedro de Alvarado, November 29, 1540, transcribed and translated as Document 20 in *Documents*, 271–84.

27. Tello, *Crónica miscelánea*, 368–71.

28. Pacheco, Cárdenas, and Torres de Mendoza, *Colección de documentos inéditos*, 15: 378–79.

29. Vasco de Puga, *Provisiones, cédulas, instrucciones para el gobierno de la Nueva España* (México, D.F.: Pedro Ocharte, 1563; facsimile edition, Madrid: Ediciones Cultura Hispánica, 1945), fol. 26v.

30. Oviedo y Valdés, *Historia general*, 4: 300.

31. Visita of don Antonio de Mendoza, 1546, Letter from fray García de Loaysa, president of the Consejo de Indias, to Antonio Mendoza, Madrid, June 10, 1540, fol. 1r.

32. As is seen in the next chapter, some royal funds were given to members of the Coronado expedition, but they amounted to only a small fraction of the enterprise's cost.

Chapter 5: Raising a Force and Paying for It

1. Testimony of Witnesses in Havana regarding fray Marcos's Discoveries, fol. 68r (*Documents*, 99, 103).

2. Disposal of the Juan Jiménez Estate, fol. 7r (*Documents*, 335, 358).

3. Castañeda de Nájera, fols. 16r–16v (*Documents*, 389, 440).

4. AGI, Guadalajara, 46, N.8, Testimony Taken by Order of the Cabildo of San Miguel de Culiacán, 1566.

5. AGI, Justicia, 259, Pieza 3, Charges against Mendoza and Rebuttals of the Viceroy, June 21, 1546, fol. 10r.

6. See Appendix 3 in *Documents*, 605–15.

7. George P. Hammond and Agapito Rey, eds. and trans., *Narratives of the Coronado Expedition, 1540–1542* (Albuquerque: University of New Mexico Press, 1940), 340 n. 2; AGI, Justicia, 1021, N. 2, Pieza 5, Proof of Service Made at the Request of don García López de Cárdenas, 1547–1548.

8. Castañeda de Nájera, fol. 18r (*Documents*, 389, 441); Visita of don Antonio de Mendoza, 1546.

9. AGI, Patronato, 74, N.1, R.11, Proof of Service of Tristán de Arellano, 1575. Luna y Arellano came to the New World on the same ship as don Luis and later lodged in don Luis's house. They remained friends throughout their lives. Herbert Ingram Priestly, "Historical Introduction," in Herbert Ingram Priestly, trans. and ed., *The Luna Papers: Documents Relating to the Expedition of don Tristán de Luna y Arellano for the Conquest of La Florida in 1559–1561*, 2 vols. (De Land, Fla.: Florida State Historical Society, 1928; reprint, Freeport, N.Y.: Books for Libraries Press, 1971), 1: xxiv.

10. See introduction to Document 12 in *Documents*, 135–38, as well as note 30 to that document, 639.

11. Tello, *Crónica miscelánea*, 135, 407–11; AGI, México, 1088, L.1bis., Royal *Cédula*, August 31, 1531, fols. 113r–113v.

12. AGI, Patronato, 60, N.5, R.4, Proof of Service of Juan de Zaldívar, February 1566; Donald E. Chipman, "The Oñate-Moctezuma-Zaldívar Families of Northern New Spain," *New Mexico Historical Review* 52, no. 4 (1977): 304–5; Castañeda de Nájera, fol. 18r (*Documents*, 389, 441); Tello, *Crónica miscelánea*, 531. don Diego de Guevara, brother of the viceroy of Navarra, was said at the time to be "so noble and important that no one was ahead of him"; truly he was from the cream of Spanish society. Thomas Hillerkuss, *Diccionario biográfico del occidente novohispano, siglo XVI*, 3 vols. (Zacatecas: Universidad Autónoma de Zacatecas, 2001), 2: 324.

13. For this and the other five preexisting companies, see AGI, Guadalajara, 5, R.1, N.7, Muster Roll of the Expedition, February 22, 1540, transcribed and translated as Document 12 in *Documents*, 135–63.

14. Cristóbal Bermúdez Plata, *Catálogo de pasajeros a Indias durante los siglos XVI, XVII, y XVIII*, 3 vols. (Sevilla: Editorial de la Gavidia, 1940 and 1942), 2: 74–78.

15. AGI, México, 206, N.12, Proof of Service of Juan Troyano, February 20, 1560, transcribed and translated as Document 31 in *Documents*, 527–32.

16. Reports of the Conquistadores and Settlers of the Ciudad de México, fol. 270r.

17. Visita of don Antonio de Mendoza, 1546. Because some men had the same names, it is possible that a few of those identified here as former members of Mendoza's personal guard were not in fact guardsmen. But without evidence to the contrary, there is no reason to exclude any specific person from the list.

18. AGI, Justicia, 339, N.1, R.1, Residencia of Francisco Vázquez de Coronado, 1544 and 1545, translated in Hammond and Rey, *Narratives*, 375–76.

19. AGI, Justicia, 1021, N.2, Pieza 6, Proof Taken by the *Fiscal* Villalobos, 1547.

20. Proof of Service Made at the Request of don García López de Cárdenas, 1547–1548.

21. The known and probable father-and-son pairs were Alonso Sánchez and his unnamed son, Jorge Báez and Rodrigo de Trujillo, Francisco and Pedro de Castro, two men named Alonso González, Pedro Mayoral and Pedro Márquez, Sebastián Roxo and Francisco Roxo Loro, and Andrés de Salinas and an unnamed son.

22. The known and probable pairs of brothers were Rodrigo and Velasco de Barrionuevo, Antón and Cristóbal García, Miguel Hernández and Francisco Hernández de Arriba, Antón Ruiz and Gonzalo Yáñez, and Bartolomé and Rodrigo Sánchez.

23. The known and probable sets of cousins were Pedro de Benavídes and Cristóbal Mayorga; Alonso González and Diego Hernández; Alonso and Juan Jiménez; Andrés and Francisco Martín; Francisco Martín and Pedro Martín de la Bermeja; and Hernando (Martín) Bermejo, Juan Martín (Bermejo de la Fuente del Arco), and Pero Martín Cano.

24. The men with known and probable origins in Guadalcanal were Francisco Rodríguez, Antón Ruiz, Gonzalo Yáñez, Juan Gallego, Fernánd González, Francisco González, Martín Hernández Chillón, Pero Hernández de Guadalajara, Alonso Jiménez, Juan Jiménez, Alonso López, Francisco López, and Diego Núñez de Mirandilla. The likely natives of Llerena were Juan Barragán, Juan de Céspedes, Hernán García de Llerena, Francisco Gómez, and Gerónimo Ramos. From Azuaga probably came Andrés Hernández de Encinasola, Hernán Pérez, Bartolomé Sánchez, and Rodrigo Sánchez. And another four were likely natives of Fuente del Arco: Hernando (Martín) Bermejo, Juan Martín (Bermejo de la Fuente del Arco), Pero Martín Cano, and Pedro González.

25. AGI, Justicia, 276, N.2, Visita of Alonso Pérez Tamayo, 1545; AGI, Justicia, 269, Pieza 2, Book of the Residencia Secreta, 1544.

26. Cristóbal de Escobar's Proof of Service (*Documents*, 554–80).

27. Proof of Service of Juan de Zaldívar, February 1566.

28. Of the 194 European expeditionaries for whom place of origin is known, 22 percent were from Extremadura, 18 percent from Castilla y León, and 17 percent from Andalucía. Shirley Cushing Flint, "Putting Faces on the Coronado Expedition, Part 1: The Expedition as a Whole," paper presented to the Hispanic Genealogical Society of New Mexico, Albuquerque, July 10, 2004.

29. Ibid.

30. Hearing on Depopulation Charges, fol. 2r (*Documents*, 175, 181).

31. AGI, México, 204, N.33, Proof of Service of Pedro de Benavídez, 1551, fols. 1r, 1v, 6v.

32. Fray Angelico Chavez confusingly discussed a mythical fifth friar, Juan de la Cruz, who was later said to have accompanied the expedition. Chávez, *Coronado's Friars*, 32–36.

33. Juan Jaramillo's Narrative, fol. 5r (*Documents*, 517, 524).

34. Chávez, *Coronado's Friars*, 12–13, 14–17.

35. Tello, *Crónica miscelánea*, 484.

36. Residencia of Francisco Vázquez de Coronado; Chávez, *Coronado's Friars*, 30–31.

37. Juan Jaramillo's Narrative, fols. 5r, 5v (*Documents*, 517, 524).

38. Proof of Service of Pedro de Benavídez, 1551; AGI, Patronato, 121, R.8, Proof of Service of Miguel de Entrambasaguas, December 11, 1577; Melchior Pérez's Petition for Preferment, 1551 (*Documents*, 533–53); Proof of Service of Juan Troyano, 1560.

39. Residencia of Francisco Vázquez de Coronado, fol. 288v; Proof of Service Made at the Request of don García López de Cárdenas, 1547–1548.

40. AGI, Patronato, 63, R.5, Proof of Service of Juan de Paladinas [sic], June 6, 1560; Proceso of Francisco Vázquez de Coronado, fols. 6v–10v (*Great Cruelties*, 58–62); AGI, México, 168, Investigation concerning Francisco Vázquez, March 1547; Reports of the Conquistadores and Settlers of the Ciudad de México, fol. 228r.

41. Bolton, *Coronado*, 319. See also *Great Cruelties*, 55 and 591, chapter 4, n. 4.

42. Reports of the Conquistadores and Settlers of the Ciudad de México, fol. 200r, Alonso Sánchez.

43. Proof Taken by the *Fiscal* Villalobos, 1547.

44. Proof of Service of Juan de Paladinas, 1560, fol. 1r.

45. Reports of the Conquistadores and Settlers of the Ciudad de México, fol. 228r; AGI, México, 168, Letter from Juan Troyano to the King, Ciudad de México, December 20, 1568, fol. 6v.

46. For a modern example, see Jared Diamond, *Guns, Germs, and Steel: The Fates of Human Societies* (New York: W. W. Norton, 1999), 67–68.

47. Castañeda de Nájera, fols. 16r, 16v (*Documents*, 389, 440).

48. Administrative Review of the Viceroy and *Oidores*, fols. 432r, 494r. Relying only on hearsay, Iñigo López de Anuncibay declared that the number was between 4,000 and 5,000.

49. Ibid., fol. 494r.

50. In substantial agreement with Serván Béjarano in his estimate are two statements in Castañeda de Nájera's narrative (fols. 16r, 16v, *Documents*, 389, 440).

51. Castañeda de Nájera, fol. 41r (*Documents*, 395, 449).

52. Administrative Review of the Viceroy and *Oidores*, fol. 605v.

53. Ibid., fols. 602r–638r.

54. Fray Angelico Chavez, trans. and ed. *The Oroz Codex* (Washington, D.C.: Academy of American Franciscan History, 1972), 314; Hanke, *México*, 1: 70.

55. Administrative Review of the Viceroy and *Oidores*, fol. 616v.

56. Ibid., fol. 626r.

57. Tello, *Crónica miscelánea*, 485. Both Lucas and Andrés escaped unharmed from Quivira after the killing of fray Juan de Padilla.

58. Administrative Review of the Viceroy and *Oidores*, fol. 617r.

59. René Acuña, ed., *Relaciones geográficas del siglo XVI: Nueva Galicia* (México, D.F.: Universidad Nacional Autónoma de México, 1988), 57–70; Thomas Hillerkuss, *Documentalia del sur de Jalisco (siglo XVI)* (Zapopan, Jalisco: Colegio de Jalisco, 1994), 82.

60. Administrative Review of the Viceroy and *Oidores*, fol. 605v.

61. Marc Simmons, "Tlascalans in the Spanish Borderlands," *New Mexico Historical Review*, 39, no. 2 (1964): 101–10; Rudolfo Hernández and José Francisco Román, "Presencia Tlaxcalteca en Nueva Galicia," in María Isabel Monroy Castillo, ed., *Constructores de la nación: La migración tlaxcalteca en el norte de la Nueva España* (San Luis Potosí: Colegio de San Luis and Gobierno del Estado de Tlaxcala, 1999), 19.

62. Glasgow University Library, MS Hunter 242 (U.3.15), The Tlaxcala Codex, fol. 317r. The Tlaxcala Codex accompanies the *Descripción de la ciudad y provincia de Tlaxcala*, written by Diego Muñoz Camargo, the *mestizo* interpreter at Tlaxcala from the 1570s to the 1590s.

63. Library of the British Museum, Add MSS 31219, Codex Aubin, Chronicle of Mexican History to 1576, continued to 1607, fols. 46v and 47r, transcribed and translated as Document 13 in *Documents*, 169–70.

64. Diego Pérez de Luxán, "Diego Pérez de Luxán's Account of the Antonio de Espejo Expedition into New Mexico, 1582," in George P. Hammond and Agapito Rey, *Rediscovery of New Mexico, 1580–1594: The Explorations of Chamuscado, Espejo, Castaño de Sosa, Morlete, and Leyva de Bonilla and Humaña* (Albuquerque: University of New Mexico Press, 1966), 184.

65. Antonio de Espejo, "Report of Antonio de Espejo," in George P. Hammond and Agapito Rey, *Rediscovery*, 225.

66. Juan Jaramillo's Narrative, fol. 5v (*Documents*, 517, 524).

67. Obregón, *Historia*, 71, 74–75.

68. Administrative Review of the Viceroy and *Oidores*, fols. 616v and 617r.

69. Proceso of Francisco Vázquez de Coronado, fol. 102v (*Great Cruelties*, 280, 297).

70. UCB, Ban., M-M 93, Memorial of the Indians concerning Their Services, c. 1563, published in Robert H. Barlow and George T. Smisor, eds. and trans., *Nombre de Dios, Durango: Two Documents in Nahuatl concerning Its Foundation* (Sacramento: House of Tlaloc, 1943), 3, 31.

71. Andrés Pérez de Ribas, *History of the Triumphs of Our Holy Faith amongst the Most Barbarous and Fierce Peoples of the New World*, trans. and eds., Daniel T. Reff, Maureen Ahern, and Richard K. Danford (Tucson: University of Arizona Press, 1999), 104, 238.

72. Administrative Review of the Viceroy and *Oidores*, fols. 602r–638r.

73. Muster Roll of the Expedition, February 22, 1540 (*Documents*, 135–63); Disposal of the Juan Jiménez Estate (*Documents*, 326–77); Richard Flint, "Armas de la Tierra: The Mexican Indian Component of Coronado Expedition Material Culture," in Flint and Flint, *Coronado Expedition to Tierra Nueva*, 57–70.

74. Castañeda de Nájera, fol. 27v (*Documents*, 392, 444).

75. Contrary to the Viceroy's assertion, Vázquez de Coronado and don Luis de Castilla both testified in 1546 that *tamemes* were provided for the expedition. Their testimony is amply confirmed by statements made by Indian *principales* before the *visitador* Francisco Tello de Sandoval. Charges against Mendoza and Rebuttals of the Viceroy, June 21, 1546, fol. 10r; Administrative Review of the Viceroy and *Oidores*, fols. 602r–638r; AGI, Justicia, 263, Pieza 1, Rebuttals of Viceroy Mendoza, 1546.

76. Muster Roll of the Expedition, fol. 9v (*Documents*, 150, 162).

77. Castañeda de Nájera, fol. 149v (*Documents*, 395, 432).

78. Shirley Cushing Flint, "The Financing and Provisioning of the Coronado Expedition," in Flint and Flint, *Coronado Expedition from the Distance of 460 Years*, 47.

79. The amount of the ransom distributed to the conquerors of Cajamarca, minus the king's fifth, was approximately 1.16 million pesos. Lockhart, *Men of Cajamarca*, 80.

80. However, during 1539 and early 1540, 43 men who became members of the expedition did receive amounts from the royal treasury ranging from 50 to 200 pesos each. Ostensibly the payments were not linked to participation in the expedition, but they were made almost exclusively to future expeditionaries and only shortly before their departure. Administrative Review of the Viceroy and *Oidores*, fols. 796r–801r.

81. S. Flint, "Financing and Provisioning," 44–48.

82. AGI, Justicia, 259, Pieza 4, Certification of a Suit concerning Tlapa, 1544.

83. Peter Gerhard, *A Guide to the Historical Geography of New Spain*, rev. ed. (Norman: University of Oklahoma Press, 1993), 323.

84. Berdan and Anawalt, *Essential Codex Mendoza*, 86.

85. Investigation concerning Nuño de Chávez, fol. 10v (*Great Cruelties*, 359, 379).

86. Proof of Service of Juan de Zaldívar, February 1566.

87. Proof of Service of Juan de Paladinas, 1560; Reports of the Conquistadores and Settlers of the Ciudad de México, fols. 252r, 280v, 281r; Melchior Pérez's Petition for Preferment, 1551; AGI, Patronato, 87, N.1, R.5, Proof of Service of García Rodríguez and His Grandson, 1617.

Chapter 6: Avoiding Provocation, Demanding Submission

1. AGI, México, 96, Letter from Jerónimo López to the King, México, February 25, 1545. Published in Spanish in Francisco del Paso y Troncoso, *Espistolario de Nueva España, 1505–1818*, 2nd series, 16 vols. (México, D.F.: José Porrúa e Hijos, 1939–1942), 4: 161, 164. Published in English in John H. Parry and Robert G. Keith, *New Iberian World,* 5 vols. (New York: Times Books, 1984), 3: 447–48.

2. Relación de Antonio de Mendoza a Luis de Velasco, in Hanke, *México*, 1: 38.

3. Castañeda de Nájera, fol. 20r (*Documents*, 390, 442).

4. AGI, Justicia, 263, Pieza 1, Rebuttals of Viceroy Mendoza, 1546.

5. Ibid.; AGI, Justicia, 264, Pieza 3, Proof Assembled in the Name of don Antonio de Mendoza, 1547; Administrative Review of the Viceroy and *Oidores*.

6. For the beginning date of the Spanish year, see Russell J. Barber and Frances F. Berdan, *The Emperor's Mirror: Understanding Cultures through Primary Sources* (Tucson: University of Arizona Press, 1998), 87. For Mendoza's arrival in Pátzcuaro, see AGI, Justicia, 129, N.3, Records of the Case between the Bishop and City of Michoacán and Juan Infante, 1540. Also see Fintan B. Warren, *Vasco de Quiroga and His Pueblo-Hospitals of Santa Fe* (Washington, D.C.: Academy of American Franciscan History, 1963), 99.

7. The directive referred to here must have included a provision requiring use of the *requerimiento*, or formal demand for submission, which since 1513 was to be given to and employed by all expeditions of reconnaissance and conquest and which the Coronado expedition routinely read to the native people it encountered. The full directive does not accompany the copy of Vázquez de Coronado's appointment that has been preserved. Nevertheless, it probably included many of the specific provisions of the then-current regulations governing conquests. See Lewis Hanke, *The Spanish Struggle for Justice in the Conquest of America* (Boston: Little, Brown, 1965), 30–36.

8. Biblioteca del Escorial, códice &-II-7, Doc. LXVII, The Viceroy's Instructions to Hernando Alarcón, 1541, fol. 2r, transcribed and translated as Document 16 in *Documents*, 227, 230, 231.

9. Investigation concerning Nuño de Chávez, fol. 3r; Report Extracted from the Affidavit Prepared for don García Ramírez de Cárdenas, fol. 1r (*Great Cruelties*, 352, 372, 437, 447).

10. Proceso of Francisco Vázquez de Coronado, fol. 102r (*Great Cruelties*, 279, 296).

11. Castañeda de Nájera, fol. 24r (*Documents*, 391, 443).

12. Investigation concerning Nuño de Chávez, fol. 3r (*Great Cruelties*, 352).

13. Ibid., fol. 13v (*Great Cruelties*, 362).

14. For a detailed history and analysis of the *requerimiento*, see Hanke, *Spanish Struggle for Justice*, 29–36. See also Seed, *Ceremonies of Possession*, 3–99.

15. For a complete transcript and translation of an early-sixteenth-century copy of the *requerimiento*, see Appendix 4 in *Documents*, 616–19.

16. Bartolomé de las Casas, *Historia de las Indias*, ed. Juan Pérez de Tudela Bueso (Madrid: Ediciones Atlas, 1992), Libro 3, Capítulo 58; Hanke, *Spanish Struggle for Justice*, 35.

17. Specifically, Alarcón reported that the *navío San Gabriel* was dedicated to carrying food supplies for the expedition. Ramusio, *Navigationi et viaggi*, Narrative of Alarcón's Voyage, 1540, fol. 363r, transcribed and translated as Document 15 in *Documents*, 188, 206.

18. Proceso of Francisco Vázquez de Coronado, fol. 100v (*Great Cruelties*, 278, 295). Other contemporary documents place the number of Europeans in the advance guard at between 70 and 100. See note 4, chapter 7.

19. Castañeda de Nájera, fol. 27v (*Documents*, 392, 444).

20. Proceso of Francisco Vázquez de Coronado, fol. 101v (*Great Cruelties*, 278–79).

21. Ibid., fol. 110v (*Great Cruelties*, 287, 304–5).

22. Ibid., fol. 111r (*Great Cruelties*, 287, 305).

23. *Great Cruelties*, 528.

Chapter 7: Almost a Highway

1. Muster Roll of the Expedition, fol. 10r (*Documents*, 151, 162).

2. Castañeda de Nájera, fol. 25r (*Documents*, 391, 444).

3. Juan Jaramillo's Narrative, fol. 1r (*Documents*, 512, 519).

4. Contemporaneous estimates of the number of men-at-arms in the advance guard range from Castañeda de Nájera's 50 and Jaramillo's 60 to the 105 reported in the anonymous "Traslado de las Nuevas." Castañeda de Nájera, fol. 27v (*Documents*, 392, 444); Juan Jaramillo's Narrative, fol. 1r (*Documents*, 512, 519); AGI, Patronato 20, N.5, R.8, Traslado de las Nuevas, 1540, fol. 1r, transcribed and translated as Document 22 in *Documents*, 291, 294.

5. Vázquez de Coronado's Letter to the Viceroy, August 3, 1540, fol. 359v (*Documents*, 254, 263).

6. Ibid., fol. 360r (*Documents*, 255, 264). Conclusions from archaeological research in the Río Sonora Valley seem to confirm that it was indeed the location of the large settlements of Los Corazones, Señora, and Ispa visited by the Coronado expedition. William E. Doolittle, *Pre-Hispanic Occupance in the Valley of Sonora, Mexico: Archaeological Confirmation of Early Spanish Reports* (Tucson: University of Arizona Press, 1988).

7. Juan Jaramillo's Narrative, fol. 1v (*Documents*, 513, 519).

8. Ibid. (*Documents*, 513, 520).

9. Castañeda de Nájera, fol. 30r (*Documents*, 393, 445). Recent recovery of artifacts related to the Coronado *entrada* strongly suggest that the burned Kuykendall Ruin, situated on the eastern margin of Sulphur Springs Valley east of Sunizona, Arizona, is the site known to the expeditionaries of the early 1540s as Chichilticale. Nugent Brasher, "The Chichilticale Camp of Francisco Vázquez de Coronado," *New Mexico Historical Review* 82, no. 4 (2007):433–68.

10. Castañeda de Nájera, fol. 12v (*Documents*, 388, 439).

11. Polo, *Travels*, 90.

12. Cristóbal de Escobar's Proof of Service, fol. 4v (*Documents*, 558, 570). The deaths of blacks and Indians during this stretch suggests that their food was cut while the Europeans continued on more normal rations.

13. AGI, Patronato 20, N.5, R.8, Relación del Suceso, 1540s, fol. 1r, transcribed and translated as Document 29 in *Documents*, 497, 503.

14. Castañeda de Nájera, fol. 29v (*Documents*, 392, 445). Castañeda's statement here implies that fray Marcos, the Díaz-Zaldívar party, and the advance guard all traveled generally the same route.

15. Investigation concerning Nuño de Chávez, fol. 21v (*Great Cruelties*, 93, 101).

16. Ibid., fol. 54r (*Great Cruelties*, 166, 179).

17. Ibid., fol. 102v (*Great Cruelties*, 280, 297).

18. Modern archaeologists disagree about how much turquoise found in Mesoamerica can really be identified as coming from sources in the American Southwest. For a range of positions on this question, see George Harbottle and Phil C. Weigand, "Turquoise in Pre-Columbian America," *Scientific American* 26, no. 2 (1992): 78–85. See also S. M. Young, David Phillips, and Joan Mathien, "Lead Isotope Analysis of Turquoise Sources in the Southwestern U.S.A.," poster presented at the 29th International Symposium on Archaeology, Ankara, Turkey, 1994 (cited and summarized in Curtis F. Schaafsma and Carroll L. Riley, "Analysis and Conclusion," in Curtis F. Schaafsma and Carroll L. Riley, eds., *The Casas Grandes World* (Salt Lake City: University of Utah Press, 1999), 247.

19. For discussion of some of the protohistoric indigenous trade and communication routes in northwestern Mexico and the American Southwest, see

Carroll L. Riley and Joni L. Manson, "The Sonoran Connection: Road and Trail Networks in the Protohistoric Period," in Charles D. Trombold, ed., *Ancient Road Networks and Settlement Hierarchies in the New World* (Cambridge: Cambridge University Press, 1991), 132–44; and Carroll L. Riley and Joni L. Manson, "The Cíbola-Tiguex Route: Continuity and Change in the Southwest," *New Mexico Historical Review* 58, no. 4 (1983): 347–67.

20. Narrative of Alarcón's Voyage, fols. 368v–369r (*Documents*, 201, 218).

21. Narrative Account by fray Marcos de Niza, fol. 3v (*Documents*, 69, 82).

22. Castañeda de Nájera, fol. 45r (*Documents*, 397, 451).

23. Investigation concerning Nuño de Chávez, fol. 102v (*Great Cruelties*, 279, 297).

24. Castañeda de Nájera, fol. 85v (*Documents*, 410, 466).

25. Investigation concerning Nuño de Chávez, fol. 102v (*Great Cruelties*, 280, 297).

26. Castañeda de Nájera, fol. 50v (*Documents*, 399, 453).

27. The major languages the expedition encountered were Acaxee, Xixime, Pima, Ópata-Eudeve, Seri, Cahitan, Tepehuan, Seri, Yuman, ancestral Apache, Zunian, Hopi, Keresan, Tanoan, Teya, Quiviran (Wichita), and Harahey (Pawnee). Carroll L. Riley, *The Frontier People: The Greater Southwest in the Protohistoric Period*, rev. ed. (Albuquerque: University of New Mexico Press, 1987), 47, 102–3, 176, 221–23, 252; Susan M. Deeds, *Defiance and Deference in Mexico's Colonial North: Indians under Spanish Rule in Nueva Vizcaya* (Austin: University of Texas Press, 2003), 43, 47–48; Edward H. Spicer, *Cycles of Conquest: The Impact of Spain, Mexico, and the United States on the Indians of the Southwest, 1533–1960* (Tucson: University of Arizona Press, 1962), 10–11; Robert W. Young, "Apachean Languages," in Alfonso Ortiz, ed., *Handbook of North American Indians*, vol. 10, *Southwest* (Washington, D.C.: Smithsonian Institution, 1983), 393–400.

28. Investigation concerning Nuño de Chávez, fol. 84v (*Great Cruelties*, 236, 244).

29. Ibid., fol. 37v (*Great Cruelties*, 129, 135).

30. Ibid., fol. 56v (*Great Cruelties*, 169, 182).

31. Narrative Account by fray Marcos de Niza, fol. 2r (*Documents*, 67, 80).

32. Ibid., fols. 5r, 5v (*Documents*, 72, 73, 84, 85).

33. Ibid., fol. 5v (*Documents*, 73, 85).

34. Ibid., fol. 3v (*Documents*, 70, 82). This statement suggests that hundreds of years before an international border was laid out across the region, natives of Sonora traveled into the American Southwest for seasonal employment. It provides an extremely rare glimpse of how closely linked disparate parts of the region were during protohistoric times.

35. Ibid., fol. 5v (*Documents*, 72, 84).

36. Ibid., fol. 6r (*Documents*, 73, 85).

37. That Marcos de Niza is not included in this list of those familiar with the route beyond Chichilticale is yet another indication that he did not reach Cíbola before July 1540. Castañeda de Nájera, fol. 30r (*Documents*, 393, 445).

38. See Castañeda de Nájera, fols. 35v, 45r, 50v, 51v (*Documents*, 394, 397, 399, 400, 447, 451, 453); Relación del Suceso, fol. 2v (*Documents*, 499, 504).

39. See, for example, the case of two boatmen who tricked the hero Esplandián and his companion Sargil at the beginning of their adventures, as told to a sixteenth-century Spanish readership. Rodríguez de Montalvo, *Sergas de Esplandián*, fol. 4v.

CHAPTER 8: BY SEA TO CHICHILTICALE

1. Alarcón was an important member of Mendoza's personal guard. Visita of don Antonio de Mendoza, 1546.

2. BNM, MS 716, Rôles d'Oléron, fol. 91, quoted in Pérez-Mallaína, *Spain's Men of the Sea*, 192; Narrative of Alarcón's Voyage, fol. 363v (*Documents*, 189, 207).

3. Narrative of Alarcón's Voyage, fol. 363v (*Documents*, 189, 207).

4. Ibid., fol. 365r (*Documents*, 192, 210).

5. See Carroll L. Riley, "Early Spanish-Indian Communication in the Greater Southwest," *New Mexico Historical Review* 46, no. 4 (1971): 302. Riley also suggests that Piman dialects might have served as traders' languages throughout the protohistoric American Southwest and Mexican northwest.

6. Hernán Cortés, "Tercera Carta-Relación—15 de Mayo de 1522," in Hernán Cortés, *Cartas de relación* (México, D.F.: Editorial Porrúa, 1993), 158; Adorno and Pautz, *Cabeza de Vaca*, 1: 165, 203; Obregón, *Historia*, 180; Fernando Cervantes, *The Devil in the New World: The Impact of Diabolism in New Spain* (New Haven, Conn.: Yale University Press, 1994), 13.

7. Narrative of Alarcón's Voyage, fol. 366r (*Documents*, 195, 213).

8. Ibid., fol. 369r (*Documents*, 202, 219).

9. Ibid., fols. 367r, 368r (*Documents*, 197, 199, 215, 216).

10. Ibid., fol. 368v (*Documents*, 201, 218).

11. Ibid., fol. 370r (*Documents*, 204, 221).

12. Ibid. (*Documents*, 205, 221).

13. Many, if not all, of these cross locations were plotted on the map subsequently prepared by the pilot Domingo del Castillo. An eighteenth-century copy of that map was published in Francisco Antonio Lorenzana, *Historia de Nueva España escripta por su esclarecido conquistador Hernán Cortés: Aumentada con otros documentos y notas* (México, D.F: Imprenta del Superior Gobierno, 1770). See also *Documents*, 187.

14. Castañeda de Nájera, fol. 37r (*Documents*, 394, 448).
15. Ibid., fol. 37v (*Documents*, 395, 448).
16. Ibid., fols. 38r, 38v (*Documents*, 395, 448).
17. Ibid., fol. 71v (*Documents*, 406, 460).
18. Narrative of Alarcón's Voyage, fols. 363v–364r (*Documents*, 189, 207).
19. Ibid., fol. 367r (*Documents*, 196, 214).
20. Ibid., fol. 365r (*Documents*, 192, 210).
21. Ibid., fols. 364r, 364v, 367v (*Documents*, 189, 191, 198, 207, 209, 215).
22. *Documents*, 648, Document 16, n. 19.
23. Viceroy's Instructions to Hernando Alarcón, 1541, fol. 1v (*Documents*, 226, 230).
24. Ibid., fol. 2v (*Documents*, 228, 231).
25. The historian Harry Kelsey has argued that Alarcón indeed attempted the second voyage. In addition to the evidence he provides, there is this statement in a March 1542 letter from Antonio de Mendoza: "The ships I sent to relieve [Vázquez de Coronado] broke all their masts and remain on the island of the marqués [California]." Harry Kelsey, *Juan Rodríguez Cabrillo* (San Marino, Calif.: Huntington Library, 1998), 85; AHN, Diversos-Colecciones, 22, N.36, Letter from Mendoza to Francisco de Cobos, March 10, 1542, fol. 2r.
26. Peter Gerhard, *The North Frontier of New Spain*, rev. ed. (Norman: University of Oklahoma Press, 1993), 112; Tello, *Crónica miscelánea*, 339.
27. José López-Portillo y Weber, *La Rebelión de la Nueva Galicia* (México, D.F.: Instituto Panamericano de Geografía e Historia, 1939), 435–46.

Chapter 9: Inside Cíbola

1. Carroll L. Riley, *Rio del Norte: People of the Upper Rio Grande from Earliest Times to the Pueblo Revolt* (Salt Lake City: University of Utah Press, 1995), 120.
2. Edmund J. Ladd, "Zuni on the Day the Men in Metal Arrived," in Flint and Flint, *Coronado Expedition to Tierra Nueva*, 227. On the subject of communication between protohistoric tribes of northwestern Mexico and the American Southwest, see also Riley, *Frontier People*, 313–19.
3. For a summary of current thought on diffusion of some cultural traits from Mesoamerica into the Pueblo world, see Riley, *Rio del Norte*, 49–72.
4. T. J. Ferguson and E. Richard Hart, *A Zuni Atlas* (Norman: University of Oklahoma Press, 1985), 57.
5. Narrative Account by fray Marcos de Niza, fol. 6r (*Documents*, 74, 85).
6. Ladd, "Zuni on the Day the Men in Metal Arrived," 229.

7. Viceroy's Letter to the King, April 17, 1540, fol. 2v (*Documents*, 238, 241).

8. Castañeda de Nájera, fol. 30v (*Documents*, 393, 445).

9. Vázquez de Coronado's Letter to the Viceroy, August 3, 1540, fol. 360v (*Documents*, 256, 265).

10. Proceso of Francisco Vázquez de Coronado, fol. 84v (*Great Cruelties*, 235, 244).

11. Castañeda de Nájera, fol. 31v (*Documents*, 393, 446).

12. For a generalized version of the Zuni ceremonial calendar, see Barton Wright, *Kachinas of the Zuni* (Flagstaff, Ariz.: Northland Press, 1985), 9. Failing to make allowance for the offset between celestial events such as the summer solstice and the Julian calendar, Ed Ladd suggested that the eight-day solstice ceremonial itself was in progress when the vanguard of the Coronado expedition arrived. Instead, they arrived in the equivalent of mid-July when synchronized to the solar calendar. Ladd, "Zuni on the Day the Men in Metal Arrived," 231.

13. "The *ciudad* had been cleared of men older than sixty years and younger than twenty [years] and of women and children." Traslado de las Nuevas, 1540, fol. 1r (*Documents*, 292, 294).

14. "I think they have turquoise in quantity. By the time I arrived, this had disappeared, along with the rest of their possessions, except the corn." Vázquez de Coronado's Letter to the Viceroy, August 3, 1540, fol. 361v (*Documents*, 259, 267).

15. "They packed up their belongings and food and fled to the hills [with] their women and children, leaving their towns almost deserted, so that none remained except a few of them." Ibid., fol. 362r (*Documents*, 260–61, 268). There has been considerable discussion over the last century about the number and identity of the seven (or six) *ciudades* of Cíbola. Chalo:wa is often omitted from lists of Zuni pueblos that were inhabited into the sixteenth century. The most recent archaeological conclusion on this point, by archaeologist Keith Kintigh, who has done decades of fieldwork on the Zuni Reservation and in its vicinity, places the end of Chalo:wa's occupation "sometime near A.D. 1540." Keith W. Kintigh, *Settlement, Subsistence, and Society in Late Zuni Prehistory* (Tucson: University of Arizona Press, 1985), 68, 81.

16. In the face of a similar threat from outside in the 1680s and 1690s, the Ashiwi once again physically relocated to Dowa Yalanne. This time, when hostilities between the Ashiwi and returning Spanish colonists concluded, the native people of Cíbola did not redisperse to scattered pueblos. Instead, maintaining the strength of their numbers, they all took up residence together at the site of modern Zuni Pueblo. From then on the shared political structure of Shíwana, which previously had been only inferable to outsiders, became an open and obvious fact.

17. Ptolemy, *Geography*, 26, 51, and "Europe, Secunda tabula."

18. Vázquez de Coronado's Letter to the Viceroy, August 3, 1540, fol. 361r (*Documents*, 258, 267).

19. Ibid., fol. 362r (*Documents*, 261, 268).

20. Castañeda de Nájera, fol. 106r (*Documents*, 417, 474).

21. Edmund J. Ladd, "Zuni Social and Political Organization," in Alfonso Ortiz, ed., *Handbook of North American Indians*, vol. 9, *Southwest* (Washington, D.C.: Smithsonian Institution, 1979), 488–89.

22. Narrative Account by fray Marcos de Niza, fol. 5v (*Documents*, 73, 85); Castañeda de Nájera, fols. 12v, 104r (*Documents*, 388, 417, 437, 473).

23. This is the same river Vázquez de Coronado called the Río del Lino. Vázquez de Coronado's Letter to the Viceroy, August 3, 1540, fol. 360v (*Documents*, 256, 265).

24. Castañeda de Nájera, fol. 31r (*Documents*, 393, 446).

25. Vázquez de Coronado's Letter to the Viceroy, August 3, 1540, fol. 360v (*Documents*, 257, 265). Ed Ladd interpreted these columns of smoke as indications of activities of Shu'la:witsi, a masked impersonator of the Zuni fire deity. But Ladd ignored the fact that the European calendar was badly out of synchrony with the solar calendar used by the Zunis. Shu'la:witsi would have been setting little ritual fires a couple of weeks before the arrival of the Spanish-led *entrada*, rather than as it entered Cíbola. Ladd, "Zuni on the Day the Men in Metal Arrived," 231–32.

26. Ferguson and Hart, *Zuni Atlas*, 36, 37.

27. Ibid., 42–49.

28. Ibid., 57, 58.

29. Ibid., 20–27.

Chapter 10: Refusal to Submit

1. Proceso of Francisco Vázquez de Coronado, fol. 102v (*Great Cruelties*, 280, 297).

2. That the vanguard came at Hawikku from the southwest in its final approach is suggested by a single documentary statement: AGI, Justicia, 336, N.1, Vázquez de Coronado's Petition for Recovery of Encomiendas, 1553, fol. 10v, published in part in *Great Cruelties*, 468, 489. There is no other surviving evidence of the direction of approach.

3. Vázquez de Coronado's Letter to the Viceroy, August 3, 1540, fol. 360v (*Documents*, 256, 265).

4. Proceso of Francisco Vázquez de Coronado, fol. 103r (*Great Cruelties*, 280, 297).

5. Castañeda de Nájera, fols. 31r–31v (*Documents*, 393, 446).

6. Administrative Review of the Viceroy and *Oidores*, fols. 606v–607r, 94th witness, Martín Caccol, indio.

7. Proceso of Francisco Vázquez de Coronado, fols. 84v, 103r–103v (*Great Cruelties*, 236, 244, 280, 298). See also Traslado de las Nuevas, 1540, fols. 1r–1v (*Documents*, 292, 294); Castañeda de Nájera, fol. 31v (*Documents*, 393, 446); Report Extracted from the Affidavit Prepared for don García Ramírez de Cárdenas, fol. 1v (*Great Cruelties*, 438–39, 448).

8. *Documents*, 617–18.

9. Proceso of Francisco Vázquez de Coronado, fol. 84v (*Great Cruelties*, 236, 244); Vázquez de Coronado's Letter to the Viceroy, August 3, 1540, fol. 360v (*Documents*, 257, 265).

10. Vázquez de Coronado's Letter to the Viceroy, August 3, 1540, fol. 361r (*Documents*, 257, 266).

11. Ibid.

12. Proceso of Francisco Vázquez de Coronado, fol. 104r (*Great Cruelties*, 281, 298); Castañeda de Nájera, fol. 32r (*Documents*, 393, 446).

13. According to Daniel Judkins, trauma coordinator and head injury epidemiologist at the University Medical Center in Tucson, Arizona, Vázquez de Coronado "sustained no serious head injury. Nothing beyond a mild concussion, at least. In a mild concussion, you can have a brief (seconds or minutes) loss of consciousness, or just dizziness, seeing stars, etc." Personal communication, March 4, 2004.

14. Castañeda de Nájera, fol. 32r (*Documents*, 393, 446). Evidence of the battle has been recovered archaeologically at Hawikku, first between 1917 and 1923 and again since 2002. That evidence consists primarily of crossbow dart points and lead shot flattened by impact against the pueblo's outer walls. See Watson Smith, Richard B. Woodbury, and Nathalie F. S. Woodbury, *The Excavation of Hawikuh by Frederick Webb Hodge: Report of the Hendricks-Hodge Expedition, 1917–1923* (New York: Museum of the American Indian–Heye Foundation, 1966); Jonathan E. Damp, *The Battle of Hawikku: Archaeological Investigations of the Zuni-Coronado Encounter at Hawikku, the Ensuing Battle, and the Aftermath during the Summer of 1540*, Zuni Cultural Resource Enterprise Report 884 (Zuni, N.M.: Zuni Cultural Resource Enterprise, 2005).

15. This is according to the 1544 testimony of Pedro de Ledesma. Other expeditionaries, including Juan Troyano and Melchior Pérez, vaguer in their accounts, said simply that the Indians submitted and withdrew from the pueblo. Ledesma also claimed that the captain general was aware that the Cíbolans were escaping and ordered them not to be pursued. This does not jibe with his widely acknowledged unconsciousness throughout the battle and occupation of Hawikku. Proceso of Francisco Vázquez de Coronado, fols. 55r, 74r, 85r (*Great Cruelties*, 167, 180, 211, 221, 236–37, 245).

16. Vázquez de Coronado's Letter to the Viceroy, August 3, 1540, fol. 361r (*Documents*, 257–58, 266).

17. Ibid., fol. 361v (*Documents*, 259, 267).

18. Relación del Suceso, fol. 1v (*Documents*, 498, 504).

19. Vázquez de Coronado's Letter to the Viceroy, August 3, 1540, fol. 361r (*Documents*, 258, 267); Relación del Suceso, fol. 1v (*Documents*, 498, 504).

20. Vázquez de Coronado's Letter to the Viceroy, August 3, 1540, fol. 361v (*Documents*, 259, 267).

21. Castañeda de Nájera, fol. 117v (*Documents*, 422, 478).

22. Vázquez de Coronado's Letter to the Viceroy, August 3, 1540, fol. 360r (*Documents*, 255, 264).

23. Ibid., fol. 362r (*Documents*, 260, 268).

24. Ibid.

25. Ibid. (*Documents*, 260–61, 268).

26. Ibid. (*Documents*, 261, 268).

27. Ibid.

28. Ibid., fol. 362v (*Documents*, 261, 269).

29. Ibid., fol. 361v (*Documents*, 260, 267).

Chapter 11: In the Wake of Disillusionment

1. Vázquez de Coronado's Letter to the Viceroy, August 3, 1540, fol. 362v (*Documents*, 261, 269).

2. Castañeda de Nájera, fols. 42r–42v, 45r (*Documents*, 396, 397, 450, 451).

3. Tello, *Crónica miscelánea*, 491.

4. Vázquez de Coronado's Letter to the Viceroy, August 3, 1540, fol. 362v (*Documents*, 261, 269).

5. Castañeda de Nájera, fol. 42v (*Documents*, 396, 450).

6. Ibid., fol. 43r (*Documents*, 396, 450).

7. John Otis Brew, "The History of Awatovi," in Ross Gordon Montgomery, Watson Smith, and John Otis Brew, *Franciscan Awatovi: The Excavation and Conjectural Reconstruction of a Seventeenth-Century Spanish Mission Establishment at a Hopi Indian Town in Northeastern Arizona* (Cambridge, Mass.: Peabody Museum, Harvard University, 1949), 3.

8. Castañeda de Nájera, fol. 43r (*Documents*, 396, 450).

9. Ibid., fol. 47v (*Documents*, 398, 452).

10. Relación del Suceso, fol. 2r (*Documents*, 498, 504).

11. Vázquez de Coronado's Letter to the Viceroy, August 3, 1540, fol. 362r (*Documents*, 260, 268).

12. AGI, Patronato, 26, R.23, Hernando de Alvarado's Narrative, 1540, fol. 1r, transcribed and translated as Document 24 in *Documents*, 305, 307.

13. Vázquez de Coronado's Letter to the Viceroy, August 3, 1540, fol. 363r (*Documents*, 262, 270).

14. Linda S. Cordell, *Prehistory of the Southwest* (New York: Academic Press, 1984), 246.

15. Frederick W. Hodge, *Circular Kivas near Hawikuh, New Mexico* (New York: Museum of the American Indian, Heye Foundation, 1923).

16. Frank H. H. Roberts Jr., *Village of the Great Kivas* (Washington, D.C.: Bureau of American Ethnology, 1932).

17. Some scholars are convinced that the place where Marcos was told about Marata was in the Santa Cruz Valley rather than on the San Pedro. In either case the ruins of Paquimé would have lain to the southeast, in today's Mexican state of Chihuahua. Hartmann, "Pathfinder for Coronado," 95–100.

18. Narrative Account by fray Marcos de Niza, fol. 5r (*Documents*, 72, 84).

19. Riley, *Rio del Norte*, 152.

20. Michael E. Whalen and Paul E. Minnis, "Investigating the Paquimé Regional System," in Curtis F. Schaafsma and Carroll L. Riley, eds., *The Casas Grandes World* (Salt Lake City: University of Utah Press, 1999), 54–62.

21. Narrative Account by fray Marcos de Niza, fol. 5r (*Documents*, 72, 84).

22. Ibid., fol. 7r (*Documents*, 75, 87).

23. Cordell, *Prehistory of the Southwest*, 277–83.

24. M. Jane Young, *Signs from the Ancestors: Zuni Cultural Symbolism and Perceptions of Rock Art* (Albuquerque: University of New Mexico Press, 1988), 117.

Chapter 12: Overture from Cicuique

1. Castañeda de Nájera, fol. 48v (*Documents*, 398, 452).

2. Proceso of Francisco Vázquez de Coronado, fols. 55v–56v, 85v, 119r (*Great Cruelties*, 168, 180–81, 237, 245, 315–16, 321).

3. Castañeda de Nájera, fol. 48r (*Documents*, 398, 452).

4. Ibid., fol. 48v (*Documents*, 398, 452).

5. Proceso of Francisco Vázquez de Coronado, fol. 105v (*Great Cruelties*, 282, 300).

6. Ibid., fol. 56r (*Great Cruelties*, 168, 181).

7. Ibid., fols. 38v–39r, 45v, 56r, 85v (*Great Cruelties*, 130, 135, 147, 155, 168, 181, 237, 245–46).

8. Ibid., fol. 105v (*Great Cruelties*, 282, 300).

9. UTA, Ben., JGI 31 XVI C, Relación Postrera de Cíbola, 1540s, fol. 124v, transcribed and translated as Document 23 in *Documents*, 300, 302.

10. Proceso of Francisco Vázquez de Coronado, fols. 105v–106r (*Great Cruelties*, 282, 300).

11. Hernando de Alvarado's Narrative, fol. 1r (*Documents*, 305, 307).

12. Ibid.

13. Ibid.; Juan Jaramillo's Narrative, fol. 2v (*Documents*, 514, 521).

14. Relación del Suceso, fol. 3r (*Documents*, 499, 505).

15. Castañeda de Nájera, fol. 115v (*Documents*, 421, 478).

16. Ibid., fol. 109v (*Documents*, 419, 475).

17. Hernando de Alvarado's Narrative, fol. 1r (*Documents*, 305, 307).

18. Proceso of Francisco Vázquez de Coronado, fol. 74v (*Great Cruelties*, 211, 222).

19. Ibid., fol. 68r (*Great Cruelties*, 194, 201).

20. Castañeda de Nájera, fol. 51r (*Documents*, 399, 453).

21. Ibid., fol. 116r (*Documents*, 421, 478).

22. Bakewell, *A History of Latin America*, 151.

23. Castañeda de Nájera, fol. 117v (*Documents*, 422, 478).

24. Proceso of Francisco Vázquez de Coronado, fols. 75r–75v (*Great Cruelties*, 212, 222).

25. Castañeda de Nájera, fol. 112r (*Documents*, 420, 476).

26. Proceso of Francisco Vázquez de Coronado, fol. 106r (*Great Cruelties*, 283, 300).

27. Relación del Suceso, fol. 3v (*Documents*, 499–500, 505).

28. Castañeda de Nájera, fols. 150v–151r (*Documents*, 432, 491).

29. Proceso of Francisco Vázquez de Coronado, fol. 56v (*Great Cruelties*, 169, 181).

30. Castañeda de Nájera, fols. 53v–54r (*Documents*, 400, 454).

31. Proceso of Francisco Vázquez de Coronado, fol. 107v (*Great Cruelties*, 284, 302).

32. Ibid., fol. 57v (*Great Cruelties*, 169, 182).

33. Castañeda de Nájera, fol. 51v (*Documents*, 400, 453).

34. The name Nanapagua has not been correlated with any extant pueblo or any known archaeological site. The name does not appear in other documents of the Coronado expedition or in later Spanish documents.

35. Proceso of Francisco Vázquez de Coronado, fols. 57v–58r (*Great Cruelties*, 169–70, 182).

36. Ibid., fol. 58r (*Great Cruelties*, 170, 183).

37. Ibid., fol. 108v (*Great Cruelties*, 285, 302–3).

38. Ibid., fol. 31r (*Great Cruelties*, 112, 120).

39. Ibid., fol. 68v, Testimony of Rodrigo de Frías (*Great Cruelties*, 194, 202).

40. Proceso of Francisco Vázquez de Coronado, fols. 47v, 109v (*Great Cruelties*, 148, 156, 285–86, 303).

41. Ibid., fol. 58v (*Great Cruelties*, 170, 183).

42. Ibid., fol. 94r (*Great Cruelties*, 256, 265).

Chapter 13: The Heart of the Land of Flat-Roofed Towns

1. Juan Jaramillo's Narrative, fol. 2r (*Documents*, 513, 520).

2. Castañeda de Nájera, fols. 51v, 52r (*Documents*, 400, 453).

3. Report Extracted from the Affidavit Prepared for don García Ramírez de Cárdenas, fols. 2r–2v (*Great Cruelties*, 440, 449).

4. Castañeda de Nájera, fol. 52r (*Documents*, 400, 453).

5. The late Dee Brecheisen of Peralta, New Mexico, an avid metal detectorist, collected at least 23 copper crossbow boltheads and dozens of lead balls from property immediately adjacent to Santiago Pueblo (LA 326). Among the lead balls, at least 19 had been flattened by impact. This strongly suggests that fighting took place between members of the Coronado expedition and the residents of Santiago-Coofor. Further suggestion of a violent expulsion comes from a mid-eighteenth-century history by an official of the Audiencia de Guadalajara, Matías Ángel de la Mota López Padilla. He had access to no-longer-extant manuscript documents prepared by one or more members of the Coronado expedition. With regard to their removal from Coofor, he wrote that the Pueblo owners-residents were "evicted" (*los indios los desembarazaron*). Matías de la Mota y Padilla, *Historia de la conquista del reino de la Nueva Galicia*, ed. José Ireneo Gutiérrez (Guadalajara, México: Talleres Gráficos de Gallardo y Alvarez del Castillo, 1920), 226; A. Grove Day, "Mota Padilla on the Coronado Expedition," *Hispanic American Historical Review* 20, no. 1 (1940): 98.

6. For further discussion of cornstalk use as a source of conflict, see *Great Cruelties*, 525–26.

7. Elinore M. Barrett, *The Geography of Rio Grande Pueblos Revealed by Spanish Explorers, 1540–1598* (Albuquerque: Latin American Institute, University of New Mexico, 1997), 8–9.

8. Carla R. Van West and Henri D. Grissino-Mayer, "Dendroclimatic Reconstruction," in *Archaeological Data Recovery in the New Mexico Transportation Corridor and First Five-Year Permit Area, Fence Lake Coal Mine Project, Catron County, New Mexico*, vol. 2, part 1, *Draft Report* (Tucson, Ariz.: Statistical Research, 2004).

9. Castañeda de Nájera, fol. 115v (*Documents*, 421, 478). This count did not include several groups of pueblos that the expedition apparently did not visit, including the Tompiros of the Estancia Basin and several Tewa and northern Tiwa pueblos.

10. Elinore M. Barrett, *Conquest and Catastrophe: Changing Rio Grande Pueblo Settlement Patterns in the Sixteenth and Seventeenth Centuries* (Albuquerque: University of New Mexico Press, 2002), 12. By no means is the population of the Pueblo world in 1540 a settled fact. Both sixteenth-century Spanish observers and modern archaeologists have offered widely varying estimates. The most likely range is between 60,000 and 100,000. For discussion of the many estimates, see Albert H. Schroeder, "Pueblos Abandoned in Historic Times," in Ortiz, *Handbook of North American Indians*, vol. 9, *Southwest*, 236–54; Riley, *Frontier People*, 177–79, 230–32, 259.

11. Castañeda de Nájera, fol. 115r (*Documents*, 421, 477); Juan Jaramillo's Narrative, fol. 2v (*Documents*, 514, 521); Proceso of Francisco Vázquez de Coronado, fol. 17r (*Great Cruelties*, 80, 85).

12. Proceso of Francisco Vázquez de Coronado, fol. 109v (*Great Cruelties*, 286, 303).

13. Castañeda de Nájera, fols. 113v–114r (*Documents*, 420–21, 477).

14. Proceso of Francisco Vázquez de Coronado, fol. 77r (*Great Cruelties*, 213, 224).

15. Castañeda de Nájera, fol. 118r (*Documents*, 422, 479).

16. Ibid., fol. 56v (*Documents*, 401, 455).

17. Remains of what are likely these structures were exposed during a highway widening project on New Mexico Highway 528 west of Bernalillo in early spring 1986. Subsequent excavation by Museum of New Mexico archaeologists determined that they dated from the time of the Coronado *entrada*. Bradley J. Vierra, *A Sixteenth-Century Spanish Campsite in the Tiguex Province*, Laboratory of Anthropology Notes 475 (Santa Fe: Museum of New Mexico, Research Section, 1989).

Chapter 14: Vassalage Denied

1. Castañeda de Nájera, fol. 58v (*Documents*, 402, 456).

2. Investigation concerning Nuño de Chávez, fol. 6r (*Great Cruelties*, 354, 363, 375, 383). Juan Alemán's indigenous name is provided by a 1546 deposition made by the former *maestre de campo*, don García López de Cárdenas. AGI, Justicia, 1021, Pieza 1, Deposition of don García López de Cárdenas, Pinto, February 20, 1546, translated in Hammond and Rey, *Narratives*, 359.

3. Castañeda de Nájera, fol. 58v (*Documents*, 402, 456).

4. Ibid.

5. Ibid., fol. 59r (*Documents*, 402, 456); Proof Taken by the *Fiscal* Villalobos, 1547.

6. Castañeda de Nájera, fols. 59r–59v (*Documents*, 402, 456).

7. Proceso of Francisco Vázquez de Coronado, fol. 59r (*Great Cruelties*, 171, 183).

8. Ibid., fol. 31v (*Great Cruelties*, 113, 121).

9. Ibid., fol. 87v (*Great Cruelties*, 238, 247).

10. Relación del Suceso, fol. 3v (*Documents*, 500, 506).

11. The coordinated action of the Tiguex people, like that of the people of Cíbola-Shíwana, is highly suggestive of what archaeologist David Wilcox posited as "confederations of ethnically identical village clusters" throughout the protohistoric Pueblo world. David R. Wilcox, "Changing Perspectives on the Protohistoric Pueblos, A.D. 1450–1700," in David R. Wilcox and W. Bruce Masse, eds., *The Protohistoric Period in the North American Southwest, A.D. 1450–1700* (Tempe: Arizona State University, 1981), 378–409. Carroll Riley recently outlined the case for the existence of protohistoric Pueblo confederations among settlements speaking the same language. Carroll L. Riley, *Becoming Aztlan: Mesoamerican Influence in the Greater Southwest, AD 1200–1500* (Salt Lake City: University of Utah Press, 2005), 106. The concept of protohistoric Pueblo confederations has been further amplified in Katherine A. Spielmann, "Clustered Confederacies: Sociopolitical Organization in the Protohistoric Rio Grande," in Wirt H. Wills and Robert D. Leonard, eds., *The Ancient Southwestern Community: Models and Methods for the Study of Protohistoric Social Organization* (Albuquerque: University of New Mexico Press, 1994), 45–54. Spielmann suggested that protohistoric Puebloan confederacies might have been similar to those of the Huron in eastern North America. Consolidation of the disparate pueblos of Cíbola into a single large pueblo at Zuni after the Pueblo Revolt of 1680 and the ease with which the various Jemez pueblos later amalgamated add further credence to the existence of some sort of interpueblo, but intraethnic, governance at the time of the Coronado expedition and for centuries before and afterward.

12. Castañeda de Nájera, fol. 61r (*Documents*, 403, 457).

13. Proceso of Francisco Vázquez de Coronado, fol. 24v (*Great Cruelties*, 96, 104).

14. Investigation concerning Nuño de Chávez, fol. 4v (*Great Cruelties*, 353, 374).

15. Hammond and Rey, *Narratives*, 357.

16. Ibid., 355.

17. Proceso of Francisco Vázquez de Coronado, fols. 60r–60v (*Great Cruelties*, 172–73, 184–85).

18. Disposal of the Juan Jiménez Estate, fol. 3r (*Documents*, 332, 356). Further, Francisco Gorbalán testified in 1546 that the Tiguex had vacated three pueblos for the expedition's use during its first winter in Tierra Nueva. Testimony of Francisco Gorbalán, in UCB, Ban., C-B 840, Item 398, H. E. Bolton Papers, Part I, AGI, Justicia, 1021, N.2, Pieza 3, Report Prepared on Behalf of don García Ramírez de Cárdenas, transcription by Agapito Rey.

19. Proceso of Francisco Vázquez de Coronado, fols. 110v–112r (*Great Cruelties*, 287–88, 305–6).

20. Hammond and Rey, *Narratives*, 358.

21. In some documents deriving from the expedition, Moho is also called Pueblo del Cerco. *Great Cruelties*, passim. This meeting between Juan Alemán–Xauian and the *maestre de campo* is the subject of the cover illustration for this book.

22. Castañeda de Nájera, fols. 64r–65r (*Documents*, 404, 458).

23. Ibid., fols. 66r–66v (*Documents*, 404, 458–59).

24. Investigation concerning Nuño de Chávez, fol. 14r (*Great Cruelties*, 362, 383); Relación del Suceso, fol. 4r (*Documents*, 500, 506). It is possible that the ruins of this pueblo are located on Santa Ana Mesa overlooking modern San Felipe Pueblo near the confluence of the Rio Grande and the Jemez River. *Documents*, 677, Document 28, n. 265.

25. Castañeda de Nájera, fol. 66v (*Documents*, 404, 459).

26. Ibid., fols. 68v–69r (*Documents*, 405, 459).

27. Ibid., fol. 66v (*Documents*, 404, 459).

28. Proceso of Francisco Vázquez de Coronado, fol. 69v (*Great Cruelties*, 195, 203).

29. Castañeda de Nájera, fol. 75v (*Documents*, 407, 462).

30. Ibid.

Chapter 15: To the Farthest Edge

1. Relación del Suceso, fol. 4r (*Documents*, 500, 506).

2. Castañeda de Nájera, fol. 75v (*Documents*, 407, 462).

3. AGI, Patronato, 184, R.34, Vázquez de Coronado's Letter to the King, October 1541, fol. 1r, transcribed and translated as Document 27 in *Documents*, 319, 323.

4. Proceso of Francisco Vázquez de Coronado, fol. 58v (*Great Cruelties*, 171, 183). Castañeda de Nájera gave a different story, saying that when Vázquez de Coronado went to Cicuique for the purpose of releasing Bigotes, the pueblo "was at peace and supplied foodstuffs." Castañeda de Nájera, fol. 77r (*Documents*, 407, 462–63).

5. Castañeda de Nájera, fol. 93r (*Documents*, 413, 469).

6. For a detailed discussion of this portion of the expedition's route, see Richard Flint and Shirley Cushing Flint, "The Coronado Expedition: Cicúye to the Río de Cicúye Bridge," in Flint and Flint, *Coronado Expedition to Tierra Nueva*, 262–77.

7. See Richard Flint, "Who Designed Coronado's Bridge across the Pecos River?" *Kiva* 57, no. 4 (1992): 331–42.

8. Castañeda de Nájera, fols. 77v–78r (*Documents*, 408, 463).

9. Ibid., fols. 78v–79r (*Documents*, 408, 463).

10. Vázquez de Coronado's Letter to the King, October 1541, fol. 1r (*Documents*, 319, 323).

11. A travois is a dragged litter consisting of two long poles bound together at one end and a platform or net for carrying goods near the opposite end. The bound end is attached to a harness on a dog or other animal, which pulls the litter and its contents.

12. Castañeda de Nájera, fol. 79r (*Documents*, 408, 463).

13. Ibid., fols. 118v–119r (*Documents*, 422, 479).

14. Vázquez de Coronado's Letter to the King, October 1541, fol. 1v (*Documents*, 320, 324).

15. Jaramillo's Narrative, fol. 3r (*Documents*, 515, 522).

16. Some researchers have taken this dispatch of scouting parties as an indication that the guides were lost. Instead, the expeditionaries did not know which guide to believe. Unbeknownst to them, El Turco was leading the expedition straight for the summer territory of the Teyas. For those members of the expedition familiar with Marco Polo's *Travels*, Haya must have sounded tantalizingly like Ayas, a key entrepôt in Lesser Armenia, on the very fringe of Greater India. Polo, *Travels*, 37, 38, 46.

17. Matías Ángel de la Mota López Padilla, the eighteenth-century lawyer and descendant of members of the Coronado expedition, had access to sixteenth-century documents no longer known to exist, including papers of Pedro de Tovar. Evidently on the basis of those sources, he provided details about the arrival at this "first *barranca*" and the subsequent hailstorm there. Mota y Padilla, *Historia*, 230.

18. The expedition met two distinct communities of bison-hunting nomads during the summer of 1541, the first along the western margin of the Llano Estacado and the second on its eastern edge. The names of both groups used throughout the surviving contemporaneous documents, Teyas and Querechos, are names applied by the Pueblos of the Rio Grande region. Juan Jaramillo's Narrative, fol. 2v (*Documents*, 514, 521); Castañeda de Nájera, fols. 83v, 113v, 120r (*Documents*, 410, 420, 423, 465, 477, 479).

19. Castañeda de Nájera, fol. 83v (*Documents*, 410, 465). Recent researchers, Carroll Riley and anthropologist Nancy Hickerson prominent among them, have concluded instead that the Teyas spoke a language related to that of the Tompiro Pueblos of New Mexico's Tularosa Basin. Riley, *Rio del Norte*, 100; Nancy Parrott Hickerson, *The Jumanos: Hunters and Traders of the South Plains* (Austin: University of Texas Press, 1994), 24.

20. Castañeda de Nájera, fols. 81v–82r (*Documents*, 409, 464); Juan Jaramillo's Narrative, fol. 3r (*Documents*, 515, 522).

21. Castañeda de Nájera, fol. 81v (*Documents*, 409, 464).

22. Mota y Padilla, *Historia*, 230. The detail about the time of day may have come from papers written by Captain Pedro de Tovar, to which Mota y Padilla had access, although that is uncertain because the papers have since disappeared.

23. Castañeda de Nájera, fols. 82r–82v (*Documents*, 409, 464–65).

24. See Donald J. Blakeslee, Richard Flint, and Jack T. Hughes, "Una Barranca Grande: Recent Archeological Evidence and a Discussion of Its Place in the Coronado Route," in Flint and Flint, *Coronado Expedition to Tierra Nueva*, 370–83.

25. Castañeda de Nájera, fol. 85r (*Documents*, 410, 466). Other contemporary sources report numbers of as many as 40 for this detachment. Including Mexican Indians, it may have exceeded 100. Investigation concerning Nuño de Chávez, fols. 9v, 17v (*Great Cruelties*, 357, 365, 378, 386).

26. Vázquez de Coronado's Letter to the King, October 1541, fols. 1v–2r (*Documents*, 320, 324).

27. Investigation concerning Nuño de Chávez, fol. 9v (*Great Cruelties*, 358, 378).

28. Castañeda de Nájera, fol. 122v (*Documents*, 423, 480). As mentioned in note 19, this chapter, the suggestion that the Teyas spoke a Caddoan dialect is not accepted by other researchers whose opinions I respect highly. In this case, though, I am not persuaded by their arguments for a linguistic connection between the Teyas and the Tompiro Pueblos. The Caddoan linguistic affiliation has been maintained most strongly by historian Albert Schroeder and archaeologist Jack Hughes. Albert H. Schroeder, "A Re-analysis of the Routes of Coronado and Oñate into the Plains, 1541 and 1601," *Plains Anthropologist* 7, no. 15 (1962): 2–23; Jack T. Hughes, "Prehistoric Cultural Developments on the Texas High Plains," *Bulletin of the Texas Archaeological Society* 60 (1991): 1–55. For a discussion of the difficulties involved in assigning cultural and linguistic affiliations to the protohistoric peoples of the southern Great Plains, see Donald J. Blakeslee et al., "Bison Hunters of the Llano in 1541: A Panel Discussion," in Flint and Flint, *Coronado Expedition from the Distance of 460 Years*, 164–86. In the end, which language the Teyas spoke is not crucial here. What is important is that they had cordial relations with El Turco and people from Pecos, as well as with the Quivirans. Such relations were not dependent on a shared language.

29. Vázquez de Coronado's Letter to the King, October 1541, fols. 1v–2r (*Documents*, 320, 324). It should be pointed out that cultural similarity does not necessarily imply linguistic identity. The language of the Teyas is still very much a matter for investigation, although I lean toward their having been Caddoan speakers. See notes 19 and 28, this chapter.

30. Castañeda de Nájera, fol. 87r (*Documents*, 411, 467).

31. Ibid., fol. 88r (*Documents*, 411, 467).

32. Vázquez de Coronado's Letter to the King, October 1541, fol. 2r (*Documents*, 320, 324).

33. Proceso of Francisco Vázquez de Coronado, fol. 35r (*Great Cruelties*, 115, 124).

34. Vázquez de Coronado's Letter to the King, October 1541, fol. 2r (*Documents*, 321, 324–25).

35. Juan Jaramillo's Narrative, fol. 4r (*Documents*, 516, 522).

36. Ibid. (*Documents*, 516, 523).

37. Proceso of Francisco Vázquez de Coronado, fol. 81v (*Great Cruelties*, 217, 228). See also fol. 89v (*Great Cruelties*, 240, 249).

38. Juan Jaramillo's Narrative, fol. 4v (*Documents*, 516, 523).

39. Report Extracted from the Affidavit Prepared for don García Ramírez de Cárdenas, fol. 4v (*Great Cruelties*, 445, 454).

40. Proceso of Francisco Vázquez de Coronado, fol. 34v (*Great Cruelties*, 115, 123).

41. Ibid., fol. 117v (*Great Cruelties*, 293, 311).

42. Ibid., fol. 61v (*Great Cruelties*, 173–74, 186).

43. Ibid., fol. 99r (*Great Cruelties*, 260, 269).

44. Ibid., fol. 35r (*Great Cruelties*, 115, 124).

45. Juan Jaramillo's Narrative, fol. 4v (*Documents*, 516, 523).

46. John L. Kessell, *Kiva, Cross, and Crown: The Pecos Indians and New Mexico, 1540–1840* (Albuquerque: University of New Mexico Press, 1987), 18; Riley, "Spanish-Indian Communication," 305; Mildred Mott Wedel, "The Indian They Called Turco," in Don G. Wyckoff and Jack L. Hofman, eds., *Pathways to Plains Prehistory: Anthropological Perspectives of Plains Natives and Their Pasts* (Duncan, Okla.: Cross Timbers Press, 1982), 154–55.

47. Gentleman from Elvas, "The Account by a Gentleman from Elvas," in Lawrence A. Clayton, Vernon James Knight Jr., and Edward C. Moore, *The De Soto Chronicles: The Expedition of Hernando de Soto to North America in 1539–1543*, 2 vols. (Tuscaloosa: University of Alabama Press, 1993), 1: 112–13.

48. Ibid., 1: 118.

49. Wedel, "Turco," 155.

50. Gentleman from Elvas, "Account," 1: 89, 120.

51. Biloine Whiting Young and Melvin L. Fowler, *Cahokia: The Great Native American Metropolis* (Urbana: University of Illinois Press, 2000), 310.

52. Ibid., 132

53. Proceso of Francisco Vázquez de Coronado, fol. 57r (*Great Cruelties*, 169, 182).

54. Ibid., fol. 56v (*Great Cruelties*, 169, 181).

55. See, for instance, ibid., fol. 46r (*Great Cruelties*, 147, 155); also Castañeda de Nájera, fol. 51r (*Documents*, 399, 453).

56. Riley, *Frontier People*, 278.

57. James F. Brooks, *Captives and Cousins: Slavery, Kinship, and Community in the Southwest Borderlands* (Chapel Hill: University of North Carolina Press, 2002), 54.

58. A related arrangement of intercultural marriage between Kiowa and Comanche bands two and a half centuries later is reported in Brooks, *Captives and Cousins*, 170–71.

59. Such arrangements were within the repertoire of social and political relations between Pueblos and plains tribes. In discussing intertribal relations of the historic period, for example, anthropologist Charles Lange referred to "prisoner exchanges, bartering of slaves, extended periods of captivity and various forms of adoption." Charles H. Lange, "Relations of the Southwest with the Plains and Great Basin," in Ortiz, *Handbook of North American Indians*, vol. 9, *Southwest*, 203. More recently, James F. Brooks, relying on sources from the nineteenth century, provided an equally complex description of intertribal slavery and assimilation as fictive kin. Brooks, *Captives and Cousins*, 185–86.

60. Proceso of Francisco Vázquez de Coronado, fol. 23r (*Great Cruelties*, 94, 103).

61. Bolton, *Coronado*, 301–2.

62. Riley, *Rio del Norte*, 180.

63. Vázquez de Coronado's Letter to the King, October 1541, fol. 2r (*Documents*, 321, 325).

64. Report Extracted from the Affidavit Prepared for don García Ramírez de Cárdenas, fol. 4v (*Great Cruelties*, 445, 454).

65. Recent archaeological research provides yet another reason for a route by way of the Teyas rather than the Querechos. Ceramic analysis by archaeologist Kathryn Leonard strongly suggests that the people of Cicuique-Pecos maintained long-standing trade relations with several Teya–Garza Complex communities but had no such direct relationship with Querecho–Tierra Blanca Complex settlements. Kathryn Leonard, "Directionality and Exclusivity of Plains-Pueblo Exchange during the Protohistoric Period, AD 1450–1700," in Judith A. Habicht-Mauche,

Suzanne L. Eckert, and Deborah L. Huntley, eds., *The Social Life of Pots: Glaze Wares and Cultural Dynamics in the Southwest, AD 1250–1680* (Tucson: University of Arizona Press, 2006), 232–52.

66. See, as but two of countless examples, the case of two boatmen who trick the hero Esplandián and his companion Sargil at the very beginning of their adventures and the case of the treacherous female guide who leads King Lisuarte into a misadventure that is told among the tales of Esplandián's father, Amadís. Rodríguez de Montalvo, *Sergas de Esplandián*, fol. 4v; Anónimo, *Amadís de Gaula*, ed. Ángel Rosenblat (Barcelona: Losada, 1998), 145–47.

67. One possibility that would have been "under the Europeans' radar" is friction between the Quivirans and the expedition's Indian allies. But in the absence of even the slightest hint of such a development in the documentary record, to offer that as realistic would be gratuitous.

68. Proceso of Francisco Vázquez de Coronado, fols. 61v–62r (*Great Cruelties*, 174, 186).

CHAPTER 16: WHAT WAS SEEN AND WHAT WAS NOT

1. Castañeda de Nájera, fol. 91v (*Documents*, 412, 468).

2. Introduction to Castañeda de Nájera's narrative, *Documents*, 380.

3. Castañeda de Nájera, fol. 102v (*Documents*, 416, 472).

4. Ibid., fols. 100v, 102v (*Documents*, 416, 472). A royal *provisión* of 1526, still the prevailing law in 1539–42, specifically designated homosexuality, or the *pecado nefando*, as one of the "vices" among American natives that it was permissible to suppress by means of force. AGI, Indiferente, 421, L.11\1, Real Provisión dada por don Carlos, que dispone y trata la orden que antiguamente se tenia en los descubrimientos y poblaciones que se hacían en Indias, y en el buen tratamiento de sus naturales, 1526, fol. 335v. For an insightful look at homosexual lives at Zuni Pueblo, see Will Roscoe, *The Zuni Man-Woman* (Albuquerque: University of New Mexico Press, 1991).

5. Castañeda de Nájera, fol. 104r (*Documents*, 417, 473).

6. Vázquez de Coronado's Letter to the Viceroy, August 3, 1540, fol. 360v (*Documents*, 256, 265).

7. Castañeda de Nájera, fol. 105v (*Documents*, 417, 474); Vázquez de Coronado's Letter to the Viceroy, August 3, 1540, fol. 361v (*Documents*, 260, 268).

8. During the seventeenth century, with a decline in Spanish colonists' expectations and the rise of relatively nearby Spanish markets for New Mexican products such as wool and salt, 13 *encomiendas* were established in New Mexico. None was very prosperous, and the *encomienda* system in the province ended with the Pueblo Revolt of 1680. H. Allen Anderson, "The Encomienda in New Mexico, 1598–1680," *New Mexico Historical Review* 60, no. 4 (1985): 353–77.

9. Vázquez de Coronado's Letter to the Viceroy, August 3, 1540, fol. 362r (*Documents*, 260, 268).

10. Ibid., fol. 51r (*Documents*, 399, 453).

11. Ibid., fol. 111r (*Documents*, 420, 476).

12. Relación del Suceso, fol. 3r (*Documents*, 499).

13. Polo, *Travels*, 57.

14. Castañeda de Nájera, fol. 110v (*Documents*, 419, 475).

15. Ibid., fol. 116v (*Documents*, 422, 478).

16. Codex Aubin, fols. 46v, 47r (*Documents*, 169).

17. Ibid.

18. Francisco de Sandoval Acazitli, "Relación de la jornada que hizo don Francisco de Sandoval Acazitli . . . ," in Joaquín García Icazbalceta, ed., *Colección de documentos para la historia de México*, 2 vols. (México, D.F.: Antigua Librería, 1866), 2: 328.

19. That some of the Indian allies remained in Tierra Nueva is treated at greater length in chapter 18.

20. Castañeda de Nájera, fol. 118v (*Documents*, 422, 479).

21. Riley, *Frontier People*, 215.

22. It is especially remarkable that the expeditionaries were never aware of the Cerrillos lead and turquoise mines, because recent archaeological analysis has shown that all the Pueblos of the Galisteo Basin and many from the neighboring Rio Grande Valley made use of lead from those mines in their manufacture of decorated ceramics. Archaeologists Kit Nelson and Judith Habicht-Mauche have gone so far as to conclude that the lead was acquired by persons from the various pueblos who actually traveled to the mines and extracted the ore themselves, rather than obtaining it through trade. Thus, many native people would have been aware of the mines' precise locations, yet none evidently disclosed that information to members of the expedition. Kit Nelson and Judith A. Habicht-Mauche, "Lead, Paint, and Pots: Rio Grande Intercommunity Dynamics from a Glaze Ware Perspective," in Habicht-Mauche, Eckert, and Huntley, *Social Life of Pots*, 197–215.

23. Relación del Suceso, fol. 5v (*Documents*, 502).

24. Castañeda de Nájera, fols. 92r, 108v (*Documents*, 412, 418, 468, 475).

25. Ibid., fols. 110r–110v (*Documents*, 419, 475).

26. James Lockhart, "The Post-Conquest Period of Mexican History," in "A Scholarly Debate: The Origins of Modern Mexico—Indígenistas vs. Hispanistas," *The Americas* 48, no. 3 (1992): 327.

27. Vázquez de Coronado's Letter to the King, October 1541, fol. 2r (*Documents*, 321).

28. Ibid., fols. 2r–2v (*Documents*, 321).

29. October 20 is the date on the original letter. It is in the Julian calendar and so is the equivalent of October 30 according to the modern calendar.

30. Vázquez de Coronado's Letter to the King, October 1541, fol. 2r (*Documents*, 321).

Chapter 17: Disintegration and Withdrawal

1. Castañeda de Nájera, fols. 92v–93r (*Documents*, 413, 469).

2. Ibid., fol. 94r (*Documents*, 414, 469).

3. Ibid., fol. 93v (*Documents*, 413–14, 469).

4. Vázquez de Coronado's Letter to the King, October 1541, fol. 2r (*Documents*, 321, 325).

5. Ibid.

6. Castañeda de Nájera, fol. 90v (*Documents*, 412, 468).

7. Proceso of Francisco Vázquez de Coronado, fol. 51r (*Great Cruelties*, 151, 159–60).

8. Ibid., fols. 95v, 113r (*Great Cruelties*, 257, 266, 289, 307).

9. Henri D. Grissino-Mayer, "A 2129-Year Reconstruction of Precipitation for Northwestern New Mexico, USA," in Jeffrey S. Dean, D. M. Meko, and T. W. Swetnam, eds., *Tree Rings, Environment, and Humanity* (Tucson: Department of Geosciences, University of Arizona, 1996), 191–204.

10. Investigation concerning Nuño de Chávez, fol. 9v (*Great Cruelties*, 358, 378).

11. Disposal of the Juan Jiménez Estate (*Documents*, 326–77).

12. Castañeda de Nájera, fols. 128v–129r (*Documents*, 425, 482).

13. According to trauma nurse Dan Judkins, "it is most likely Coronado experienced a moderate cerebral contusion, or maybe a small subdural hematoma that gradually resolved. He did recover enough to be able to decide to return to Mexico and to travel back there and go about usual daily functions. He likely had some personality change or mild cognitive deficit, and if so, this would imply that the most likely injury was a frontal contusion. Contusion to the frontal lobe often is associated with a 'flat' personality affect and other behavior changes. Coronado seems to have lost his ambition for the project, and his enthusiasm declined. This fits very well with frontal lobe injury." Personal communication, March 4, 2004.

14. Castañeda de Nájera, fols. 129r–129v (*Documents*, 425, 483).

15. Proceso of Francisco Vázquez de Coronado, fol. 73r (*Great Cruelties*, 210, 220).

16. Castañeda de Nájera, fols. 133v–134v (*Documents*, 427, 484).

17. AGI, México, 228, N.23, Reports Made on behalf of Diego Gutiérrez de Bocanegra, 1608.

18. Tello, *Crónica miscelánea*, 443.

19. Castañeda de Nájera, fol. 130v (*Documents*, 426, 483).

20. Ibid., fol. 129v (*Documents*, 425, 483).

21. Proceso of Francisco Vázquez de Coronado, fol. 9v (*Great Cruelties*, 61, 69).

22. Castañeda de Nájera, fols. 138r–139r (*Documents*, 428, 489).

23. Riley, *Rio del Norte*, 213–14.

24. Hammond and Rey, *Rediscovery of New Mexico*, 184–86, 225.

25. Castañeda de Nájera, fol. 138r (*Documents*, 428, 486).

26. Ibid., fol. 147r (*Documents*, 431, 489).

27. Ibid., fol. 139v (*Documents*, 428, 486).

28. Proceso of Francisco Vázquez de Coronado, fol. 14r (*Great Cruelties*, 65, 73–74).

29. Ibid., fol. 10v (*Great Cruelties*, 61, 70).

30. Castañeda de Nájera, fol. 140v (*Documents*, 429, 487).

31. *Documents*, 605–15.

32. Castañeda de Nájera, fols. 143r–143v (*Documents*, 430, 488).

33. Ibid.

34. Ibid.

Chapter 18: Upshot

1. Relación del Suceso, fol. 4r (*Documents*, 500, 506).

2. Vázquez de Coronado's Letter to the King, October 1541, fols. 2r–2v (*Documents*, 321, 325).

3. Castañeda de Nájera, fol. 130v (*Documents*, 426, 483).

4. Ibid., fol. 123r (*Documents*, 423, 480).

5. Francisco López de Gómara, *Historia general de las Indias* (Zaragosa: Miguel de Zapila, 1555; facsimile edition, Lima: Comisión Nacional del V Centenario del Descubrimiento de América-Encuentro de Dos Mundos, 1993), fol. 18r.

6. AGI, Guadalajara, 5, R.1, N.5, Letter from Vázquez de Coronado to the King, December 1538, fols. 1r–2r, transcribed and translated as Document 1 in *Documents*, 23–24, 27–28.

7. Melchior Pérez's Petition for Preferment, fol. 3v (*Documents*, 537, 547).

8. Proof of Service of Juan de Paladinas, 1560.
9. Cristóbal de Escobar's Proof of Service, fol. 15v (*Documents*, 564, 577).
10. Vázquez de Coronado's Petition for Recovery of Encomiendas, fol. 1r (*Documents*, 584, 587).
11. Kelsey, *Cabrillo*, 101–3.
12. *Documents*, 534.
13. Ibid., 554–55.
14. Vázquez de Coronado's Petition for Recovery of Encomiendas, fol. 2v (*Documents*, 584, 587).
15. Castañeda de Nájera, fols. 131r–131v (*Documents*, 426, 483) and fols. 139v–140r (*Documents*, 429, 486–87).
16. *Documents*, 611.
17. Ibid.
18. Ibid., 609.
19. *Great Cruelties*, 250–52.
20. During the ambush of Juan de Zaldívar at Acoma Pueblo, for instance, shortly after Juan de Oñate and his colonists arrived in New Mexico in 1598, Acoma warriors called down from their mesa to European attackers below, using epithets in Nahuatl. George P. Hammond and Agapito Rey, *Don Juan de Oñate, Colonizer of New Mexico, 1595–1628*, 2 vols. (Albuquerque: University of New Mexico Press, 1953), 1: 438.
21. Richard Flint, "The Coronado and de Soto Expeditions: A Contrast in Attitudes or Difference in External Conditions? Part 1. Relative Humanity of the Expeditions." *El Viaje* 1, no. 2 (1992): 6–7.
22. Hammond and Rey, *Rediscovery of New Mexico*, 105–6.
23. Daniel T. Reff, "The Relevance of Ethnology to the Routing of the Coronado Expedition in Sonora," in Flint and Flint, *Coronado Expedition to Tierra Nueva*, 165–76.
24. After decades of overemphasis of the role of disease in the depopulation of native America, the tide seems to have turned. Suzanne Alchon, for instance, recently and eloquently pointed out—I think correctly—that in addition to epidemic disease, "other factors specific to the phenomenon of European colonialism also played a significant role" in the drastic demographic decline suffered by Native Americans during the sixteenth and seventeenth centuries. Those factors included warfare, dislocation, slavery, and forced labor. Suzanne Austin Alchon, *A Pest in the Land: New World Epidemics in a Global Perspective* (Albuquerque: University of New Mexico Press, 2003), 144.

25. For a fuller discussion of the question of the effect of Old World infectious diseases in New Mexico, see Ann F. Ramenofsky, "The Problem of Introduced Infectious Diseases in New Mexico, A.D. 1540–1680," *Journal of Anthropological Research* 52 (1996): 161–84.

CHAPTER 19: ONE OF A HUNDRED AND THIRTY

1. For a provisional list of such expeditions, the names of their leaders, and the regions they covered, see Appendix 1.

2. Morison, *Southern Voyages*, 204.

3. I have not counted subsidiary expeditions, such as the Díaz trip to the lower Colorado River and the Tovar and López de Cárdenas trips to Tusayán, in the case of the Coronado expedition, separately. If they were counted separately, then the total number of expeditions would easily be two or three times greater than the 15 given here.

4. Gentleman of Elvas, "Account," 1: 48–49.

5. "Concession made by the King of Spain to Hernando de Soto of the government of Cuba and the conquest of Florida, with the title of Adelantado," in Clayton, Knight, and Moore, *De Soto Chronicles*, 1: 362.

6. Henry R. Wagner, *Spanish Voyages to the Northwest Coast of America in the Sixteenth Century* (San Francisco: California Historical Society, 1929), 11.

7. Kelsey, *Cabrillo*, 110.

8. Oviedo y Valdés, *Historia general*, 5: 235–36; Gaspar Carvajal, "On the Voyage of Francisco de Orellana down the Amazon in 1542," in John H. Parry and Robert G. Keith, eds., *New Iberian World*, vol. 5, *Coastlines, Rivers, and Forests* (New York: Times Books, 1984), 187–217.

9. Oviedo y Valdés, *Historia general*, 5: 240–41.

10. Matthew Restall, *Maya Conquistador* (Boston: Beacon Press, 1998), 9–13.

11. Howard, *Conquistador in Chains*, 109.

12. Cabeza de Vaca, *Naufragios y comentarios*, 215.

13. José Ignacio Avellaneda, *The Conquerors of the New Kingdom of Granada* (Albuquerque: University of New Mexico Press, 1995), 41, 47, 121.

14. Carlos Monge Alfaro, *Historia de Costa Rica*, 10th ed. (San José, Costa Rica: Imprenta Trejos, 1960), 53–55.

15. "Pedro de Valdivia to the Emperor, on His Conquest of Chile," in Parry and Keith, *Coastlines, Rivers, and Forests*, 343–55.

16. Howard, *Conquistador in Chains*, 110, 128.

17. Avellaneda, *Conquerors*, 42, 47.

18. Robert S. Chamberlain, *The Conquest and Colonization of Yucatan, 1517–1550* (Washington, D.C.: Carnegie Institution of Washington, 1948), 211.

19. "Pedro de Valdivia to the Emperor," 346.

20. Pedro de Cieza de León, *The Discovery and Conquest of Peru*, trans. and eds. Alexandra Parma Cook and Noble David Cook (Durham, N.C.: Duke University Press, 1998), 384.

21. Jared Diamond, *Guns, Germs, and Steel: The Fates of Human Societies* (New York: W. W. Norton, 1999), 74.

22. Oviedo y Valdés, *Historia general*, 5: 36; Cieza de León, *Discovery and Conquest of Peru*, 177.

23. Cieza de León, *Discovery and Conquest of Peru*, 171, 173, 177.

24. J[ohn] H. Elliott, *Imperial Spain, 1469–1716* (London: Penguin, 1990), 48.

25. Juan Bethencourt Alonso, *La conquista de las Islas Canarias* (La Laguna, Tenerife: Francisco Lemus, 1997), passim.

26. For example, see Thomas, *Conquest*, 207; also William H. Prescott, *The Conquest of Mexico* (Garden City, N.Y.: Doubleday, Doran and Company, 1934; first published 1843), 78.

27. The 1555 edition of the *Relación*, prepared by Cabeza de Vaca himself, includes specific reference to the maize road. Álvar Núñez Cabeza de Vaca, *The Account: Álvar Núñez Cabeza de Vaca's Relación*, eds. and trans. Martin A. Favata and José B. Fernández (Houston: Arte Público Press, 1993), 103; also Adorno and Pautz, *Cabeza de Vaca*, 1: 227.

28. Pero Hernández, "Up the Paraguay River and His [Cabeza de Vaca's] Arrest and Expulsion from Asunción," in Parry and Keith, *Coastlines, Rivers, and Forests*, 298.

29. Avellaneda, *Conquerors*, 47.

30. Gentleman of Elvas, "Account," 1: 77.

31. Oviedo y Valdés, *Historia general*, 5: 244–46.

32. Avellaneda, *Conquerors*, 47.

33. José Ignacio Avellaneda, *Los Sobrevivientes de la Florida; The Survivors of the de Soto Expedition* (Gainesville, Fla.: P. K. Yonge Library of Florida History, 1990), 6–10.

34. Oviedo y Valdés, *Historia general*, 5: 239.

35. Francisco López de Gómara, *Historia de la conquista de México*, 2 vols., ed. Joaquín Ramírez Cabañas (México, D.F.: Editorial Pedro Robledo, 1943), 2: 202. "Estuvieron en este viaje un año entero, y no trajeron nueva de ninguna tierra buena. Más fué el ruido que las nueces."

36. Adorno and Pautz, *Cabeza de Vaca*, 1: 411.
37. "Pedro de Valdivia to the Emperor," 349.
38. Avellaneda, *Conquerors*, 43.
39. "Pedro de Valdivia to the Emperor," 349.
40. AGI, México, 907, Proof of Service of Rodrigo Álvarez, 1575, translated in Chamberlain, *Conquest and Colonization of Yucatan*, 218.
41. Restall, *Maya Conquistador*, 18.
42. See Inga Clendinnen, *Ambivalent Conquests: Maya and Spaniard in Yucatán, 1517–1570* (Cambridge: Cambridge University Press, 1987).
43. See, for instance, Robert Ricard's discussion of Bernardino de Sahagún's belief that use of native languages and images by friars led to "confusions . . . among the Indians" and "errors" committed by the missionaries. Ricard, *Spiritual Conquest*, 273–74, 286.
44. Proof of Service of Rodrigo Álvarez, 1575, in Chamberlain, *Conquest and Colonization of Yucatan*, 218.
45. Compiled by John R. Swanton, *Final Report of the United States De Soto Expedition Commission* (Washington, D.C.: Smithsonian Institution, 1939; reprint 1985), 88.
46. Chamberlain, *Conquest and Colonization of Yucatan*, 216.
47. "Pedro de Valdivia to the Emperor," 346.
48. Ibid.
49. Restall, *Maya Conquistador*, 115.
50. Howard, *Conquistador in Chains*, 127.
51. Restall, *Maya Conquistador*, 113, 115.

Chapter 20: Discontinuity at Mid-Century

1. See Formation of Company between Mendoza and Pedro de Alvarado, November 29, 1540 (*Documents*, 271–84).
2. Aiton, *Mendoza*, 131–36.
3. Morison, *Southern Voyages*, 402–20.
4. That proof came as a result of a voyage by Vitus Bering in 1728. He demonstrated that even at their closest approach, Asia and North America were separated by the strait that today bears the Danish-Russian navigator's name. Orcutt Frost, *Bering: The Russian Discovery of America* (New Haven, Conn.: Yale University Press, 2003), 48–62.

5. It has been suggested that the López de Villalobos and Cabrillo voyages were coordinated in a pincer strategy for the purpose of settling the question of whether Asia and America were indeed separate. Kelsey, *Cabrillo*, 103.

6. Simpson, *Encomienda*, 5.

7. Ibid., 9–39.

8. Henry Stevens and Fred W. Lucas, trans. and eds., *The New Laws of the Indies for the Good Treatment and Preservation of the Indians* (London: Chiswick Press, 1893; reprint, Amsterdam: N. Isreal, 1968).

9. Hanns J. Prem, "Disease Outbreaks in Central Mexico during the Sixteenth Century," in Noble David Cook and W. George Lovell, eds., *"Secret Judgments of God": Old World Disease in Colonial Spanish America* (Norman: University of Oklahoma Press, 1992), 33. Recent epidemiological research suggests that the 1545–48 epidemic was not typhus or any other Old World disease but rather a rodent-spread "indigenous hemorrhagic fever," perhaps similar to hantavirus or arenavirus. Rodolfo Acuña-Soto et al., "Megadrought and Megadeath in Sixteenth-Century Mexico," *Emerging Infectious Diseases* 8, no. 4 (2002): 360–62.

10. Daniel T. Reff, *Disease, Depopulation, and Culture Change in Northwestern New Spain, 1518–1764* (Salt Lake City: University of Utah Press, 1991), 114–17.

11. W. George Lovell, "Disease and Depopulation in Early Colonial Guatemala," 49–83; Linda A. Newson, "Old World Epidemics in Early Colonial Ecuador," 84–112; and Juan A. Villamarín and Judith E. Villamarín, "Epidemic Disease in the Sabana de Bogotá, 1536–1810," 113–41; all in Cook and Lovell, *"Secret Judgments of God."*

12. Peter Bakewell, *Silver Mining and Society in Colonial Mexico: Zacatecas, 1546–1700* (Cambridge: Cambridge University Press, 1971), 4, 13.

13. Ibid., 268.

14. Bakewell, *History of Latin America*, 176.

15. Phelan, *Millennial Kingdom*, 1970, 111.

16. The years of death of Los Doce are as follows: fray Juan Suárez and fray Juan de Palos, both in 1528; fray Martín de Valencia, 1534; fray García de Cisneros, 1536; fray Francisco Jiménez, 1530s?; fray Martín de Jesús, 1541?; fray Luis de Fuensalida, 1545; fray Francisco de Soto, 1551; fray Antonio de Ciudad Rodrigo, 1553; fray Juan de Ribas, 1562; fray Toribio de Benavente, 1565; and fray Andrés de Córdoba, unknown. Chávez, *Oroz Codex*.

17. Ricard, *Spiritual Conquest*, 58.

18. Richard F. Greenleaf and Neal Kaveny, eds. and trans., *Zumárraga and His Family: Letters to Vizcaya, 1536–1548* (Washington, D.C.: Academy of American Franciscan History, 1979), xxvii; Phelan, *Millennial Kingdom*, 46.

19. Aiton, *Mendoza*, 13, 100, 192; Phelan, *Millennial Kingdom*, 63.

20. Francisco Morales Valerio, "Criollización de la orden Franciscana en Nueva España, Siglo XVI," *Archivo Ibero-Americano* 48 (1988): 672.

21. Elliott, *Imperial Spain*, 210.

22. Ibid., 224–31.

23. "Ordinances for New Discoveries," in John H. Parry and Robert G. Keith, eds., *New Iberian World*, vol. 1, *The Conquerors and the Conquered* (New York: Times Books, 1984), 366–71.

24. The changes discussed in this chapter, as well as others that took place during the same period, marked a general watershed in Spain and its worldwide dominions. For the transformation in Spain itself, see, for example, Erika Spivakovsky, *Son of the Alhambra: Diego Hurtado de Mendoza, 1504–1575* (Austin: University of Texas Press, 1971), 333–50.

Chapter 21: Enduring Life of Rumor

1. Day, *Coronado's Quest*, 318; Janet Lecompte, "Coronado and Conquest," *New Mexico Historical Review* 64, no. 3 (1989): 279–304.

2. Castañeda de Nájera, fol. 1r (*Documents*, 384, 435).

3. Codex Aubin (*Documents*, 169, 170).

4. Administrative Review of the Viceroy and *Oidores*.

5. The five relevant documents that Ramusio published were Marcos de Niza's *Relación*; Letter of Vázquez de Coronado to the Viceroy, March 8, 1539; Letter of the Viceroy to the King, 1539; Narrative of Alarcón's Voyage, 1540; and Vázquez de Coronado's Letter to the Viceroy, August 3, 1540. Ramusio, *Navigationi et viaggi*.

6. Ramusio, *Navigationi et viaggi*, fol. 359r, English translation by Richard Flint and Shirley Cushing Flint (see *Documents*, 63–64).

7. Bartolomé de las Casas, *Apologética historia sumaria* (edición de Vidal Abril Castelló et al.), vol. 7 of *Obras completas* (Madrid: Alianza, 1992), 556.

8. Abraham Ortelius, *Americae Sive Novi Orbis, Nova Descriptio* (Amsterdam, 1570).

9. AHN, Diversos-Colecciones, 24, N.51, Fray Cyndos to the King, July 20, 1561.

10. Viceroy Luis de Velasco had adopted a similar procedure earlier in the 1550s before he commissioned Luis Cortés to reconnoiter toward the north. About ten years later Velasco granted to Francisco de Ibarra the right to lead an *entrada* north. That expedition departed in April 1564 from the mines of San Martín. Obregón, *Historia*, 40–45.

11. It has been suggested that the "exalted person" to whom the *Relación* is addressed could have been Francisco de Ibarra, who was governor of the new

and rival *provincia* of Nueva Vizcaya and who mounted an expedition to the north between 1564 and 1566. However, considerable animosity existed between Ibarra and the residents of Culiacán at the time. In 1566 the *cabildo* of Culiacán took testimony in support of its formal complaints against Ibarra, who was accused of luring away residents of Culiacán. The most vociferous witness during that testimony was Pedro de Nájera. Considering his clear rancor against Ibarra, it seems unlikely that Castañeda de Nájera would have so cordially supplied information to him about the expedition to Tierra Nueva. Obregón, *Historia*, 45–238; Testimony Taken by Order of the Cabildo of San Miguel de Culiacán, 1566.

12. Almost certainly what the expeditionaries saw at Yuque Yunque was either lead from the Cerrillos Hills or mica from the Jemez Mountains. See Ann F. Ramenofsky and C. David Vaughan, "Jars Full of Shiny Metal: Analyzing Barrionuevo's Visit to Yuque-Yunque," in Flint and Flint, *Coronado Expedition from the Distance of 460 Years*, 116–39.

13. AHN, Diversos-Colecciones, 24, N.45, Memorial by licenciado Zorita concerning Florida and New Mexico, 1560–1561. See also AGI, Justicia, 1029, N.7, R.1, Proof of Service of Alonso de Zorita, 1560s.

14. Nueva Vizcaya comprised the territory that much later was to become the Mexican states of Sinaloa, Sonora, Durango, Chihuahua, and part of Coahuila. Gerhard, *North Frontier*, 161, 245.

15. Proof of Service of Alonso de Zorita, 1560s.

16. Obregón, *Historia*, 40–62.

17. Ibid., 41.

18. The leaders of the four unsuccessful attempts to colonize Nuevo México in the 1580s and early 1590s were Francisco Sánchez Chamuscado and fray Agustín Rodríguez (1581); Antonio de Espejo (1582); Gaspar Castaño de Sosa (1590–91); and Francisco Leyva de Bonilla and Antonio Gutiérrez de Humaña (1593–94). Hammond and Rey, *Rediscovery of New Mexico*.

19. The Mexican historian Jesús Amaya Topete asserted more than 50 years ago that Juan Gutiérrez Bocanegra was a son of Diego Gutiérrez de la Caballería. That cannot have been the case, because Juan was born nearly a decade after Diego's death. Nevertheless, Juan's surnames and place of origin, Ciudad Real in Spain—also Diego's birthplace—make it all but certain that the two were relatives. The exact nature of their relationship remains to be determined. Jesús Amaya Topete, *Bioteca de occidente: Conquistas y poblazones al poniente de México* (México, D.F., 1951), 75.

20. Hammond and Rey, *Don Juan de Oñate*, 1: 17, 320.

21. Juan Jaramillo's Narrative, fol. 2r (*Documents*, 514, 520).

22. Richard Hakluyt, ed. and trans., *The Principal Navigations, Traffiques, and Discoveries of the English Nation Made by Sea or Over-land to the Remote and

Farthest Distant Quarters of the Earth at any Time within the Compass of these 1600 Yeeres. 12 vols. (Glasgow: James MacLehose and Sons, 1903–4).

23. Juan Páez, "Relation of the Voyage of Juan Rodríguez Cabrillo, 1542–1543," in Herbert E. Bolton, ed., *Spanish Explorations in the Southwest, 1542–1706* (New York: Charles Scribner and Sons, 1916), 23.

Chapter 22: Violence, Expected but Not Sought

1. Liss, *Isabel*, 297–99.

2. "The Laws of Burgos," in Parry and Keith, *Conquerors and the Conquered*, 336–47.

3. Hanke, *Spanish Struggle for Justice*, 17–22.

4. Real Provisión dada por don Carlos, 1526, images 669–78.

5. J[ohn] H. Parry, *The Age of Reconnaissance* (Cleveland, Ohio: World Publishing, 1963), 308.

6. Stevens and Lucas, *New Laws*, xviii.

7. Ibid., xii.

8. *Great Cruelties*, chapter 3, 26–53.

9. Ibid., chapter 17, 325–35.

10. Ibid., chapter 18, 336–41.

11. Ernesto Schäfer, *El Consejo Real y Supremo de las Indias: Su historia, organización y labor administrativa hasta la terminación de la Casa de Austria*, 2 vols. (Sevilla: Universidad de Sevilla, 1935), 1: 351.

12. Hearing on Depopulation Charges, fol. 2r (*Documents*, 175, 181).

13. United Nations General Assembly, "Universal Declaration of Human Rights," Resolution 217 A (III), December 10, 1948.

Glossary

adelantado. Government: a person authorized by the Spanish crown to settle a new territory and be its perpetual governor, with both military and civil authority. The office was assumed to be heritable.

Akumeca. Society: native name of the people of Acoma Pueblo.

alarde. Society: a roster, list, or muster roll.

alcalde. Government: a judge-administrator. *Alcaldes* served at many levels of government, from the royal court to the smallest towns.

alcalde mayor. Government: a royal functionary who had administrative and judicial jurisdiction over a community or group of communities and was responsible for tribute collection on the king's behalf. See also *corregidor*.

alguacil. Government: a law enforcement officer or constable.

alguacil mayor. Government: chief law enforcement officer.

Ashiwi. Society: native name of the people of Zuni Pueblo.

audiencia. Government: the governing body of a *provincia-* or *reino-*size jurisdiction within the Spanish Empire; the highest regional appellate court. In conjunction with a viceroy or president, the *audiencia* exercised both legislative and judicial authority.

bachiller. Education: an academic title roughly equivalent to the modern university level of bachelor's degree, but held much more rarely than today.

barranca. Geography: a canyon or ravine; gorge.

caballero. Society: an *hidalgo* of proven nobility. The designation derives from a Roman term for those in the equestrian order who were granted special privileges and status.

cabildo. Government: the governing council of a community. In the context of towns, it exercised authority over the urban area and its surroundings. In the largest cities it was composed of 24 members, including *regidores* and *alcaldes*. A *cabildo* exercised administrative, legislative, and judicial authority and was responsible for granting *vecino* status and for distributing land to *vecinos*. The same term was applied to the governing body of a religious or other organization.

cacicazgo. Government: the community governed by a *cacique* or the office of such a ruler.

cacique. Government: an Arawak word meaning "headman," widely used in Spanish America. Usually a native ruler with vassals or someone understood by Spaniards to have such status.

capitulación. Government: a formal agreement between a monarch and a subject; a royal document conferring a privilege or establishing an obligation, specifying the term and conditions of the arrangement.

casa. Geography: in its basic sense, a house or residential structure; in extended usage, any structure, whether physical or not.

castellano. Monetary unit: the most common form of gold coinage in Spain. In the Spanish colonies it came to be called a *peso de oro*, or unit of gold of a specified weight, valued during the sixteenth century at between 450 and 480 *maravedíes*.

cédula. Government: a written order, often from the king or the royal court.

censo. Finance: an arrangement in which one party assigned to another for a specified period the right to collect tribute or other income owed to the first party, in exchange for a set payment made at the beginning of the period. Also, the document recording such an arrangement.

ciudad. Political geography: a status conferred on a settlement by the king, indicating its relatively large size and great importance and usually accompanied by the concession of a coat of arms, escutcheon, and honorific titles. Use of the word *ciudad* throughout the Coronado expedition documents is significant. In Spanish usage of the day the term applied only to communities of the highest political and social rank, ordinarily administrative and commercial centers. In Nueva España in 1540 the term was applied only to the Ciudad de México and Puebla de los Ángeles. Its use in relation to Cíbola indicates the expectations Europeans held concerning the wealth, size, and sophistication of Tierra Nueva.

codex. Literature: a manuscript book; in the case of Spain's American colonies, usually a book written in a native language or with symbols rather than alphabetic words.

codo. Weights and measures: a length roughly equal to the distance from a person's elbow to the tips of the outstretched fingers.

compañera. Society: a domestic partner, whether within the ecclesiastical prescriptions of matrimony or not.

comunidad. Political geography: in modern Spain, one of the 17 semiautonomous political units into which the country is divided, analogous to the states of the United States.

conquistador. Society: participant in an enterprise of conquest and reconnaissance, especially in Mexico, Peru, and other regions of Spain's overseas empire.

Consejo de Indias. Government: the king's royal council exercising ultimate administrative and judicial authority over Spanish colonial jurisdictions in the Americas and the Philippines. The Consejo's actions and decisions could be reversed by the king and sometimes by other royal councils.

contador. Government: an accountant; one of four standard royal offices established in each overseas Spanish colony, the other three being the *veedor*, *factor*, and *tesorero*.

convento. Religion: the communal residence of members of a religious order, a friary or nunnery.

corregidor. Government: a salaried, royally appointed official who administered an *encomienda* held directly by the crown. This person served at the pleasure of the king and the Consejo de Indias as the chief administrator and justice for the native community embraced by the *encomienda*.

criado. Society: literally a servant, but more often a henchman or retainer; a full-time employee or dependent who might function in a variety of capacities, including tradesman, artisan, and apprentice; sometimes a poor or orphaned relative. Equivalent to and cognate with the archaic English usage of "creature," meaning a retainer.

de oficio. Judicial: a modifier applied to witnesses, testimony, or exhibits initiated at the request of the court in the course of a legal case, often for purposes of verifying information provided by private parties. The term also applied to what today would be called testimony for the prosecution.

de parte. Judicial: a modifier applied to witnesses, testimony, or exhibits initiated at the request and on behalf of a private party to a legal case—for instance, testimony offered to support a party's claim or to refute that of another party or a charge leveled by the *fiscal* or investigating judge. The term also applied to what today would be called testimony for the defense.

despoblado. Geography: a region devoid of permanent human settlement. In sixteenth-century usage it included territory occupied and used by nomadic or semi-nomadic peoples.

donado. Religion: a person who, without taking vows, served in a religious house and wore a habit of sorts.

duque. Society: the highest nobel rank, a duke.

encomendero. Government: a person holding and exercising an *encomienda*.

encomienda. Government and geography: a grant of the right to collect tribute, labor, or both from an indigenous community, usually granted by the king as reward for service; limited to a specific native polity. The grant entailed responsibility for providing defense and religious instruction to the community. The term also applied to the community and its territory so granted. In the sixteenth century, also called *repartimiento*.

entrada. Society: an expedition penetrating new territory.

escribano. Government: a combination secretary, scribe, and notary; could be either a governmental or a public position. For centuries this was the most abundant class of bureaucratic functionary.

estancia. Geography: a stock ranch.

estufa. Architecture: the word members of the Coronado expedition and later *entradas* applied to separate, sometimes subterranean ceremonial chambers found in the pueblos of New Mexico and Arizona, usually known today as kivas. The heat of such chambers, sometimes crowded with ceremonial performers and superheated by smoky fires, inspired the Spaniards to apply the word *estufa*, or "sweating room."

explorador. Society: an explorer, a person engaged primarily in reconnaissance of territory.

factor. Government: royal official charged with collecting tribute owed to the king. One of four standard royal offices established in each overseas Spanish colony, the other three being the *veedor*, *contador*, and *tesorero*. Also, an agent for the king who reports on the results of an expedition.

fiscal. Government: court official roughly equivalent to a prosecuting attorney.

guardián. Religion: among the Franciscans, the superior of a *convento*.

hidalgo. Society: a person of the lower nobility in Spain.

hombres libres. Society: independent actors at greater liberty than most of society to choose the trajectory of their lives; usually restricted to persons of moderate or higher economic status.

Hopitu. Society: the native name for the Hopi people as a whole.

indios amigos. Society: native warriors and other native persons serving as allies of the Spaniards. Such allies often had only recently been subjugated themselves but were nominally Christian.

jacal. Architecture: a type of construction in which walls are made of upright poles chinked and at least partially covered with adobe.

junta. Government: a meeting or council; in the context of the Coronado expedition and similar enterprises, a council of high-status members with whom the leader consulted on all important matters.

ladino. Society: a Native American who has become culturally Spanish, or at least mostly so, especially one who is Catholic, speaks Spanish, and dresses in European clothing.

Los Doce. Religion: the first contingent of 12 Franciscan priests sent to México-Tenochtitlan in 1524.

lugar. Political geography: status conferred on a settlement by the king, indicating its small size; smaller than a *villa*; a hamlet.

macana. Military: a weapon common to indigenous central and western Mexico, analogous to a European sword, made from a flat wooden club studded on its edges with obsidian blades.

maestre de campo. Military: field commander; the second in command after a general or captain general.

manta. Clothing: a shawl-like article of indigenous clothing common during and before the Spanish colonial period; frequently used as the unit of tribute.

marqués. Society: a title of nobility with status inferior to that of a *duque* and superior to that of a *conde*, or count.

mayordomo. Society: a foreman or custodian of public or private property, including religious property.

mestizo. Society: in Latin America, a person of racially mixed ancestry, Native American and European.

Mexica. Society: the Nahuatl-speaking people who founded Tenochtitlan and dominated most of central Mexico before the arrival of Europeans; often called Aztecs.

Nahua. Society: any native speaker of Nahuatl or one of its dialects. Use of the name usually implies practice of a broad culture spread throughout much of a band running across central Mexico.

navío. Watercraft: an ocean-going, high-sided, square-rigged, three-masted sailing vessel of around 100 *toneladas* in capacity, manned by a crew of 20 or more; also called a *nao*.

oidor. Government: a judge and legislator who was a member of an *audiencia*.

Ópata. Society: an indigenous linguistic and cultural group that, in the sixteenth century, occupied much of the central and northern part of what is now the Mexican state of Sonora.

Otomí. Society: an indigenous, non-Nahua linguistic and cultural group that, in the sixteenth century, occupied the western and northern fringes of the Basin of Mexico; also the language spoken by these people.

palmo. Weights and measures: a unit of length equal to approximately 7 centimeters, or 2.75 inches. The measurement derived from the concept that the width of four fingers made a palm, or *palmo*. There was also a *palmo mayor*, which equaled 8.25 inches.

peñol. Geography: a steep-sided, often flat-topped hill; a butte.

pesquisa secreta. Judicial: an official investigation or inquiry in which witnesses were not permitted to hear one another's testimony.

piloto mayor. Government: a royal official charged with certifying pilots as competent at navigation. He also maintained an up-to-date compendium of sailing instructions and maps for reaching all ports of the world. This post was often combined with that of royal cosmographer.

pintado. Society: adjective meaning tatooed or painted; applied as a name to Indians who practiced this type of body decoration. In the context of the Coronado expedition, the term referred specifically to non-Ópata natives of interior Sonora.

pitahaya. Food: the edible fruit of any of several giant cacti, including the organ pipe cactus and *cardón*.

pregonero. Government: a public crier, usually a man with a loud and sonorous voice, who made public announcements. The office was often held by a black person.

principal. Government: an indigenous leader, usually one of several in a community.

provincia. Political geography: a political division of a *reino* administered by a governor. When the term was applied in indigenous contexts, a similar political hierarchy was assumed.

pueblo. Geography: a status conferred on a settlement and its hinterland by the king, indicating its intermediate size and importance. When applied to indigenous settlements, a similar hierarchical relation was assumed.

ramada. Architecture: an open-sided shelter composed of a roof of brush or branches supported by upright posts; most common in desert and tropical regions.

real. Military: an encampment formed of interconnected pavilions, or any major encampment.

reconquista. Political: the sporadic reconquest of the Iberian Peninsula from Moorish-Islamic sovereignty by Christian-Visogothic armies between the 700s and 1492.

regidor. Government: an elected member of the *cabildo* of a municipality (*ciudad*, *pueblo*, or *villa*). Upon leaving office the incumbent often nominated his successor; the office was often hereditary.

reino. Political geography: a semiautonomous region subject to the Spanish monarchs. When applied to an indigenous political unit, an analogous overarching authority was assumed to exist.

relación. Literature: an example of a literary genre comprising narrative accounts of exotic places and peoples, usually written by firsthand observers though often also incorporating journalistic elements.

repartimiento. Government and geography: literally a "distribution"; in the sixteenth century, a synonym for *encomienda*.

requerimiento. Government: a formal summons to submit to the authority of the king of Spain. A text specified by law was in use from 1513 until 1573, although increasingly infrequently as time passed.

residencia. Government: a judicial review of the performance of a royal official, held at the end of his term in office and sometimes conducted by his successor.

tamemes. Commerce: indigenous load bearers common in Mesoamerica from prehistory through much of the Spanish colonial period. The tradition of human transport of goods, sometimes over sizable distances, was fostered by the lack of domesticated beasts of burden in most of the Western Hemisphere prior to the arrival of Europeans.

Tarascos. Society: the indigenous, Purépecha-speaking people of Michoacán. In prehistoric times they maintained a state independent of the larger Mexica empire, which virtually surrounded them.

Tenochca. Society: the indigenous name of the Mexica group that dwelled in Tenochtitlan, occupying the southern portion of the island of México in Lake Texcoco at the time of Spanish conquest. After the conquest, many Tenochca lived in barrios of the Ciudad de México.

tierra caliente. Geography: the tropical and semitropical coastal lowlands of Mexico, known for hot, humid summers.

tierra de guerra. Political geography: territory not yet brought under Spanish control; therefore, a land where warfare would be expected if Spaniards were to enter.

Tlaxcalteca. Society: the indigenous, Nahuatl-speaking people of Tlaxcala. In prehistoric times, like the Tarascos, they maintained a state independent of the larger Mexica empire, which virtually surrounded them. After bloody fighting with the Cortés expedition in 1519, they consistently served as allies of Spaniards against other native groups.

Turkomans. Society: a Turkic-speaking, traditionally pastoral people inhabiting the portion of central Asia east of the Caspian Sea.

vecino. Government: a person with full political rights in a municipality. Such rights were not automatic but granted by the *cabildo* after payment of a fee and the making of a pledge to establish and maintain a residence for a certain length of time. Residents without full political rights were *estantes*.

versillo. Military: a small-bore swivel gun or cannon most commonly used on the gunwales of ships; the same or similar cannon when used on land, ordinarily transported on horse- or muleback.

villa. Political geography: a status conferred on a settlement and its hinterland by the king, indicating its inferior size and importance; smaller than both a *ciudad* and a *pueblo*. In the Coronado expedition documents, often used to distinguish a small Spanish community from an indigenous one of similar size and importance (a pueblo).

visita. Government: an extraordinary judicial review of the performances of officials.

visitador. Government: a special investigator dispatched to make an inspection of a *reino*, a *provincia*, or some part thereof, whether secular or ecclesiastical; often sent to resolve a particular problem or complaint.

REFERENCES

ARCHIVAL MATERIAL

AGI, Contratación, 199, N.23, Goods of the Deceased, Bartolomé Sánchez, 1561.

AGI, Contratación, 5575, N.24, Disposal of the Juan Jiménez Estate, 1542 [copy, 1550]. Transcribed and translated as Document 27 in *Documents*, 330–77.

AGI, Guadalajara, 5, R.1, N.5, Letter from Vázquez de Coronado to the King, December 1538. Transcribed and translated as Document 1 in *Documents*, 23–30.

AGI, Guadalajara, 5, R.1, N.6, Letter of Vázquez de Coronado to the King, July 15, 1539. Transcribed and translated as Document 3 in *Documents*, 39–44.

AGI, Guadalajara, 5, R.1, N.7, Muster Roll of the Expedition, February 22, 1540. Transcribed and translated as Document 12 in *Documents*, 139–63.

AGI, Guadalajara, 46, N.8, Testimony Taken by Order of the Cabildo of San Miguel de Culiacán, 1566.

AGI, Indiferente, 421, L.11\1, Real Provisión dada por don Carlos, que dispone y trata la orden que antiguamente se tenía en los descubrimientos y poblaciones que se hacían en Indias, y en el buen tratamiento de sus naturales, 1526.

AGI, Justicia, 129, N.3, Records of the Case between the Bishop and City of Michoacán and Juan Infante, 1540.

AGI, Justicia, 258, Pieza 1, Administrative Review of the Viceroy and *Oidores* . . . Conducted by Tello de Sandoval, 1546.

AGI, Justicia, 259, Pieza 2, Visita of don Antonio de Mendoza, 1546.

AGI, Justicia, 259, Pieza 3, Charges against Mendoza and Rebuttals of the Viceroy, June 21, 1546.

AGI, Justicia, 259, Pieza 4, Certification of a Suit concerning Tlapa, 1544.

AGI, Justicia, 263, Pieza 1, Rebuttals of Viceroy Mendoza, 1546.

AGI, Justicia, 264, Pieza 3, Proof Assembled in the Name of don Antonio de Mendoza, 1547.

AGI, Justicia, 267, N.3, Proceso of Francisco Vázquez de Coronado, 1544. Published in *Great Cruelties*, passim.

AGI, Justicia, 269, Pieza 2, Book of the Residencia Secreta, 1544.

AGI, Justicia, 269, Pieza 4, Visita of Luis de la Torre, 1545.

AGI, Justicia, 270, Pieza 4, Residencia of Gerónimo de Medina, 1546.

AGI, Justicia, 276, N.2, Visita of Alonso Pérez Tamayo, 1545.

AGI, Justicia, 336, N.1, Vázquez de Coronado's Petition for Recovery of Encomiendas, 1553.

AGI, Justicia, 339, N.1, R.1, Residencia of Francisco Vázquez de Coronado, 1544 and 1545.

AGI, Justicia, 1021, N.2, Pieza 2, Report Extracted from the Affidavit Prepared for don García Ramírez de Cárdenas [1540s]. Published in *Great Cruelties*, passim.

AGI, Justicia, 1021, N.2, Pieza 5, Proof of Service Made at the Request of don García López de Cárdenas, 1547–1548.

AGI, Justicia, 1021, N.2, Pieza 6, Proof Taken by the *Fiscal* Villalobos, 1547.

AGI, Justicia, 1029, N.7, R.1, Proof of Service of Alonso de Zorita, 1560s.

AGI, México, 96, Letter from Jerónimo López to the King, México, February 25, 1545. Published in Spanish in Francisco del Paso y Troncoso, *Espistolario de Nueva España, 1505–1818*, 2nd series, 16 vols., 4: 150–79. México, D.F.: José Porrúa e Hijos, 1939–1942. Published in English in John H. Parry and Robert G. Keith, *New Iberian World*, 5 vols., 3: 4446–53. New York: Times Books, 1984.

AGI, México, 97, R.1, Proof of Service of Tristán de Luna y Arellano, 1559.

AGI, México, 168, Investigation concerning Francisco Vázquez, March 1547.

AGI, México, 168, Letter from Juan Troyano to the King, December 20, 1568.

AGI, México, 204, N.14, Cristóbal de Escobar's Proof of Service, 1543. Transcribed and translated as Document 33 in *Documents*, 556–80.

AGI, México, 204, N.33, Proof of Service of Pedro de Benavídez, 1551.

AGI, México, 206, N.12, Proof of Service of Juan Troyano, February 20, 1560. Transcribed and translated as Document 31 in *Documents*, 527–32.

AGI, México, 228, N.23, Reports Made on behalf of Diego Gutiérrez de Bocanegra, 1608.

AGI, México, 1064, L.1, Reports of the Conquistadores and Settlers of the Ciudad de México, ca. 1547.

AGI, México, 1088, L.1bis., *Cédula*, August 31, 1531.

AGI, México, 1088, L.3, Royal *Cédula*, November 22, 1538.

AGI, Patronato, 20, N.5, R.8, Juan Jaramillo's Narrative, 1560s. Transcribed and translated as Document 30 in *Documents*, 512–24.

AGI, Patronato 20, N.5, R.8, Relación del Suceso, 1540s. Transcribed and translated as Document 29 in *Documents*, 494–507.

AGI, Patronato 20, N.5, R.8, Traslado de las Nuevas, 1540. Transcribed and translated as Document 22 in *Documents*, 289–95.

AGI, Patronato 20, N.5, R.10, The Viceroy's Instructions to fray Marcos de Niza, November 1538. Transcribed and translated as Document 6 in *Documents*, 65–66, 78–79.

AGI, Patronato, 20, N.5, R.10, Narrative Account by fray Marcos de Niza, August 26, 1539. Transcribed and translated as Document 6 in *Documents*, 59–88.

AGI, Patronato, 21, N.2, R.3, Hearing on Depopulation Charges, February 26, 1540.

AGI, Patronato, 21, N.2, R.4, Testimony of Witnesses in Havana regarding fray Marcos's Discoveries, November 1539. Transcribed and translated as Document 8 in *Documents*, 95–105.

AGI, Patronato, 21, N.2, R.4, Litigation of the Marqués del Valle, Nuño de Guzmán, and the *adelantados* Soto and Alvarado concerning reconnaissance of Tierra Nueva, 1541. Published in Joaquín F. Pacheco, Francisco de Cárdenas, and Luis Torres de Mendoza, eds., *Colección de documentos inéditos relativos al descubrimiento, conquista y organización de las antiguas posesiones españoles de América y Oceania*, Series 1, 42 vols., 15: 300–408. Madrid: José María Pérez, 1864–1884.

AGI, Patronato, 21, N.2, R.4\2, Hernán Cortés's Brief to Carlos V concerning the Injuries Done to Him by the Viceroy of Nueva España, June 25, 1540. Transcribed and translated as Document 18 in *Documents*, 242–51.

AGI, Patronato, 21, N.3, R.2, Formation of Company between Mendoza and Pedro de Alvarado, November 29, 1540. Transcribed and translated as Document 20 in *Documents*, 271–84.

AGI, Patronato, 26, R.23, Hernando de Alvarado's Narrative, 1540. Transcribed and translated as Document 24 in *Documents*, 303–8.

AGI, Patronato, 56, N.3, R.2, Proof of Service, Pedro Jerónimo, 1542.

AGI, Patronato, 60, N.5, R.4, Proof of Service of Juan de Zaldívar, February 1566.

AGI, Patronato, 63, R.5, Proof of Service of Juan de Paladinas [sic], June 6, 1560.

AGI, Patronato, 74, N.1, R.11, Proof of Service of Tristán de Arellano, 1575.

AGI, Patronato, 79, N.3, R,2, Proof of Service of Francisco de Santillana, 1594.

AGI, Patronato, 87, N.1, R.5, Proof of Service of García Rodríguez and His Grandson, 1617.

AGI, Patronato, 121, R.8, Proof of Service of Miguel de Entrambasaguas, December 11, 1577.

AGI, Patronato, 184, R.27, Letter of Mendoza to the King, December 10, 1537.

AGI, Patronato, 184, R.31, The Viceroy's Letter to the King, April 17, 1540. Transcribed and translated as Document 17 in *Documents*, 233–41.

AGI, Patronato, 184, R.34, Vázquez de Coronado's Letter to the King, October 1541. Transcribed and translated as Document 26 in *Documents*, 317–25.

AGI, Patronato, 216, R.2, Investigation concerning Nuño de Chávez. Published in *Great Cruelties*, 344–431.

AGN, Hospital de Jesús, 123, Expediente 31, *Cédula* of July 10, 1540. Published in José Luis Martínez, ed., *Documentos cortesianos*, 4 vols., 4: 216–19. México, D.F.: Universidad Nacional Autónoma de México, 1992.

AHN, Diversos-Colecciones, 22, N.36, Letter from Mendoza to Francisco de Cobos, March 10, 1542.

AHN, Diversos-Colecciones, 24, N.45, Memorial by licenciado Zorita concerning Florida and New Mexico, 1560–1561.

AHN, Diversos-Colecciones, 24, N.51, Fray Cyndos to the King, July 20, 1561.

Biblioteca del Escorial, códice &-II-7, Doc. LXVII, The Viceroy's Instructions to Hernando Alarcón, 1541. Transcribed and translated as Document 16 in *Documents*, 223–32.

BNM, MS 3042, Relación de Antonio de Mendoza a Luis de Velasco al término de su Gobierno. Sin fecha, ca. 1550 ó 1551. Transcribed as Documento Número 5 in Lewis Hanke, ed., *México: Los virreyes españoles en América durante el gobierno de la Casa de Austria*, 5 vols., 1: 38–57. Madrid: Ediciones Atlas, 1976.

Biblioteca Real, Madrid, II/3042, Gonzalo Fernández de Oviedo y Valdés, *Historia general y natural de las Indias*, Tercera Parte, Libro XL, Capítulo I, 1547, Letters from Antonio de Mendoza and Rodrigo de Albornoz, October 18, 1539. Transcribed and translated as Document 7 in *Documents*, 89–94.

Glasgow University Library, MS Hunter 242 (U.3.15), The Tlaxcala Codex.

Library of the British Museum, Add MSS 31219, Codex Aubin, Chronicle of Mexican History to 1576, continued to 1607. Transcribed and translated as Document 13 in *Documents*, 164–70.

Pedro de Castañeda de Nájera's Narrative, 1560s [copy, 1596]. Transcribed and translated as Document 28 in *Documents*, 378–493.

UCB, Ban., C-B 840, Item 398, H. E. Bolton Papers, Part I. AGI, Justicia, 1021, N.2, Pieza 3, Report Prepared on Behalf of don García Ramírez de Cárdenas. Transcription by Agapito Rey.

UCB, Ban., M-M 93, Memorial of the Indians concerning Their Services, c. 1563. Published in Robert H. Barlow and George T. Smisor, eds. and trans., *Nombre de Dios, Durango: Two Documents in Nahuatl concerning Its Foundation*, 2–45. Sacramento: House of Tlaloc, 1943.

UCB, Ban., M-M 1714, Melchior Pérez's Petition for Preferment, 1551. Transcribed and translated as Document 32 in *Documents*, 533–53.

UTA, Ben., JGI 31 XVI C, Relación Postrera de Cíbola, 1540s. Transcribed and translated as Document 23 in *Documents*, 296–302.

Published Material

Acuña, René, ed. *Relaciones geográficas del siglo XVI: Nueva Galicia*. México, D.F.: Universidad Nacional Autónoma de México, 1988.

Acuña-Soto, Rodolfo, David W. Stahle, Malcolm K. Cleaveland, and Matthew D. Therrell. "Megadrought and Megadeath in Sixteenth-Century Mexico." *Emerging Infectious Diseases* 8, no. 4 (2002): 360–62.

Adorno, Rolena, and Patrick Charles Pautz. *Álvar Núñez Cabeza de Vaca: His Account, His Life, and the Expedition of Pánfilo de Narváez*. 3 vols. Lincoln: University of Nebraska Press, 1999.

Aiton, Arthur S. *Antonio de Mendoza: First Viceroy of New Spain*. Durham, N.C.: Duke University Press, 1927.

Aiton, Arthur S., and Agapito Rey. "Coronado's Testimony in the Viceroy Mendoza Residencia." *New Mexico Historical Review* 12 (July 1937): 288–329.

Alchon, Suzanne Austin. *A Pest in the Land: New World Epidemics in a Global Perspective*. Albuquerque: University of New Mexico Press, 2003.

Amaya Topete, Jesús. *Bioteca de occidente: Conquistas y poblazones al poniente de México*. México, D.F., 1951.

Anónimo. *Amadís de Gaula*. Ed. Ángel Rosenblat. Barcelona: Losada, 1998.

Avellaneda, José Ignacio. *The Conquerors of the New Kingdom of Granada*. Albuquerque: University of New Mexico Press, 1995.

———. *Los Sobrevivientes de la Florida; The Survivors of the de Soto Expedition*. Gainesville, Fla.: P. K. Yonge Library of Florida History, 1990.

Bakewell, Peter. *A History of Latin America: Empires and Sequels, 1450–1930*. Oxford: Blackwell, 1997.

———. *Silver Mining and Society in Colonial Mexico: Zacatecas, 1546–1700*. Cambridge: Cambridge University Press, 1971.

Barber, Russell J., and Frances F. Berdan. *The Emperor's Mirror: Understanding Cultures through Primary Sources*. Tucson: University of Arizona Press, 1998.

Barlow, Robert H., and George T. Smisor, eds. and trans. *Nombre de Dios, Durango: Two Documents in Nahuatl concerning Its Foundation*. Sacramento, Calif.: House of Tlaloc, 1943.

Barrett, Elinore M. *Conquest and Catastrophe: Changing Rio Grande Pueblo Settlement Patterns in the Sixteenth and Seventeenth Centuries.* Albuquerque: University of New Mexico Press, 2002.

———. *The Geography of Rio Grande Pueblos Revealed by Spanish Explorers, 1540–1598.* Albuquerque: Latin American Institute, University of New Mexico, 1997.

Berdan, Frances F., and Patricia Rieff Anawalt, eds. *The Essential Codex Mendoza.* Berkeley: University of California Press, 1997.

Bermúdez Plata, Cristóbal. *Catálogo de pasajeros a Indias durante los siglos XVI, XVII, y XVIII.* 3 vols. Sevilla: Editorial de la Gavidia, 1940 and 1942.

Bethencourt Alonso, Juan. *La conquista de las Islas Canarias.* La Laguna, Tenerife: Francisco Lemus, 1997.

Blakeslee, Donald J., Douglas K. Boyd, Richard Flint, Judith Habicht-Mauche, Nancy P. Hickerson, Jack T. Hughes, and Carroll L. Riley. "Bison Hunters of the Llano in 1541: A Panel Discussion." In Richard Flint and Shirley Cushing Flint, eds., *The Coronado Expedition from the Distance of 460 Years,* 164–86. Albuquerque: University of New Mexico Press, 2003.

Blakeslee, Donald J., Richard Flint, and Jack T. Hughes. "*Una Barranca Grande*: Recent Archaeological Evidence and a Discussion of Its Place in the Coronado Route." In Richard Flint and Shirley Cushing Flint, eds., *The Coronado Expedition to Tierra Nueva: The 1540–1542 Route across the Southwest,* 370–83. Niwot, Colo.: University Press of Colorado, 1997.

Bloom, Lansing B. "Was Fray Marcos a Liar?" *New Mexico Historical Review* 16 (April 1941): 244–46.

Bolton, Herbert E. *Coronado: Knight of Pueblos and Plains.* Albuquerque: University of New Mexico Press, 1949.

Brasher, Nugent. "The Chichilticale Camp of Francisco Vázquez de Coronado." *New Mexico Historical Review.* 82, no. 4 (2007): 433–68.

Brew, John Otis. "The History of Awatovi." In Ross Gordon Montgomery, Watson Smith, and John Otis Brew, *Franciscan Awatovi: The Excavation and Conjectural Reconstruction of a Seventeenth-Century Spanish Mission Establishment at a Hopi Indian Town in Northeastern Arizona,* 1–43. Reports of the Awatovi Expedition 3. Cambridge, Mass.: Peabody Museum, Harvard University, 1949.

Brooks, James F. *Captives and Cousins: Slavery, Kinship, and Community in the Southwest Borderlands.* Chapel Hill, N.C.: University of North Carolina Press, 2002.

Cabeza de Vaca, Álvar Núñez. *The Account: Álvar Núñez Cabeza de Vaca's Relación.* Eds. and trans. Martin A. Favata and José B. Fernández. Houston: Arte Público Press, 1993.

———. "Account of the Disasters (*Relación de los Naufragios*)." In Alex D. Krieger, ed., *We Came Naked and Barefoot: The Journey of Cabeza de Vaca across North America,* 155–241. Austin: University of Texas Press, 2002.

———. *Naufragios y comentarios con dos cartas*. 9th ed. México, D.F.: Espasa-Calpe Mexicana, 1985.

Caro Baroja, Julio. *Los Moriscos del reino de Granada*. Madrid: Ediciones Istmo, 1991.

Carvajal, Gaspar. "On the Voyage of Francisco de Orellana down the Amazon in 1542." In John H. Parry and Robert G. Keith, eds., *New Iberian World*, vol. 5, *Coastlines, Rivers, and Forests*, 187–217. New York: Times Books, 1984.

Cervantes, Fernando. *The Devil in the New World: The Impact of Diabolism in New Spain*. New Haven, Conn.: Yale University Press, 1994.

Chamberlain, Robert S. *The Conquest and Colonization of Yucatan, 1517–1550*. Washington, D.C.: Carnegie Institution of Washington, 1948.

Chávez, Fray Angélico. *Coronado's Friars*. Washington, D.C.: Academy of American Franciscan History, 1968.

———, trans. and ed. *The Oroz Codex*. Washington, D.C.: Academy of American Franciscan History, 1972.

Chipman, Donald E. *Nuño de Guzmán and the Province of Pánuco in New Spain, 1518–1533*. Glendale, Calif.: Arthur H. Clark, 1967.

———. "The Oñate-Moctezuma-Zaldívar Families of Northern New Spain." *New Mexico Historical Review* 52, no. 4 (1977): 297–310.

Cieza de León, Pedro de. *The Discovery and Conquest of Peru*, trans. and eds. Alexandra Parma Cook and Noble David Cook. Durham, N.C.: Duke University Press, 1998.

Clendinnen, Inga. *Ambivalent Conquests: Maya and Spaniard in Yucatán, 1517–1570*. Cambridge: Cambridge University Press, 1987.

———. *Aztecs: An Interpretation*. Cambridge: Cambridge University Press, 1991.

Cordell, Linda S. *Prehistory of the Southwest*. New York: Academic Press, 1984.

Cortés, Hernán. "Tercera carta-relación—15 de Mayo de 1522." In Hernán Cortés, *Cartas de relación*. México, D.F.: Editorial Porrúa, 1993.

Cuevas, Mariano, ed. *Documentos inéditos del siglo XVI para la historia de México*. México, D.F.: Museo Nacional de Arqueología, Historia y Etnología, 1914.

Damp, Jonathan E. *The Battle of Hawikku: Archaeological Investigations of the Zuni-Coronado Encounter at Hawikku, the Ensuing Battle, and the Aftermath during the Summer of 1540*. Zuni, N.M.: Zuni Cultural Resource Enterprise, 2005.

Day, A. Grove. *Coronado's Quest: The Discovery of the Southwestern States*. Berkeley: University of California Press, 1940.

———. "Mota Padilla on the Coronado Expedition." *Hispanic American Historical Review* 20, no. 1 (1940): 88–110.

Deeds, Susan M. *Defiance and Deference in Mexico's Colonial North: Indians under Spanish Rule in Nueva Vizcaya*. Austin: University of Texas Press, 2003.

Diamond, Jared. *Guns, Germs, and Steel: The Fates of Human Societies.* New York: W. W. Norton, 1999.

Díaz del Castillo, Bernal. *The Discovery and Conquest of Mexico,* trans. and ed. A. P. Maudslay. New York: Farrar, Straus and Cudahy, 1956.

Doolittle, William E. *Pre-Hispanic Occupance in the Valley of Sonora, Mexico: Archaeological Confirmation of Early Spanish Reports.* Tucson: University of Arizona Press, 1988.

Dunn, Oliver, and James E. Kelley Jr., trans. and eds. *The Diario of Christopher Columbus's First Voyage to America, 1492–1493.* Norman: University of Oklahoma Press, 1989.

Durán, Diego. *The History of the Indies of New Spain.* Trans. and ed. Doris Heyden. Norman: University of Oklahoma Press, 1994.

Elliott, J[ohn] H. *Imperial Spain, 1469–1716.* London: Penguin Books, 1990.

Engstrand, Iris H. W. "John Sutter: A Biographical Examination." In Kenneth N. Owens, ed., *John Sutter and a Wider West,* 76–92. Lincoln: University of Nebraska Press, 1994.

Espejo, Antonio de. "Report of Antonio de Espejo." In George P. Hammond and Agapito Rey, *Rediscovery of New Mexico, 1580–1594: The Explorations of Chamuscado, Espejo, Castaño de Sosa, Morlete, and Leyva de Bonilla and Humaña,* 213–31. Albuquerque: University of New Mexico Press, 1966.

Ferguson, T. J., and E. Richard Hart. *A Zuni Atlas.* Norman: University of Oklahoma Press, 1985.

Flint, Richard. "The Coronado and de Soto Expeditions: A Contrast in Attitudes or Difference in External Conditions? Part 1, Relative Humanity of the Expeditions." *El Viaje* 1, no. 2 (April 1992): 4–8.

_____. *Great Cruelties Have Been Reported: The 1544 Investigation of the Coronado Expedition.* Dallas: Southern Methodist University Press, 2002.

_____. "What's Missing from this Picture? The *Alarde,* or Muster Roll, of the Coronado Expedition." In Richard Flint and Shirley Cushing Flint, eds., *The Coronado Expedition from the Distance of 460 Years,* 57–80. Albuquerque: University of New Mexico Press, 2003.

_____. "Who Designed Coronado's Bridge across the Pecos River?" *Kiva* 57, no. 4 (1992): 331–42.

Flint, Richard, and Shirley Cushing Flint. "The Coronado Expedition: Cicúye to the Río de Cicúye Bridge." In Richard Flint and Shirley Cushing Flint, eds., *The Coronado Expedition to Tierra Nueva: The 1540–1542 Route across the Southwest,* 262–77. Niwot, Colo.: University Press of Colorado, 1997.

_____, eds. *The Coronado Expedition from the Distance of 460 Years.* Albuquerque: University of New Mexico Press, 2003.

———, eds. *The Coronado Expedition to Tierra Nueva: The 1540–1542 Route across the Southwest*. Niwot, Colo.: University Press of Colorado, 1997.

———, trans. and eds. *Documents of the Coronado Expedition, 1539–1542: "They Were Not Familiar with His Majesty, nor Did They Wish to Be His Subjects."* Dallas: Southern Methodist University Press, 2005.

Flint, Shirley Cushing. "The Financing and Provisioning of the Coronado Expedition." In Richard Flint and Shirley Cushing Flint, eds., *The Coronado Expedition from the Distance of 460 Years*, 42–56. Albuquerque: University of New Mexico Press, 2003.

———. "Putting Faces on the Coronado Expedition, Part 1, The Expedition as a Whole." Paper presented to the Hispanic Genealogical Society of New Mexico, Albuquerque, July 10, 2004.

Frost, Orcutt. *Bering: The Russian Discovery of America*. New Haven, Conn.: Yale University Press, 2003.

Fuson, Robert H., trans. and ed. *The Log of Christopher Columbus*. Camden, Me.: International Marine Publishing, 1992.

Gandía, Enrique de. *Historia crítica de los mitos de la conquista americana*. Buenos Aires: Juan Roldán, 1929.

García Ormaechea y Quero, Carmen. "The Far East." Trans. coordinated by Oliver Strunk. In *Art and Culture around 1492*, 44–53. Sevilla: Sociedad Estatal para la Exposición Universal Sevilla 92, 1992.

Gentleman from Elvas. "The Account by a Gentleman from Elvas." In Lawrence A. Clayton, Vernon James Knight Jr., and Edward C. Moore, *The De Soto Chronicles: The Expedition of Hernando de Soto to North America in 1539–1543*, 2 vols., 1: 19–219. Tuscaloosa: University of Alabama Press, 1993.

Gerhard, Peter. *A Guide to the Historical Geography of New Spain*. Rev. ed. Norman: University of Oklahoma Press, 1993.

———. *The North Frontier of New Spain*. Rev. ed. Norman: University of Oklahoma Press, 1993.

Gibson, Charles. *The Aztecs under Spanish Rule: A History of the Indians of the Valley of Mexico, 1519–1810*. Stanford, Calif.: Stanford University Press, 1964.

Greenleaf, Richard E., and Neal Kaveny, eds. and trans. *Zumárraga and His Family: Letters to Vizcaya, 1536–1548*. Washington, D.C.: Academy of American Franciscan History, 1979.

Grissino-Mayer, Henri D. "A 2129-Year Reconstruction of Precipitation for Northwestern New Mexico, USA." In Jeffrey S. Dean, D. M. Meko, and T. W. Swetnam, eds., *Tree Rings, Environment, and Humanity*, 191–204. Tucson: Department of Geosciences, University of Arizona, 1996.

Hakluyt, Richard, ed. and trans. *The Principal Navigations, Traffiques, and Discoveries of the English Nation Made by Sea or Over-land to the Remote and

Farthest Distant Quarters of the Earth at any Time within the Compasse of these 1600 Yeeres. 12 vols. Glasgow: James MacLehose and Sons, 1903-4.

Hallenbeck, Cleve. *The Journey of Fray Marcos de Niza.* Dallas: Southern Methodist University Press, 1949. Reprint with introduction by David J. Weber, Southern Methodist University Press, 1987.

Hammond, George P., and Agapito Rey, eds. and trans. *Don Juan de Oñate: Colonizer of New Mexico, 1595-1628.* 2 vols. Albuquerque: University of New Mexico Press, 1953.

———. *Narratives of the Coronado Expedition, 1540-1542.* Albuquerque: University of New Mexico Press, 1940.

———. *The Rediscovery of New Mexico, 1580-1594: The Explorations of Chamuscado, Espejo, Castaño de Sosa, Morlete, and Leyva de Bonilla and Humaña.* Albuquerque: University of New Mexico Press, 1966.

Hanke, Lewis. "Introducción." In Bartolomé de las Casas, *El único modo de atraer a todos los pueblos a la verdadera religión,* 17-60. México, D.F.: Fondo de Cultura Económica, 1942.

———, ed. *México: Los virreyes españoles en América durante el gobierno de la Casa de Austria.* 5 vols. Madrid: Ediciones Atlas, 1976.

———. "Pope Paul III and the American Indians." *Harvard Theological Review* 30 (1937): 65-102.

———. *The Spanish Struggle for Justice in the Conquest of America.* Boston: Little, Brown, 1965. Edition with new introduction and supplementary material, Dallas: Southern Methodist University Press, 2002.

Hartmann, William K. "Pathfinder for Coronado: Reevaluating the Mysterious Journey of Marcos de Niza." In Richard Flint and Shirley Cushing Flint, eds., *The Coronado Expedition to Tierra Nueva: The 1540-1542 Route across the Southwest,* 73-101. Niwot, Colo.: University Press of Colorado, 1997.

Hartmann, William K., and Richard Flint. "Before the Coronado Expedition: Who Knew What and When Did They Know It?" In Richard Flint and Shirley Cushing Flint, eds., *The Coronado Expedition from the Distance of 460 Years,* 20-41. Albuquerque: University of New Mexico Press, 2003.

Headley, John M. *The Emperor and His Chancellor: A Study in the Imperial Chancellery under Gattinara.* Cambridge: Cambridge University Press, 1983.

Hernández, Pero. "Up the Paraguay River and His [Cabeza de Vaca's] Arrest and Expulsion from Asunción." In John H. Parry and Robert G. Keith, eds., *New Iberian World,* vol. 5, *Coastlines, Rivers, and Forests,* 284-307. New York: Times Books, 1984.

Hernández, Rudolfo, and José Francisco Román. "Presencia Tlaxcalteca en Nueva Galicia." In María Isabel Monroy Castillo, ed., *Constructores de la nación: La migración tlaxcalteca en el norte de la Nueva España,* 17-33. San Luis Potosí, México: Colegio de San Luis and Gobierno del Estado de Tlaxcala, 1999.

Hickerson, Nancy Parrott. *The Jumanos: Hunters and Traders of the South Plains.* Austin: University of Texas Press, 1994.

Hillerkuss, Thomas. *Diccionario biográfico del occidente novohispano, siglo XVI.* 3 vols. Zacatecas: Universidad Autónoma de Zacatecas, 2001.

_____. *Documentalia del sur de Jalisco (siglo XVI).* Zapopan, Jalisco: Colegio de Jalisco, 1994.

Himmerich y Valencia, Robert. *The Encomenderos of New Spain, 1521–1555.* Austin: University of Texas Press, 1991.

Hodge, Frederick W. *Circular Kivas near Hawikuh, New Mexico.* New York: Museum of the American Indian, Heye Foundation, 1923.

Howard, David A. *Conquistador in Chains: Cabeza de Vaca and the Indians of the Americas.* Tuscaloosa: University of Alabama Press, 1997.

Hudson, Charles. *Knights of Spain, Warriors of the Sun: Hernando de Soto and the South's Ancient Chiefdoms.* Athens, Ga.: University of Georgia Press, 1997.

Hughes, Jack T. "Prehistoric Cultural Developments on the Texas High Plains." *Bulletin of the Texas Archaeological Society* 60 (1991): 1–55.

Kelsey, Harry. *Juan Rodríguez Cabrillo.* San Marino, Calif.: Huntington Library, 1998.

Kessell, John L. "Foreword." In Herbert E. Bolton, *Coronado: Knight of Pueblos and Plains,* ix–xxiv. Albuquerque: University of New Mexico Press, 1990.

_____. *Kiva, Cross, and Crown: The Pecos Indians and New Mexico, 1540–1840.* Albuquerque: University of New Mexico Press, 1987.

Kintigh, Keith W. *Settlement, Subsistence, and Society in Late Zuni Prehistory.* Tucson: University of Arizona Press, 1985.

Krieger, Alex D., ed. *We Came Naked and Barefoot: The Journey of Cabeza de Vaca across North America.* Austin: University of Texas Press, 2002.

Ladd, Edmund J. "Zuni on the Day the Men in Metal Arrived." In Richard Flint and Shirley Cushing Flint, eds., *The Coronado Expedition to Tierra Nueva: The 1540–1542 Route across the Southwest,* 225–33. Niwot, Colo.: University Press of Colorado, 1997.

_____. "Zuni Social and Political Organization." In Alfonso Ortiz, ed., *Handbook of North American Indians,* vol. 9, *Southwest,* 482–91. Washington, D.C.: Smithsonian Institution, 1979.

Lange, Charles H. "Relations of the Southwest with the Plains and Great Basin." In Alfonso Ortiz, ed., *Handbook of North American Indians,* vol. 9, *Southwest,* 201–5. Washington, D.C.: Smithsonian Institution, 1979.

las Casas, Bartolomé de. *Apologética historia sumaria* (edición de Vidal Abril Castelló et al.). Vol. 7 of *Obras completas.* Madrid: Alianza, 1992.

_____. *Del único modo de atraer a todos los pueblos a la verdadera religión.* México, D.F.: Fondo de Cultura Económica, 1942.

———. *The Devastation of the Indies: A Brief Account.* Trans. Herma Briffault. Baltimore, Md.: Johns Hopkins University Press, 1992.

———. *Historia de las Indias.* Ed. Juan Pérez de Tudela Bueso. Madrid: Ediciones Atlas, 1992.

"The Laws of Burgos." In John H. Parry and Robert G. Keith, eds., *New Iberian World*, vol. 1, *The Conquerors and the Conquered*, 336–47. New York: Times Books, 1984.

Lecompte, Janet. "Coronado and Conquest." *New Mexico Historical Review* 64, no. 3 (July 1989): 279–304.

Leonard, Kathryn. "Directionality and Exclusivity of Plains-Pueblo Exchange during the Protohistoric Period, AD 1450–1700." In Judith A. Habicht-Mauche, Suzanne L. Eckert, and Deborah L. Huntley, eds., *The Social Life of Pots: Glaze Wares and Cultural Dynamics in the Southwest, AD 1250–1680*, 232–52. Tucson: University of Arizona Press, 2006.

Liss, Peggy K. *Isabel the Queen: Life and Times.* Oxford: Oxford University Press, 1992.

Lockhart, James. *The Men of Cajamarca: A Social and Biographical Study of the First Conquerors of Peru.* Austin: University of Texas Press, 1972.

———. "The Post-Conquest Period of Mexican History." In "A Scholarly Debate: The Origins of Modern Mexico—Indígenistas vs. Hispanistas," *The Americas* 48, no. 3 (1992): 323–30.

López de Gómara, Francisco. *Cortés: The Life of the Conqueror by His Secretary.* Trans. and ed. Lesley Byrd Simpson. Berkeley: University of California Press, 1964.

———. *Historia de la conquista de México.* 2 vols. Edited by Joaquín Ramírez Cabañas. México, D.F.: Editorial Pedro Robledo, 1943.

———. *Historia general de las Indias.* Zaragosa: Miguel de Zapila, 1555. Facsimile edition, Lima: Comisión Nacional del V Centenario del Descubrimiento de América–Encuentro de Dos Mundos, 1993.

López-Portillo y Weber, José. *La rebelión de la Nueva Galicia.* México, D.F.: Instituto Panamericano de Geografía e Historia, 1939.

Lorenzana, Francisco Antonio. *Historia de Nueva España escripta por su esclarecido conquistador Hernán Cortés: Aumentada con otros documentos y notas.* México, D.F: Imprenta del Superior Gobierno, 1770.

Lovell, W. George. "Disease and Depopulation in Early Colonial Guatemala." In Noble David Cook and W. George Lovell, eds., *"Secret Judgments of God": Old World Disease in Colonial Spanish America*, 49–83. Norman: University of Oklahoma Press, 1992.

Martínez, José Luis, ed. *Documentos cortesianos.* 4 vols. México, D.F.: Universidad Nacional Autónoma de México, 1992.

Menzies, Gavin. *1421: The Year China Discovered America*. New York: Harper Collins, 2002.

Morales Valerio, Francisco. "Criollización de la orden Franciscana en Nueva España, siglo XVI." *Archivo Ibero-Americano* 48 (1988): 661–84.

Morison, Samuel Eliot. *The European Discovery of America: The Northern Voyages, 1492–1616*. New York: Oxford University Press, 1974.

———. *The European Discovery of America: The Southern Voyages, 1492–1616*. New York: Oxford University Press, 1974.

Mota y Padilla, Matías de la. *Historia de la conquista del reino de la Nueva Galicia*. Ed. José Ireneo Gutiérrez. Guadalajara: Talleres Gráficos de Gallardo y Alvarez del Castillo, 1920.

Nelson, Kit, and Judith A. Habicht-Mauche. "Lead, Paint, and Pots: Rio Grande Intercommunity Dynamics from a Glaze Ware Perspective." In Judith A. Habicht-Mauche, Suzanne L. Eckert, and Deborah L. Huntley, eds., *The Social Life of Pots: Glaze Wares and Cultural Dynamics in the Southwest, AD 1250–1680*, 197–215. Tucson: University of Arizona Press, 2006.

Newson, Linda A. "Old World Epidemics in Early Colonial Ecuador." In Noble David Cook and W. George Lovell, eds., *"Secret Judgments of God": Old World Disease in Colonial Spanish America*, 84–112. Norman: University of Oklahoma Press, 1992.

Obregón, Baltasar de. *Historia de los descubrimientos antiguos y modernos de la Nueva España, escrita por el conquistador en el año de 1584*. Ed. Mariano Cuevas. México, D.F.: Editorial Porrúa, 1988.

"Ordinances for New Discoveries." In John H. Parry and Robert G. Keith, eds., *New Iberian World*, vol. 1, *The Conquerors and the Conquered*, 366–71. New York: Times Books, 1984.

Ortelius. *Americae Sive Novi Orbis, Nova Descriptio*. Amsterdam, 1570.

Oviedo [y Valdéz], Gonzalo Fernández de. *Historia general y natural de las Indias*. Ed. Juan Pérez de Tudela Bueso. 5 vols. Madrid: Ediciones Atlas, 1992.

Pacheco, Joaquín F., Francisco de Cárdenas, and Luis Torres de Mendoza, eds. *Colección de documentos inéditos relativos al descubrimiento, conquista y organización de las antiguas posesiones españoles de América y Oceania*. Series 1. 42 vols. Madrid: José María Pérez, 1864–1884.

Páez, Juan. "Relation of the Voyage of Juan Rodríguez Cabrillo, 1542–1543." In Herbert E. Bolton, ed., *Spanish Explorations in the Southwest, 1542–1706*, 13–39. New York: Charles Scribner and Sons, 1916.

Parry, J[ohn] H. *The Age of Reconnaissance*. Cleveland, Ohio: World Publishing, 1963.

Pérez de Luxán, Diego. "Diego Pérez de Luxán's Account of the Antonio de Espejo Expedition into New Mexico, 1582." In George P. Hammond and Agapito

Rey, *Rediscovery of New Mexico, 1580–1594: The Explorations of Chamuscado, Espejo, Castaño de Sosa, Morlete, and Leyva de Bonilla and Humaña*, 153–212. Albuquerque: University of New Mexico Press, 1966.

Pérez de Ribas, Andrés. *History of the Triumphs of Our Holy Faith amongst the Most Barbarous and Fierce Peoples of the New World*. Trans. and eds. Daniel T. Reff, Maureen Ahern, and Richard K. Danford. Tucson: University of Arizona Press, 1999.

Pérez-Mallaína, Pablo E. *Spain's Men of the Sea: Daily Life on the Indies Fleets in the Sixteenth Century*. Trans. Carla Rahn Phillips. Baltimore, Md.: Johns Hopkins University Press, 1998.

Phelan, John L. *The Millennial Kingdom of the Franciscans in the New World*, 2nd ed. Berkeley: University of California Press, 1970.

Polo, Marco. *The Travels*. Ed. and trans. Ronald Latham. New York: Penquin, 1958.

Prem, Hanns J. "Disease Outbreaks in Central Mexico during the Sixteenth Century." In Noble David Cook and W. George Lovell, eds., *"Secret Judgments of God": Old World Disease in Colonial Spanish America*, 20–48. Norman: University of Oklahoma Press, 1992.

Prescott, William H. *The Conquest of Mexico*. Garden City, N.Y.: Doubleday, Doran, 1934. First published 1843.

Priestly, Herbert Ingram, trans. and ed. *The Luna Papers: Documents Relating to the Expedition of don Tristán de Luna y Arellano for the Conquest of La Florida in 1559–1561*. 2 vols. De Land, Fla.: Florida State Historical Society, 1928. Reprint, Freeport, N.Y.: Books for Libraries Press, 1971.

Ptolemy, Claudius. *The Geography*. Trans. and ed. Edward Luther Stevenson. New York: Dover, 1991.

Puga, Vasco de. *Provisiones, cédulas, instrucciones para el gobierno de la Nueva España*. México, D.F.: Pedro Ocharte, 1563. Facsimile edition, Madrid: Ediciones Cultura Hispánica, 1945.

Ramenofsky, Ann F. "The Problem of Introduced Infectious Diseases in New Mexico, A.D. 1540–1680." *Journal of Anthropological Research* 52 (1996): 161–84.

Ramenofsky, Ann F., and C. David Vaughan. "Jars Full of Shiny Metal: Analyzing Barrionuevo's Visit to Yuque-Yunque." In Richard Flint and Shirley Cushing Flint, eds., *The Coronado Expedition from the Distance of 460 Years*, 116–39. Albuquerque: University of New Mexico Press, 2003.

Ramusio, Giovanni Battista. *Terzo volume delle navigationi et viaggi*. Venice: Stamperia de Giunti, 1556.

Reff, Daniel T. *Disease, Depopulation, and Culture Change in Northwestern New Spain, 1518–1764*. Salt Lake City: University of Utah Press, 1991.

———. "The Relevance of Ethnology to the Routing of the Coronado Expedition in Sonora." In Richard Flint and Shirley Cushing Flint, eds., *The Coronado Expedition to Tierra Nueva: The 1540–1542 Route across the Southwest*, 165–76. Niwot, Colo.: University Press of Colorado, 1997.

Restall, Matthew. *Maya Conquistador*. Boston: Beacon Press, 1998.

Ricard, Robert. *The Spiritual Conquest of Mexico: An Essay on the Apostolate and the Evangelizing Methods of the Mendicant Orders in New Spain, 1523–1572*. Trans. Lesley Byrd Simpson. Berkeley: University of California Press, 1966.

Riley, Carroll L. *Becoming Aztlan: Mesoamerican Influence in the Greater Southwest, AD 1200–1500*. Salt Lake City: University of Utah Press, 2005.

———. "Coronado in the Southwest." In M. S. Duran and David T. Kirkpatrick, eds., *Archaeology, Art, and Anthropology: Collected Papers in Honor of J. J. Brody*, 147–56. Albuquerque: Archaeological Society of New Mexico, 1992.

———. "Early Spanish-Indian Communication in the Greater Southwest." *New Mexico Historical Review* 46, no. 4 (1971): 285–314.

———. *The Frontier People: The Greater Southwest in the Protohistoric Period*. Rev. ed. Albuquerque: University of New Mexico Press, 1987.

———. *Rio del Norte: People of the Upper Rio Grande from Earliest Times to the Pueblo Revolt*. Salt Lake City: University of Utah Press, 1995.

Riley, Carroll L., and Joni L. Manson. "The Cíbola-Tiguex Route: Continuity and Change in the Southwest." *New Mexico Historical Review* 58, no. 4 (1983): 347–67.

———. "The Sonoran Connection: Road and Trail Networks in the Protohistoric Period." In Charles D. Trombold, ed., *Ancient Road Networks and Settlement Hierarchies in the New World*, 132–44. Cambridge: Cambridge University Press, 1991.

Roberts, Frank H. H. Jr. *Village of the Great Kivas*. Bureau of American Ethnology, Bulletin 111. Washington, D.C., 1932.

Rodríguez de Montalvo, Garci. *Las sergas de Esplandián*. Zaragosa: Casa de Simon de Portonariis, 1587. Facsimile, Madrid: Ediciones Doce Calles, 1998.

Roscoe, Will. *The Zuni Man-Woman*. Albuquerque: University of New Mexico Press, 1991.

Rossabi, Morris. "The Silk Trade in China and Central Asia." In James C. Y. Watt and Anne E. Wardwell, eds., *When Silk Was Gold: Central Asian and Chinese Textiles*, 7–19. New York: Metropolitan Museum of Art, 1997.

Sahagún, Bernardino de. *Primeros Memoriales*. Trans. Thelma D. Sullivan. Norman: University of Oklahoma Press, 1997.

Sauer, Carl O. "The Credibility of the Fray Marcos Account." *New Mexico Historical Review* 16 (April 1941): 233–43.

Schaafsma, Curtis F., and Carroll L. Riley. "Analysis and Conclusion." In Curtis F. Schaafsma and Carroll L. Riley, eds., *The Casas Grandes World*, 237–49. Salt Lake City: University of Utah Press, 1999.

Schaafsma, Polly. *Warrior, Shield, and Star: Imagery and Ideology of Pueblo Warfare*. Santa Fe, N.M.: Western Edge Press, 2000.

Schäfer, Ernesto. *El Consejo Real y Supremo de las Indias: Su historia, organización y labor administrativa hasta la terminación de la Casa de Austria*. 2 vols. Sevilla: Universidad de Sevilla, 1935.

Schroeder, Albert H. "Pueblos Abandoned in Historic Times." In Alfonso Ortiz, ed., *Handbook of North American Indians*, vol. 9, *Southwest*, 236–54. Washington, D.C.: Smithsonian Institution, 1979.

———. "A Re-analysis of the Routes of Coronado and Oñate into the Plains, 1541 and 1601." *Plains Anthropologist* 7, no. 15 (1962): 2–23.

Schroeder, Albert H., and Dan S. Matson. *A Colony on the Move: Gaspar Castaño de Sosa's Journal, 1590–1591*. Santa Fe, N.M.: School of American Research, 1965.

Seed, Patricia. *Ceremonies of Possession in Europe's Conquest of the New World, 1492–1640*. Cambridge: Cambridge University Press, 1995.

Simmons, Marc. "Tlascalans in the Spanish Borderlands." *New Mexico Historical Review* 39, no. 2 (1964): 101–10.

Simpson, J[ames] H. "Coronado's March in Search of the 'Seven Cities of Cibola' and Discussion of Their Probable Location." In *Annual Report of the Board of Regents of the Smithsonian Institution for 1869*, 309–40. Washington, D.C., 1872.

———. *Navaho Expedition: Journal of a Military Reconnaissance from Santa Fe, New Mexico, to the Navaho Country, Made in 1849*. Ed. Frank McNitt. Norman: University of Oklahoma Press, 1964.

Simpson, Lesley Byrd. *The Encomienda in New Spain: The Beginning of Spanish Mexico*. Berkeley: University of California Press, 1966.

Smith, Watson, Richard B. Woodbury, and Nathalie F. S. Woodbury. *The Excavation of Hawikuh by Frederick Webb Hodge: Report of the Hendricks-Hodge Expedition, 1917–1923*. New York: Museum of the American Indian, Heye Foundation, 1966.

Spicer, Edward H. *Cycles of Conquest: The Impact of Spain, Mexico, and the United States on the Indians of the Southwest, 1533–1960*. Tucson: University of Arizona Press, 1962.

Spielmann, Katherine A. "Clustered Confederacies: Sociopolitical Organization in the Protohistoric Rio Grande." In Wirt H. Wills and Robert D. Leonard, eds., *The Ancient Southwestern Community: Models and Methods for the Study of Protohistoric Social Organization*, 45–54. Albuquerque: University of New Mexico Press, 1994.

Spivakovsky, Erika. *Son of the Alhambra: Diego Hurtado de Mendoza, 1504–1575.* Austin: University of Texas Press, 1971.

Stevens, Henry, and Fred W. Lucas, trans. and eds. *The New Laws of the Indies for the Good Treatment and Preservation of the Indians.* London: Chiswick Press, 1893. Reprint, Amsterdam: N. Isreal, 1968.

Stevens, Thomas Wood. *The Entrada of Coronado: A Spectacular Historic Drama.* Albuquerque, N.M.: Coronado Cuarto Centennial Commission, 1940.

Swanton, John R. *Final Report of the United States De Soto Expedition Commission.* Washington, D.C.: Smithsonian Institution, 1939. Reprint, 1985.

Taylor, William B. "Santiago's Horse: Christianity and Colonial Indian Resistance in the Heartland of New Spain." In William B. Taylor and Franklin Pease G. Y., eds., *Violence, Resistance, and Survival in the Americas: Native Americans and the Legacy of Conquest*, 153–89. Washington, D.C.: Smithsonian Institution Press, 1994.

Tello, fray Antonio. *Libro segundo de la Crónica miscelánea, en que se trata de la conquista espiritual y temporal de la santa provincia de Xalisco en el nuevo reino de la Galicia y Nueva Vizcaya y descubrimiento del Nuevo México.* México, D.F.: La Republica Literaria, 1891. Reprint, México, D.F.: Editorial Porrúa, 1997.

Ternaux-Compans, Henri, trans. and ed. "Relation de la navigation et de la découverte faite par le capitaine Fernando Alarcon." In *Voyages, relations et memoires originaux pour servir a l'histoire de la decouverte de l'Amerique.* 10 vols., 9: 299–348. Paris: A. Bertrand, 1838.

Thomas, Hugh. *Conquest: Montezuma, Cortés, and the Fall of Old Mexico.* New York: Simon and Schuster, 1993.

Turner, Frederick Jackson. *History, Frontier, and Section: Three Essays.* Albuquerque: University of New Mexico Press, 1993.

United Nations General Assembly. "Universal Declaration of Human Rights." Resolution 217 A (III), December 10, 1948.

Van West, Carla R., and Henri D. Grissino-Mayer. "Dendroclimatic Reconstruction." In *Archaeological Data Recovery in the New Mexico Transportation Corridor and First Five-Year Permit Area, Fence Lake Coal Mine Project, Catron County, New Mexico*, vol. 2, part 1, *Draft Report.* Tucson: Statistical Research, 2004.

Vierra, Bradley J. *A Sixteenth-Century Spanish Campsite in the Tiguex Province.* Santa Fe: Museum of New Mexico, Research Section, 1989.

Villamarín, Juan A., and Judith E. Villamarín. "Epidemic Disease in the Sabana de Bogotá, 1536–1810." In Noble David Cook and W. George Lovell, eds., *"Secret Judgments of God": Old World Disease in Colonial Spanish America*, 113–41. Norman: University of Oklahoma Press, 1992.

Wagner, Henry R. "Fr. Marcos de Niza." *New Mexico Historical Review* 9 (April 1934): 184–227.

———. *Spanish Voyages to the Northwest Coast of America in the Sixteenth Century.* San Francisco: California Historical Society, 1929.

Walsh, Jane MacLaren. "Myth and Imagination in the American Story: The Coronado Expedition, 1540–1542." Ph.D. diss., Catholic University of America, 1993.

Warren, Fintan B. *Vasco de Quiroga and His Pueblo-Hospitals of Santa Fe.* Washington, D.C.: Academy of American Franciscan History, 1963.

Wedel, Mildred Mott. "The Indian They Called Turco." In Don G. Wyckoff and Jack L. Hofman, eds., *Pathways to Plains Prehistory: Anthropological Perspectives of Plains Natives and Their Pasts*, 153–62. Duncan, Okla.: Cross Timbers Press, 1982.

West, Delno C. "Medieval Ideas of Apocalyptic Mission and the Early Franciscans in Mexico." *The Americas* 45 (January 1989): 293–313.

Whalen, Michael E., and Paul E. Minnis. "Investigating the Paquimé Regional System." In Curtis F. Schaafsma and Carroll L. Riley, eds., *The Casas Grandes World*, 54–62. Salt Lake City: University of Utah Press, 1999.

Wilcox, David R. "Changing Perspectives on the Protohistoric Pueblos, A.D. 1450–1700." In David R. Wilcox and W. Bruce Masse, eds., *The Protohistoric Period in the North American Southwest, A.D. 1450–1700*, 378–409. Anthropological Research Paper 24. Tempe: Arizona State University, 1981.

Winship, George Parker, ed. and trans. *The Coronado Expedition, 1540–1542.* In *Fourteenth Annual Report of the Bureau of American Ethnology of the Smithsonian Institution, 1892–1893, Part 1.* Washington, D.C.: Smithsonian Institution, 1896. Reprint, Chicago: Rio Grande Press, 1964.

Woodward, David. "The Renaissance Geographic and Cartographic Background to the First Century of Greater Southwest Discovery and Cartography." In Dennis Reinhartz and Gerald D. Saxon, eds., *The Mapping of the Entradas into the Greater Southwest*, 3–29. Norman: University of Oklahoma Press, 1998.

Wright, Barton. *Kachinas of the Zuni.* Flagstaff, Ariz.: Northland Press, 1985.

Young, Biloine Whiting, and Melvin L. Fowler. *Cahokia: The Great Native American Metropolis.* Urbana: University of Illinois Press, 2000.

Young, M. Jane. *Signs from the Ancestors: Zuni Cultural Symbolism and Perceptions of Rock Art.* Albuquerque: University of New Mexico Press, 1988.

Young, Robert W. "Apachean Languages." In Alfonso Ortiz, ed., *Handbook of North American Indians*, vol. 10, *Southwest*, 393–400. Washington, D.C.: Smithsonian Institution, 1983.

Zumárraga, Fray Juan de. "Carta a un ecleciástico desconocido, April 1537." In Mariano Cuevas, ed., *Documentos inéditos del siglo XVI para la historia de México*, 83–84. México, D.F.: Museo Nacional de Arqueología, Historia y Etnología, 1914.

INDEX

Abuy, Francisco (*indio amigo*), 59

Acuco, Acoma (NM): cotton at, 120; description of, 130, 132; distance from Cíbola, 104; food of, 120; peaceful reception at, 130; population of, 113, 132, 174; poverty of, 104; route to, 128; skirmish at in 1598, 313

Acus (reino), 33, 34, 36, 44; chimera, 125, 195, 229; identified with Acuco, 120; reported wealth of, 37, 119

Aguas Calientes, *provincia* (NM): pueblos of, 113

Ahacus, 34

Akumeca (people), 130, 321

Alarcón, Hernando de (capt.): abandoned voyage, 90, 268; brevity of stay with Indians, 94; *criado* of Mendoza, 52; described as son of the sun, 89; heard about Christians at Cíbola, 79, 89–90; instructions from Mendoza, 67–68; interrogated by Indians, 88–89; markers left by, 90, 91; member of Mendoza's personal guard, 53; peaceful relations with Indians, 88, 91, 93–94; reluctant to engage in warfare, 93, 246; report on voyage, 91, 172; planned second voyage, 94, 294n25; searched for by Díaz, 91, 119, 187; sent to Autlán, 95; to resupply exp., 71, 87, 95, 290n7; told natives about Christian ritual, 88, 94; tried to send people to Cíbola, 90; use of interpreters, 88–90

Albaicín, (Granada, Spain): compared to Cíbola, 113

Albornoz, Rodrigo de (*contador*), 39; on Cabeza de Vaca's information, 28; on competition for conquest, 42

Alcaraz, Diego de (capt.): blamed for uprising at Suya, 187; killed at San Gerónimo, 187–88; in charge at San Gerónimo, 187, 202

Alemán, Juan, Xauían, Juan Emán, Juan Loman, Jumena (pueblo leader), 140, 201; at Arenal, 148; at Coofor, 145; at Moho, 151, 153; attempted to kill López de Cárdenas, 151, 304n21; reason for name, 145; response to demand for clothing, 145–46

Alonso, don (*indio amigo*): from Pátzcuaro, 59

Alvarado, Hernando de (capt. of artillery), 1; accompanied Bigotes to pueblos, 81, 130–33, 171; arrival at Tiguex, 130; at Quivira, 160; imprisoned and set dogs on Bigotes, 137, 138, 144; on difficult ascent at Acoma, 130; protected Vázquez de Coronado at Cíbola, 112; reached Cicuique, 132

Alvarado, Pedro de (*adelantado* of Guatemala), 95, 262, 263; contract to sail to Orient, 45; contract with Mendoza, 46, 199, 219; contribution to the enterprise, 64; death of, 46, 189; rivalry with Mendoza, 42, 45; ships of, 46

Álvarez (exp. members): Lorenzo, 69; Rodrigo, 217

Amazons, 20, 209

Andrés (*indio amigo*), 60; stayed in Quivira, 7, 59, 287n57

Antilia, 17, 20, 24, 56, 274n28; conflated with Cíbola and Aztlán, 21, 26; goal of the exp., 20; seven cities of, 19, 267

Antón (*indio amigo*), 60

Antonio, fray, de Castilblanco (de Vitoria), 56

Antonio, fray, de Ciudad Rodrigo (provincial), 31, 317n16

Arahey, Haraee, Harahey (Great Plains), 292n27; governor of thought to be Christian, 160; home of El Turco, 133

347

348 ■ INDEX

Arellano, Tristán de (Luna y) (capt.), 1, 51, 52, 284n9; arrival at Cíbola, 140; arrival at Tiguex, 143; at San Gerónimo, 116; company of, 200; return to Tiguex, 158, 171; skirmish at Cicuique, 183

Arispe, Arispa, Ispa (SON, Mexico), 291n6

Arms and armor: *armas de la tierra* carried by Europeans and natives alike, 62; arquebuses, 62, 111, 140, 301n5; crossbows, 62, 111, 112, 140, 282n6, 297n14, 301n5; *macanas*, 62; scarcity of European arms and armor, 62; quilted cotton armor, 62; *versillos*, 111, 112

Ashiwi (people of Zuni/Cíbola), 97–105

Asia: as contiguous with the Americas, 18, 22, 317n5; distance from the Americas, 197, 220, 316n4

Aztlán, Teocolhuacan, Chicomoztoc (legendary origin of the Mexica), 21; conflated with Cíbola, 21, 231

Awatovi (AZ), 118

Báez, Jorge (exp. member): death of during exp., 186, 192; son, Rodrigo de Trujillo, 285n21

Barahona, Hernando de (exp. member), 52

Barragán, Juan (exp. member), 285 n, 24

Barrancas (TX): exp. split at, 158, 184; first, 157, 305n17; second, 158–59, 186

Barrionuevo (exp. members): Rodrigo de, 285n22; Velasco (Francisco) de (capt.), 1, 51, 52, 285n22; exp. to Valladolid/Taos, 171

Basalt Point Pueblo (NM): as Moho, xi

Behaim, Martin, or Boheim (cartographer), 19

Benavente, Cristóbal de (*fiscal*): charged López de Cárdenas, 240

Benavídes, Pedro de (exp. member): cousin of Cristóbal Mayorga, 285n23; slaves of, 56

Benevolent treatment of Indians, 31; by Vázquez de Coronado, 73; instructions to Vázquez de Coronado concerning, 67–68; pledged and ordered by Vázquez de Coronado, 68; royal directives concerning, 237–39

Bigotes (*principal*), 164, 165, 183, 201; at Cíbola, 127–29; dogs set on, 137–38, 145, 240, 245; golden arm bands of, 136, 164; guide and intermediary, 81, 130–33, 171; prisoner, 137, 150; relationship with El Turco, 165–66; release of, 138, 155, 304n4; supposed plot with El Turco, 167–69

Bison, 1, 97, 128, 129, 134–36, 143, 156–57 159; hides of, 33, 78, 98, 121, 128, 143, 157, 158, 173, 174, 184, 186, 198, 228, 233; hunted by expeditionaries, 158, 186; meat of, 143, 158, 186; tattooed image of, 129

Blacks on the exp., 7, 29, 50, 56, 77, 142, 206; identity of, 29, 35, 49, 83, 84, 89, 99, 198, 291n12, 326; perceived danger from, 41; women and children, as well as men, 56

Blaque, Tomás (exp. member), 10

Boabdil, Mohamet Abdala: last emir of Granada, 4; pledge to fight against his father, 213

Body decoration: tattooing, 80, 129, 157, 229

Bow priests, 110, 115, 119; as government of Cíbola, 102; as trail guards, 99

Brava, Uraba, Yuraba, Taos, *provincia* and *pueblo* (NM), 141; called Valladolid, 171; population of, 113; visited by Alvarado and Barrionuevo, 131, 171

Bridge, 53; built by exp., 156

Caballero, Lope de (exp. member): Indian wife of, 57

Cabeza de Vaca, Álvar Nuño (treasurer of Narváez exp.), 28–30, 44, 89, 129, 211, 213, 218, 263, 264, 268; at Los Corazones, 76; encouraged Soto exp., 43–44; governor of Río de la Plata, 209, 215; relations with Indians, 31; report of, 27, 28; told of northern cities, 25, 36, 37, 208; visited Teyas, 157

Cabrillo, Juan Rodríguez (capt.), 207, 208–9, 213, 220, 264, 268, 317n5

Cacique (*principal*), 164, 183; dogs set on, 137–38, 145, 240, 245; prisoner, 137; released, 150

Caddoan (language): as language of the Teyas, 157, 159; language of the proto-Wichita, 156, 168, 306n28, 307n29

Cadena, Hernando de la (exp. member), 146

Cahokia (IL), 267; source of stories about Quivira, 163–64

Calendars, Gregorian, 269; Julian, 100, 105, 155, 157, 161, 191, 295n12, 311 n, 29

Campo, Andrés de (exp. member): accompanied Padilla to Quivira, 7

Canary Islands (Spain), 20; conquest of, 213, 267

Cannibalism, 175

Carlos I of Spain, Carlos (Holy Roman Emperor), xiii, 23, 47, 241, 267–69; abdication of, 225, 269; attitudes of, 14–15, 221, 237–39; received firsthand account of exp., 182; rewarded Cortés, 45

Castañeda de Nájera, Pedro de (exp. member): accused Vázquez de Coronado of deceit, 194; on poverty and small population of Tierra Nueva, 113, 132, 133, 141, 172, 175–76, 196; reliability as narrator, 136; settled at Culiacán, 198; wrote his *relación* for Dr. Zorita, 230

Castilla, don Luis de (associate of Mendoza), 52; key role of, 51; sent ahead of exp. to hire *tamemes*, 12, 66–67, 288n75; supplied a ship for Alarcón's intended second voyage, 94

Castillo, Domingo del (pilot): prepared map of Gulf of California, 293n13; with Alarcón and Ulloa, 88

Castillo Maldonado, Alonso (capt.), 28, 157, 208, 268; survivor of Narváez exp., 25; not interested in further travel, 30

Castro, Francisco de (exp. member), 285n21

Castro, Pedro de (exp. member), 285n21

Castroverde, Hernando de (exp. member), 52

Casualties during Coronado exp., xiv, 56, 69, 75, 77, 95, 147, 151, 187, 188, 196–97

Cathay, China, 17–19, 22, 184

Cepeda, Juan de (exp. member), 52, 53

Cerrillos turquoise mines (NM), 319n12; not seen by exp., 133, 179, 310n22

Céspedes, Juan de (exp. member), 285n23

Chaco Canyon, culture of (NM): age of, 267; luxury goods of, 121; relation to Cíbola, 120–22; ruins of near Cíbola, 121

Chalo:wa (NM): one of the cities of Cíbola, 100, 295n15

Chamelote (fabric): said to be made at Totonteac, 34

Chia, Zia, *provincia* and *pueblo* (NM), 113, 202; amicable relations with exp., 153; clothing purchased at, 72, 150

Chiametla (SIN, Mexico), 265; procurement of food attempted at, 69; execution of natives of, 69, 239; rendezvous with Díaz and Zaldívar at, 75; Samaniego killed at, 244

Chichilticale, Chichiltiqueale, Chichiltiecale (AZ), 84, 173, 202, 293n37; beginning of unsettled region, 103; Díaz and Zaldívar at, 40, 75; disappointment of expeditionaries at, 77; distance from Mar del Sur, 87, 99; distance to Cíbola, 76–77, 103, 192; identified as Kuykendall Ruin, 291n9; people of did not resist exp., 99; thought to be on or near the coast, 87

Cíbola, Shíwana, Zuni (NM): abandonment of, 112; advance knowledge of approach of exp., 99, 103; architecture of, 108; arrival of exp. at, 104–5, 107–8; as a *provincia*, 101; battle and capture of, 110–12; called a *ciudad*, 103; called Granada, 113; compared to Tenochtitlan, 6; corn abundant at, 112–13; death of Esteban at, 35, 99; death of natives of, 112; derivation of name, 97; distance from Chichilticale, 77; distance from Los Corazones, 77; distance to Cicuique, 127; distance to oceans, 115; government of, 102; Indian allies remained at, 12; laborers from Sonora at, 83, 98; geographical limits of, 103–4; links to Río Sonora, 98; long-distance traders at, 97; notion of time, 124; not suitable for settlement, 7; political integration of, 101–2; population of, 113; pueblos or cities of, 2, 100; *requerimiento* delivered at, 108–9; sent message to people of Chichilticale, 99; skirmish at pass, 107; source of its fame, 120–22; summer ceremonial at, 100; turquoise trade, 78–79; women of, 114

Cicuique (NM): casualties at, 183; councils at, 127; desire for Tiguex pueblo, 133; distance from Cíbola, 127; emissaries from at Cíbola, 127–29; population of, 113; skirmish at, 183

Ciudad de México (DF, Mexico): anticipation in, 36; as a *ciudad*, 322; built on ruins of Tenochtitlan, 268; departure of expedition from, 40, 66, 268; jail of, 54; population of, 275; recruitment of expeditionaries at, 50–51; return of the expedition to, 176–77, 194, 200

Ciudad Rodrigo, fray Antonio de (Franciscan provincial): one of Los Doce, 317; recommended fray Marcos, 31

Civilization: sixteenth-century definition of, 136, 162, 173, 175

Clothing: demands for by exp., 71, 72–73, 115, 144, 145–46, 147, 185, 210, 243–45; purchased at Chia, 72, 150; shortage of, 72, 145, 186

Coavis, Juan (*indio amigo*): from Tlatelolco, 59; on number of *indios amigos*, 59

Cocolitzli: epidemic in 1540s, 222, 268; identification of, 222

Colorado and Gila River Indians (people): assisted Alarcón, 88; languages of, 88; visits to Cíbola, 89; warfare among, 89

Columbus, Christopher (Cristóbal Colón): distributed *encomiendas*, 5; thought he had found Antilia and Asia, 18, 20, 21–22

Communication, long-distance: example from Alarcón voyage, 89–90

Compostela (NAY, Mexico), capital of Nueva Galicia, 193; departure of exp. from, 68, 71, 75; muster of exp. at, 51, 58, 75, 200, 268

Consejo Real de las Indias, Council of the Indies: Cortés's case against Mendoza, 241; dispute among Mendoza, Alvarado, Guzmán, Cortés, and Soto, 42–46

Contemporaneous expeditions: compared with Coronado exp., 205–18, 264

Continental Divide: recognized by exp., 13

Conti, Nicolo di (Venetian traveler): account of humpbacked cattle, 129

Contreras, Juan de (exp. member): member of Mendoza's guard, 53; on execution of El Turco, 161; on the setting on of dogs, 138

Coofor, Coafor, Alcanfor (NM): home of Xauían, 140; identified with Santiago Pueblo, 149, 301n5; Indians held prisoner at, 144; location of, 143, 291n6; residents of expelled by exp., 140, 144, 242; winter quarters of exp., 141, 143, 183, 185

Corazones, Los Corazones (SON, Mexico): distance to Cíbola, 140; interpreter from, 82; on Río Sonora, 76; people of friendly to exp., 193; populous place, 76; San Gerónimo established at, 76; visited by Cabeza de Vaca, 76

Cordero, Juan (exp. member), tailor, 10

Coronado Expedition: ages of members of, 55; as Holy crusade, 15; captains and companies of, 51–52; economic status of members of, 50; failure of, 195–97; financing of, 62–64, 288n80; Indian allies on, 58–62; linkages between members of, 52, 54; misconceptions about, xv; motivations of, 1–12, 14–15; not mining or exploring party, 3, 12–14, 78; occupations of members of, 2, 10, 11; occupied several Tiguex pueblos, 150, 304n18; origins of members of, 39, 54–55, 285n24; reasons for abandonment of, 2; slaves and servants on, 56–57, 90; recruiting members, 6, 49; size of, xiii, 58, 62; women and children on, 57

Cortés, Hernando (Marqués del Valle): distributed *encomiendas*, 6; attempted to colonize California, 263; dispute with Mendoza, 42–43, 241; led conquest of Tenochtitlan, 22; mistakenly credited with tactic of using *indios amigos*, 213; reconnaissance of Mar del Sur, 42; rights to conquest, 42

Cotton: in Acuco, 120, 174; in Cíbola, 173, 228; in Tiguex, 131, 132

Cornstalks: as food for livestock, 141; as fuel for Pueblos, 141; as thatch, 140

Counter-Reformation: effect of on conversion of Indians, 225

Cristóbal (Jaramillo's slave): remained with fray Luis in Cicuique, 8

Crosses: sent by Esteban, 33; set up and distributed by Alarcón, 88, 90, 94; set up and used by exp., 72, 78, 185, 293n13; to be set up by fray Luis, 7, 55; used by Indians, 149, 234

Cross-staff, 63

Cuchillo (SIN, Mexico): Indians of sent with fray Marcos, 83

Culiacán, San Miguel de (SIN, Mexico): arrival of Narváez survivors at, 25, 268; departure of fray Marcos from, 32; distance to Los Corazones, 76; resupplied by, 71; exp. split at, 71, 76; founded by Guzmán, 25; population swelled by returning expeditionaries, 197, 198; ritual battle at, 76; threatened depopulation of, 198; Tovar one of the founders of, 117

Daniel, fray: Italian lay brother, 56

Debts of expeditionaries, xiv, 64, 113, 116, 190, 198, 199, 214

Defensive strategy of Indians, 100, 110–12, 147, 151, 179, 234, 244

De la Cruz, fray Juan: mistaken identity of, 274n17

Depopulation because of departure of the exp.: consequences of, 42, 95, 189

Díaz (exp. members): Francisco, jailer, 54; Melchior (capt.), 51, 52, 117; at Chichilticale,

40; at Río del Tizón, 91; death of, 92, 95; reception of by natives, 91–92; report by, 40–41; search for Alarcón, 91, 119, 187; sent ahead of exp., 39, 72; unable to confirm Marcos's report, 40–41, 107

Díaz, Melchior and Juan de Zaldívar reconnaissance: could not reach Cíbola, 40; departure from Culiacán, 40; failed to confirm Marcos's report, 40–41, 107; met northbound exp., 75; route of, 291 n.14; sent to verify Marcos's report, 39; winter at or near Chichilticale, 40

Dorantes, Andrés (capt., Narváez exp.): arrival in Culiacán, 25, 268; declined to go to Tierra Nueva, 29, 31; owner of Esteban, 32, 83; report by, 28, 208; visited Teyas, 157

Dowa Yalanne (mesa, NM): refuge of the Ashiwi, 100, 102, 112, 114–15, 128, 151, 295n16

Easter, 33, 71, 76, 155

Encomenderos, 5–6, 210, 221–22; members of Coronado exp., 7, 64

Encomiendas, repartimientos, 2; attempts to suppress, 4–6, 221–22; 239; distributed by Cortés, 6, 24; distributed by Guzmán, 25; grant document, 5; motivation of sixteenth-century expeditions, 6, 15; not to be extended to the New World, 5; requirements of, 5–6, 238

Entrambasaguas, Miguel de (exp. member): slaves of, 56

Entrepreneurs and tradesmen on exp., 10

Escobar, Cristóbal de (exp. member): coat of arms, 199; debt of, 199; on pilfering of food from pueblos, 185; on shortage of food, 77; partnership with Domingo Martín, 54; took livestock, 10, 54

Espejo, Antonio de (leader of exp. to New Mexico), 265, 318n18; found *indios amigos* at Zuni, 60

Espinosa, Francisco de (exp. member): in jail, 54

Estancia Basin (NM): not seen by exp., 178, 302n9

Esteban, Esteban de Dorantes (slave of Andrés Dorantes): accompanied by Indians, 34, 107; accompanied Marcos de Niza, 32, 268; at Cíbola, 35, 89, 98, 121; death of, 35, 89, 99, 127; first heard name Cíbola, 33; purchased by Mendoza, 29, 32, 83; received glowing reports, 33; sent in advance of Marcos, 33, 246; survivor of Narváez exp., 25; visited Teyas, 157

Estrada, Beatriz de (wife of Vázquez de Coronado): dowry of, 64; niece of Diego Gutiérrez de la Caballería, 52, 232

Fernando II of Aragón, 267; on *encomiendas*, 5; on Indian slavery, 237

Felipe II of Spain: theologically orthodox, 225

Fioz, Juan (exp. member), 53, 54

Flint, Shirley Cushing (historian), xi, xv, 63

Franciscans, Order of Friars Minor: little contact with natives of Tierra Nueva, 196; Los Doce, 8, 224, 317n16; millenarians, 8, 223–25

Frías, Rodrigo de (exp. member): on the setting on of dogs, 138; reported force used at Tiguex, 131, 153

Gallego, Juan (capt.), 51; reached retreating exp. on relief mission, 192–93; returned to Colima with message to Mendoza, 116; skirmishes with Indians, 192

García de Plasencia, Juan (exp. member), 52

Gaspar (*indio amigo*), 60

Gila River (AZ, NM), 79, 123; led to Cíbola, 89

Golden armbands: as sign of special status, 165; told of by El Turco, 136–38, 162, 165–66; existence of denied, 137, 162, 164

Gómez, Francisco (exp. member), 53, 285n24

Gómez de Paradinas, Juan (exp. member): *criados* of, 57; debt of, 64; tailor, 10

Gómez de Salazar, Juan (exp. member), 57

González (exp. members): Alonso, man and son, 285n21; Fernand, 285n24; Francisco, 285n24; Pero (Pedro), 285n24

Gorbalán, Francisco (exp. member): on occupation of pueblos, 304n18

Granada (Spain): last moorish province in Spain, 4

Grand Canyon (AZ): description, 13; reconnoitered by López de Cárdenas, 119

Greater India: destination of exp., 17, 26; proximity to Tierra Nueva, 18, 19, 21

Great Plains: extent of, 156, 178; home of bison, 1, 129, 134; productive, 3

Group-on-group violence, 242–44

Guadalupe, Gaspar de (exp. member), 52

Guanche (people): enlisted by Spaniards to fight other Guanche, 213

Guas (people and *provincia*), 197

Guevara, Diego de (capt.), 1, 51, 52, 284n12; attacked pueblo with Zaldívar, 153

Guides and emissaries: determined what was seen, 178, 180–81; Esteban as, 83; fled, 159; required, 83, 133, 178; suspicion of, 84, 168; use of by the exp., 13, 80–85, 117, 119, 131, 133, 135, 155, 159, 161

Gulf of California: Castillo's map, 293n13; fleets sent by Cortés, 42; natives of, 80; reconnaissance of by Alarcón, 87, 90

Gutiérrez, Francisco (exp. member), 52

Gutiérrez Bocanegra, Juan (secretary of Juan de Oñate): relative of Diego Gutiérrez de la Caballería, 232, 319n19

Gutiérrez de Humaña, Antonio (leader of exp. to New Mexico), 319n18

Gutiérrez de la Caballería, Diego (capt.), 51; death of, 188; uncle of Beatriz de Estrada, 52

Guzmán, Nuño Beltrán de (former governor of Nueva Galicia): competitor of Mendoza, 42, 45; conquered Nueva Galicia, 52, 268; death of, 45; exp. of, 24–25, 45, 263; failed to find Seven Ciudades, 25; slaving activity of, 97, 99

Halona:wa (NM): one of the cities of Cíbola, 100

Hawikku, Hawikuh (NM): arrival of exp. at, 107; battle at, 110–12; called Granada by the Spaniards, 113; council held at, 100; death of Esteban at, 35, 127; distance to Dowa Yalanne, 100; evacuated, 100; one of the cities of Cíbola, 100

Haya (native community), 157, 305n16

Hernández (exp. members): Diego (*alférez*), 52; Diego, 52, 285n23; Gonzalo, 52; Manuel, 53; Miguel, 285n22; Pero, 53, 54

Hernández Chillón, Martín (exp. member), 285n24

Hernández de Arriba, Francisco (exp. member), 285n22

Hernández de Encinasola, Andrés (exp. member), 285n24

Hernández de Guadalajara, Pero (exp. member), 285n24

History: as evolving, xvi; opportunity to learn, xvi; understanding the range of behavior, xvi

Hohokam culture (AZ), 267; source of stories of Totonteac, 122–23

Hopitu, Hopi (people), 117–19

Hozes, Francisca de (exp. member), 57; on uprising at Suya, 193; wanted to stay in Tierra Nueva, 9, 190–91, 275n32; wife of Alonso Sánchez, 9, 57

Hurtado de Mendoza, Luis (capt. general of Granada): brother of Antonio de Mendoza and president of the Consejo de Indias, 241

Ibarra, Francisco (governor of Nueva Vizcaya), 89, 265, 269, 318n10 and n11

Illness and epidemic disease: among Pueblos, 202–3; experienced by exp., 186, 192; role of in Indian population decline, 202, 219, 222, 313n24, 317 n, 9

Indios amigos, Indian allies: assessment of exp. by, 176–77, 200; casualties among, 112, 147; impact on conquest, 112, 148, 201, 212; in conquest of the Inca, 212; lacked by Soto exp., 211; majority of exp., 10, 58; motivations of, 10–12, 177; numbers of on Coronado exp., 58; numbers of on sixteenth-century expeditions, 189, 211–13; origins of, 7, 58–60; organization of, 61; preceded advance guard, 61, 78; present as warriors, 61, 112, 200, 243; recruitment of, 11, 61–62; relations among, 60; remained in Tierra Nueva, 192; roles of, 61, 135; sought out combat, 147, 243; sufferings of, 72, 144; with units of exp., 91, 117, 130, 131

Indian rights movement in Spain, 30, 66, 237, 267

Individual-on-individual violence, 245

Interpreters, 60, 88, 108, 118; inability of, 82, 88; lack of, 37; reliance on, 80, 82, 83, 84, 119, 129, 135, 178, 213, 239

Isabel (queen of Castilla): on *encomiendas*, 4–5; on treatment of Indians, 221, 237

INDEX 353

Jacinto (Cyndos) de San Francisco, fray: partner of Alonso de Zorita, 230

Jaramillo, Juan (exp. member): addressed his narrative to Zorita, 230; became a capt. later, 200; narrative of, 230; opposed to abandonment of exp., 9, 275n32; reached Quivira, 160; slaves of, 7, 56

Jemez, *provincia* (NM), 113, 132, 303n11

Jimena, pueblo and *provincia* (NM), 113

Jiménez (exp. members): Alonso, 285n23 and n24; Francisco (*indio amigo*), 59; Juan, 285n23 and n24; asked for indulgence, 15; death of during exp., 186, 192; merchant, 10

Jimmy Owens Site (TX), 158

Joachim of Fiore, 8

Joint Report (of Narváez survivors), 28; told of copper, 24–25

Junta, routinely directed the exp., 1–2, 7, 9, 87, 116, 138, 151, 155, 157, 158, 161

Kechiba:wa, Kechipauan (NM): one of the cities of Cíbola, 100, 102

Khan-balik, Beijing (China): described by Marco Polo, 18

Kwa'ki'na (NM): one of the cities of Cíbola, 100

Kyaki:ma (NM): one of the cities of Cíbola, 100

La Florida, 21, 43, 156, 160, 210

Las Casas, fray Bartolomé de, 30, 66, 231, 237; advocate for peaceful conversion, 31, 238; called for suppression of *encomiendas*, 221; corresponded with fray Marcos, 31; experiment at Vera Paz, 31; on the *requerimiento*, 70

Laws of Burgos, 237–38

Ledesma, Pedro de (exp. member): criado of Mendoza, 52; debt of, 64; on the embassy from Cicuique, 127

León Romano, Juan de (*escribano* and Mendoza's secretary): sent ahead of exp. to hire *tamemes* and purchase provisions, 66

León, Luis de (*indio amigo*), 59

License for mounting an exp., 43, 46–48, 238

Livestock on exp.: cattle, sheep, rams and pigs, 63, 139, 141; horses and mules, 40, 63, 78, 107, 139, 141, 147, 148, 181, 186, 191, 192, 198; left behind, 71

Llano Estacado (TX, NM), 156–57, 167, 305n18

López (exp. members): Alonso, 53, 54, 285n24; Diego (capt.): accused Marcos of lying, 36; councilman of Sevilla, 51; interrogated El Turco, 161; served under Guzmán, 52; Francisco, 53, 285n24

López de Cárdenas, García (capt.): at Grand Canyon, 119; attacked pueblos, 148; attempted murder of, 151; confiscated livestock from Pérez, 198; convicted of abusing Indians, 240, 268; forced Indians to vacate a pueblo, 140; ignored promise of peace, 149; *maestre de campo*, 75; prepared winter quarters, 140; reconnaissance of Tusayán, 117, 119; shielded Vázquez de Coronado, 112; skirmish at "bad" pass, 107; slaves of, 56; succeeded as head of family, 184; wounded and injured, xi, 184–85

López de Palacios Rubios, Juan (legal scholar): author of the *requerimiento*, 69

López de Villalobos, Ruy (leader of voyage to the Philippines), 219, 268

Los Doce (Franciscan missionaries), 8, 224; deaths of, 317n16

Lucas (*indio amigo*): stayed in Quivira, 7, 59, 230

Luis, fray, de Úbeda: in battle at Cíbola, 108, 110; member of Zumárraga's household, 55; remained at Cicuique, 7, 191

Luisa (interpreter): fled from exp., 60

Maldonado (exp. members): don Rodrigo (capt.): attacked fleeing Indians, 152; company of, 52; raced with Vázquez de Coronado, 186; sent ahead on Plains, 157; sent to block Ulloa, 43; María, wife of Juan Gómez de Paradinas, 57

Manrique de Lara, Alonso (exp. member), 1

Marata (CHIC?, Mexico), xiii, 34; desired destination, 119; nonexistent, 120; perhaps Paquimé, 122

Marcos, fray, de Niza: accompanied by Esteban, 32, 83; accompanied by Indians, 32, 34, 80, 83; accompanied by Onorato, 32; claimed to have seen Cíbola, 35; confirmed Narváez survivors' report, 36; conversations with Mendoza and Vázquez de Coronado, 37; correspondent of Las Casas, 31; crosses and messages sent to by Esteban, 33; felt unsafe at Cíbola and fled, 108; followed trails,

78–79, 84; formal report by, 35–36; Franciscan provincial, 7, 50; in Peru, 31; issue of lying by, 35–38, 184; led exp., 55; sought populous settlements, 32; sought news of the coast, 33; theory of collusion with Mendoza, 281n51

Mar del Norte (Atlantic Ocean): distance from Cíbola, 115

Mar del Sur (Pacific Ocean): breadth of, 18, 219–20; distance from Cíbola, 115; reconnaissance of, 42

Márquez, Pedro (exp. member), 285n21

Martín, don (Indian *principal*), 59

Martín (exp. members): Andrés, 285n23; Domingo, debt of, 199; took livestock, 10, 54; Francisco, 54, 285n23

Martín Bermejo (exp. members): Hernando (Vázquez de Coronado's secretary), 108, 109, 285n23 and n24; Juan, 285n23 and n24

Martín Cano, Pero (exp. member), 285n23 and n24

Martín de la Bermeja, Pedro (Pero) (exp. member), 285n23

Mats'a:kya, Mazaque (NM): one of the pueblos of Cíbola, 100, 114, 128

Mayoral, Pedro (exp. member), 285n21

Mayorga, Cristóbal de (exp. member), 146, 285n23

Medina, Alonso de (exp. member), 52

Melgosa, Pablo de (capt.), 1, 51, 52

Mendoza, Antonio de (viceroy), 268; advice to Velasco, 27; appointed Vázquez de Coronado, 39, 67; attempted to enlist Dorantes, 29–30; conducted muster, 75; contract with Pedro de Alvarado, 46, 219; financial losses of, 228; granted a license for an exp., 46–48; instructions to Alarcón, 67–68; led exp. to Mixtón War, 60, 177, 189; major funder of exp., 63–64; on benign treatment of Indians, 31, 66; personal guard of, 53, 71; purchased Esteban, 29, 32, 83; relation to members of exp., 51–53; rivalry with Cortés, Alvarado, Guzmán, Soto, and Cabeza de Vaca, 43–45, 241; transferred to Peru, 224; tried to detain Ulloa, 43

Mercado de Sotomayor, Gerónimo (exp. member), 53

Metal: copper, 26, 27, 44, 121, 159, 163, 164; gold, xv, 6, 17, 25, 36, 135, 136, 159, 160, 163, 164, 184, 195, 228, 231; lead, 174, 179, 310n22, 319n12; silver, 3, 17, 25, 36, 135, 164, 195, 222–23, 228, 230, 231, 233

Mexica, Aztecs, Nahuas (people), 6; employed as emissaries, 78, 81; importance of war to, 11

Michoacán, *provincia* (Mexico): affected by epidemic disease, 222; origin of *indios amigos*, 12, 58, 59; *tamemes* from, 66

Miguel, Antón (exp. member), 52

Millenarianism: adherents among the Franciscan Order, 8, 223–25

Mistreatment of Indians: charges against Coronado exp., 239–40

Mixtón War: departure of exp. blamed for, 189; interrupted Alarcón's second voyage, 95; Mendoza led exp. to, 60, 177, 189; role of Caxcanes in, 188–89

Moho (NM): besieged by López de Cárdenas, 151–53, 245; flight of defenders from, 152; lack of water at, 152; possibly on Santa Ana Mesa, xi, 152; slaughter of refugees from, 152

Molestation of women, 73, 146–47, 244

Montesinos, fray Antonio de (Dominican): critical of conquistadores, 30, 237, 267

Montúfar, Alonso de (Dominican): bishop who succeeded Zumárraga, 224

Moors: conquerors of Iberian Peninsula, 4, 213, 267

Muster roll: date of, 51; many men-at-arms not listed, 51

Nahuatl (language): widely used outside central Mexico, 82; taught by missionaries, 82; understood by El Turco and Ysopete, 83, 135, 161; used at some pueblos, 201, 313n20

Nanapagua (NM): not identified, 300n34; planned attack on, 136–37

Narváez exp.: joint report, 25–26; survivors of, 25

Navarro, Juan (exp. member), 54

New Laws of the Indies (regulations governing treatment of Indians): called for suppression of *encomiendas*, 221; extract from, 221–22

Núñez de Mirandilla, Diego (exp. member), 285n24

Oñate, Cristóbal de (lieutenant governor): present at muster, 9; on members of exp., 9; reaction to Mixtón uprising, 95, 189; Juan de (colonizer of New Mexico), son of Cristóbal de Oñate, 232

Ordinances concerning New Discoveries: instituted use of term "pacification", 226

Ordinances concerning the Benevolent Treatment of Indians, 238

Oriental-style goods: sought by exp., 17–19

Ortega, Pedro de (exp. member), 53

Ovando, Francisco de (capt.), 51

Padilla, fray Juan de: at battle of Hawikku, 82; at Quivira, 7, 59, 60; death of, 56, 197, 230; leader of Franciscans of exp., 2; went to Tusayán, 130; went to Tiguex, 130

Padilla, don García de (*indio amigo*), 59

Páez, Fernán or Hernán (exp. member), 53

Painters, on Coronado exp., 10, 53

Palo Duro Canyon (TX), 158

Paniagua, Juan (exp. member), 64

Paquimé (CHIH, Mexico): perhaps Marata, 122

Paul III, Pope: bull on Indian conversion, 30–31

Paz Maldonado, Rodrigo de (exp. member), 200

Pedro, a Black (crier), 49

Pérez (exp. members): Hernán, 161, 285n24; Melchior: debt of, 64; on the uprising at Suya, 187; slaves and servants of, 7–8, 56, 198; took horses, 198; took livestock, 10

Pérez de Bocanegra, Alonso (exp. member), 55; became a *regidor*, 200

Pérez de la Torre, Diego (*licenciado*): death of, 32; former governor of Nueva Galicia, 32

Petatlán (SIN, Mexico), 172; Indians from with fray Marcos, 83

Philippines: crossing of Pacific Ocean to, 219

Piman (language): as traders' language, 293n5

Pintados (people): met and accompanied Marcos, 80; territory of, 80

Pizzigano, Zuane (cartographer), 20

Polo, Marco (merchant): co-author with Rustichello, 17, 267; *Travels* of, 17, 175, 267

Populous and wealthy peoples: lack of, 172–76; principal goal of exp., 10, 80, 92, 160, 208; reported by Cabeza de Vaca and fray Marcos, 28; sought by fray Marcos, 37

Province of the Santo Evangelio (Franciscan province in Nueva España), 30

Pueblo de la Alameda (NM): possibly occupied by exp., 150

Pueblo del Arenal (NM): besieged by López de Cárdenas, 148; execution and massacre of prisoners at, 148–49; rape of woman at, 146–47; set afire, 148

Puelles, Diego de (exp. member), 54

Querechos (people), 305n18, 308n65; compared to Turkomans, 184; enemies of Teyas, 167; tents of, 156; territory of, 167; traded with Pueblos, 143; use of bison by, 143; use of dogs by, 156

Quesada (exp. members): Cristóbal de, 10, 53; Luis de, 52, 230

Quirix, Keres, *provincia* (NM), 113, 142, 147; expansion of territory following the exp., 202; pueblos of, 150, 202

Quivira, *provincia* (KS): copper at, 159; distance from barrancas, 158; desired destination, xiii; El Turco's death at, 161; fray Juan de Padilla at, 7–8, 59, 197; gold said to be at, 135–36; guides from, 133, 161; legends of derived from Cahokia, 163–64; people of, 159; reception of exp. at, 159; summary of route to, 155–59

Ramírez de Vargas, Luis (*contador*), 1

Ramos, Gerónimo (exp. member), 285n24

Ramusio, Giovanni Battista (publisher): embellished his translations, 228–29; published documents from the Coronado exp., 228

Reconquista: use of recently subjugated fighters, 213

Religious conversion: bull of Pope Paul III, 30–31; failure of, 196; without force, 238

Requerimiento: as legal basis for conquest, 69; excerpts from, 70, 109; native response to, 108–9, 110, 118, 148; read at Cíbola, 82, 108, 111; read at Tiguex, 148, 151; read at Tusayán, 118

Río Bermejo, Little Colorado River (AZ), 99, 103

Río de Cicuique, Pecos River (NM), bridge over, 53, 156

Río de Tiguex, Río de Nuestra Señora, Rio Grande (NM), 1, 3; distance from Acuco, 130; flow of, 130; frozen, 153; headwaters of, 19; valley of, 135, 139

Río del Tizón, Río de Buena Guía, Colorado River (AZ, CA), 91; Alarcón's report of, 91; distance from Cíbola, 90; naming of, 88; size of, 88

Río Nexpa, San Pedro River (SON, Mexico and AZ), 34, 76; Indians along, 76

Río San Pedro y San Pablo (Arkansas River in KS), 159

Río Señora, Sonora (SON, Mexico): people from worked in Cíbola, 33; Spanish settlement along, 76; turquoises at, 78, 83

Ribero de Espinosa, Antonio (*factor*), 1, 53

Rodríguez, fray Agustín (leader of exp. to New Mexico), 202, 227, 232, 265

Rodríguez (exp. members): Francisco, 285n24; García, 64; Juan, 53; Sancho, 52

Roxo, Sebastián (exp. member), 285n21

Roxo Loro, Francisco (exp. member), 285n21

Ruiz (exp. members): Antón, 285n22 and n24; Juan, 53

Ruiz de Haro, Pedro (lawyer), 239

Ruiz de Rojas, Marcos (exp. member), 53

Rustichello (author): co-author with Marco Polo, 17, 267

Saldaña, Gaspar de (exp. member), 52, 53, 160

Salinas (exp. members): Andrés de, 285n21; Pedro de, 53; son of Andrés, 285n21

Salinas Pueblos (NM), 178

Salt: at Cíbola, 173; in Estancia Basin, 178

Samaniego, Lope de (capt.), 52; death of, 69, 244; *maestre de campo*, 51

Sámano, Julián de (exp. member), 53

Sánchez (exp. members): Alonso: age of, 57; debts of, 9, 190; shoemaker, 9; small merchant, 9; wanted to stay in Tierra Nueva, 9, 190, 275n32; Bartolomé: painter, 10, 285n22 and n24; Leonardo, 52; Rodrigo, 285n22 and n24; son of Alonso, 9, 285n21

Sánchez Chamuscado, Francisco (leader of exp. to New Mexico), 227, 265, 319n18

San Gerónimo (SON, Mexico): established at Los Corazones, 76; moved to Señora, 76; moved to Suya, 76, 187; native uprising at, 187–88, 244; pivotal for the exp.'s survival, 188; supply and communication base, 192, 202

Santiago Pueblo (NM): evidence for fighting at, 140, 301n5; identified as Coofor, 140

Santillana, Francisco de (exp. member): blacksmith, 10

Santovaya, Juan de (exp. member), 53

San Vitorés, Juan Bautista de (exp. member), 54

Sayavedra, Alonso de (exp. member), 146

Sebastián (*indio amigo*): remained in Quivira, 7, 60

Sebastián (Jaramillo's black slave): remained with fray Juan de Padilla, 8

Señora, Sonora (SON, Mexico): in Río Sonora valley, 291n6; San Gerónimo moved to, 76

Sergas de Esplandián (romance), 20–21

Seri (people), used as guides, 80

Sexual behavior, homosexuality, 173, 175, 309n4

Signs and sign language, use of, 77, 82, 83, 93, 120, 135, 148, 155, 156, 161, 162, 167

Simón, Rodrigo (exp. member): on embassy from Cicuique, 129

Slaves and servants of exp. members, 7–8, 55, 56–57, 64, 90

Soto, Hernando (Fernando) de (*adelantado* of La Florida): death of, 44; dispute with Mendoza, 43; leader of exp. to southeastern U.S. and Tierra Nueva, 44; offered position to Cabeza de Vaca, 29, 43

Soto, Sebastián (exp. member), 52

Suya (SON, Mexico), 172, 193, 202; native uprising at, 187–88; poison at, 187; San Gerónimo moved to, 76, 187

Tamemes: number on exp., 63; used on Coronado exp., 58, 66, 288n75

Tano (people), 142

Tejada, Lorenzo, *licenciado* (*oidor*): investigated Coronado exp., 239; recruited *indios amigos*, 61; *oidor* of royal *audiencia*, 61

Tejo (*indio*): as a merchant, 25; told about seven pueblos, 25

Tello de Sandoval, Francisco (*visitador general*): investigated exp., 241; recalled to Spain, 241

Tenochca (people): exp. members, 60; in Mixtón War, 60

Tenochtitlan, Tenuxtitan (Mexica capital), 6; compared to Cíbola, 6; size of, 23

Tents: destroyed by hail, 158

Tewa (people), 142; pueblos of, 171, 302n9

Teyas (people), 305n18, 308n65; compared to Turkomans, 184; destroyed Galisteo Basin pueblos, 128, 143; enemies of Querechos, 167; friends of El Turco, 167; furnished guides, 159; language of, 157, 306n19 and n28, 307n29; spent winter at pueblos, 143; tattooed,157; territory of, 305n16; traded with Pueblos, 308n65; use of bison by, 143; visited by Cabeza de Vaca party, 157

Tianguez: absence of in Tierra Nueva, 174; at Tenochtitlan, 174–75

Tierra Nueva, xiii; abandonment of by exp., 2, 9, 190–91; extent of pueblos in, 139, 142; goal of exp., xiii, 39; multitude of languages in, 292n27; unsuitable for settlement, 2, 113, 173, 190, 203

Tiguex, *provincia* (NM), xiii; abandonment by natives, 147; called "the best place", 182; compared to Cíbola, 139; could not support *encomiendas*, 290–91; description of, 141–42; exp.'s winter headquarters at, 139; political integration of, 147, 303n11; pueblos demolished, 153; pueblos of, 142; requisition of clothing at, 145–46; submission of, 131; uprising at, 147–53; woman raped at, 146–47

Time: difference between European and Native American conceptions of, 124–25

Tiwa (people), 102, 141, 145

Tlapa (GUE, Mexico): *encomienda* of Beatriz de Estrada, 64

Tlaxcaltecas (people): claimed to be on Coronado exp. 59; with Cortés and Guzmán, 59

Tlecanen, Juan (Mexica leader): on number of *indios amigos*, 59

Tompiro pueblos (NM): not seen by exp., 133, 178, 302n9

Toro, Alonso de (exp. member), 53

Torquemada, Juan de (*alférez*), 52

Toscanelli, Paolo dal Pozzo (cosmographer): influenced Columbus, 20

Torture: sixteenth-century use of, 43, 92, 145, 161, 245

Totonteac (AZ): described as hot lake, 120; description of, 123; desired destination, xiii; exotic fabric from, 34; possibly Hohokam communities, 122–23

Tovar, Pedro de (*alférez general*): papers of lost, 305n17; reconnaissance of Tusayán, 117–18; sent to San Gerónimo, 185; threatened Bigotes, 137

Towa (people), 142, 150

Tribute: as labor, 6; in kind, 6, 64; in Old World, 4; motive of exp., 2; preconquest, 6, 23; reduced as payment for serving on exp., 11–12, 62, 67

Troyano, Juan (exp. member): artilleryman, 52; *criado* of Mendoza, 52; *india* wife of, 57; on the setting on of dogs, 137; on Turco's revelation, 135; slaves of, 56; subsidized by Mendoza, 52

Trujillo, Rodrigo de (exp. member), 285n21

Turco (native guide): avoided Querechos, 156; confession of, 161; executed, 161; golden arm bands of, 136, 137, 164; guided Alvarado to Great Plains, 133; interpreter, 83; issue of lying, 137, 164–66; knew some Nahuatl, 161; language of, 156; led exp. to Quivira, 155–57; native of Haraee, 133; planned attack at Quivira, 160, 168–69; possible reciprocal hostage, 165–66; supposed plot with Bigotes, 167–68; told stories of Quivira, 135

Turquoise: at Cerrillos, 133, 179, 310n22; at Cíbola, 33, 98, 115, 173, 228–29; at Tiguex, 174; in Sonora, 78, 83

Tusayán, Tucano, *provincia* (AZ), xiii; distance from Cíbola, 104; government of, 102; reconnaissance by López de Cárdenas, 119; reconnaissance by Tovar, 117–19; skirmish at, 118

Tutahaco, *provincia* (NM), 113, 141

Ulloa, Francisco de (capt.): aim was to reach Tierra Nueva, 208; reconnaissance of Mar del Sur, 42, 87, 207, 264

Unsettled areas (*despoblados*), 77, 101, 103, 104, 119, 192